The Storm Birds

The Storm Birds

Soviet Postwar Defectors

Gordon Brook-Shepherd

 WEIDENFELD & NICOLSON · New York

Published by Weidenfeld & Nicolson, New York
A Division of Wheatland Corporation
841 Broadway
New York, New York 10003-4793

Published in Canada by General Publishing Company, Ltd.

Library of Congress Cataloging-in-Publication Data

Brook-Shepherd, Gordon, 1918–
    The storm birds: Soviet postwar defectors.

    Bibliography: p.
    Includes index.
        1. Defectors—Soviet Union—Biography.   2. Spies—
Soviet Union—Biography.   3. Soviet Union. Komitet
gosudarstvennoĭ bezopasnosti—Officials and employees—
Biography.   4. Soviet Union—Glavnoe razvedyvatel'noe
upravleni—Officials and employees—Biography.
5. Espionage, Russian.   I. Title.
DK268.A1B76   1989   327.1'2'0922   88-37870
ISBN 1-55584-122-8

Manufactured in the United States of America

This book is printed on acid-free paper

Designed by Irving Perkins Associates

First Edition

10 9 8 7 6 5 4 3 2 1

To the Bird-Watchers

Contents

PART FOUR: THE WHEEL TURNS

PART FIVE: FULL CIRCLE

Illustrations

Evdokia Petrov, 1954 (Associated Press)

Dr. Alan Nunn May (Keystone Collection)

Captain Nikolai Khokhlov, 1957 (Associated Press)

KGB Headquarters, Moscow (Camera Press)

H. A. R. ("Kim") Philby, 1967 (Thomson Regional Newspapers)

Oleg Lyalin (Pic Photos)

Oleg Penkovsky (Popperfoto)

Missile site in Cuba (Associated Press)

James Angleton (photograph by Raymond Rocca)

Headlines announcing Kennedy's assassination, November 23, 1963 (BBC Hulton Picture Library)

Speznaz training

Speznaz in action

The spade, traditional weapon of Speznaz training

Arkady Shevchenko, 1985 (Associated Press)

Nikita Khrushchev, October 1960 (Topham Picture Library)

Ariane rocket (Military Archive and Research Services)

Margaret Thatcher and Mikhail Gorbachev, 1984 (Associated Press)

Oleg Gordievski (Associated Press)

Foreword

TWELVE YEARS ago, I turned aside from my preoccupation with nineteenth- and early-twentieth-century European history to study a novel subject, the story of the first Soviet defectors to cross to the West. I was launched on it by the chance discovery that the pioneer of all these pioneers was still alive and well and living in Paris. Boris Bajanov was also the most important of those early cases; before his flight to British India in 1928, he had been one of Stalin's private secretaries. I learned much from him during more than thirty hours of conversation about subsequent defectors. My book *The Storm Petrels*, which appeared in 1977 and takes us down to 1941 and beyond, was the genesis of *The Storm Birds*, whose theme is the postwar Soviet defectors from 1945 right down to the Gorbachev era.

The major difference as regards the research for the present book has been the great increase in the number of principal figures dealt with who were still alive and whom it was possible to see. Bajanov had been the only "Petrel" who survived to tell his tale. The others had all died natural deaths, or had been assassinated. For the present work, I have been able to talk at length, either in America or in Europe, to no fewer than eight Soviet defectors. Their accounts have been corroborated and amplified by expert sources in Europe and America. From all that has emerged it became clear that Western intelligence has achieved steadily mounting success in this field, which has received far less attention than Western failures—either real or suspected.

There are three giants who dominate the scene. A giant I have defined as a Soviet intelligence defector (and these are my main

concern) whose contribution went far beyond his normal professional "assets" to play a certain strategic role in postwar
history as such.

I have put only three in this category without hesitation. The
first is Colonel Oleg Penkovsky, whose revelations went much
wider than his role in the 1962 Cuban missile crisis. Quite apart
from that affair, the 5,500 secret or top secret documents he
managed to photograph and pass to the West can be proved to
have been of such far-reaching military significance as to have
affected the planning of the Western alliance for years and, in
some departments, for decades ahead.

The second giant is the fascinating French case of "Farewell." His main contribution, in the eight hectic months which
preceded his self-induced destruction, was scientific and technological; yet he, too, had an added dimension in that his revelations, when shared with other NATO countries, helped to
draw the France of President François Mitterrand closer to the
Western alliance. As with Penkovsky, the true story of his fall,
told here for the first time, is more extraordinary than anything
in spy fiction.

The third giant is Oleg Gordievski, who, as KGB rezident-
designate in Britain, was the most senior Soviet intelligence
officer ever to work for the West. He is also the only one of the
trio to have survived. His strategic importance lies mainly in
the political field. He was the first man to show how the Kremlin of the early 1980s really worked and to warn his audience
about its paranoia. One of his most far-reaching disclosures,
which is described later in detail, is how, as a result of that
paranoia, the West may, quite unsuspectingly, have come un-
comfortably close to a nuclear confrontation with the Soviet
Union in November of 1983. Gordievski's warnings were heard,
and heeded, at the highest levels.

But what these defectors, be they of giant or normal stature,
have told us is only part of their story. The other side, which
I have concentrated throughout on trying to develop, is what
each was like as an individual human being and what were the
motives which caused each to turn his back on the regime of
which he was a privileged member. In some cases, which in-

clude, above all, Gordievski and Farewell, the impulse was entirely ideological, a moral revulsion against Communism because of the corruption, deceit and terror in which it was rooted.

With most of the others, a more complex pattern is evident. The great Penkovsky, for example, acted partly out of career frustration and partly out of a fantasized vanity. He was also drawn to the West, as were nearly all of the others, by the magnet of a fuller and freer life than anything offered, even to the secret police, in the Soviet world. Indeed, one of the early postwar cases, Yuri Rastvorov, was a fun-loving extrovert for whom that better life (plus the prospect of escaping from a wife he detested) was the dominant motive. He fell in love with that life as the only Soviet member of the Tokyo Tennis Club and jumped westward, so to speak, across the net. (More than thirty years later, he was still enjoying his game in America.)

The defectors' domestic situation, and the absence or presence of a love affair outside it, is another factor which always has to be weighed. An even more compelling role was played by the naked fear of being exterminated, especially during the repeated Stalinist and early post-Stalinist purges of the Soviet intelligence services. It was this terror which, in the final analysis, prompted the young cipher clerk Igor Gouzenko to snatch up his telegrams and run for his life in the streets of Ottawa in September 1945; it was also to nudge the Petrov couple (both of them KGB officers) into the hands of the Australian authorities in Canberra nine years later. (The Petrovs, incidentally, are the only defectors on whom this book has nothing very new to offer. In the wife's case, however, the tale of the flight itself, which made worldwide headlines at the time, is still a unique human drama of this genre.)

Though I did not set out with any cyclical theme in mind, a strong one emerged without being summoned over the four years the book has been in preparation. It is conveyed by the title of the last part, "Full Circle." In one technical sense, the East-West espionage conflict does move around to an exact counterpoint in this postwar era: Gordievski, the top Western agent of his day, succeeded in 1981 in getting himself appointed to precisely the same key post, the British desk of the KGB in Moscow, as was occupied in the reverse direction by Kim Philby forty years before, when the top Soviet agent of his time was put in charge of the Soviet desk in London.

But the wheel turns in a much broader sweep than that. In the wartime and early postwar period, Britain in particular had lost several privileged figures of its establishment. Men like Burgess, Maclean and Blunt had gone over to the Soviet Union out of ideological persuasion that the Communist path was the one mankind should tread. The Russians who crossed to the West at the time were workmanlike figures, who were not born into the Soviet elite and who, for the most part, defected for personal reasons or out of fear for their safety. By the late 1970s and 1980s, however, it is figures from the Soviet establishment who come to reject their system, with ideology as their main impulse. What the Kremlin is by now getting in return is agents who, despite their very considerable professional value, are shoddy human specimens, caught up in the Soviet net by greed or other defects in their character. Geoffrey Prime in Britain and Ronald Pelton or Edward Lee Howard in America are typical examples. Obviously, there could be exceptions moving in either direction at any moment. But the broad pattern, so far as the Western powers are concerned, is one where the best Russians are now turning to them, and for what they hold to be the best reasons.

My concern throughout has been with Soviet intelligence defectors (Arkady Shevchenko, the onetime under secretary-general at the United Nations, being the only odd man out, included for his personal and political significance). Every now and then, however, I have found myself brushing up against Western defectors. When this does happen, the reader will also find new material. Thus the chapter on the Volkovs, the hapless couple fingered by Philby and promptly exterminated by his KGB masters in 1945, ends with the first comprehensive "damage assessment" of Philby's betrayal as well as much fresh detail on the Volkov case itself.

As for the West's principal "suspect," the conclusive evidence which is produced to show that Colonel Penkovsky was every bit as genuine as he was important, destroys by itself the thesis that Sir Roger Hollis could have been a Soviet agent. Hollis, head of MI5 at the time, was one of the very few officers in that organization who, for operational reasons, had to be informed of the colonel's true identity and significance before his first visit was ever made to London. No secret agent working for Moscow could have failed to tip the Kremlin off to the peril, even before the enormous and broad-ranging scope of Penkovsky's revelations became clear. It is significant that all those espionage writers who suggest that Hollis was a Soviet spy have perforce to begin by casting doubts on Penkovsky's credentials, otherwise their equation simply will not balance. I hope we shall read less of their particular brand of algebra in the future.

In conclusion, I wish to thank all those, and particularly the Soviet defectors, who have given me so much of their time over the past few years, always, I may say, willingly, and usually eagerly. I have been impressed by the defectors' frankness and, as their stories unfolded, by their coolness and courage. The West as a whole owes them a very considerable debt. But my gratitude to them is personal, and all the warmer for that.

PART ONE

Sparks of War

1

Appointment at Chequers

AT NOON on Sunday, October 7, 1945, the *Queen Mary* docked at Southampton after her six-day voyage from New York. Of the hundreds of passengers disembarking, the most illustrious was the prime minister of Canada, the Right Honorable William Lyon Mackenzie King. His distinction did not arise from any great personal qualities. A shrewd and ruthless political tactician in his own domestic backyard, Mackenzie King had contrived to keep himself and his Liberal party in power for more than eighteen years. On the international scene, however, he was nervous and unsure, a pygmy among the giants who had led the Western alliance to victory over Nazi Germany. His significance was that he alone of the wartime leaders was still in power at this dawn of peace.

Two of those giants who had overshadowed him were gone already. Death had removed the American president, Franklin D. Roosevelt, back in the spring of that year. His successor, Harry Truman, was still fingering the levers of presidential power, which he would eventually wield with unexpected firmness. Another giant, Winston Churchill, the British prime minister, had been ignominiously pushed off the stage in midsummer by his own electorate (an event which had astonished Stalin, among countless other observers, and must have made the Russian dictator all the more satisfied with his Soviet way

3

of doing things). The new prime minister of Britain, the Labour party leader Clement Attlee, was no stranger to world affairs, for, as Churchill's deputy for the greater part of the war, he had been involved in every tragedy and triumph of that vast conflict. Yet he too was still feeling his way at the pinnacle and, in any case, was by nature every inch as reticent as his predecessor had been rambunctious. The third giant of the West at war, the Free French leader, General Charles de Gaulle, had yet to secure his political hold over peacetime France. Thus it was as an embodiment of the old "V for Victory" sign rather than as a statesman that Prime Minister Mackenzie King found himself surrounded by newspaper reporters as he landed.

"I have," he told them, "no special program. I just want to talk things over quietly with as many people as possible."[1] As an exercise in disinformation, that bland statement equaled anything which had been spread abroad by wartime propaganda.

Mackenzie King drove straight from the landing to the British prime minister's official country residence at Chequers. There, far from taking a leisurely look at the global scene from the peace of the Buckinghamshire countryside, he and Attlee spent most of that afternoon and evening, and early the following morning, debating the shattering event that Mackenzie King had just finished discussing with President Truman in Washington. On September 7, exactly one month earlier, a cipher clerk who had fled from the Soviet embassy in Ottawa, his head full of top secret intelligence stories and his pockets stuffed with documents, had finally succeeded, after some hair-raising adventures, in making contact with the Canadian security authorities. One story, backed up by the originals of his embassy's telegrams, was to stand out above the rest. Among the Western spies he named as having operated for the Russians throughout the war was a British scientist who had worked on the last and greatest secret of that war—the Manhattan Project, the creation of the West's atomic bomb. And there was not much, it seemed, about the production of that strategically decisive weapon of which the Kremlin was not aware.

For the three leaders of the postwar alliance, the blow had a triple impact. First was the shock that privileged and highly educated members of Western society like the British scientist, and a number of Canadians also unmasked as Soviet spies, could have betrayed their countries at all—let alone betrayed them out of ideological conviction rather than fear of blackmail or simple greed. In this respect the West, and Britain in particular, had some even nastier surprises ahead.

Second was the disquieting revelation that, throughout the war, Russia had been spying on her allies just as if they were hostile intelligence targets. This led to the equally disturbing thought that, in the Kremlin's eyes, her wartime partners, as leaders of the capitalist world, had never lost the image of enemies. It was, of course, already obvious by the autumn of 1945 that the grand alliance which had overthrown Hitler was fast dissolving into two rival power blocs, at odds over the future shape of liberated Europe. The bitter struggle between Russia and the West over the postwar regime to be set up in Poland—a struggle eventually won hands down by Stalin—underscored that conflict. But it was one thing to be involved in a quarrel over spoils, a fairly common and often short-term problem among battle partners, and quite another to confront a new enemy arising from the graveyard of that alliance partnership. Only on September 2, 1945, had Japan, her resistance broken by the atom bombs dropped on Hiroshima and Nagasaki, signed formal terms of surrender on the American battleship USS *Missouri.* Final victory over the Axis powers and, with it, global peace in the world was thus less than one week old when the bombshell of a different order had gone off in Ottawa.

Lastly, there was the momentous nature of the harm inflicted on the Western camp. So long as the West was in sole possession of the ultimate weapon of destruction in the air, it might counter the overpowering weight of Soviet military superiority on the ground. Eventually, Russia would develop the weapon herself, for science has no permanent frontiers. Indeed with this certainty in mind, there had been much agonizing in the West, while the wartime alliance had flourished, over whether and how nuclear knowledge might be shared with Moscow. President Truman was still turning over the possibility of some such open approach to the Russians when the defection of the cipher clerk revealed how much the Russians already knew. Suspicions had long existed about such nuclear and other wartime Soviet espionage; but here was the proof, and it helped to stiffen a growing mood of hard-nosed disenchantment with Moscow in the minds of both Truman and Attlee. (Mackenzie King, something of an innocent abroad, proved much slower to bite on the bullet of disillusion.)

For the Americans, the gravest matter was not the ending of any misapprehensions about a wartime partner, but the loss of a crucial strategic advantage over an ally now turned hostile rival. Two months before the first atom bomb was dropped on Japan, President Truman had been speculating to his secretary of war, Henry Stimson, that possession of the weapon would enable the United States to enforce its will on the Soviet Union in East–West confrontations stretching from Poland to Manchuria.[2] James Byrnes, the secretary of state, had put the thought in Truman's mind as soon as the new president had taken office in April. The time frame of that crucial American advantage was now seen to be shrinking alarmingly. Estimates by Western nuclear experts of how long it would take the Russians to construct their own bomb unaided varied from five years to a full generation. With the revelation that such efforts had been far from unaided, even the minimum estimates of lead time had to be reduced.

The Russians had in fact resumed work on their own long-neglected nuclear research program sometime in 1943, presumably on the strength of the first reports they had received from their agents in the West about the Manhattan Project. But there had been nothing frenzied about their efforts, even after President Truman offhandedly mentioned to Stalin at the Potsdam Conference in July of 1945 that the West had perfected a "very powerful explosive" which might well end the war with Japan. Stalin had received the information as casually as it was offered, either because he was determined to show no alarm or because he genuinely had no idea just how powerful the new weapon was to prove. Its deployment to wipe out two Japanese cities a month later cleared any doubts that might have been in his mind.

More then twenty years afterward Stalin's daughter described how, on the day of the Hiroshima explosion, she had gone to her father's dacha to find the Soviet dictator so absorbed with the implications of the bomb that he could scarcely find time for her—despite the fact that she had just presented him with a new grandchild.[3] Behind the screen of outward calm which the Soviet leaders continued to display on the subject, a frantic race was immediately begun to overtake the West by any means and with the utmost speed. To help in the race, a series of urgent and top secret messages was sent to all the Soviet Union's relevant intelligence-gathering centers in the West, ordering them to give the highest priority to getting hold of documentary material about the weapon just unleashed on the world. The text of one such message, sent on August 22, 1945, was among the documents the Russian cipher clerk escaped with only a fortnight after it had been dispatched.

Such was the global context of the Mackenzie King visit. Into it fit two other figures in particular, both of whom seemed unexceptional enough at the time but each of whom was to cast a long and extraordinary personal shadow forward. The British counterintelligence official who, on that October 7, boarded the *Queen Mary* to give the Canadian prime minister the latest briefing on the espionage crisis was none other than Roger Hollis, later to rise to the head of Britain's MI5 and to be suspected during his lifetime, and openly accused after his death, of being the Kremlin's superspy. And the British colleague who had hastily passed the whole Canadian problem over to Hollis to deal with was none other than H. A. R. ("Kim") Philby of MI6, the man revealed nearly twenty years later to have been without question the most important of all known Russian postwar agents operating in the West. Moreover, the reason for Philby's haste was his desperate need to cover his own back from the sudden threat of exposure from another defector in a totally different quarter and coming in a totally unrelated manner.

This curious confluence of espionage events will be described in a later chapter. Suffice it to note here that what was to go down in history as the Gouzenko affair was already off to a rousing start.

2

The Cipher Clerk

THE THOUGHT of defection may have flitted across the mind of Igor Sergeyevich Gouzenko even before the wheels of the plane carrying him and his master, Colonel Nikola Zabotin, from Moscow had touched down at Ottawa in June 1943. On the approach flight via the polar route over northern Canada he had seen below him dozens of towns and villages, all of them traced out in long lines and semicircles of houses, the smallest evidently a five- or six-room construction and each complete with garden and garage. These, he was repeatedly assured by the Canadians accompanying the Soviet party, were the houses of ordinary people, workers for the most part. At first, Gouzenko was incredulous. The sheer numbers of them eventually convinced the young cipher clerk on his first trip anywhere outside the Soviet Union that his hosts must be telling the truth. Yet, to live in any one of those houses, a Russian back home would need to be a member of the senior hierarchy of the Communist party or state officialdom, one of the privileged Nomenklatura. Ordinary mortals would be lucky to get even a tiny two-room apartment in which to bring up a whole family. It was a disquieting introduction to the Western world. If this was the capitalistic "exploitation of the workers," a thesis which had been dinned into him since childhood, there seemed, at first sight, much to be said for it.

Second and third impressions only hammered home the ines-

capable contrasts with life in the Soviet Union and the equally
inescapable doubts they raised. Gouzenko, then twenty-four
years old, was a married man, and his wife, Anna, who was
pregnant, had been allowed to join him soon afterward by sea.
She proved just as flabbergasted as her husband, and even more
delighted, by the shops of the Canadian capital, every one of
them an Aladdin's Cave compared with the half-empty counters
and shoddy displays of Moscow's stores. Nor was it only material things which impressed and troubled the young couple,
whose first child, Andrei, was born soon after their arrival on
Canadian soil. The hostility and surliness they had been told to
expect from their ideological enemies simply did not exist. The
airport worker who had greeted Gouzenko and his colleagues
by inquiring about their dreaded leader with a cheery "How's
Uncle Joe?" had immediately set a tone which never faltered in
the weeks and months that followed. They had come upon
friendly human beings who were, moreover, quite uninhibited,
in both public and private, about their feelings. Clearly, therefore, these were people who feared nobody, a revelation to the
young couple just arrived from a state system controlled by
terror and threaded through with suspicion, evasion and
denunciation.

   To someone of Gouzenko's background, the shock was especially strong. He was, after all, a thoroughly indoctrinated
product of that system, the perpetuation of which had been the
prime concern of all his training. Though never a member of
the Communist party (that would have come automatically had
he allowed his career to blossom), he had joined the Komsomol
or Young Communists when aged seventeen. Four years later,
Hitler invaded Russia, and Gouzenko, by now a graduate of the
Moscow Academy of Engineering, found himself selected for
military intelligence work. He was thoroughly trained in cod-
ing and decoding but only after a five-month investigation by
the Soviet secret police, known in those days by the initials
NKVD,* was he allowed to operate for the first time as a cipher

---

*For an account of the various names under which the KGB has operated in the past, see
Appendix: *Plus ça change.*

clerk at the military intelligence HQ of the Red Army in Moscow. From there he was posted to the battlefield, and while he was at the front the authorities decided he was good enough at his job and reliable enough in his loyalties to be sent abroad. A second prolonged vetting process followed to establish the latter point beyond any shadow of Soviet doubt. The final seal of approval for such foreign postings had to be given either by, or in the name of, the head of the Foreign Branch of the Communist party himself. Such was the choice product of the Soviet system, described as a "civilian employee" but now, in reality, Lieutenant Gouzenko of the GRU, or Main Intelligence Directorate of the General Staff, who found himself transported more or less straight from Hitler's war front to the tranquil capital of Ottawa in the summer of 1943.[1]

The work he now took over amply explained—had Gouzenko ever needed the explanation—why he had been put for so long under the police microscope before being sent on such a mission abroad. His superior, Colonel Zabotin, fulfilled the formal function of military attaché in the large redbrick house at 285 Charlotte Street which had been opened up as the new Soviet embassy when diplomatic relations were established between Ottawa and Moscow the year before. But, as Gouzenko was well aware, Zabotin was, above and beyond this, the head of the GRU's secret operations against the West in Canada, with the code name "Grant." (Gouzenko's own code name was "Klark," a somewhat disingenuous label, given the nature of his duties.) As he was also well aware, the NKVD maintained its own parallel but entirely separate espionage network within the embassy and, on the counterespionage side, watched over everybody, including "Grant" and his fourteen-man team. Indeed, Gouzenko himself was to trip up badly over an NKVD security hurdle. In all, if the secret and straightforward sections of the embassy were counted up, there were no fewer than five distinct Soviet networks based at 285 Charlotte Street, each reporting directly by its own ciphers to five separate centers in Moscow, from where five separate sets of instructions flowed back. The man nominally in charge of the whole mission, Ambassador George Zarubin, had neither detailed knowledge of nor direct responsibility for what went on in the intelligence sections. This was just as well for him when disaster struck one of those departments.*

Gouzenko's own office was in Room 12, one of eight rooms on the second floor of the embassy, the entire section of which was closed off by a double steel door, with iron bars, reinforced at night by steel shutters across all the windows. A hidden bell brought a guard's eye to a keyhole before access was given. This was the claustrophobic cell in which the young lieutenant worked for fifteen months, enciphering and deciphering all the GRU's telegrams to and from Moscow. Though for the most part he knew only the code names and not the real identities of Zabotin's agents (whom the colonel had mostly inherited from his predecessor, Major Sokolov), Gouzenko was either familiar with or could learn about every other detail of the network. In the safe of Room 12 were the colonel's secret diary, all his agents' records and all the other key documents of the GRU's operations. The actual cipher books, together with the day's telegram traffic to and from Moscow, were placed in a sealed bag each night and handed to a security man for safe overnight keeping.

The private life which Igor Gouzenko was allowed to lead stood in complete contrast to his tense, padlocked existence within his own mission and among his own colleagues. The time was to come when, partly because of Gouzenko's actions, all cipher clerks in every Soviet mission abroad were to be compulsorily billeted, with their families, inside the official compound and required to be accompanied whenever allowed to step outside. But these were early days and Canada was formally an Allied power. It would have been embarrassing to the Kremlin to have demanded the construction of a separate Soviet enclave in Ottawa when the mission was opened; in any case, there was no time. So it was that many of the staff were scattered in private accommodations all over the capital. Colonel Zabotin had a house to himself at 14 Range Road, where he did much of his work. Gouzenko lived with his wife and infant

---

*Zarubin's career as a diplomat was unaffected by the traumas of the Gouzenko affair. Though in 1945 he did not know a word of English, he was to end up as Soviet ambassador in both London and Washington.

son in a comfortable apartment block at 511 Somerset Street, in the suburbs of the capital. On all sides, he had ordinary Canadians living just through the walls—a circumstance that was to prove his salvation.

It is probable, as Gouzenko constantly asserted when he was safely in Western hands, that he would have defected anyway sooner or later, even had no emergency arisen. There was always one painful check on his actions, the thought of the family "hostages" in Russia. His own mother and sister were still there. Anna had left behind both her parents as well as a sister and brother. He could be fairly certain that any or all of them would be persecuted and perhaps liquidated by Joseph Stalin's police state if he both turned his back on the regime and seriously damaged it in the process.[2] Yet, despite this, the outward and inner blessings of living right in among a society so prosperous, so open and so carefree compared with anything he had known at home or expected abroad were like a master spring coiling slowly inside him to impel him to defection. The more he identified with this society as a human being, the more repugnance he felt at helping to spy on it, with the ultimate objective of bringing it down. But what triggered the spring to push him across the line was fear.

Before leaving Moscow, he had been told that he could expect to remain at his post for two to three years. In September 1944, when he had been in Ottawa for only fifteen months, he was called into Colonel Zabotin's office and told that a message had just arrived from Moscow ordering the immediate recall of the cipher clerk and his family for no stated reason.[3] It was the sort of chilling, unexplained summons back into the void which every Soviet official serving abroad dreaded to receive. The colonel himself lived under the same fear. Indeed, he began to breathe easily only after receiving, out of the blue, both the Order of the Red Banner and that of the Red Star as a reward for his good work. "Now," the military attaché exclaimed openly in his office, "I have nothing to fear in returning to Moscow." As things turned out, the poor man was to depart in justified dread for his life. But in the autumn of 1944 the colonel's prestige and influence were good enough for him to persuade Moscow to change its mind and allow Gouzenko to stay on for the time being, in view of the heavy workload in the department and the shortage of trained staff. Whether this amounted to a security clearance or, as Gouzenko's wife suspected, only a temporary reprieve from danger, the incident decided the pair to seek Canadian asylum "when the time came."

It came the following summer. Gouzenko had gone home from the embassy one evening carelessly leaving behind him a secret document buried among a pile of unimportant papers on his desk. To his immense relief, the slipup appeared to have gone unnoticed when he discovered the document still there the next morning. It *had* been noticed, by a "charlady" who was in fact one of the security team working in the building. She told neither the military attaché nor the ambassador but only her own master, Vitaly Pavlov, who, under the guise of a second secretary, headed the NKVD team at the mission. He, in turn, informed only his own masters in Moscow through his own private channels. The reaction came within a week. Colonel Zabotin (who had indulgently let Gouzenko off with a private rebuke when his cipher clerk dutifully confessed his mistake) got a reprimand for not reporting such a grave matter. The culprit himself was recalled to Moscow, this time unequivocally. It was an order which, in the circumstances, was useless to question but perilous to obey. Far from escaping with rebukes, Soviet cipher clerks had been executed for such negligence. Apart from fear, there was one final spur to defection. Gouzenko's wife had told him that she was expecting a second child. They determined that it should not only, like the first, be born on Canadian soil but be given the chance to spend all its life there.

Gouzenko now set one pattern which was to be followed by nearly all the premeditated, as opposed to the so-called impulse, defectors who were to follow his example in the years ahead. He prepared a dowry of intelligence material to present to the arbiters of his fate. In the short time which remained to him before his GRU replacement, one Lieutenant Koulakov, arrived from Moscow, he went carefully through the files, turning over the edges of more than a hundred documents he would want to remove at short notice. The choice was shrewdly made. The bulk of the material was picked for its direct interest to the Canadian authorities in whose hands he was placing his future; but he also selected a handful of documents which were of vital concern to the West in general, and it was one of these, coupled with his own verbal testimony, which, as we have seen, contained the real dynamite.

There was some shrewdness too in the defection itself, but also a small dose of naïveté and a much larger dose of muddle.[4] He chose an evening when Lieutenant Koulakov, now arrived, was working at Colonel Zabotin's house and when the colonel himself, a genial fellow with a very busy social life, was attending a party. Gouzenko also knew that several of his colleagues would definitely be out of the embassy that night, attending an Ottawa cinema show. The date was September 5, 1945.

He got a nasty shock, as he signed himself in, to see the mission's NKVD boss, Vitaly Pavlov, still lingering in the building. But on the pretext of "having just a couple of telegrams to do" he got through the steel doors and into his office. He duly enciphered two telegrams, to ward off any immediate suspicion, then stuffed his pockets and the inside of his shirt with the papers already selected for removal. He handed over to the duty officer the prepared telegrams, together with the sealed bag containing the military attaché's cipher codes for safe overnight keeping. Everything, except for his bulging clothes, looked normal as he walked downstairs. Fortunately, the doorman, another NKVD security man, noticed nothing odd. Fortunately, too, the dreaded Pavlov had gone. It was soon after 8 p.m. that Gouzenko stepped out into Charlotte Street.

What he did next can only be understood when we remember that Gouzenko was the first of the postwar defectors. Even the word "defection" was a new one. It still had an unfamiliar and, for some in the West, a somewhat discordant ring. The remarkable Russian who, in prewar days, had blazed the trail of flight to the West less than twenty years before had actually been looked down upon, to begin with, as a turncoat.[5] A little of that same repugnance was still in the air in 1945, in the aftermath of a war in which, seemingly, the Soviet Union had been nothing but a great and glorious ally. As for Gouzenko, he had no previous examples to guide him. So he acted by instinct, and those instincts were still the ones which had been bred in him by a totalitarian society. Despite everything that he had seen and welcomed about Western freedom (and that summer he had even witnessed the amazing spectacle of a truly democratic election being enacted all around him in Canada), Gouzenko could not bring himself to believe that the police in any country were people who were on your side. He had, however, come to believe in the independence of the Canadian press. So, instead of going straight to the authorities, he took a tram to the Queen Street offices of the *Ottawa Journal,* the more solid and more conservative of the capital's two daily papers, to present his case there.

On the first visit, his courage simply failed him as he was about to knock on the door marked "Editor," and he fled home to Anna to calm his nerves and clean up his precious documents, some of which had become soaked in his own perspiration. When he returned to the *Ottawa Journal,* the editor had already left and the night staff, busy making up the next day's paper, had neither time nor comprehension for this strange figure, waving papers written in a language they could not read, and talking excitedly of Soviet espionage and Canadian treachery. Nonetheless, they put him on the right track by persuading him to go to the Royal Canadian Mounted Police and tell his story there. But it was past midnight by the time Gouzenko made his first contact with officialdom by accosting a uniformed policeman on duty outside the Justice Ministry. He was told to come back the next day. There was nothing for it but to take himself and his documents, which had now begun to feel more dangerous than precious, back to his Somerset Street apartment for the night. His absence from duty, and the gaps in the files in Room 12 would, in the normal course of events, not be noticed until sometime the following morning. He still had a few hours left.

The next day, September 6, was a defector's nightmare.[6] The couple decided to make the expedition a family affair, partly to avoid leaving anyone behind and partly to add to the force of their appeal for asylum. So Anna, seven months pregnant, and the two-year-old Andrei both set out with him for the Ministry of Justice. Anna, who was clearly a good woman to have along-side one in an emergency, insisted on carrying the documents herself so that, if they were caught on the streets by any NKVD pursuers, she might slip away with both their infant and their evidence. As ill-luck would have it, the new session of the Canadian Parliament was convening at 11 A.M. that very morning and no minister was at his normal desk. However, they made enough of an impression at the Ministry of Justice, their first port of call, for a secretary to take them over to Parliament Hill. Here, they made more pleas, in yet another anteroom, to be allowed to tell their story and present their documents to the minister, Louis St. Laurent, in person, only to be told, after more telephone calls, that he would be unable to see them.*

Back they trudged to their original haven, the *Ottawa Journal.* This time, they managed to get their documents shown to the editor, only to have them returned with the comment that they just "did not register." Even that conservative journal did not want to be seen attacking the Soviet Union so soon after the Allied victory. The Gouzenkos were, by now, in a pitiful state, but all that the sympathetic newspaper staff could suggest was that they try to take out Canadian naturalization papers in order to protect themselves. Protection of some sort was directly needed. The morning was over. The Soviet embassy and both its secret intelligence networks would already be in an uproar over their disappearance. They were now hunted people, more fugitives than defectors.

After a break for food, they finally made contact with the correct department, the office of the crown attorney in Nicholas Street. Here they faced a new hurdle: bureaucracy. Their application had to be processed even if it was, in truth, a scream for help. They were asked to fill in appropriate forms and return

---

*The minister was later to tell Parliament that he had felt "unable to receive an official from a friendly embassy bearing tales of the kind described." The prim naïveté of the reaction shows what the Gouzenkos, and anyone trying to spread the truth about Stalin's Russia, were up against in 1945.

with photographs the following day. The desk clerk had no idea whether or when Canadian citizenship would be granted and he had to point out that it might well take months. Anna's composure gave way for the first time and she broke into tears. It was the best thing she could have done. The crown attorney's secretary, Mrs. Fernande Joubarne, was a perceptive woman whose desk was in the same office. She proved the most sympathetic audience to date for the Gouzenkos' story and also, so far as they could judge, the first person in all Ottawa to take it seriously. But even Mrs. Joubarne could not provide instant protection, let alone instant citizenship. All that she could and did promise was to make more efforts on their behalf. It was a very despondent and very frightened couple who returned, by the back entrance, to Somerset Street, collecting Andrei, whom they had left in another apartment over lunchtime.

They had not been home for long when the expected threat came. There was a loud hammering on the front door downstairs. Gouzenko heard his name shouted out with the order, in Russian, to open up. He recognized at once the voice of Colonel Zabotin's driver. A few minutes before, peeping out of the window, he had seen two men sitting on a bench on the opposite sidewalk with their eyes glued on his apartment. It seemed all too clear that the NKVD had arrived in force to get him.

There was nothing to do but turn to his neighbors for help. Luckily for the Gouzenkos, the couple who lived next door in Apartment 5 were a Royal Canadian Air Force sergeant and his wife. Sergeant Maine soon put down his newspaper and evening pipe when told by the young Soviet tenant that his Russian masters were probably about to kill both him and his wife; in which case would somebody please look after their little child? The sergeant pondered this astonishing story for a short while before deciding that, in all decency, he had to help them all. At this point, a lady tenant from across the hall appeared on the scene and there was a general conference. It was agreed that all three Gouzenkos should move into her Apartment 6 while Sergeant Maine set off on his bicycle to fetch the local police.

Between 11:30 and midnight these two worlds—the NKVD hovering outside and the Canadian neighbors furnishing protection—collided in earnest. Vitaly Pavlov appeared in person in the corridor, together with Lieutenant Colonel Rogov, the assistant air attaché, who was in uniform, and two other henchmen. They demanded to know Gouzenko's whereabouts. When told by the good sergeant, who slammed his door on them, that he had no idea where his neighbor was, the quartet proceeded to smash their way into Apartment 4 by force. They were busy ransacking the empty rooms when they were interrupted by Constables Walsh and McCullock from the municipal police. The two men, alerted by Sergeant Maine earlier that evening, had already made contact with the Gouzenkos in their hiding place and had agreed to keep the building under surveillance. A fairly calm discussion followed between the intruders, who claimed they were merely inspecting Russian property (with the absent tenants' permission), and the policemen, who pointed to the clear signs of unauthorized entry. Then, things grew more tense. The Russians ordered the constables out. The constables refused to go before the arrival of their own superior officer. Finally, the Russians melted away after a police inspector duly appeared on the scene and announced that he would have to make "further inquiries."

Igor and his family had been only a few yards away in Apartment 6 during the entire confrontation. But their troubles were over. There could be no doubt, after what had just happened, that the couple really were in danger at the hands of their own countrymen, nor that Gouzenko himself was a person of importance. The family stayed in their place of asylum overnight, but now under police guard. There was one more discreet knock on the door of Apartment 4 during the night, but the caller retired when he got no answer.

After breakfast the next morning another police inspector arrived, this time to collect the fugitives for a talk with the Canadian security authorities at the Ministry of Justice, the building they had besieged in vain the previous day. The Gouzenkos left Somerset Street and the NKVD behind them for good.

They had not in reality been so unprotected during that terrible night as they had imagined. Glimpsed through the cur-

tains by Gouzenko, the two figures sitting on a park bench
opposite were not, as he supposed, Russians, but Canadian security men. And the last visitor to Apartment 4 who had quietly
tapped on the door in the small hours and then disappeared into
the night was one of the most influential figures in the espionage world on that side of the Atlantic: Sir William Stephenson,
who coordinated Western intelligence and security operations
from an office in New York. He happened to be a Canadian,
which had perhaps strengthened his interest in the matter. But
the greatest stroke of fortune for the Gouzenkos was that Stephenson had picked that very time to be on a brief liaison visit
to Ottawa. On arrival, he had got in touch with Norman Robertson, the permanent under secretary at the Canadian Ministry of External Affairs, as was his usual practice. He had immediately been given the highly unusual news about a would-be
Soviet defector wandering around Ottawa with a bundle of
sensational documents in his pockets which he wanted to swap
for asylum. For his part, Robertson had been alerted by those
apparently noncommittal officials the Gouzenkos had pleaded
with at the Ministry of Justice. The good Mrs. Joubarne from
the crown attorney's office had also played her part. But it was
the felicitous arrival on the Ottawa scene of Stephenson (code-
named "Intrepid" in intelligence parlance because of his exploits as a young fighter pilot in the 1914–18 war) which set the
rather hesitant Canadian security machinery moving in top
gear. Gouzenko had been instantly recognizable to the expert
as manna falling from heaven upon his own secret world.

What is interesting, and possibly unique, about the Gouzenko
case is that it was officials who decided the issue against all the
first instincts and, indeed, the first decisions of their political
masters. The bland hands-off attitude of the Canadian minister
of justice toward both the intelligence offerings and the human
plight of the Gouzenkos has already been noted. Even more
remarkable in its naïveté was the initial reaction of the prime
minister himself. When told by Robertson on the sixth that an
employee of the Soviet embassy was scurrying around Ottawa
seeking refuge and would probably do away with himself if

refused, Mackenzie King seems almost to have wished for that suicide in order to keep himself out of the unaccustomed glare of world publicity. "If suicide took place," he wrote in his diary, "let the city police take charge and secure whatever there was in the way of documents, but on no account let us take the initiative." As for the value of those documents, Mackenzie King noted that he simply did not believe Gouzenko's story.[7]

It was an extraordinary reaction from someone who had already been prominent in Canadian politics in the early 1930s when Richard Bedford Bennett's Conservative government of the day had outlawed Canada's small but virulent Communist party and jailed some of its leaders on clear evidence that they were engaged in subversion, directed and financed from Moscow. True, it had been Mackenzie King's own Liberal government of 1936 which had withdrawn that ban, although only to reimpose it in 1940 inasmuch as the Nazi-Soviet pact of 1939 remained in force during the first phase of the Western struggle against Hitler.* Moreover, one might have supposed that, despite the second phase of that struggle, when the Soviet Union had been the wartime partner of the democracies, Mackenzie King would have learned that Russia had not abandoned her bad old habits. As it was, recognition of that fact and with it the need for action had to be extracted from him like a wisdom tooth.

Even when told, early on the morning of September 7, what had gone on in Somerset Street the previous night, the prime minister of Canada remained as cautious as a rabbit. He was still thinking in terms of handing back Gouzenko's documents to the Soviet embassy, having perhaps taken photostats. As he later sought to explain:

> I felt that the situation with which we were confronted could not be viewed too circumspectly. I felt that we must make sure what type of person Gouzenko was and what the motive was which

*Britain and France declared war on Germany on September 3, 1939, and Canada followed suit a week later, on September 10. Russia was not brought in on the Allied side until June of 1941, when Hitler's invasion decided matters for her.

had prompted his action. One had to consider other nations as well as one's own before taking a step that might be considered premature.[8]

It was the involvement of those other nations which drew King out of his rabbit warren. One good look at the material Gouzenko had brought with him was enough to convince the security authorities that everything the defector had claimed about the range and depth of Soviet penetration was true. The defector was driven with his wife and son that same day under armed guard to a safe house, a Special Operations training camp near Oshawa on the shores of Lake Ontario, several hundred miles from Ottawa. There, his in-depth interrogation began. His bundle of documents stayed behind in the capital for translation and evaluation.

The ring of Canadian citizens revealed as Soviet agents in those papers was surprising for its size and cohesion, though not for some of its names. The leading people involved were familiar Communist figures, already arrested for subversion in the 1930s: people like Sam Carr, organization secretary of the Canadian Communist party since January 1937, who had been briefly jailed as a security risk in 1942; Fred Rose, another prominent Communist who, despite a long history as a political suspect, had been elected to the Canadian Parliament in 1943 and reelected in the June 1945 voting which had so impressed Gouzenko. Both were Jewish immigrants of the 1920s. More significant were the areas from which they had emigrated. Carr's real name was Schmil Kogan, born in the Soviet Ukraine. Rose had started life as the son of Jacob Rosenberg, a native of Lublin in Poland. Several of their colleagues or helpers uncovered by Gouzenko's documents had similar origins: Samuel Gerson, though born in Montreal, was the son of Russian immigrants from Kiev; Emma Woiken was also of Russian parentage; Isadore Gottheil had a Polish father and a Russian mother. It was an early lesson for Western intelligence that the pull of Slavdom can easily jump over a generation of living abroad.

More disturbing were those impeccably native Canadian or Anglo-Saxon agents now identified, with their code names, in the papers from Colonel Zabotin's desk. David Gordon Lunan, for example, who headed his own little espionage group of four, came from pure Scottish stock in Kirkaldy; although acquitted on the main charge of treason, he was later jailed for refusing to testify against Rose. Matthew Nightingale, who had served in the Royal Canadian Air Force, was the son of a Canadian couple who had moved to Alabama. Agents like Lunan had dropped into the GRU network not out of nostalgia for Russia but out of ideological enthusiasm for a Soviet Union they had never seen. Neither money nor blackmail had encouraged their recruitment. Of the whole bunch, only Emma Woiken was not a member of the Canadian Communist party but, like the rest, she put Communism before Canada. The discovery of so much flagrant disloyalty astounded the handful of Canadians privy to these disclosures, most of all the prime minister himself. Describing the morning when Norman Robertson had come over to Parliament and first told him of the Gouzenko affair, Mackenzie King wrote in his diary:

> It is all very terrible and frightening. . . . I can see that from now until the end of my days it will be with this problem more than any other that, in all probability, I shall be most concerned. . . .
>
> As I dictate this note I think of the Russian Embassy being only a few doors away and of there being a centre of intrigue. During this period of war, while Canada has been helping Russia and doing all we can to foment Canadian–Russian friendship, there has been one branch of the Russian service that has been spying on us . . . and yet another branch intended as a secret service, spying on themselves. . . . The amazing thing is how many contacts have been successfully made with people in key positions in government and industrial circles. . . .[9]

Although Mackenzie King and his officials were sufficiently agitated about Canada's own vulnerability, it was when her allies were shown to be involved that the wires really began to hum. A lead to the United States cropped up in one of the Moscow telegrams to "Grant," abstracted by his cipher clerk, in which the Soviet military attaché was, for once, given a professional task to his liking. He was ordered, among other intelligence priorities, to get "information as to the transfer of American troops from Europe to the United States and the Pacific," together with the locations and movement orders of twenty specified American army formations and headquarters. The order ended with the command "Hurry!" Quite apart from the general gravity of Gouzenko's disclosures, this telegram by itself meant that the first person Mackenzie King would have to discuss the crisis with was his neighbor President Truman in the White House.

The leads to Britain were even more alarming, for they concerned not information requested by Moscow but top secret information already betrayed to Moscow over the years. The first British name to come out of Gouzenko's brimming hat, with the code name "Ellie" (or "Elli"), was Kathleen Mary Willsher, a trusted employee in the office of the British High Commission in Ottawa. Her downfall was the story of the lonely female yearning for something dramatic to happen in life, a story that was to be repeated several times in the long East-West espionage tussle which lay ahead. Her boss, British High Commissioner Malcolm MacDonald, was to sum up her vulnerability thus:

> She was a respectable and quite brainy spinster, nearer forty than thirty years old. A pleasant if rather plain, spectacled woman, she perhaps suffered from a double sense of frustration. First, being a single female with no apparent prospect of marriage, and also with no boy-friend, she never received any satisfaction for her romantic instincts. Second, although she was a quite capable graduate of the London School of Economics, she had not achieved the promotion in government service which she felt was her due. In both the emotional and the intellectual spheres, therefore, she probably nursed grievances. . . .[10]

What the high commissioner (himself the son of the ideologically befuddled British Labour Prime Minister Ramsay MacDonald) did not point out was that it was in the London School of Economics of the 1920s, a bastion of prewar radical thought, where Kathleen Willsher had first imbibed her left-wing sympathies. These were duly converted into outright Communist loyalties when, in 1936, six years after her arrival in Ottawa, she became a member of the Labour-Progressive party, as the Canadian Communists styled themselves. At that time, she was still a stenographer, but that was good enough for the Communist MP Fred Rose (cover names "Fred" or "Debouz" in Gouzenko's list), who, the year before, had already persuaded her to hand over information, ostensibly just for party use and all in the cause of solidarity with the Russian Communists. The long-term investment of time, sympathy and flattery which Rose and his minions put into Miss Willsher proved well worthwhile. In 1939, she was transferred to the Registry Division of the office, where she had access to much of its secret material. In 1944, she was appointed assistant registrar with the duty of actually filing all such material. Thus, through the personal complexes of a British spinster in Ottawa, first Fred Rose, then his espionage master Colonel Zabotin and finally Moscow acquired another useful window on the political aims of their wartime allies.

The wretched woman certainly had no idea that she had ended up as a direct tool of Soviet intelligence. But it strains credulity too far to suggest that the thought had never crossed her mind that her Canadian Communist comrades might not keep everything she told them to themselves. When asked by the investigating commissioners whether she had not felt a conflict between her loyalty to the Crown and that to her political convictions, she gave the frankly revealing reply: "Yes, it was a struggle; it is always a struggle."[11]

On Thursday, September 6, the Canadian authorities first got down to studying Gouzenko's hoard of documents, and early that same evening MacDonald was called in by them and given a briefing. It seems to have been in general terms, with only Miss Willsher mentioned by name. The high commissioner was asked to report her case immediately by top secret telegram to his prime minister and, in the meantime, to ensure, without arousing any suspicion, that no more classified information came her way.

The irony of the occasion was that MacDonald had just come from an official garden party given at his official residence Earnscliffe to celebrate the first month of peace in the world. Among those present was the Soviet ambassador and his interpreter, none other than "Second Secretary" Vitaly Pavlov. Knowing that Zarubin was a passionate angler, and noting that he appeared somewhat bleary-eyed, MacDonald, still unaware of the earthquake which had shaken the Soviet embassy, quipped that his guest looked as though he "had been out fishing all night," and with no success.[12] He later learned that Pavlov's men had indeed been searching the banks of the Ottawa River throughout the small hours in case their missing cipher clerk had thrown himself or his papers into the water.

MacDonald was duly concerned, but not shattered, by the news that his assistant registrar had been passing information to the Russians. Nor was there any great alarm in London when his telegram reporting the fact was received there. The first supporting message, sent on September 9 by Norman Robertson, the Canadian permanent under secretary for external affairs, to his British opposite number, Sir Alexander Cadogan, likewise did little to raise the temperature. Gouzenko was referred to, not by name, only as a clerical officer of the Soviet embassy, and the only reference to his revelation was that the Russians had been enjoying "a certain access to the contents of secret telegrams exchanged between London and Ottawa." In other words, Miss Willsher only.

The next day, September 10, the really lethal news was learned in London. The defector was now correctly described as a cipher officer, which, to anyone with the barest knowledge of intelligence, meant that his information was probably twenty-two-carat gold. Moreover, though Gouzenko himself was, very properly, still not identified, it was now revealed that one of the Soviet agents he had named was Alan Nunn May, described as a doctor of physics at Cambridge University and operating for the Russians in Canada under the code name "Alek." They needed no telling in London what the professor's operations were. Nor did they need reminding, as the Canadians had somewhat unnecessarily pointed out, that the vetting of UK scientists sent out to Canada on any joint project was a British responsibility.

May was no ordinary scientist, and he had not been sent out on any ordinary joint project. Dr. Alan Nunn May was a nuclear physicist. Moreover, since January of 1945 he had been a group leader, under a fellow Cambridge don, Professor John Cockcroft, with the Allied team working full time at the Canadian National Research Council in Montreal on the construction of the atom bomb. The Russians had got wind of this project, through other agents, before the transfer to Canada had taken place. They knew that Western scientists (notably in Britain, Germany, France and America) had all been working at atomic physics since before the war, as had their own experts. They might easily have assumed that wartime research would be concentrated in Canada, not only because that country provided locations which lay beyond the reach of the Luftwaffe's bombers, but also because it possessed both the essential element of uranium, near the Great Bear Lake, and a uranium laboratory. But the West had always assumed that Soviet knowledge of their operations was fairly general. The scale of the Western program, the billions of American dollars being poured into it, above all the successful testing of the first device on a New Mexico desert in July 1945, were believed to be secrets known to only a handful of British, Canadian and American scientists, service officers and statesmen.

By this last year of the war, with the inter-Allied struggle for supremacy in occupied Europe already shaping up, there was evidently no Western endeavor which the Russians were as anxious to learn about. Now, suddenly, it seemed clear that, throughout the last months of the A-bomb's perfection and deployment, they had been doing their learning from a high-level source uniquely placed in the heart of all the experiments. The Western powers were faced with the first of their major postwar espionage challenges.

3

The Professor

MUCH DEBATE and some confusion ensued over how the challenge should be met. Zabotin had got the West off to a good start by an extraordinary lapse of security. Gouzenko had known only May's code name and the nature of his work. However, one of the telegrams he brought over with him provided Alek's colleagues with an instant personal identification. The message, sent by the colonel to his masters in Moscow in early August, read:

> We have worked out the conditions of a meeting with Alek in London. Alek will work in King's College, Strand. It will be possible to find him there through the telephone book. . . . He cannot remain in Canada. At the beginning of September he must fly to London. Before his departure, he will go to the uranium plant in the Petawawa district where he will be for about two weeks. . . . We handed over 500 dollars to him.[1]

There followed a long rigmarole about contact arrangements.

It so happened that there was only one man who was due to leave the Allied team in Canada in September to take up a lecturing appointment at King's College, and that was Dr. May. Had Zabotin exercised more professional caution he would at least have divided his information between separate telegrams, saving the crucial item about Alek's new job for a final message.

But when he sent off that bulletin to Moscow the GRU had as little inkling that it was harboring a key defector in its midst as did the West that the Russians possessed a high-level atomic spy in their own innermost scientific circle.

Now the cat was out of the bag, or rather the twenty cats, counting Miss Willsher and the principal Canadians named by Gouzenko and his material. What had to be decided was how and when to net them, and whether separately or together; if and when to make the scandal public; how to tackle the crisis with the Soviet Union and how to deal with it as between the Western governments themselves. This last issue was an equally delicate one. The Canadians, for example, had immediately suggested that, as May was a British traitor, it should be left to the British to brief the American secretary of state, James Byrnes.

Two threads of Western policy evolved over the weeks and months ahead. Matters were not simplified by the fact that they occasionally got entangled with each other. On the professional front, there was a brisk response from the British side. Peter Dwyer, the highly capable head of the MI6 station in Washington who was also dealing with MI5 matters, flew up to Ottawa immediately after the news of Gouzenko's defection broke. He and William Stephenson formed a powerful duo of on-the-spot advisers. From London, two British code names were issued for the principals in the affair. Gouzenko was henceforth to be referred to only as "Corby." May became "Primrose." The question was how Primrose should be plucked.

Let us start with the reactions of Kim Philby, the Kremlin's ace spy in the West, who at this time held the key position of head of Section 9, the Russian department of MI6. Through normal channels, he had received Dwyer's first two messages about Gouzenko on September 9 and 10. It needs stressing that, at this juncture, Philby did *not* know (as has been stated even in very reputable accounts)[2] that his own position had come under serious threat from another and totally unconnected would-be Soviet defector. That dreadful crisis only confronted him ten days later and is dealt with in the chapter which follows. To begin with, therefore, Philby was able to play the

Gouzenko affair dead straight, which he proceeded to do, with that icy professionalism which characterized all his double-dealing.

The one thing he wanted to avoid was to be sent out to Ottawa himself, for this would remove him from the London center, from where every Western move in the crisis could be monitored by him and passed on to his Soviet contacts. Zabotin's clerk, he told his colleagues, was clearly a mine of valuable information, and a really expert person ought to be sent out from London to help with the investigation there. He threw two names in the ring. The first was Jane Archer, the redoubtable Soviet expert who had given the prewar defector Walter Krivitsky the only thoroughly professional debriefing which he was ever to receive in the West.[3] But he felt she might be a little out of touch and recommended that his MI5 colleague Roger Hollis should go instead.* This was agreed, and out Hollis went, flying from Prestwick on September 16.

Philby was less successful with another suggestion he started peddling. This was that the whole of Operation Corby should be taken out of Foreign Office hands and left with the intelligence communities. This solution would obviously have suited him and his Soviet masters to perfection; yet it was never a starter, as Philby himself soon came to realize. It was not just foreign ministers but presidents and prime ministers who were to become personally involved. The overriding priorities and the crucial decisions in the crisis had to be political.

Back in Ottawa, the Canadian authorities and their Allied advisers, now strengthened by the arrival of Hollis, had to decide what should be done in the short term. As more and more of Gouzenko's pilfered messages were translated, it became clear that Primrose, as we can now call him, had not only told Moscow the broad technical details of the New Mexico trial explosion and of the actual bomb dropped on Japan but had

---

*In view of the later controversy over whether Hollis was or was not a Soviet agent it should be noted that the suggestion by Philby that he be given the job was in no way incriminating. Hollis was, in fact, the obvious candidate in counterintelligence, being then the head of the 2B anti-Soviet division, and he appears to have discharged the task quite straightforwardly.

even managed to secure and pass on a sample of the key raw material used in preparing the devices, "162 micrograms of uranium 233 in the form of oxide in a thin lamina," to quote Colonel Zabotin's accompanying telegram.[4] This was in response to messages from the KGB's Moscow Center urging the colonel to get everything he could out of their agent before his departure for England.

There was some discussion among the Canadian authorities about whether Primrose should be allowed to make that trip or not. One argument against letting him travel was that the Soviet secret police might succeed in capturing him en route. Another was the legalistic point that, as his offenses had been committed in Canada, it might be easier to try him there. But the professional view prevailed that, as in all such cases where the full extent of the plot was still unknown, he should be allowed to cross the Atlantic under close surveillance in the hope that, once in London, his contacts there would provide more knowledge about Soviet penetration. This view was reinforced by the precise arrangements for making those contacts, as revealed in other telegrams provided by Gouzenko. Moscow had agreed with Zabotin's suggestion that the secret meeting should take place on October 7 in front of the British Museum. But the Russians altered practically everything else in the colonel's proposals (which added up to another very slapdash exercise). The meeting was to be at 8 P.M., not 11 P.M. (when it would be too dark). The professor was to identify himself by carrying a copy of the London *Times* under his left arm whereas his contact man would be carrying, in his left hand, a copy of *Picture Post*. The password concerned "the shortest way to the Strand."[5] Clearly, if that meeting ever did take place and the scientist was seen to be handing anything over, there would be no option but to arrest him on the spot: such a situation would comprise any spy catcher's dream, seizing an agent in flagrante. Nonetheless, it was agreed that, if possible, all the Soviet agents, British and Canadian, should be taken simultaneously in one coordinated swoop.

However, those decisions still lay ahead. For a tense week after Gouzenko's defection, May was played fairly loose in case he became suspicious and tried to flee the country,* that is, until he was finally put on his plane for London on September 16. A droll episode surrounded the departure from Montreal's Dorval Airport, scheduled for 11 A.M. Detective Sergeant Bayfield of the Canadian Mounties was detailed to fly on the same plane as surveillance, though obviously sitting elsewhere and in mufti. Malcolm MacDonald remembered that the British group captain of a Royal Air Force unit operating from the same airfield knew the detective well. Had the supposedly innocent passenger been greeted with his real identity, May would have taken fright on the spot. So the group captain found himself invited to the British High Commission and there detained with drinks and amicable conversation until the telephone rang to say that May's plane had just taken off. It duly landed at Prestwick, where British officials were lurking to have Primrose pointed out to them by the unknown Bayfield. The identification process between the security men was somewhat labored:

> British contact man: How do you like our lowlands weather?
> Bayfield: I haven't seen much of it yet but it's rather like our Maritime Province.

Ten days later, May was seen in London by the head of the British Atomic Council, Mr. Akers. The meeting was routine enough, but Akers was instructed to give his impressions of the new recruit to King's College. He reported that May appeared to have absolutely nothing on his mind.

A lot of high-level diplomacy needed to be got out of the way before, on October 7, Primrose was due to appear in front of the British Museum clutching his copy of *The Times*. It so happened that a meeting of the Foreign Ministers Council of the wartime Allied powers convened in London just after Gouzenko defected. By now, the Western Allies were growing soberly disenchanted over the prospect of getting any concessions out of the

---

*May's boss in Montreal at the Canadian National Research Council, Professor John Cockcroft, had of course to be told, in great secrecy, of May's treachery. This task was allotted to Malcolm MacDonald, who later wrote that he would never forget Professor Cockcroft's "jump of astonishment."

Russians at these gatherings. Still, they reasoned, the timing could be awkward. If the Gouzenko affair were revealed instantly, this could be exploited by the Kremlin as a deliberate Western move to sabotage the talks. As we have seen, there were technical reasons, which fluctuated in importance, why disclosure was delayed; but the political problem—to what extent could the West afford to offend the Russians, impossible though they had become as peacetime partners?—was always there.

In Ottawa, the Russian embassy, immediately after Gouzenko's disappearance, had embarked on a course of action which was to become something of a stereotype in handling future defections from their ranks. The ambassador, in demanding the cipher clerk's return, alleged that he was needed to answer criminal charges, as he had stolen money from the embassy safe. The Russians followed this up with a second note demanding Gouzenko's arrest and surrender "for deportation." Both requests were easily stalled. An irony of this tense situation which had sprung up between wartime allies was that the same ambassador, Zarubin, had just informed Mackenzie King that Stalin wished to confer a high Soviet decoration on General Henry D. G. Crerar, the officer who had commanded the Canadian army in Europe in the common fight against Hitler.

Meanwhile, solid ranks had to be formed within the Western camp itself. Remarkably, it seems that it was only on September 21 that the Americans were informed that a cipher clerk from the office of the Soviet military attaché in Ottawa was in Canadian hands, and had already provided some "useful information." Not a word, as yet, about the treachery of a British spy operating from the center of the American-financed and American-launched Allied atomic weapon. Not until nine days after that, on September 30, did Mackenzie King fly to Washington for the first top-level discussions on the issue with President Truman, whom he had not previously met.

At a talk in the White House Oval Office which lasted well over two hours on that Sunday morning, President Truman was at last given a full political briefing on the Gouzenko affair. The president was naturally interested above all in the American ramifications. What were the links with Soviet consulates in places like Chicago and New York? What precisely had the Russians been interested in discovering about the shipping movements of U.S. forces out of Europe? No decisions emerged from the meeting, if only because Truman wanted to hear the views of the British prime minister before authorizing any action. This, he stressed, should not be premature and must, above all else, be taken on a coordinated basis.

In the immediate prelude to this meeting, some very strange ideas had been passing to and fro across the Atlantic. Thus, on September 26, Malcolm MacDonald in Ottawa had proposed three alternative courses of action over the affair, presumably after discussions with other Allied officials on the spot. The first was to deal with Primrose on the quiet and not let the Russians know what had happened to him. The second was to publish the whole story. The third was an elaborate compromise between these two opposing options. According to option three, President Truman and Prime Minister Attlee would jointly inform Stalin and his intractable Foreign Minister Vyacheslav Molotov what had happened in Ottawa, yet at the same time offer to hush it up in the cause of postwar solidarity between Russia and the West. As a quid pro quo for this concession, the Russians were to be asked to abandon forthwith any and all espionage activities against the Western powers, wherever these might exist. This third choice was recommended as probably the best under the circumstances. Indeed, the pious hope was expressed that, if this gesture were to be combined with an offer to share some of the atomic-bomb secrets with Russia,* this might even bring about a complete change of heart in the Kremlin. The wobbly well-intentioned hand of Mackenzie King was probably behind this.

Apparently it was Ernest Bevin, Attlee's superbly down-to-earth foreign secretary, who first blew these gathering cobwebs of compromise aside in one great puff. When the solution pro-

---

*The consensus view among May's scientific colleagues working in Canada, men like Oppenheimer and Fermi, was that the Russians would have the bomb anyway by 1950. In fact, the Soviet Union exploded its first atomic device in August 1949.

posed by Ottawa was put to him, he retorted that the only thing to do in the crisis was to proceed quite normally. If the West had a proper legal case against any of the individuals named by Gouzenko, they should be arrested and brought to trial. As regards the impact of this course of action on relations with the Soviet Union (about which Bevin was anyway pessimistic, having already endured countless hours of hostile stonewalling at Molotov's hands), the British foreign secretary felt quite ready to accept any consequences. He made a point of asking that Mackenzie King be told of this. This blast of common sense set the tone for Allied policy in the coming weeks and months. Mackenzie King immediately caved in. Truman, though he saw good reasons for delaying police action, probably needed little persuasion at heart that Bevin had got it right. The British miner's son and the farmer's boy from Independence, Missouri, were carved from the same grain of solid wood.

It will be noted that October 7, 1945, the day Mackenzie King arrived in England to discuss the crisis with Attlee, was by coincidence the same day that the principal British villain in the drama, Dr. May, was due to meet his Soviet contact. May had obviously been kept under keen but discreet Special Branch watch ever since his arrival, with Lieutenant Colonel Leonard Burt and Detective Inspector William Whitehead of Scotland Yard in charge. The two officers got confirmation from the faculty lists of King's College that Dr. May, formerly working in Montreal, had indeed been appointed as university reader for physics at the college. The register also gave his London address, in Stafford Terrace, and noted that he was working as a senior member of the Nuclear Physics Division at Imperial Chemical Industries.

They thus had three places to keep their eyes glued on: the college in the Strand; the ICI building on the Embankment close to Parliament; and the solid, bourgeois Kensington flat. They were not really surprised, on the evening of that October 7, to see that their quarry did not move out of Stafford Terrace but remained, easily in view, in an armchair of his ground-floor sitting room, puffing at his pipe and perusing a book. Nor was there any surprise when the police undercover men, posing as passersby or window-shoppers in nearby antique shops, reported that nobody had appeared outside the British Museum's main entrance in Great Russell Street carrying a copy of *Picture Post* under his left arm. By now, the Moscow Center had known for almost two months of the incriminating telegrams Gouzenko had handed over. The Russians were all too aware that May—Alek to them and now Primrose to the West—had been blown as high as the Geneva waterspout. Though he always refused to name any of his Soviet contacts, it is evident that one of them in London had been in touch, suggesting, at the least, that any rendezvous must be postponed.

At that same hour, eight o'clock on the Sunday evening, the agitated Mackenzie King was sitting down to dinner with the normally unflappable Clement Attlee. Mackenzie King found the British prime minister in thorough agreement with the case put by Truman (and, of course, by his own intelligence chiefs), namely, that before the Allies pounced in unison they should try to discover everything possible about the nature and extent of the Soviet penetration. But Attlee, unlike the Canadian, was in no way overawed by the political ramifications of the crisis. He felt that it was time anyway for a showdown with the Kremlin and this could give the justified pretext. Success in war seemed to have gone to the Russians' head and they had a strong inferiority complex which made things even more difficult. Attlee also told his guest (who noted all this down in his diary) that the Russians had absolutely "no true conception of democracy." East and West "were talking about different things while they used the same words."[6]

Mackenzie King spent a month in Britain, with Corby (to give the cipher clerk his new code name) flitting in and out of all the discussions he had with Cabinet ministers and security officials alike. At one point, the latter had proposed waiting no longer and pouncing on all the suspects as early as October 18. But the more it was examined the more the affair emerged as something highly political which only a top-level meeting between the three Western leaders involved could resolve. This was accordingly arranged for mid-November, Mackenzie King returning comfortably to America by ship and Attlee flying straight out to Washington.

Obviously, no mention of the Corby crisis appeared in any of the bland communiqués issued about these White House meetings. There is nothing of note about the affair in the memoirs of either Truman or Attlee, while Mackenzie King's diary—useful despite all its subjective slants—inconveniently starts a six-week break just before the summit begins. But it seems that Attlee and Mackenzie King put an agreed Anglo-Canadian program to the American president: coordinated arrests in Britain, America and Canada, to be followed in all three countries by prosecution where warranted; the establishment of a Royal Commission in Canada to go into the whole matter; and a formal Canadian protest to Russia, demanding, among other things, the recall of Colonel Zabotin.

The president had already been receiving energetic promptings from J. Edgar Hoover, his own powerful and ambitious FBI chief, for tough public action, including arrests with full publicity. It is possible therefore that the handcuffs would have been issued straight from the summit but for one complication. Elizabeth Bentley, a well-bred New England Vassar graduate who had fallen into the clutches of the American Communist party in the 1930s, chose this moment to see the light and give herself up to the FBI.[7] A startled J. Edgar Hoover now learned that, throughout the war, she had been feeding the NKVD with secret data from the U.S. War Department, Air Force, War Production Board and Departments of the Treasury, Agriculture and Commerce, using left-wing sympathizers as her sources. Unlike Gouzenko, this devastating self-confessed Soviet agent brought no documentary material over with her. All she could do was promise to tell all. Miss Bentley had indeed plenty to tell,* though that does not concern us here. Her only effect on the Corby case was to persuade Truman to call for a little more time. He did not want the forthcoming tripartite

---

*Elizabeth Bentley was later a key witness in proceedings which, in 1948, incriminated several U.S. officials, including Harry Dexter White.

wave of arrests to trample out any specifically American treason trails which the FBI might get onto as a result of the Bentley confessions, and he had received a first digest of these only
on November 8.

And so, in the event, Christmas 1945 came and went and 1946,
the first year of peace, dawned with the suspects still at large
on both sides of the Atlantic, four months after the start of the
affair. One key figure had, however, already disappeared from
the scene. Colonel Zabotin was removed under escort from
Ottawa, without any notification to the Canadian authorities to
whom he was accredited. He was taken to New York, where,
on a December evening, he boarded the Soviet freighter *Aleksandr Suvorov*, which then slipped away, without lights, down
the Hudson River into the Atlantic, en route for home and the
reckoning for the highly decorated colonel. Nobody in the West
knows for certain what happened to him. Malcolm MacDonald
heard soon afterward that the colonel had jumped overboard in
midocean, preferring a watery grave to an MGB (secret police)
interrogation cell. According to another report, Zabotin
reached Moscow but died "of heart failure" four days after
getting there. One way or the other, it seems clear that he paid
with his life for his cipher clerk's disclosures.

In the end, it was a media leak which precipitated action by
the Western leaders. On the evening of February 3, 1946, the
unscrupulous, often scurrilous but always highly influential
American commentator Drew Pearson had gone on the air in
his weekly broadcast to reveal that Mackenzie King's visit to
Washington the previous November had been to warn the
American president about the discovery of widespread Soviet
subversion. The columnist, claiming that he "didn't like to report" what was coming, went on with gusto:

> A Soviet agent surrendered some time ago to Canadian authori-
> ties and confessed a gigantic Russian espionage network inside
> the United States and Canada. . . . They had maps of this coun-
> try, which is next door to Siberia. Perhaps even more important,
> this Russian told Canadian authorities about a series of agents

planted inside the American and Canadian governments who are working with the Soviets. . . . All this points to the belief on the part of high American officials that a small group of military-minded men near the top in Russia apparently are determined to take over not merely Iran, Turkey and the Balkans, but perhaps dominate other areas of the world.

Pearson's involvement in the affair had in fact been known to a handful of officials in Washington for more than three weeks. As early as January 10, the FBI was getting reports that the columnist knew more about both the Gouzenko and Bentley cases (or "Corby" and "Speed" in the codebooks) than he ought to. The question was: where was the leak coming from? Subsequently, Sir William Stephenson, the man who had tapped on Gouzenko's door after midnight when the cipher clerk was in fear of his life, was named as the informant. But, active and pervasive though he was, Intrepid is often put across by his admirers as a bit too ubiquitous to be true.

Another, equally likely, source for the leak was J. Edgar Hoover himself. We have seen how, during the November summit over the crisis, the FBI chief was already urging the president to make the scandal public, and thus push the Russians on the defensive before world opinion. Nor would Hoover have been concerned only with psychological warfare at this juncture. He was fighting a personal power battle of his own to gain control over all overseas American intelligence as well as his existing domain of national security. It was a struggle he was finally to lose the following year when the Central Intelligence Agency was established as a separate organization to cover the nondomestic field. But the issue was far from settled at the beginning of 1946 and Hoover, it was felt, may well have been tipping off Drew Pearson to a story he anyway wanted uncovered in order to win the powerful Washington columnist over to his side. Certainly, the subjective style of the leak, with its urgent message that active operational measures needed to be taken in various overseas theaters, reflected Hoover's ambitions precisely.

The revelations caused relatively little excitement in the public domain. The Canadian embassy in Washington, for example, received only a scattered handful of inquiries over the broadcast. These it was easily able to brush aside with the tart response that it never commented on Pearson's stories. But it was a different matter in the worlds of Western politics and intelligence. There was no telling what the columnist might go on to reveal; he might even alert some of the quarries if he dug deeper and disclosed anything further. In any case, he was stealing the thunder of three Allied leaders. The program provisionally agreed upon among those leaders in November was accordingly wheeled into operation.

Mackenzie King, though not yet formally constituting his Royal Commission of Inquiry, set it in motion by appointing two Canadian Supreme Court judges, Robert Taschereau and R. L. Kellock, as commissioners, with an appropriate legal staff. Gouzenko was brought back from Lake Ontario to start giving formal evidence to the Royal Canadian Mounted Police. Finally, in the early morning of February 15, the twelve principal Canadian suspects, plus the British woman Kathleen Willsher, were all taken into custody in a dawn swoop on their dwellings. The day was a Friday. The RCMP had originally elected for Sunday, February 17. They brought it forward forty-eight hours just in case any of their quarries did not intend to return from a weekend's absence. Everyone on the list had, after all, been given a plain hint that trouble was brewing for them ever since Drew Pearson's broadcast nearly a fortnight before.

On that same Friday, Dr. May was tackled for the first time. Colonel Burt called on him at Shell Mex House, the ICI London headquarters, and asked him straight out whether he was aware that there had been "a leakage of information from Canada relating to atomic energy." The scientist was also asked, to bring matters to a sharper point, whether, in this connection, he had not failed to keep an appointment with "someone in London." May flatly denied any wrongdoing. He assured Burt that he had only just heard for the first time of any information leakage over atomic energy and was even prepared to sign a statement swearing that he had never at any time had contact with any Russian official or intelligence officer.

Five days later, however, when confronted on February 20 with some of the detailed evidence passed on from Ottawa against him, he suddenly changed his tune and, in the same calm style, confessed, even admitting to providing his Russian agents with the uranium samples for Moscow. He had done so, he said, because he believed that the Soviet Union "had a right to share in the secret." Though kept under an even closer watch from then on, he was not actually taken into custody until March 4, the day all the detainees being held in Canada were also formally charged.

When he heard that Primrose had confessed, Mackenzie King's first concern was that the scientist should be brought to justice in his own country and not in Canada, where his offenses had been committed. Mackenzie King told his diary on February 21, 1945:

> Let them see that everything is not put off on Canadians. When he is arrested and his trial comes, *bring home Britain's responsibility and this is certain to lead very far in the U.S.* *[8]

This was a spiteful reaction indeed. It is explicable (apart from Mackenzie King's own parochial nature) only in terms of the spiritual and political isolation postwar Canada was already faced with, wishing, on the one hand, to lean back from Britain without on the other hand toppling over into the arms of America.

May's plea that he had acted only in the broader interests of humanity was incorporated in his written confession:

> I gave and had given very careful consideration to the correctness of making sure that development of atomic energy was not confined to the U.S.A. I took the very painful decision that it was necessary to convey general information on atomic energy and

---

*Author's italics.

make sure it was taken seriously. . . . The whole affair was
extremely painful to me and I only embarked on it because I felt
that this was a contribution I could make to the safety of mankind. I certainly did not do it for gain.*[9]

This was the best, indeed the only, point which could be
pleaded on his behalf and when, on May 1, 1946, he was brought
up for trial at the Old Bailey before Mr. Justice Oliver, his
defense counsel Gerald Gardiner KC (later to become lord
chancellor) made the most of it. Scientists, he argued, were like
doctors, who may take the view that, if they have discovered
something of benefit to mankind, then they were under an
obligation to see that it was used for mankind.

The judge would have none of this. In his eyes, May was a
dishonorable man who had signed a pledge of official secrecy
and then "had the crass conceit . . . the wickedness, to arrogate
to himself a decision of this sort," while still drawing pay for
years to keep his bargain with his own country. He sentenced
May to ten years' penal servitude.† May did not appeal and was
removed to Wakefield Prison to serve out his term. He was in
fact released at the end of 1952, having gained more than three
and a half years' remission of sentence due to model behavior.
He was visited once by security authorities while in jail, in an
attempt to draw him out about his Soviet contacts. But he stuck
to his original pledge and refused to yield up any details.

After his release, this balding, mild-looking academic returned to the obscurity from which Igor Gouzenko had suddenly lifted him. His Viennese wife, Dr. Hildegarde Broda (the
female Austrian connection was to become a recurring theme

---

*May had, in fact, accepted 500 dollars (quite a useful sum then) in early August of 1945 from
Colonel Zabotin. It is a pity that he had not preserved his idealism by insisting on handing
this money back.

†May changed his original plea from not guilty to guilty on the day of the trial. This was
almost certainly the result of plea bargaining with the British authorities who wanted a
swift clean finish to the case, avoiding the possible embarrassment of cross-examination
by defense counsel had the original plea stood. The sentence was exceptionally mild. Any
of the several treason charges laid against the accused would normally have carried a
fourteen-year term. If served consecutively they would have kept May behind bars for
most of his life.

in Western security cases), held a medical post in Cambridge, and it was there he returned to live with her and their seven-year-old son. He unsuccessfully applied for a post at Khartoum University but in 1962 managed to get himself appointed professor of physics at the University of Ghana, as the old British colony of the Gold Coast had just become. His term there was extended, partly because the new state had great need of the medical skills of his wife. He vanished completely from view after returning to England. One possible final trace surfaced in 1982 when a brief letter signed by a Dr. A. May appeared in the Chinese Communist organ *Peking Daily*. If the writer really was the onetime Soviet agent, that would have been an appropriate farewell wave.

Igor Gouzenko's life followed a very different path. In that he and his family had to live in secret under assumed identities, the path lay in deep darkness. Yet every now and then, without his whereabouts ever being revealed, it was lit up by the full glare of the media, as he published autobiographical books or was called upon for comment when even bigger spy sensations than his own filled the headlines.

It was fitting that Gouzenko should have been inspired to write his own life story after reading, during his first months in Canadian hands, the memoirs of an earlier Soviet defector in North America. Victor Kravchenko was not an intelligence officer and his defection took place in wartime—two reasons why his case gets only an honorable mention in this study, and then only because of its connection with Gouzenko. Yet Kravchenko's case deserves to be recorded, however briefly, if only because of the date. It was on Monday, April 3, 1944, when the American press reported that "Victor A. Kravchenko, an official of the Soviet Purchasing Commission in Washington, announced his resignation yesterday and placed himself 'under the protection of the American people.' "

In April 1944 the war against Hitler had a full year to run. Disenchantment with Stalin's Russia had not begun to set in, except among a handful of Western statesmen and senior officials who had been trying to sort out the shape of the postwar world in secret parleys with the Soviet dictator. To the Western public at large, the Russians, now slowly grinding their way back through the mass of German invaders, were the heroes of the hour. The complementary Allied attack against the Atlantic flank of Hitler's Europe, the Anglo-American landing in Normandy, had not yet been launched. Russia as a wartime ally had never loomed larger nor ever held a stronger hold on Western gratitude. By choosing this moment to defect, Kravchenko ran the serious risk of being handed straight back to the Soviet authorities. Instead, he was to be sheltered by an America which, despite everything it owed to Russia, had not forgotten a deeper and older debt to individual liberty.

There was little in Kravchenko's story that came new to Gouzenko: a childhood spent in the traumas of the First World War, the fall of tsarist Russia and the triumph of Bolshevism, indoctrination through the Komsomol, or Communist youth movement, culminating in admission to the Party itself, the elite of the new Russia; then the growing disenchantment as he witnessed the brutal extinction of the peasantry and saw the first of Stalin's political purges, in the course of which he himself was beaten up by the secret police; then the panics and triumphs of the war against Hitler, where he realized that it was Russian patriotism, not Soviet ideology, which had carried the day; and finally the posting to America, where, just as with Gouzenko, the free, unfearing world of the "capitalist arch-enemy" had captivated him almost at first sight and breath.*

But if the ex-cipher clerk could learn little from Kravchenko's revelations, his countryman's earnings as the author of a best-seller on the American market were an eye-opener. His own book, *This Was My Choice*, came out in 1948 and was a commercial success despite the fact that much of the story had already been published. Indeed, he went one better than Kravchenko inasmuch as a film, *The Iron Curtain*, was based on his memoirs. Yet

---

*The Russians were rash enough to try to discredit Kravchenko by inspiring stories in the French Communist weekly *Les Lettres Françaises* that he was nothing more than an American agent provocateur. He sued for libel and not only cleared his name but produced in his defense much more evidence condemning the Soviet regime, which he later published in book form—*I Chose Freedom* (London, 1951).

he had only the one story in him, his own, and subsequent attempts to write political novels about Russia had less impact.

His later life was blighted by illness, money problems and frustration. The illness was diabetes, which made him blind during his last years. His Western hosts could do little about this, beyond making sure that he was given proper medical treatment. As for money, there was an odd announcement in the Montreal press on March 17, 1947, stating that "an anonymous Canadian has purchased an annuity equivalent to £25 a month for Igor Gouzenko, which will provide him an income for life, and his wife and two children for 20 years should he die in that time."[10] The "anonymous Canadian" could well have been the Canadian government trying to give Gouzenko financial as well as physical security. The snag was that 25 pounds a month, though adequate in 1947, gradually became very inadequate indeed as inflation gnawed away at its value.

Nor—and in this aspect too his case set the pattern for many later ones—did Gouzenko find it easy to settle down in the world of freedom which he had embraced after the world of regimentation which he had repudiated. Being unable to operate in the open was one obvious handicap. Another was the psychological problem of adapting to a totally unfamiliar economic and social order. Here, it was private initiative which brought rewards proportionate to effort or luck. There was no membership in state and Party hierarchy to guarantee the basic comforts of life, provided the member kept his nose ideologically clean.* It was not surprising that when he tried to move outside his professional ambit and took up farming, the venture failed.

But when, in June 1982, he died, "near Toronto," at the rela-

---

*It should be stressed, contrary to many accounts, that Gouzenko did *not* implicate the other British atomic spies, notably Dr. Klaus Fuchs, who was convicted of espionage and sentenced at the Old Bailey to fourteen years' imprisonment in 1950. There was in fact a "trace," in that Fuchs's name appeared in a notebook belonging to Israel Halperin, one of the Canadians accused (and one of nine acquitted). But the trace was not given any importance at the time and Fuchs's downfall was brought about in 1949 by messages from Moscow read when the Western Allies broke the Soviet codes.

tively young age of sixty-three, it was the frustration which probably had troubled him the most of his afflictions. His testimony and his armfuls of pilfered documents had achieved much. A powerful Soviet spy ring in Canada had been crushed and broken apart. Nine of the accused had been convicted under the Official Secrets Act, and its most prominent figure, the Communist MP Fred Rose, sent to prison for six years. In the United States, leads supplied by Gouzenko had, among other things, helped in the uncovering of the Gold-Greenglass-Rosenberg espionage network, which had begun to penetrate the Western atomic project in 1944, in an operation quite separate from anything being conducted at the time by the ill-fated Colonel Zabotin. Then there was the exposure of by far the most dangerous of the agents, Alan Nunn May himself, in recognition of which Gouzenko and his family were awarded British citizenship.

All that, one might have thought, would have represented achievement and satisfaction enough for an ex-cipher clerk. Yet Gouzenko died still somewhat embittered that one final coup against the Kremlin was being denied to him—the unmasking of a Soviet agent operating in the highest echelons of the British Secret Service. The flight of the British spy duo, Guy Burgess and Donald Maclean, to the Soviet Union in 1951 stirred Gouzenko into action, for the controversy raged then, and has still not died down today, over who had tipped them off. In May of 1952, he wrote a memorandum for the Canadian authorities stating that, during his wartime service in the Moscow Intelligence Directorate, he had learned, both by reading telegrams and by a whispered conversation with a fellow GRU cipher clerk, one Lieutenant Liubimov, that there was a Soviet spy working in wartime British counterintelligence. According to Liubimov: "This man has something Russian in his background." At the time (1942–43) that description fitted none of the men who later came to be suspected of working for Moscow or those who, like Anthony Blunt, actually confessed to having done so.

It is curious that, whereas in this 1952 statement Gouzenko was unable to remember the spy's code name, in a fuller version of his debriefing, released in Ottawa nearly thirty years later, he identified the alias unequivocally as "Elli," the same name under which Kathleen Willsher had operated. On the face of things, it would appear as strange for two British spies to be entered on the Moscow books using the same basic cover as for two British racehorses to be registered in the bloodstock lists with identical names. Gouzenko's final contribution to the mystery, made only the year before his death, was to help others point the finger at Roger Hollis, the MI5 officer sent out from London to interrogate him and who later rose to be director-general of MI5 from 1956 to 1965. Hollis, he now claimed, might well have been the second Elli, because the 1945 MI5 interrogation report, which Gouzenko was shown in the 1970s, appeared to him to have been distorted.

The evidence leaves an obscure riddle, probably because Gouzenko was seeking to regain the limelight with his now muddled memories. Had Hollis falsified Gouzenko's testimony (and there is no evidence that he did) he would only have drawn suspicion against himself. Whatever allegations the cipher clerk was making to Hollis in 1945 were being made also to the Royal Canadian Mounted Police and, among others, to that extremely percipient MI6/MI5 officer, Peter Dwyer. Any crass discrepancy in the reports could not fail to attract attention. Gouzenko achieved much that was clear-cut. Yet in the British spy controversy he only added fuel to the blaze without revealing any clear images behind the flames.

It is, however, to a fully proven British spy, indeed the most powerful of all the agents known to have worked for Moscow, that we must turn now, for the next Soviet defector to be reported to British intelligence had come straight up against Kim Philby. Philby escaped with a bad scare; the result for the defector was disaster.

4

The Wrecker

IN THE memoirs written after he was safely ensconced in Moscow, Philby wrote in lovingly misleading detail about the Volkov drama. His account,[1] like the rest of the book, is a continuation from enforced exile of his lifelong feud with Western democracy. It is a web of lies and half-truths spun around the bones of an authentic happening. What follows is the first full story of the Volkov affair, with Philby's principal deceptions noted in passing.

Konstantin Petrovich Volkov, accompanied by his wife Zoya, arrived in Istanbul from Moscow on May 19, 1945. They traveled on Soviet diplomatic passports numbered 10408 and 10409 and the husband's appointment was given as vice-consul at the Soviet consulate general. In fact, Volkov, then in his early thirties, was a lieutenant colonel in the Soviet NKVD intelligence service, had worked at its headquarters in Moscow and had been sent to Turkey for his first posting as a field officer. It is clear from what transpired that he had decided in advance that it would be his last.

Though Volkov's case exploded only a fortnight later than Gouzenko's and can therefore be taken up after the Ottawa affair, it actually began twelve days before, on August 27, 1945. On that day, C. H. Page, the British vice-consul in Istanbul and technically therefore Volkov's opposite number in the diplomatic community, received a letter from his Soviet colleague asking to be received at 10 P.M. that same night or the following morning on "urgent and important business." Volkov attached his official visiting card and requested the presence at the meeting of a Russian interpreter, preferably an Englishman. To confirm, Page was asked either to send his visiting card to the Soviet consulate general, or else to ring up and ask for an official there to appear at the British consulate "for negotiations over a Soviet citizen."

To understand this elephantine approach, it is important to bear in mind the climate of the immediate postwar months. Defection was a novelty in concept and practice. Just as Gouzenko had wasted hours by fleeing first to a newspaper office, Volkov wasted days by dropping his visiting card with no clear indication of what it was all about. That, at any rate, was how Page received this mysterious missive. He discussed it with his consul general, L. S. Hurst, and the two men agreed to ignore it completely. If they had any theory on the matter, it was that some prankster was taking Volkov's name in vain.

Again, the tenor of the times must be recalled. Neither of these two officials had anything to do with British intelligence, which, in 1945, was itself somewhat out of touch with the phenomenon of defectors from the other camp. The last Soviet intelligence officer to approach the British over asylum was probably George Agabekov, who, in 1930, offered to come across and tell all, if only Whitehall would help him to marry an English woman, Isabel Streater, with whom he had fallen in love. As it happened, there was a strong Turkish connection in that case too, for the young woman in question was the daughter of an earlier British consul in Istanbul. But Hurst and Page can be forgiven for not recalling the affair. Agabekov's strange case was hardly a familiar precedent. Nothing like it had happened before, or has ever happened since, in the espionage world.[2]

As it was, Volkov's first approach, either filed away or thrown away, was simply ignored. The Russian waited in vain a full fortnight for some response. Then his patience snapped and he decided to raise both the stakes and the risks. On September 4 he arrived unannounced at the British consulate. When he reached Page's office, an interpreter was produced in the person of a British member of the consulate staff, J. L. Reed, who spoke quite good Russian.

The moment Volkov started talking, it became obvious to Page how unwise they had been not to follow up the August approach. Volkov declared at the outset that he was not vice-consul but deputy chief of the Soviet intelligence station in Turkey and that he had information of vital importance to give to Britain, provided the British government would furnish him with appropriate rewards in return.

For his part, he offered to name 314 Soviet agents in Turkey and no fewer than 250 Soviet agents in Britain. (Those names, he said, were locked in a suitcase in an empty flat in Moscow; which, if true, proved that he had been planning his move for a long time.) Of the agents in Britain, two, he claimed, worked in the Foreign Office. Seven more were "inside the British intelligence system," of whom one was "fulfilling the function of head of a section of British counterespionage in London."*

As a bonus, Volkov offered to throw in details about the intelligence headquarters in Moscow and about current Soviet operations in the Near East and Iran, complete with specimens of Soviet official seals, rubber stamps and identity documents.

There was one more startling piece of information, which was to complicate fatally the transaction. For the last two and a half years, Volkov assured his listeners, the Russians had been reading all cipher traffic, both on the normal diplomatic channel and on the special intelligence ones, which had passed between the British embassy in Moscow and London. (This claim was never verified but, in view of Volkov's service inside the Moscow Center, was taken very seriously. It would have meant, for example, that the Kremlin had been aware, before the Teheran, Yalta and Potsdam summits, what the Western negotiating position was.)

---

*The two inside the Foreign Office were later taken to be Burgess and Maclean. The counterespionage official (the Russian phrase had been difficult to translate precisely) was probably Philby, though the description could have fitted Roger Hollis.

The complication which now arose was that, because of his knowledge of the Moscow-London cipher break, Volkov feared that telegrams between the British consulate in Istanbul and the Foreign Office might be being tapped as well. He therefore insisted that no word about his offer be sent by cipher message but that everything be conveyed to London by the slow but safe route of the diplomatic pouch.

For his reward, Volkov required a guarantee of asylum in Britain and safe-conduct there. He also demanded "at least £50,000 in sterling" to compensate him for the loss of his job. Although that represented around 1 million pounds in present-day values, it would have been cheap at the price.* Having made his offer, which he left behind in Russian in writing, Volkov cheerfully departed. He would call again in a few days, he told the two Britons. He assured them that he felt perfectly safe in returning to the Soviet mission because "only my wife knows what I am doing." That proved in the end to be a catastrophic mistake, though, at the time, Volkov could scarcely be blamed for making it.

Clearly, the British consulate general now had something enormous on its hands and, equally clearly, it could no longer continue to sit on those hands. The ambassador to Turkey, Sir Maurice Peterson, was away at the time, so the consular officials took their extraordinary story to the counselor and chargé d'affaires, Alexander Knox-Helm. What he did was almost equally extraordinary. Though British intelligence had its own station in Istanbul, headed by one Cyril Machray, the embassy proper did not think it wise or essential to inform or consult him about what was so obviously a professional espionage matter. Instead, Volkov's offer was dispatched by the slow overland route with a covering letter from Knox-Helm addressed to William Melville Codrington, an acting assistant under secretary at the Foreign Office. It took nearly a fortnight to reach its target and was then passed, via the usual channels of the permanent under secretary's office, to the head of MI6. It was not until September

*Some accounts erroneously put Volkov's cash demand at 27,500 pounds.

19 (and not, as Philby states, "one August morning") that Sir Stewart Menzies opened the Volkov file and immediately sent for the head of his Russian section to consult.

It will be remembered that when, only nine days before, the gravity of Gouzenko's defection became apparent, Philby deliberately avoided going to Ottawa himself (getting Roger Hollis sent there instead) so that he could remain at the center of things at his desk in London, from where he could report to his Soviet masters just what the cipher clerk had revealed and what the Western Allies proposed to do about it. But the bombshell of this second threatened defection in Turkey had blown quite a different crater in Philby's world. Gouzenko had named various Canadians, a British woman registrar and a British atomic scientist as Soviet agents. Nothing suggested anything cancerous in the heart of British intelligence. But now Volkov, as was plain from the documents on Menzies' desk, was describing as traitors British officials, one of whom might be taken for Philby himself, as well as pointing a finger at two agents he knew all about in the Foreign Office. He had to do two things. The first was to alert Moscow immediately to the danger. The second was to get out to Istanbul himself, by hook or by crook, in order to assess and help deal with the danger on the spot.

There are moments when spies seem to have a guardian angel on their side, the same ironical protector who saves drunkards from tumbling off parapets or falling in front of trains. At all events, extraordinary salvation appeared at Philby's side now. A minor stroke of good fortune was when Menzies acquiesced in Philby's taking the whole Volkov file home with him overnight in order to study it at his leisure and "make recommendations in the morning." Philby writes: "That evening, I worked late. The situation seemed to call for urgent action of an extracurricular nature."[3] What he did not specify was the sort of action he took. In fact, on that night of September 19, Philby held one of his rare emergency meetings with his case officer at the Soviet embassy, who, it is now known, was Boris Mikhailovich Krotov. The details of the Volkov crisis were flashed that same night to Moscow.

A greater stroke of luck concerned the question of who was

to be sent to Istanbul. Menzies' first choice had fallen on Brigadier Douglas Roberts, the head of R5, or counterespionage in the Middle East, a fluent Russian-speaker who was then in London ending a spell of leave. But Roberts was also a former pilot who had survived three crashes in his life. Nothing that Menzies could say about the importance of the Istanbul affair would persuade him to climb into an airplane again. He was returning, as he had come, by sea. That left the road unexpectedly clear for Philby to propose himself. This was accepted by his chief on September 22. Four days later (there were some bureaucratic delays, which entirely suited Philby's purposes) he left by air for Istanbul via Cairo. He carried with him a letter of introduction from Sir Alexander Cadogan, the Foreign Office permanent under secretary, to Knox-Helm saying that London thought Volkov was probably genuine and would therefore have information of great value to impart. In fact, Philby's real masters were already busy ensuring that Volkov would impart nothing.

In his memoirs, Philby describes his proposed plan of action in these words: "It involved meeting Volkov, bedding him down with his wife in one of our safe houses in Istanbul, and spiriting him away, with or without the connivance of the Turks, to British-occupied territory in Egypt."[4] It was a very different bedding-down which Philby had already launched for the would-be defectors.

It was learned only later (unfortunately much later, for the trace back to Philby would have been fairly clear and incriminating at the time) that, forty-eight hours after receiving the alarming news from London, the Kremlin put into action a drastic crash program to deal with the threat. On September 21, 1945, the Turkish consulate in Moscow issued visas for two Soviet "diplomatic couriers" to proceed to Istanbul at once. The passports they presented identified them (probably falsely) as "Andrei Baiko" and "Aleksandre Danilov." The Turks were puzzled, as neither name figured on the list of regular Soviet Foreign Ministry couriers. This was not surprising. Both were secret-police hatchet men. "Baiko" may in fact have been Colonel Andrei Mikhailovich Otroschenko in person, the head of the

department responsible for murders and kidnappings, who was
known from several sinister missions in the Middle East.

Four days later, on September 25, these two thugs arrived at
Istanbul's Yesilkoy Airport on a Soviet aircraft type DC-47, No.
800 25640, coming from Bulgaria. With them was a senior doctor
of the Red Army medical corps, one Colonel Petriny. The
plane, a military one, had arrived without warning and was
nearly fired on by the Turks. It left again at 4:50 the following
afternoon. Two limp and bandaged passengers were carried
aboard on stretchers. By a fluke, Volkov was recognized, despite
the bandages, by John Bennett, an assistant press counselor at
the British consulate in Istanbul who had just landed from
Cairo. He knew the Soviet vice-consul well by sight and was
certain that the male stretcher case was Volkov. There seemed
to Bennett little doubt that Volkov, though under sedation (that
would have been Colonel Petriny's job), was still alive. This was
only to be expected. Stalin's secret police would want to beat
the daylights out of the prisoner in Moscow to extract from him
every detail of what he had passed on to London. Only when
he had been squeezed dry would Volkov become expendable,
and probably, together with his wife, expended.

Whether the Russians risked trying to get a message to Philby
that he now had nothing to worry about is not known. Philby
had gone ahead as though his task really was, as he blandly
described it, "solely to get Volkov away to safety." But he took
every opportunity that arose to waste just a little more time on
discussions with the British ambassador, with the consulate and
with his own intelligence colleagues in Istanbul (now belatedly
briefed on the affair). Thus, it was not until September 29, three
days after the Volkovs had been abducted, that the first British
inquiries were made. By agreement with Philby, Vice-Consul
Page, the original British contact, phoned the Soviet consulate
general and asked to speak to Volkov. He was told that Volkov
was "not in." Page tried again later and this time was answered
by a voice claiming to be the elusive Russian. He now knew that
something had gone badly wrong. The man had replied in English. Volkov spoke no English. Two days later, on October 1,
Page was finally told by the Soviet switchboard that Vice-

consul Volkov was now in Moscow. Professing surprise and disappointment, Philby returned to London to draw up his report on "the failure of his mission." Volkov, he suggested, must have betrayed himself by his nervousness or else have been trapped by a bugging device planted in his room. He might even have repented and confessed. The account in his memoirs concludes:

> Another theory—that the Russians had been tipped off about Volkov's approach to the British—had no solid evidence to support it. It was not worth including in my report.*[5]

In fact, Philby's chief in London had immediately suspected some sort of leak the moment he learned that their quarry had disappeared, but the "solid evidence," in the form of the hatchet men's lightning mission from Moscow, was not then known. In August 1951, when Philby had been brought back from America and was already under suspicion, Volkov's ghost did stir. How many people, the British investigators asked themselves, had known about the Volkov case before Philby's arrival in Istanbul? They came up with only three names for certain: Sir Stewart Menzies; his deputy, Colonel Vivian; and Philby himself. Unfortunately, there remained a possibility that one or two other British officials in London (apart, of course, from those in the Istanbul embassy) were aware of the case.

All this was for the future. In October of 1945, Philby succeeded in convincing his chief that the Volkovs had somehow betrayed themselves. Having laid this firm false trail, he was soon able, thanks to another stroke of luck, to confuse matters further. On February 20, 1946, British passport control reported that a Soviet citizen named "Constantine Volkov" had boarded the Russian vessel *Yakutsk* at Woolwich, heading for America. Could he be the missing man? Philby knew perfectly well that he was not, but he briskly passed the query to Washington as a lead worth following up. Months went by while attempts

---

*The account of the Volkov affair given with Philby's unrevealing reminiscences in the London *Sunday Times* (April 10, 1988) is equally false. This states that the Volkovs were abducted "several weeks after" Philby's return to London.

were made to get a photograph of this new Volkov and compare it with pictures of the old one. It was not until June 1948 that it was finally established that the two were quite different individuals. For more than two years, Philby had had a lively hare running up and down his false trail.

There was only one point on which Philby and all his colleagues were agreed. By imposing a delay on the consideration of his case, Volkov had greatly increased the risk to himself. Taken together with the fact that, earlier in that same September of 1945, the runaway Gouzenko had been under surveillance for twenty-four hours by the local NKVD, who came within a whisker of actually seizing him at his flat, it was clear that, in the future, the whole process of clearing would-be defectors for protection and asylum would have to be speeded up. Speeded up it steadily was over the years, so that today the necessary instructions can be flashed out from London to Washington or any other major Western capital involved within hours—and, if need be, within the hour.

Philby and Istanbul also figure in the story of another Soviet defector and, because of that double coincidence, his case comes in here, naturally if not chronologically. Ismail Akhmedov, a lieutenant colonel in the GRU, arrived in the former Turkish capital in 1941. He had been through a nightmare summer of somersaults. When it began, he had been working in Berlin, officially in harmony with the Germans, in view of the Nazi-Soviet pact. Then, on Sunday, June 22, after Hitler's invasion of Russia, he found himself arrested by the Gestapo as an "enemy alien" and sent to a prisoner-of-war camp where, because (as a Moslem) he was circumcised, he found himself grouped with the Jewish inmates and assigned to latrine duty. A week later, everything changed again. Buses arrived at the camp and all the Soviet prisoners were assembled: they were to be exchanged, on neutral Turkish soil, for an equal number of German citizens who had been trapped inside the Soviet Union when war was declared. Once in Turkey, however, Akhmedov did not move across the Soviet border with the others. Special orders arrived from Moscow. He was to stay on in Turkey using the name of George Nikolayev, an alias he had already employed when working undercover as a Tass correspondent. The Tass correspondent now operated under the cover of press attaché at the Soviet embassy in Istanbul with the main task of recruiting French, Poles, Czechs, Yugoslavs and any other refugees from occupied Europe who were willing to be trained in underground operations and smuggled back to fight the Germans.

It was congenial work inasmuch as he disliked Nazis. Yet for Akhmedov, a Tatar Moslem, who had been drafted into intelligence rather against his will in 1940, soon after graduating from the General Staff War Academy, it was not congenial enough to keep his mind entirely on the job. The delights of life in the easygoing cosmopolitan city, where his fellow Moslems were not only free and uninhibited but the sole rulers of the country, were growing steadily irresistible. In his memoirs, he cites two things which severed his last personal ties with the Soviet Union. One was the death, back in Russia, of his wife Tamara; the other, which happened only a week later, was America's entry into the war in December 1941. The day after the second event, he describes making a call on the United States consulate general in Istanbul and offering to serve anywhere, and with any rank, in the American army.[6] Not surprisingly, nothing came of this extraordinary gesture, though one may be sure that his call was noted for other purposes.

Akhmedov may well have been perfectly sincere when he assured the elderly American diplomat that he had no further desire to serve the Soviet regime because "Hitler and Stalin are both dictators, and there is no real difference between the Gestapo and the NKVD."[7] As a devout Moslem and a proud Tatar, he was instinctively anti-Russian in the religious and ethnic sense. Moreover, as a trained engineer and a General Staff graduate, he had never felt at ease with intelligence work.

Nonetheless, what turned his disenchantment into the sudden decision to jump was fear for his own neck. In May 1942 friction with his superiors culminated in a chilling summons of

recall to Moscow—chilling because he was told that two Soviet
diplomatic couriers would be acting as "escort."* Akhmedov
managed to get his forty-eight hours' notice extended to five
days, then took a train to Ankara and contacted his good friend
Vladimir Perich at the Yugoslav mission, with whom he had
been working on the partisan recruitment program. Perich put
him in touch with a British intelligence officer, who wished him
well, though asylum seems neither to have been requested nor
offered. Akhmedov had anyway made up his mind in which
direction he would jump. Two days later, back in Istanbul, he
tidied his desk, settled his financial accounts to the last penny,
wrote two letters of resignation to Moscow (in which he also
renounced his Soviet citizenship) and then drove to the Turkish
police headquarters to ask for asylum as a professed Moslem of
pure Turkic blood. The police chief, who knew Akhmedov and
liked him, took him in on the spot and hid him under strong
guard while formal approval was sought from Ankara. Akhmedov had found a sure refuge. The Turkish authorities held
him safe as a political refugee until he was finally granted Turkish citizenship eight years later.

Before that, however, Kim Philby had crossed his path. For
a time during the war, the British and Americans received
copies of the material Akhmedov had produced for his Turkish
hosts; then he dropped off the Western screen. Early in 1947,
there was revived interest in him but, unhappily for both Akhmedov and British intelligence, this coincided with Philby's
posting to Ankara in February of that year as head of station.†
Philby now had to face the problem of either blunting or blocking London's desire for a fuller debriefing of the Russian. He

---

*By now, there was quite a dossier of incriminating evidence against Akhmedov's name.
His visit to the American consulate general had been noted and he was suspected of
contacts with British intelligence and of sympathies with the royalist Yugoslav cause.
Moreover, though he was not personally involved in the affair, his position had certainly
been compromised indirectly by the scandal over the botched attempt to murder the
German envoy, Franz von Papen, on February 24, 1942. The Turkish assassin was a
Communist and one of his accomplices was revealed as an NKVD man, operating under
cover of the Soviet Trade Mission. Akhmedov feared Moscow might need him as a scape-
goat for the fiasco.

†He remained in Turkey until September 1949.

succeeded mainly through his mastery of Whitehall's bureaucratic machine, including the remarkable indulgence it could display toward its "Pending" trays.

It is now known that Philby went to Ankara to meet Akhmedov under Turkish auspices in June 1947. For months, silence reigned on his part about the meeting until, in October, he admitted to London that it had taken place but that the report he had written had somehow got lost. He was unable to explain this puzzling situation. Matters had to be put right and, eventually, in January 1948,[8] Philby held a long debriefing session with Akhmedov in Istanbul which lasted for nine days. Philby was introduced to Akhmedov by the local head of Turkish security with his correct name and full credentials—chief of the British Secret Service in Turkey and son of the respected Arabic scholar St. John Philby, who had himself become a Moslem. The Englishman, he was told, had specially requested that all the conversations should take place without the presence of any Turkish representatives and this, the Turks told Akhmedov, they had accepted. It is small wonder that the Russian refugee did not suspect this distinguished visitor, presented to him in such flattering terms.

Looking back on those meetings many years later, Akhmedov chided himself for not realizing the significance of an omission on his interrogator's part. In defiance of normal professional practice whereby the questioner would begin by examining, at great length and in minute detail, every aspect of his subject's family history, education and official career, Philby took only the most cursory interest in all this. These facts were, of course, well known to his masters in Moscow and it was irrelevant that they were also known in the West. What the Russians were after was how much Akhmedov had passed on under the main headings Philby concentrated on: the Soviet High Command, its General Staff, its military schools and academies, its research organizations, its leading personalities and so on. Similar questionnaires had been prepared by Philby regarding Akhmedov's old service, the GRU, and its sister service for political intelligence. Philby's task was to discover how many red cats Lieutenant Colonel Akhmedov had let out of the bag.

He also popped up, from time to time, with questions which very much concerned H. A. R. Philby personally. "How do the Soviets treat their double agents?" he suddenly inquired at one stage. He returned to the same point later. "Please, tell me again . . . how the Soviet intelligence treats foreigners working for them."[9] It is unlikely that Moscow had asked him to pose those particular queries.

When it was all over, Philby showed particular delight when told that Akhmedov had never been subjected to such a broad-ranging interrogation by the Turks, who had shown little interest in anything outside their own sphere. That meant that the nine-day British debriefing just completed was the only one in existence and could not therefore be checked out against any other model. Well might Philby be pleased. It meant he could do with the material what he wished. As a result, he was able to delay sending any report at all for nearly six months. When it did emerge, in June of 1948, the nine days of continuous interrogation—all taken down by a woman stenographer Philby brought with him—were compressed into a document of only thirty-nine pages. Prudent as ever, he covered himself against any future queries by noting that a considerable amount of raw material had been omitted. One can assume that Moscow got it all.

When, in parting, Akhmedov showed interest in moving on from Turkey, it only remained to dissuade him from going to England, where he might be a time bomb. Getting to England, Philby declared, was "impossible." Turkey was the place to stay in, he told Akhmedov. To underline the point, he handed the fugitive 500 dollars in Turkish lira.[10]

Philby's treacheries did not begin or end there. The previous year, apparently, he had been responsible for fingering Sublieutenant Vladimir Aleksandrovich Skripkin, a young English-speaking GRU agent who was posted to Tokyo at the beginning of 1946 with the Soviet military mission. His duties were partly overt, to help oversee Japanese demilitarization, but partly covert, to conduct military intelligence operations against the

Western powers. He lost little time in pursuing those tasks for a very different purpose.

On May 9, 1946, he made a furtive evening call at the British embassy and had a talk with a British naval officer there. He left a confusing impression that he wanted to cooperate in some way, though without giving any firm commitment. Skripkin had been putting out simultaneous feelers to the all-powerful American occupation authorities in Tokyo and, at a meeting with them on May 17, came out with it: he was "sick and tired" of the Stalinist regime in the Soviet Union and was only waiting for his wife to join him in Tokyo before applying for asylum in the United States for both of them. He made his third contact with the West when he called again at the British embassy, in a state of some agitation, at nine o'clock in the morning of June 19. His wife had not been allowed to join him in Tokyo. Meanwhile, he himself had been recalled to Moscow and was due to leave the very next day. He wanted, he said, to put himself at the service of British intelligence, whom he promised to get in touch with as soon as he could arrange for another foreign assignment with his wife. It was only because of her that he was returning at all. He handed over his Moscow address just in case it was possible for him to be contacted there.

That was in fact the last anyone heard of Sublieutenant Skripkin, who was seized on arrival in Moscow. Two defectors who later made it to the West, Rastvorov* and Golitsyn,† both confirmed that Skripkin's offer of services had been passed to the Russians by a British intelligence source. Philby, who had access to the Skripkin reports as head of Section 5 of MI6, was very likely to have been that source.

Philby's operational betrayals to Moscow had begun in earnest when he was first transferred to Section 5 in September 1941, three months after the German invasion of the Soviet Union. He is believed to have told his Russian controllers everything he safely could about the British offensive against the Abwehr, the German intelligence system, including details of

*See chapter 5.
†See chapter 11.

the top secret "Double Cross system," under which German agents captured in Britain were "turned" to feed false information back to Berlin. Though Russia and Britain were by now wartime allies, this was information which London would never have volunteered to Moscow.

After the war, Philby was able to betray a number of ground operations to his Soviet masters. Thus, he used his posting as head of station to pass on information about the West's anti-Soviet operations throughout the Middle East and, in particular, to betray the "climbers," the name given to Western agents infiltrated across the Caucasus Mountains into the Soviet Union. Only two of the cases he betrayed in 1948–49 survived.

Later, when posted to Washington, his scope for operational betrayals was widened. He was in intimate contact with the fledgling CIA, some of whose leading officials, like James Angleton, had sat admiringly at his feet when working with the wartime American OSS* in London. Their trust in him was complete and it gave him the opportunity to monitor all of America's early postwar operations against the Soviet bloc. These included, notably, their attempts to destabilize the newly established Communist regime of Enver Hoxha in Albania, though the fiasco of the CIA parachute squads, nearly all of which dropped straight into the fire of waiting trigger fingers on the ground, cannot be laid entirely at Philby's door. The feuding anti-Communist resistance groups in that luckless mountain state did quite enough mutual betrayal on their own, some of it through the sheer inability to keep their mouths shut.

Finally, Philby was undoubtedly able to inflict damage on the esoteric but increasingly vital front of signals intelligence. One of the most spectacular successes registered against the Russians on this front had begun just before Philby arrived in Washington. Meredith Gardner, an American cryptoanalyst who was to become a legend in his profession, had succeeded in breaking into the Russian intelligence cipher by analyzing the remains of a Red Army codebook found on the Finnish battlefront. "Venona," as the subsequent Anglo-American decrypting exer-

*Office of Strategic Services, forerunner of the CIA.

cise was called, remained a break-in rather than a breakthrough, as only a tiny fraction of KGB messages was ever deciphered. Even so, some of the leads it yielded were momentous, pointing the finger, for example, at Maclean as a British traitor and at Klaus Fuchs and the Rosenbergs as part of the Soviet nuclear espionage network in America. All this material would have passed over Philby's desk in the Washington embassy, though the real betrayal to Moscow of Meredith Gardner's coup was probably performed by a suspected double agent, then using the alias of "William Weissband."

Yet all this catalog of damage, proven or supposed, which Philby inflicted on the West does not surpass one ultimate exercise in treachery which went unclaimed by him and unrevealed by his former colleagues. This concerns top-level intelligence, potentially of great harm to the Soviet cause, which he succeeded in blocking on its way up to the top in Whitehall.

The case, of truly major significance, concerns the evidence, gathered by MI6 during the war, of Russian intentions after victory was won. By 1943, there was ample material from a variety of British intelligence sources that the Soviet Union was preparing to seize as much of Eastern, Central and Southeast Europe as it could, irrespective of any agreed-upon Allied strategy. Moreover, the evidence showed that the Kremlin had resolved to hold onto this great swath of territory for good, by the establishment of puppet Communist regimes installed by the Red Army, whatever political complications might ensue with the West. A paper was prepared for submission to the prime minister setting out these firm predictions and the facts to back them up. It got as far as Philby's desk on its way to the top, but no further. Again displaying his mastery of the Whitehall mentality and the Whitehall machine, Philby, far from deriding the paper, commended it as worthy of the closest attention. Indeed, so important did he consider it to be that he suggested further research in one or two key areas so that the department could submit an amplified report to its political masters with complete confidence. The delays he induced did the trick. The paper, which only surfaced by accident twenty years later, never reached the prime minister.

Yet 1943–44 was the period when Churchill, sensing these very dangers, was urging President Roosevelt to be less complacent about Stalin and pleading the cause of an Allied landing in the "soft underbelly" of occupied Europe, in order to strike out toward Vienna, Budapest and Prague ahead of the Red Army. It is possible that nothing would have changed the president's mind or produced a better balance in the last and decisive phase of Allied grand strategy. But what is certain is that the British prime minister could have presented his case with greater conviction had that paper from his own intelligence service been in his hands. There are former colleagues of Philby who believe that preventing this was the greatest single blow he delivered to the West. It is not surprising he was never allowed to boast of it. This would have revealed the implacably imperialist aims of his Soviet masters.

PART TWO

Quintet

Introduction

THE DECADE after Gouzenko's dramatic escape in Ottawa and Volkov's tragic attempt to follow his example from Istanbul presents a contrasting picture of ebb and flow which is unique in the history of postwar defection. For nine years after these two cases had occurred almost simultaneously, the roll call of defectors remains nearly blank. Only two Soviet intelligence officers are recorded as having reached the West from any jumping-off point during this period, and neither was of great significance.* Then, in the winter of 1954, came an unprecedented surge when five defectors, coming from all corners of the earth, crossed over within three months of one another.

They will be introduced separately in the pages which follow. It might, however, be a useful introduction, without going into their names at this point, to examine briefly what the members of this 1954 quintet had in common and where their cases differed. After they had reached the West, most of them declared, first in secret debriefings and then in public writings, that mounting ideological disenchantment with Soviet Communism was the main reason for their flight. This cannot be dismissed as being merely the Cold War propaganda dividend which their hosts expected them to pay on arrival in the West. Disenchantment (in varying degrees of intensity) certainly played its part in their decisions. In most cases, this was material as well as spiritual. It was not only personal freedoms they

---

*Anatoly Granovsky of the MGB, who arrived in the United States in 1946 from Sweden, and another MGB man, Boris Ivanovich Bakhlanov, who defected to the UK from Austria in July 1947, taking the pseudonym "Romanov."

67

wanted but the certainty of those higher living standards they had witnessed for themselves in foreign postings. In only one of the five cases was moral repugnance for the work on hand a dominant force, but he had had by far the dirtiest work to do.

Domestic considerations, above all the state of their marriages, played varying roles. One defector managed, albeit with great difficulty, to persuade his wife to follow his example on the spot. Another spoke frankly of dislike, almost hatred, for his wife, who had not accompanied him abroad and whom he wished never to see again. A third, who abandoned wife and infant daughter when fleeing his foreign post, admitted to a marriage which was going downhill anyway. On the other hand, one among the batch, the same one whose conscience pricked him the hardest, tried to move heaven and earth to get a well-loved wife and child out of the Soviet Union to join him in the West—all in vain. None of the quintet was bribed to defect. None (contrary to Communist allegations) had committed criminal acts by bringing hoards of official Soviet funds out with him. All were quite sane and in good health.

The most important element they shared is that suggested by the timing of their defections, the early months of 1954. This followed immediately upon the official announcement from Moscow on December 23, 1953, that Stalin's security chief Lavrenty Beria, under whom they had all served, had been executed for treason, along with his senior aides. The announcement came as the climax to nine months of purges and counterpurges in the Soviet intelligence world which had followed Stalin's death in March of 1953. Even those members of the group who did not fear actual arrest on returning home felt trepidation at the prospect. Moscow from afar seemed as though it were enveloped in a menacing fog of chaos. No career seemed safe, no life or liberty guaranteed, even for members of this Communist elite. The strongest common factor which the quintet demonstrated was, quite simply, their survival instinct, stirred by feelings which ranged from mere anxiety to downright panic. They were no lesser prizes for that.

5

Tokyo

On JANUARY 29, 1954, reports began to appear in the Western press that a second secretary of the Soviet mission in Tokyo had disappeared. One of the first with the news was *The Times* of London. The paper incorrectly spelled the man's name as "Rastzorov" but correctly reported that the Soviet authorities had approached the Japanese police to help find the missing man, who, the Russians were claiming, was "mentally deranged."[1] By the beginning of February, the press had not got much further with the name—Rastovorov was the new version—but it was in a position to flesh out the story considerably. S. I. Runov, spokesman for the Soviet mission, was now openly accusing "American espionage organs" of kidnapping their colleague "with the aim of causing a provocation of the Soviet Union." Backing this up without the propaganda, the Western newspaper reports began to talk of "growing speculation" in Tokyo that the official had asked the United States for political asylum, and indeed might already have been flown out to Okinawa, the main American Pacific base some seven hundred miles south of the Japanese capital.[2] Other versions added that he had been "a genial thirty-four-year-old tennis-playing member of the Soviet mission" and that he had vanished on the eve of his recall to Moscow, an event to which, according to the Russians, he was happily looking forward.[3]

There was a brief spell of evasiveness by the United States

government (President Dwight D. Eisenhower was quoted on February 3 as saying he had as yet received no reports on the matter but presumed he would be informed in due course). Then, on February 5, the Americans came out with it. The mystery man was indeed in their hands. Moreover, as the Soviet Union's "chief espionage agent in Japan," his defection represented a great American triumph. One American source was even quoted as comparing it with historic Second World War victories: "It is the intelligence equivalent of a Midway or a Normandy."[4]

The comparison grossly overstated the case, though MGB Lieutenant Colonel Yuri Alekseyevich Rastvorov (to give him his proper name and status) was turning out to be an important prize. He was not, however, properly speaking, an American prize, though that has been the received version in every reference to him from that day to this. But as Rastvorov was happy to admit, more than thirty years after the event, he had originally defected to British intelligence, whose agents had been cultivating him assiduously for months. Once he was in British hands, a preplanned operation had been set in motion to get him out of the country through exclusively British channels. It was frustrated on the crucial night only by a freak happening beyond anyone's power to foresee or prevent.

Before coming to the saga of his escape from Tokyo, we must look at who he was and how he got there in the first place. By the proletarian standards of the Bolsheviks, Rastvorov's pedigree was distinctly mixed. He was born on July 11, 1921, at Dmitrovsk in the Central Russian province of Orel, the son of a Red Army veteran of the revolution.[5] So far, so good. His mother, however, was the daughter of a stationmaster, already less "pure" than the peasant/worker ideal, and later, as a qualified physician, had joined the ranks of the professional classes. The boy remembered one occasion when she nearly exposed the whole family to a dangerous display of gentility. She had decided to give a dinner party and, in an attempt to show that the Rastvorov household was a civilized place, she had dug some linen napkins out of an old trunk and set them on the table. Her husband, who arrived just ahead of the guests, was horrified at what his wife had done. "The comrades will take us for despicable bourgeois," he shouted, and swept the offending objects out of sight.

But the real blot on Yuri's family escutcheon turned out to be his grandfather, on whose humble farm he had spent his first years. In the mid-1920s, when Stalin's savage collectivization drive was under way, the old man was unjustly branded as a kulak. His property was confiscated and he eventually starved to death. Yuri's father was apparently too terrified of being branded as a "counterrevolutionary" to come to the rescue. Not that this excessive display of caution did anyone much good in the long run. Ten years later, when Stalin's political purges were at their height, the father was in turn hounded for his suspect "social origins" and had to struggle for months to keep his Party membership—the key to existence in the Soviet Union at anything above a primitive level.

Yuri himself was intelligent enough and self-motivated enough to head for the uplands of the Communist elite, having first passed through the early training grounds of the Young Pioneer movement and the Komsomol youth organization. Like millions of others all over the world, his life was transformed by the outbreak of Hitler's war. When it broke out in 1939, he had just graduated from high school and had enrolled as an engineering student at Moscow's Geodetic Institute. His account of the next few years makes rather muddled reading, largely because the events themselves came tumbling on top of each other.

He was first drafted into the Moscow Proletarian Division and took part in the Red Army campaign which overran the Baltic states. Then, in September 1940, without any application on his part, he was transferred to military intelligence and sent to the Institute of Oriental Languages to study Japanese. Though he was never to complete the four-year course, he was thus a product of the first intake of what the West later identified as the top secret School 101 of Soviet intelligence. He estimated that there were between fifty and sixty students drafted in with him. Between a dozen and fifteen were also studying Japanese; the remainder were working on Chinese, Hindi, Pashto and the like. Nobody in the group was allowed to choose his specialty; each was allotted a language. Rastvorov's link with the Far East, which was to last for most of his professional career, was thus simply clamped on him as a bright and likely-looking soldier.[6]

The German invasion of Russia in June 1941 dislocated his academic studies. He was first sent to a Red Army training school outside Moscow for a course in guerrilla warfare. Then—an operation not mentioned in his writings—he was posted to Outer Mongolia with a special unit preparing leaflets and other propaganda material against the Japanese. It was his operational debut against Japan, though he did not see his target country for the first time until early in 1946, when he arrived in Tokyo as one of the huge four-hundred-strong Soviet mission headed by General Derevyanko, who had represented Stalin at the formal surrender of Japan to the Allies the previous year. By now, Rastvorov, aged twenty-four, was a career officer in MGB Soviet intelligence, which he had joined in 1943. He was also a candidate for membership in the Communist party.

His first spell in Tokyo lasted only a year but it was more than enough to leave lasting impressions behind, none of them favorable to the Soviet Union. He saw how gauche his superiors were—and above all the blockheaded Derevyanko—in Western company. He saw how, to a man, everyone in the mission embarked on frenetic shopping campaigns to collect every item of Japanese or American clothing and equipment they could lay their hands on, against the day when they would have to return to a bleak Moscow, with its scarcity, shoddiness and perpetual queues. Yakov Malik, the general's political adviser, was observed leaving Tokyo in 1946 with no fewer than sixty-five trunks stuffed with trophies from the decadent capitalist world.

At the end of that year, Rastvorov himself was suddenly summoned home in circumstances that did nothing to enamor him of the regime. A board of inquiry which had been examining his credentials unearthed the fact that his father had been suspended from membership in the Communist party ten years before, while his grandfather had been branded as a kulak. Rastvorov had failed to include either of these blemishes in his personal history file. He had to endure a humiliating investigation before he was forgiven and, in 1947, accepted as a full member of the Party. Even so, it was not until 1950, after three years at the Japanese desk of intelligence headquarters, that he was allowed abroad again, on a second tour of duty in Tokyo. His wife, a ballerina called Galina Andreevna Godova, opted to stay behind with their five-year-old daughter; her career meant more to her than a family life which had already turned sour.

Rastvorov explained in later years that this failed marriage was one factor in the decision, which was already forming in his mind on leaving Moscow, that he would never return there.[7] The other main element was the growing seduction of the Western way of life. He had experienced it in the flesh in one brief sojourn in American-dominated Tokyo. He was also able to experience it in Moscow on celluloid. At four o'clock in the morning, he would often accompany senior officials of the Ministry of State Security to a special "conference room" where Western films, brought back by Soviet intelligence officers from the liberated countries, were screened for a privileged few, with simultaneous translations spoken by interpreters. Like his colleagues, he had told his wife that he would be "working late."

The early propaganda techniques (later refined into a coordinated KGB program) which the regime had resorted to in its relations with the capitalist world had already instilled a certain disillusionment—though Rastvorov had never been much of an idealist. His first taste of Communist "disinformation" had come in 1942 when Wendell Willkie, on his fact-finding world tour for President Roosevelt, arrived in the Soviet Union. It was vital to send the envoy home with an enthusiastic report about America's new ally, and Rastvorov found himself helping to pull the Communist wool over the visitor's eyes. He was called away from his military training school at Stavropol, told to put on his civilian clothes and report with other soldiers, similarly garbed, to a nearby state farm which had been selected for

Willkie's inspection. There they worked away for weeks, repairing barns and stables and cleaning up the fields and roads. The final touch was to unload a special consignment of caviar, champagne and other luxuries to display at the local store, as though such items were on the normal menu of state farms. Two years later, Rastvorov heard about, though did not witness, an even more outrageous piece of disinformation practiced on Henry Wallace when the American vice president was on a tour of northeastern Siberia. As if by magic, all the slave laborers, and all the barbed wire surrounding their compounds, had been swept away from his route. It was depressing to serve a regime which had to resort to such trickery.

On his second stationing in Japan, Rastvorov was thrust by his assignments ever deeper into the glittering capitalist world to which he was already drawn. He had arrived in the guise of a third secretary, holding a proper diplomatic passport (Number 00863) despite the anomalous situation in which the Soviet mission now found itself.* His duties, of course, had nothing to do with diplomacy. He was now a major in the MVD (as the Soviet secret police were then known) and his principal task was to gather intelligence through a network of about fifty Japanese agents, most of whom had been recruited by blackmail and other forms of coercion. The need to keep in constant touch with them meant that Rastvorov was one of the few officers in his mission who could leave the building at will and move freely around the hotels and restaurants of the capital.

But it was the second task allotted to then Major Rastvorov by his superiors that they lived to regret. This other job was to make any infiltrations he could among the American-dominated Western community in the capital and, to this end, he was ordered to join the Tokyo tennis club, becoming its sole Soviet member. Apart from being gregarious and pleasure-loving by nature, Rastvorov was personable and athletic. He took to the

*The Soviet Union had refused to accept the San Francisco Treaty, which had restored Japanese national sovereignty while allowing the United States to maintain troops and bases on Japanese soil. As a result, there were no formal diplomatic relations between Tokyo and Moscow and the Soviet official preserve in Japan had only the vague status of a "representation."

game, and to the easy informality of a sports club, instantly. Tennis parties, drinks at the bar and the invitations to Western houses which naturally followed made a determined defector out of Yuri Rastvorov long before he reached the moment of actual bailout. Someone who often met him at the courts recalled that he played almost every day and had become very skillful at the game. He was known as George and, though somewhat arrogant at times (a sign probably of an inferiority complex), was a popular member, ready to chat and make up a foursome with anyone. People quite forgot that he was a Russian, which would have been a lethal intelligence weapon in his hands had he chosen to use it to serve the Soviet Union. Instead, as we shall see, he chose to use it to serve himself.

More strongly perhaps than with any of the other defectors in this 1954 group, Rastvorov's timing was determined by the prevailing political chaos in Moscow (echoed by hysterical feuding inside the Tokyo mission itself) and the fear that he would become one of its victims when his tour abroad was up. Thus, he first brought himself to the notice of the British authorities in the spring of 1953, some ten weeks after the news of Stalin's death. On the social front, the British diplomats were much preoccupied at the time with local festivities to mark the approaching coronation of Queen Elizabeth II in faraway London. They were somewhat surprised to receive, on May 19, a personal application from Yuri Rastvorov for four tickets to attend not only the Coronation Concert but the British embassy's Coronation Ball. Coming from a mere third secretary in a mission which did not even possess proper diplomatic status, this was a tall order. Too tall. The applicant was sent his tickets for the concert, but not for the ball.

Ten days later, Rastvorov, using his tennis club contacts, got himself invited to a private dinner party given by a member of the British embassy, and brought one of his colleagues, Vasily Saveliev, along with him. One of the other guests at that dinner recalls that Rastvorov was at first so nervous that he began by putting the lighted end of a cigarette in his mouth. However, after much alcohol had been consumed, everything went smoothly and merrily. There was dancing, and Rastvorov toasted "The Queen" (to which the tactful return toast was "The Russian People"). But once his tongue was loosened, Rast-vorov made it clear that he was a very discontented man indeed. He was full of complaints about his own mission. The doctor allocated to it had been recalled to Moscow, so regular medical services were nonexistent and the supply of drugs was poor. The supply of vodka was even worse. There was little personal contact of any sort with Moscow, the mail service being very erratic. Above all, he had found no proper female company in a land renowned for its geisha girls. In fact, he had still not even been to a geisha party. Could his hosts perhaps arrange one? This was an extraordinary outburst of bitterness and loneliness for any Soviet official to display to a Western audience in the middle of the Cold War. Yet, so far, his complaints seemed to point less to the ideological rebel than to the would-be man of the world yearning for the bright lights.

As the summer wore on, however, his indiscretions, usually aired at the tennis club (where there were no other Soviet mem-bers, he being the only "licensed sportsman"), became more serious. In June, he confided for the first time to one of his Western tennis friends that the situation in Moscow was now becoming so fraught that he feared for his life. "A big wind is sweeping over Russia," he said at one point, adding that the wind might carry him off if he returned. He confessed that he was drinking too heavily, that he hated his wife and that he had now found a Japanese mistress. He was also becoming increas-ingly political. He assured non-Americans that he disliked Americans; yet he also criticized British policy toward Russia, which he described as "appeasement." Over and over again, he repeated the warning: "If you do not act first, we will destroy you." Before the summer was over, he was accepting Western invitations without even referring back to his immediate supe-rior at the mission, Colonel Alexander Nosenko.

There could be little doubt by now that Yuri Rastvorov was not simply a frustrated socialite. By September, the British had marked him down accordingly as a likely defector and prepara-tions were set in train to get him out of Tokyo, together with his Japanese mistress if need be, if and when he applied for asylum. The obvious evacuation route was by air, but these were the days of propeller planes with a limited range. For a civilian aircraft, Hong Kong was the first staging post out of Tokyo to almost any destination. Even the Russians, homeward-bound for Moscow, had to use it. The British colony was likewise the initial stop on any journey Rastvorov might be making to Britain. RAF service planes flew there two or three times a week from American airfields in Japan, and it was decided, for obvious security reasons, to use one of these in preference to a BOAC commercial airliner. By the autumn, the authorities in London had become sufficiently interested in Rastvorov to send a Russian-speaking official out to Tokyo for the special purpose of handling his case and bringing him out. Interest increased sharply when the British received confirmation from the Japanese security service that their target was, as had been surmised, a Soviet intelligence officer. From now on, London awarded him the professional accolade of a code name. Getting him to the West was a full-blown operation.

All this time, office life had been getting steadily more distasteful and difficult for "Third Secretary" Rastvorov. Major General Kislenko, who had succeeded the egregious Derevyanko as head of the Soviet mission, was a somewhat timid intelligence officer seemingly dominated by his ambitious wife. He was on the worst of terms with one of his principal counselors, Colonel Pyotr Shibaev, a bull of a man who, in turn, would pick a quarrel with anyone when he was drunk.[8] But Rastvorov's biggest problem was not with the generals and colonels of his own intelligence world but with Georgi Pavlichev, the Soviet career diplomat who was acting as chargé d'affaires when the situation reached crisis point. The chargé was another Soviet official under the thumb of his wife. This meant that the political side of the mission was, in effect, run by Madame Pavlichev, and she had taken a hearty personal dislike to Rastvorov. For months, she had been egging her husband on to get rid of him on the pretext that he was so preoccupied with other duties and distractions that he did not put in even the minimum of appearances at formal functions required of any bogus diplomat. Because of the turmoil in the Soviet intelligence world, the

Foreign Ministry, which had been relatively sheltered from the storm, was able to exert much more pressure than was normal in such personnel questions.[9]

Things began to heat up for Rastvorov early in December of 1953 when he learned that Pavlichev had sent an official request to Moscow for his recall, on the grounds of incompetence and bad behavior. Part of the "bad behavior" complained of was that he preferred going out to see American films to staying behind with his colleagues to watch Soviet offerings shown at the mission's cinema. Rastvorov learned from his immediate intelligence chief, Colonel Nosenko, who still seemed well disposed toward him, that the reply from Moscow had been a cable of reprimand, with the implication that the culprit would be taken to task on his return. That return was not yet imminent, however, though Rastvorov knew that in the normal course of events his posting would expire during the next few months.

Two things brought his personal crisis to the boil. The first was the news of Beria's execution, which reached Tokyo on Christmas Eve. Rastvorov was not senior enough to feel automatically threatened by a purge; but as he had been trained on the Japan desk in Moscow under Beria's close eye, who could tell? The second and decisive event took place around midnight on January 10, 1954. Rastvorov was summoned to the political department of the mission and told that Pavlichev had now cabled Moscow to say that unless Rastvorov was recalled at once, the chargé would himself demand a transfer. This time there was little comfort to be had from Colonel Nosenko, who, by rights, ought to have insisted that the entire matter be dealt with through his own intelligence channels. Nosenko seemed evasive and Rastvorov was finally told that he would have to leave for home within a few days together with a party of fifteen Soviet ice skaters who had been in Tokyo for the world speed-skating championships. Rastvorov found this proposed escort more menacing than droll. There were, as usual, plenty of Soviet security officials in the visiting group. It seemed clear that one of their tasks was to make sure that he left for home as well.[10]

It is from this point onward that Rastvorov's published account of his escape differs from the truth (doubtless for reasons which seemed valid enough at the time). The story he wrote for his American audience talks merely of being unable to fly out with the skaters—who duly left aboard a BOAC airliner on January 23—because the British consular authorities in Tokyo had been slow in issuing him the necessary transit visa for Hong Kong. But on his return to the mission, Colonel Nosenko informed him that he would definitely be leaving the next day, Sunday the twenty-fourth. A tough-looking member of the skating team had been left behind to escort him. At this point, the story goes on, Rastvorov contacted his "closest American friend," a Mrs. Browning (her real name was, in fact, Burns), a middle-aged lady from Texas who taught at the American Ernie Pyle School. They regularly met at the Old Kaito Hotel to exchange lessons in Russian and English and, so far, politics had been avoided. Now, on this fraught Sunday he told her, first, that he wanted to escape to the West and, second, that he was an intelligence officer. She promised him that everything would be taken care of. Rastvorov then states that he returned to the mission to burn his papers before leaving again to keep a street-corner rendezvous which the teacher had arranged for him at 8 P.M. A car duly arrived to pick him up with the obliging "Mrs. Browning" inside. "A short time afterward," Rastvorov's version concludes, "I was on a plane bound for the American West Coast."[11]

This version was produced, with American help, for an American audience only months after his arrival in the United States. In fact, as he now gladly admits, the timing is at least twenty-four hours off and the true sequence of events very different. Even he was probably unaware at the time of everything that was going on, though he was well aware that the place where it was going on was the British embassy.

What had happened was that on Monday the eighteenth the embassy had received an urgent request from the Soviet mission for a Hong Kong transit visa to be issued to Yuri Rastvorov for travel on the twenty-second or soon after. The intelligence officer sent from London to handle his case decided that the time for him to jump had arrived. Rastvorov was clearly of the same opinion when he met his British contact on Wednesday. He was now, he said, afraid for his life. He added that, if he were not flown out to the West, he would be shipped back home under guard in a Soviet vessel during the following week. He pleaded that those menacing skaters should be got out of Tokyo ahead of him, a plea which was easily fulfilled, as the British held the key weapon of the Hong Kong visa.[12] The following day, the Royal Air Force was alerted and flew a plane into the U.S. Air Force base at Tachikawa, near Tokyo, especially to pick up the Russian. Still, however, Rastvorov had not agreed to apply formally for asylum in Britain, though he was emphatic that he did not want to go to America.

It was on Saturday the twenty-third, the day the skaters flew off (with a very relieved Rastvorov bidding them farewell at the airport), that he agreed to defect. The time was originally fixed for 5 P.M., but, in the end, it was not until two hours later that the pickup in Tokyo was made and he was driven straight out to Tachikawa and the waiting RAF plane. Unhappily, it had to go on waiting, for at this point a deus ex machina intervened which was as insuperable as it was unexpected. The snow which had started to fall went on falling ever thicker, whipped up by a blizzard. In all, 12.2 inches of it fell that night, the heaviest fall recorded since the weather bureau had opened in Tokyo in 1875.

Rastvorov was now "Gustav Rutte," a notional Scandinavian, with all the papers to prove it and the necessary visas to take him through Hong Kong to Singapore and Colombo en route to London. But in the face of this blizzard they were of no immediate use. Rastvorov spent eleven nail-biting hours, from 9 P.M. on Saturday, waiting to take off. Then, at 8 A.M. on Sunday, he announced that he was calling it off for the day, saying he would return to his mission for appearances' sake and try the same escape route again on the twenty-fifth. The British party (it included a vice-marshal of the RAF) was most reluctant to let him out of their hands. They suggested asylum overnight in the British Chancery building but he rejected that as being too risky. At one point, his "minders" even wondered among themselves whether they might not persuade the American military, whose air base this was, to hold Rastvorov there, by force if need be. But there was one huge snag to this. The Americans at the airfield had not been informed who the mysterious passenger was and why it was so important to fly him out. Nor was the American embassy in Tokyo any wiser. British-American intelligence cooperation was close, especially in this postwar decade. But it was not that close. Each service, then as now, had secrets of its own; in this case, unfortunately for the British side. The best they could get out of Rastvorov as he disappeared in the snow was that he would be at the Tokyo rendezvous again that afternoon. He neither kept the appointment nor passed any message explaining why.

It was now the turn of the British to be left in the dark. By January 26, they had given Rastvorov up sufficiently to cancel the special RAF plane. The next week was spent in rueful speculation. Had Rastvorov been captured by the Soviet mission and was being held captive? Had he been shipped back on that Soviet vessel he had mentioned? Had he committed suicide? Or was it possible that he was still alive and free and in hiding? It was not until February 5, 1954, three days after the leaks had begun to appear all over the Western press, that the Central Intelligence Agency informed its British colleagues in London that Yuri Rastvorov was safely out of Japan and in their hands. One can hardly blame the Americans for waiting until the last minute. It was a natural tit for tat among friends.

What had happened was that Rastvorov, after the failure of his first escape plan, had decided it was too risky to try the same route a second time and had turned instead to his backup saviors, the Americans. Like a good professional, he had also kept a noncommittal line out to them for several months, and not simply to Mrs. Burns. For their part, the CIA in Tokyo, alerted by his general behavior, had made at least one attempt in the summer of 1953 to "sign him up." The middleman they chose was Captain Norman Reilly, a military doctor who played tennis with the Russian at the club. Reilly had in fact refused to cooperate, but, given Rastvorov's gregarious and uninhibited life-style, there had been no shortage of other opportunities. The Americans, after all, still ran Tokyo in 1954.

Many years afterward, Rastvorov told what really took place when he left the British on the morning of January 24. He did not, of course, show his face again at the Soviet mission, least of all to start burning papers; this despite the fact that he had deliberately left 400 dollars behind to make both his absence and return look plausible. Instead, he alerted his American contacts, who whisked him off to spend the night at an American safe house in the Washington Heights district of Tokyo. The next morning he was driven to a U.S. naval base and flown straight out to Okinawa. By the twenty-fifth, the blizzard, which had deprived the British of their prize, had lifted, enabling the Americans to take possession instead.

The intelligence value of that prize was considerable, if mainly short-term and restricted in scope. Japan was the country Rastvorov had been trained for throughout his time in Moscow and it was the only foreign country in which he had ever set foot. The main operational result of his defection was therefore the destruction of the network of Japanese agents which he had helped to develop and exploit. The bulk of them were successfully rounded up during the summer of 1954, including three officials in the Japanese Foreign Ministry. Rastvorov was also able to throw new light, based on firsthand information gained while in Tokyo, on certain Far East questions, such as the Korean War. He described how Stalin had launched the North Koreans on their offensive, hoping to keep the entire operation under Russian control, and how, after General Douglas MacArthur's counteroffensive had driven the invaders back to their own frontier, Stalin had been forced to turn to the Chinese to bail him out. The broad story was, of course, known to the West; what Rastvorov supplied was confirmation and firsthand details, gleaned partly from his colleague at the Tokyo mission, Colonel Shibaev, whom he described as "one of Stalin's confidential trouble-shooters in the Far East."[13]

Much else of what he had to tell was, of necessity, secondhand. Thus his version (at least in its published form)[14] of the power struggle in Moscow after Stalin's death had to be based entirely on snippets picked up while in Tokyo, and he had himself complained of how cutoff the Soviet mission there had always felt. In any case, fuller accounts of this battle of the Kremlin titans were to be brought to the West within weeks by other defectors who followed on Rastvorov's heels.

However, though his eyes had always been glued on Japan, during his years at the Moscow Center his ears had picked up a lot of general information there which was of interest to his hosts. Part of this debriefing was repeated at his public hearing before the U.S. Senate's Subcommittee on Internal Security which took place two years after his arrival in the United States.[15] He ticked off the list of all the heads of Soviet intelligence in America from Ovakimyan, who left in 1941, through Zarubin (using the alias of Zubilin), Dolbin, Sokolov and Panyushkin, who took over the espionage job in 1949 despite the fact that he was also the accredited Soviet ambassador—a rare duality of posts. He provided a broad outline of how the Soviet intelligence network operated in the United States and was probably the first defector to confirm that this included a special section working within the United Nations in New York, which operated separately from the organization controlled through the Soviet embassy in Washington. He was also, in all probability, the first of a long series of sources who exposed the Soviet news agency Tass as a principal front for Soviet espionage throughout the world. Up to 90 percent of Tass staff correspondents abroad, he told the astonished Senate subcommittee, were in fact agents of the Soviet political or military intelligence services.[16]

Nearly all this information was of considerable value at the time. But it is the human aspect of Rastvorov's defection which had the greatest long-term significance. Quite apart from his fears about his future and distaste for his collapsed marriage, the point to grasp about his case is a seemingly trivial one: he did not jump across the Iron Curtain but over a tennis net. Yuri Rastvorov was a seeker after the carefree pleasures of this world. He had found precious little of that in the Soviet Union, but, even from the samples he had experienced in and around the Tokyo sports club, he guessed—and guessed rightly as it turned out—that he would find it among the capitalists. This does not make him a simon-pure ideologist, yet there remains a basic ideological message behind his conversion. The West was the place for a full and fearless life.

6

Vienna

SOON AFTER dawn on February 17, 1954, the Red Army patrols at all checkpoints leading out of Vienna were suddenly strengthened, and Russian soldiers and security men began a meticulous search of everything on wheels which approached the barriers by road or rail. There was nothing to be done about the holdups. Austria was still, nine years after the war, under four-power occupation.* Though the capital itself was under quadripartite administration, it lay, like Berlin, in the middle of the Soviet zone. The Russians thus controlled all the allotted access routes leading west and south to the provinces occupied by the three Western powers.

A clampdown of this severity was, however, unusual. It lasted for the best part of a week, with rummaging among truckloads and car trunks and the strictest scrutiny of all travel documents, whether of Austrians or Allied personnel. Clearly, the Russians were in a panic to prevent somebody of importance from escaping their net. After three days, a carefully distorted version of the truth came out. A general press release in Vienna reported that the Soviet authorities there had asked the Austrian police to join them in tracking down "two Russian factory officials who vanished after a drunken nightclub spree

---

*This was not ended until the autumn of the following year, after the conclusion of the Austrian State Treaty in June of 1955.

and who may try and escape to the West."[1] The charge was made, later to become familiar in such cases, that the absconders had made off with government funds. The fugitives were named simply as Skachkov and Deriabin.

Needless to say, neither was a mere "factory official." Anatoly Skachkov worked in the headquarters of the Soviet petroleum administration in Vienna (the Soviet zone had important oilfields in and around Zistersdorf in Lower Austria). He often frequented nightclubs and had indeed just made his way to the West. It was the second man, with whom his departure had been fortuitously linked, who was the quarry the Russians were so desperately anxious to trap. Peter Sergeyevich Deriabin was a major in the KGB with eight years of unusually varied experience behind him and carrying, therefore, an unusually sensitive store of information in his head. To add insult to injury, his job, when he had decided to jump, was chief of the SK or Sovetskaia Koloniia intelligence section in Vienna. As such, he was charged with the security surveillance of all Soviet citizens in Austria, with the supreme responsibility of preventing any defections. It was the captain of the guard who had thrown down his rifle and fled, and he had escaped under the noses of his pursuers.

In his principal book of memoirs, Deriabin relates[2] how with "skillfully forged credentials" he left Vienna twenty-four hours after contacting the Americans, disguised as an Austrian civilian and traveling on the westbound Orient Express. That version was a deception deemed prudent when the book was written. In fact, Deriabin left not on the ordinary train but on the so-called Mozart Express, the military train reserved exclusively for American personnel, which left the Westbahnhof each day bound for the American zone. And he traveled, not in a passenger compartment, but in a wooden packing case loaded into the freight car. Deriabin had been popped inside, with water, sandwiches and cigarettes to sustain him, and air holes drilled for him to breathe through. This strange cargo was then cased up, labeled to Camp Trustcott in Salzburg and guarded at each end of the car by an American soldier once the train had moved off. The guards were careful not to accompany the packing case on board. The loading was done by Austrian freight handlers in order not to arouse the suspicion of the Soviet agents patrolling the platform. Looking back on the journey many years later, Deriabin described the one moment of anxiety in an otherwise trouble-free escape. The American zone did not actually begin until the western bank of the Enns River, but all trains were always halted two miles short of that, at the Soviet checkpoint at St. Valentin. After the train had duly stopped and then moved on, Deriabin, believing himself already in freedom and being anyway unable to control his nerves any longer, lit up a cigarette. Smoke began to ooze out of the crate, which looked as though it might have mysteriously caught fire while still in the Soviet zone. The guards managed to signal him to put his cigarette out and, a few minutes later, the Mozart Express clattered over the Enns railway bridge to safety.[3]

This ingenious escape route had held risks from the start, but the Americans had seen no alternative. Their light landing strip in the U.S. sector of Vienna was out of action, due to bad weather. The U.S. Air Force had regular facilities at Tulln airport, but that lay in the middle of the Soviet zone and was thus approachable only through the Russian roadblocks. Though no intelligence officer had had the chance to talk at length with Deriabin, the intensive search operation which had been launched to seize him indicated that he was indeed a prize of considerable value. The Americans even feared that, if the Russians came to suspect he was on board an American military plane which had taken off from Tulln, they would force the aircraft down with their fighters at a Soviet airfield, despite the diplomatic incident this would provoke. These were desperate calculations indeed, but when the debriefing started in earnest, Major Deriabin soon convinced his hosts that he had been worth all the trouble they had taken over him.

Simply put, he enabled the Western powers to emerge fully from that dark intelligence tunnel they had been plunged into after acquiring the Soviet Union as a wartime ally thirteen years before. The exigencies of the struggle against Hitler had meant that, in Britain, for example, the security and information-gathering apparatus had been switched almost entirely onto Nazi targets, leaving only one official to maintain a desk and some semblance of continuity at what had been, in prewar times, the critical and well-staffed Soviet section. During the war, the Western powers carried out hardly any hostile espionage against the Russians, in contrast to the intensive and increasing spying which the Soviet Union, for its part, was conducting against the West. The immediate postwar period had done little to redress the balance. If we glance back at the principal intelligence leaks from that time, Igor Gouzenko had brought little with him apart from his sheaf of telegrams, vital though those were in the short term. A junior officer who had never before stepped outside the hothouse of the cipher world, his vision was limited. Konstantin Volkov had seen much more and would have revealed much more, but his voice had been stopped in good time by Philby. There had then been a gap of nearly a decade before the westward flow of Soviet intelligence officials started up again, as though a sluice had opened up, in the midwinter of 1954. However, Rastvorov, the defector who had preceded Deriabin in this sudden procession, had been restricted in experience almost entirely to Far Eastern matters, while the one who was immediately to succeed him had been concerned principally with murder.

Indeed, for the man capable of giving them their last authoritative picture, in breadth and depth, as to how the Soviet police state operated, Western experts had to look back to Aleksandr Orlov, a three-star general, no less, in the NKVD. He had defected in Paris in July 1938 after a brilliant career under Stalin which had culminated in the hijacking of the entire gold reserves of Republican Spain.[4] Deriabin had no exploit like that to boast of, and he was three ranks below a general. Nonetheless, he could provide the same wealth of detail over the same broad canvas. This was due to an extraordinary career which had taken him, as a security officer or unit Party secretary, into the rubble of Stalingrad, the remoteness of Russia's Asian borders, the inside of both the Moscow intelligence headquarters and the Kremlin itself, all in addition to a final spell of field experience abroad. The whole of his professional career was one unbroken seam of information.

There was an individualistic stamp about his origins which was never quite pressed flat, despite the weight of the ideological steamroller which later passed over him. The time and place of his birth, and the home of his childhood, all left their permanent marks. He was born at Lokot, a farming hamlet in southwestern Siberia, on February 13, 1921,[5] which was, as it happened, the time of the first armed rebellion against the Communist regime, the mutiny of the Red Fleet at Kronstadt. He thus belonged to that in-between generation of Russians who followed those grown to maturity under the tsar but preceded those who were to know nothing but the seemingly ironclad world of Stalin. When Deriabin was in his cradle, Russia was shaking all around him as marauding bands of robbers, condottieri, and the last of the White Army forces struggled with the Bolsheviks for the control of the countryside. Yet because Lokot was in the remote border territory of the Altai, well to the south of the hotly contested Trans-Siberian railway, these upheavals barely disturbed it. Nor, for a while, did the new order. For several years, the officials in Barnaul, the provincial capital, simply went about their administrative business, interpreting Moscow's orders as best they could, without feeling much of Moscow's hand in the process. This meant that Deriabin's infancy was passed largely in the atmosphere of a vanished age.

His father's influence only increased the illusion of living in a time warp. Sergey Deriabin had served as a sergeant major in the imperial army. Though a pragmatic man, concerned mainly with the welfare of himself and his family, he continued, as far as he safely could, in the ways of his forefathers. Young Peter was baptized, and icons hung in the family home long after the regime launched its all-out onslaught against religion. Above all, the boy, like his father, carried with him throughout his life something of the independent spirit of a hardy frontier people. The high flat Altai, with its long arctic winters and short searing summers, its lack of proper medical facilities (doctors were almost unknown) and the rapacious packs of wolves in its deep forests, was like primitive pioneer country. Sergey, a carpenter as well as a small farmer, built with his own hands the log cabins which were their homes, first at Lokot and then at nearby Ovsyaikov. Only three of the eleven children which his wife Stepanida bore him lived into their teens. Those who survived in the Altai carried about them a stubborn pride. All these factors need bearing in mind when we come to look at Peter Deriabin, the man in the Communist machine.

That machine first caught up with him, and the family as a whole, when in 1928 his father decided to send him to the village school. The machine soon made up for lost time. Young Deriabin was a model pupil, ideologically as well as academically. At nine, he ran home in triumph with the red scarf of the Young Pioneers around his neck. The old tsarist sergeant major was sarcastic, calling it a "dog's leash" which his son was showing off. This reaction had no effect on the boy, though it could have caused a painful conflict of loyalty. It was precisely the sort of subversive remark which all Pioneers were supposed to report to their leaders. His mother's efforts to counter the antireligious campaign in the classroom by taking the boy in secret for Bible lessons from a former novice nun were an equally plain case for denunciation. Peter never informed on his family; but, in his six years with the Pioneers, he could not avoid absorbing something of the hostile, chronically suspicious Party attitude toward the citizenry in general. He could, at this stage, find nothing wrong with such attitudes or with the Marxist New World in general. Aged fifteen, he applied for membership in the Komsomol, the youth movement which was the breeding tank for full-grown Communist specimens.

No one [he later wrote] could have argued me out of joining. . . . My only goal was to be in the ranks of those fighting to build Communism. I accepted completely the idea of the class struggle and the creation of the classless society. I was thirsty for knowledge and I had always tried to be at the top. So I worked hard to be in the front ranks of Communism.[6]

Academically, his hard work got him top honors when he graduated from the Ovsyaikov high school in 1937 and brought him a teacher's certificate a year later. It was this qualification, added to his Komsomol record and his impeccable proletarian background (his father, having sold off most of his smallholding, could be described as a plain carpenter, while his mother was a former servant girl), which stood him in good stead when Hitler's war erupted over Europe in September 1939. Within a month of being called up into the army, Peter Deriabin was made deputy political commissar for the noncommissioned officers' school where he had been sent for training. It was the beginning of a professional lifetime spent, almost entirely, in the surveillance of his fellow Russians. In May 1941, now Komsomol secretary of an engineers' battalion, Deriabin applied for full membership in the Communist party. It was one month before the war engulfed the Soviet Union itself. By the time his Party card, Number 4121243, was issued, the German advance was already threatening Moscow.

The emotions which now swept over Deriabin were affecting tens of millions of Russians, Party members and ordinary citizens alike. The "Great Patriotic War" united the country as it had never before been united, at least (ironically enough) not since the day, in August of 1914, when the nation-in-arms had marched into battle against the German and Austrian empires. Yet there was a difference in reaction between the watchers and the watched-over. For the ordinary Russian, cowed by the savagery of Stalin's purges and his mass extermination of the peasantry, and cynical about his promises to bring them a better life, the war represented a truce, a suspension of disbelief between regime and people. But for the Communist zealot, it only fired and hardened his ideological faith anew. The gap between rulers and ruled, though bridged, was not filled in. Deriabin was one of the zealots. He carried *War and Peace,* in several tattered volumes, around the battlefields with him, convinced that Stalin was re-created in the mold of Kutusov and all Tolstoy's other heroes put together.

He had what British officers would have described, with la-

conic Anglo-Saxon approval, as "a good war." Deriabin, a battalion political officer by the autumn of 1941, was badly
wounded in the leg in the battle before Moscow; the following
autumn, which brought him formal appointment as junior political commissar, with officer's rank, saw him in the thick of the
murderous struggle for Stalingrad, where he was promoted
again. His last front-line encounter with the Germans was the
worst. In April of 1944, his division, the 284th, was forcing a
crossing of the swampy Bug River as part of the operation to
free the Black Sea port of Odessa. His reconnaissance detachment reached the far bank but then ran into a strong counterattack. Deriabin was shot in the back as he struggled to regain
the Soviet side and he fell helpless in the marsh. A passing
German soldier stripped him of his new American combat
boots, shot him again, and then, taking him for dead, rifled his
pockets. The tough Siberian somehow survived, though all he
could move at first was his head. After five hours lying in the
swamp, one bullet through his shoulder blades and the second
through his lung, he was found at 11 P.M. by his own men and
moved to safer and firmer ground. Even here, he had to last out
the night alone before managing to get to his feet in the morning and stagger, barefoot, back to the main Russian lines.

When he emerged from the hospital, even his superior officers urged him to call it a day, as regards front-line service.
They suggested a post in military security instead. He was in
no mood to object. Not for the last time in his career, Deriabin,
having shown that he could stand up to fire, decided to duck out
from under the shrapnel. In June 1944, just as the Red Army's
final surge westward toward the heartland of Nazi-occupied
Europe was beginning, he passed, with high honors, into the
Higher Military Counterintelligence School. By the time he
finished his career in the redbrick building at 19 Stanislavskaya
Street in Moscow, it was April of 1945. The fighting was as good
as over and the Hitler menace banished. The regime had a new
security priority—its own people.

Deriabin was now a full-fledged "cheka," the name given to
Feliks Dzerzhinsky's first Bolshevik security policemen (Cheka)
of 1918 and a label still used by their successors, despite the

frequent changes in their nomenclature.* As such, he was pledged with every thought in his brain and every drop of blood in his body to protect the regime which had chosen him as one of its guardians. It was not just the outside world which was supposed to remain eternally polarized between socialist and capitalist forces, despite the temporary alliance, rapidly drawing to its close, between them. Within the country, as he now had to recognize, there was an equally iron division between the Communists and non-Communists of the Soviet Union.

Like the capitalists outside Russia, the ordinary citizens inside constituted a threat to the system, and one made many times more dangerous by their wartime exposure to the Western world. Hundreds of thousands of Red Army soldiers were about to be demobilized and reabsorbed into their Communist homeland (though several thousand were, in fact, to desert and remain in the West). The homecomers had all seen for themselves the fiction of their "workers' paradise" exposed. Some of the great cities they had entered in Central and Southeastern Europe were, like Prague, almost undamaged. Some were landscapes of smoking ruins, like Berlin itself. Yet, whether they were walking amidst rubble or undisturbed beauty, Stalin's soldiery, and especially the more primitive ones such as the Mongolian divisions of the Third Ukrainian Army Front, were made aware that the vanquished and the liberated belonged to a higher order of culture and comfort than the Russian victors. The author remembers a classic case of this, doubtless repeated many times elsewhere, when, in the summer of 1945, the British Eighth Army took over from units of that same Ukrainian army group in Graz, the Austrian provincial capital of Styria. Even the officers had been washing and shaving themselves in the toilets of the houses they were billeted in, persuaded by the inviting pool of water that these were intended for such ablutions. By a process of elimination, they had concluded that the sinks must have been intended for the needs of nature. These were people who, in the middle of the twentieth century, had never seen proper sanitation before in their lives.

*See Appendix: *Plus ça change.*

In terms of that one stark example, Stalin's priority, from the spring of 1945 onward, was to convince the Russians that toilets were indeed better than sinks for one's ablutions or—should he decide otherwise—that the Soviet Union could anyway produce far better basins of either variety than the decadent West. Peter Deriabin, as a member of the Communist elite, had progressed beyond the primitive facilities of his native Siberian log hut. But though he had not yet been outside the Soviet Union, he too was already growing aware of the huge gap in living standards between his motherland and the Western world. It had been shown by his American-made combat boots that the German soldier had coveted in the marshes before Odessa. It was demonstrated by the Western household equipment or Western products of any description which the Russian soldiers, in turn, coveted from their captives. Watches were the supreme prize, and Deriabin himself came back from the front with three of them strapped on his wrist.

Now, however, he had to take part in a ruthless campaign to seal Russia off entirely from all those wartime experiences and, once the vacuum had been closed up again, to re-create inside it the old lies about Communist prosperity fairly distributed. The required trick was to transform the burst of loyalty which the Great Patriotic War had produced into subservience to the regime, while annihilating all the disturbing comparisons to which the nation had been exposed by the Western alliance. The five million Red Army soldiers taken prisoner by the Germans were special targets in this reconditioning process. They were punished not so much for so-called anti-Soviet activity as for suspected contamination. Each man was given an individual "trial." Deriabin later estimated their fate as follows: 20 percent set free, though with a black mark against their name; 25 percent banished to frontier territories or consigned as work conscripts to industrial areas; up to 20 percent jailed for a minimum of five years; another 20 percent jailed for twenty-five years, or else shot. Only the severely wounded qualified for release without blame.[7]

It was a traumatic time for Deriabin, as well as for the Red Army in general. As a military counterintelligence officer, he saw from the inside how this vast Kafkaesque campaign of retribution was being waged against his former comrades-in-arms. He was committed to supporting it; he might have helped in some way to implement it; yet he cannot have been blind to its monumental injustice. The early postwar period was as bad for his conscience as it was good for his career.

This began (after a significant lapse into disenchantment when he had briefly contemplated resuming civilian life as a schoolteacher) with his posting as a State Security captain based in Barnaul, the capital of his native Siberian province. This paid more than three times the monthly salary of a teacher and made him a much privileged but also much feared official in the locality. For the first time, the truth about everything he had been taught at his counterintelligence school sank in. The regime stood implacably over and apart from the nation. From now on, he no longer belonged to the Russian people, or rather to that huge majority of it which stood outside the Party. All of the outsiders, including his childhood friends, had become surveillance targets.

He spent nearly a year in Barnaul, building up his network of agents and informers to spy on the city's two hundred thousand inhabitants, and finding the task more distasteful and embarrassing with every month that passed. But it was the loss of his wife Tanya, who died of pleurisy in the summer of 1947, which spurred him to move—not out of the intelligence world which now held him fast, but onward and upward inside it. For all the inner misgivings he doubtless felt, Captain Deriabin remained a pragmatist and, at this stage, still a Party careerist. Onward and upward meant Moscow, and it was there he went to lobby, using a stopover en route for a spell of leave in the Caucasus as a pretext for his presence. We now meet the most important person in Deriabin's official life, his "fixer." From this point forward, it becomes rewarding to add his personal amplifications to his published writings.

Deriabin always referred to his fixer in these writings as Pavel Zuikov, but the man's real name was Vladimir Petrochenkov, a friend of his from their days as students together at the counterintelligence school. Pavel or Vladimir, he was the sort of individual who, through cunning, charm, energy and a careful rationing of personal ambition, contrives to establish himself, in any great bureaucratic machine, in positions where modest rank is combined with great influence. In the case of Zuikov (as we shall continue to call him) the rank was personal assistant to the deputy minister for personnel at the Ministry of State Security, Major General Svinelupov. The influence stemmed from the fact that the deputy minister disliked hard work and avoided decisions when he could because he was disliked in turn by his ill-fated chief, Colonel General Viktor Abakumov. The effect of this was to allow the personal assistant to operate almost as though he were the deputy minister himself, signing appointments, recalls and transfer orders involving even the most senior officers in Svinelupov's name. It was no problem to move Captain Peter Deriabin from Barnaul to Moscow and put him on the staff of State Security headquarters. Here Deriabin remained for the next six years and it was this long and varied stint at the hub of the great KGB wheel which enabled Deriabin, after his escape to the West, to give such an accurate description of the twelve main departments and six special support branches into which the Moscow Center was divided in the early 1950s.

One of the first lessons Deriabin learned was that, however helpful your fixer might be, in the world of the KGB there were times when nothing could prevent your ending up as the travel baggage of your superiors. After a spell in administration, he had been assigned to work for a colonel in the Personnel Section. The appointment had barely been made when the colonel was himself switched to a post in the so-called Guard Directorate. He took Deriabin along with him. The fixer was not enthusiastic. "The Guard Directorate can be pretty sticky," he warned his friend. "It's awfully close to the top."[8]

This was, if anything, an understatement. What Deriabin's new job involved was nothing less than security surveillance over the body of handpicked janissaries who guarded the lives of the Kremlin giants. At this period, there were some fifteen thousand of these guards, whose duties ranged from making sure that no soldier carried any live ammunition at military parades* to checking all the sewers, attics and rooftops along any route to be traveled by Stalin and his principal minions. Stalin himself had a personal bodyguard of no fewer than 406 officers and men, the most select of the select. Yet somebody had to keep a wary eye even on "trusties" such as these. Deriabin was one of the watchers, the ultimate defense line drawn up at the most august level of security. His particular subsection, the fifth of thirteen such surveillance units, was responsible for the loyalty and efficiency of some 2,350 of the uniformed and plain-clothes Guard officers working in and around the Kremlin. The old question *"Quis custodiet ipos custodes?"* did have an answer in the Moscow of his day. The guardians of the guardians were Captain Deriabin and his colleagues at the Guard Directorate. All the time, of course, others were keeping an eye on them.

From this new desk of his at the Moscow Center, he learned far more interesting things than which nightclubs were frequented by Major X, or whether the wife of Lieutenant Y had a brother-in-law with distant relations living in America. He learned also of the secret city within a city which was the Kremlin complex of buildings, complete with its own barracks, power plant, communications system and even, on the outskirts of the capital, its own farms, to feed the tables of the mighty, their families and guests, in their various official residences, guesthouses and country dachas. The hidden city was served by its own army of helots—everything from specially recruited doctors and plumbers to specially recruited charwomen and prostitutes, each with his or her State Security identity card. This, the Kremlin kommandatura, with the chief task of protecting Stalin himself, was known as Okhrana No. 1.†

The special services it could provide were vividly illustrated during the visit which the Chinese Communist leaders paid to Moscow in the winter of 1949–50, before the Sino-Soviet breach. Stalin was particularly anxious to have a long talk alone with

---

*This was the security lapse that enabled the plotters to assassinate President Sadat of Egypt as he was watching a military parade in Cairo in October 1981.

†The word simply means "Guard," and was another label, and another function, with tsarist origins.

Mao Tse-tung, without the ubiquitous presence of his number two, Liu Shao-chi, getting in the way. His Guard Directorate had come up with the answer. An Okhrana refuse truck ran, carefully and gently, into the Okhrana-chauffeured limousine which was carrying Liu out to Mao's dacha, where the Communist summit was being held. The police were careful to take two hours to complete the "accident" formalities and clear the road. Stalin was thus provided with his desired tête-à-tête. To preserve appearances, Liu's chauffeur was issued a bogus dismissal order and the truck driver given an equally bogus year in jail.

Okhrana No. 2 existed to provide similar protection and special services for the hierarchs immediately below Stalin—the other members and alternate members of the Politburo, the secretaries of the Central Committee, the principal government ministers and the leading marshals of the armed forces. In nearly all cases, surveillance was added on as well. Commenting on this system in Stalin's era, Deriabin wrote in his study of protection at the Kremlin throughout the ages: "The Main Guard Directorate was probably the most perfect and sophisticated body ever organized for the personal security of a . . . leader."[9]

His first years with the Kremlin Guard Directorate seem to have passed fairly smoothly. The work was demanding but well paid; his salary of 4,000 rubles a month was more than four times that of the highest-paid factory worker in the land. He had an official car and driver and a small dacha in the pine forests of Mamontovka, twenty miles outside the capital. The only thing needed to complete this cozy picture of a contented Soviet official was a suitable spouse. This he found in June of 1948, when he married his second wife, Marina Makeyeva. Her security credentials were impeccable. They had met in the Kremlin, where she worked as a stenographer to the Politburo itself.

To work anywhere in the State Security headquarters at 2 Dzerzhinsky Square was to be surrounded by the apparatus of terror. The building also housed the dreaded Lubianka Prison, and Deriabin was well aware of what went on in the basement cells underneath his second-floor office. Indeed, some of the interrogators were his personal friends, and they would occasionally boast of the techniques they used to extract the statutory confessions from their victims. It must have been an uneasy feeling to watch from his window the prisoners shuffling around the inner courtyard when taken out for exercise—particularly when some of his former colleagues and even former bosses could be glimpsed among the sorry procession below. For gradually, as the Stalin era drew to a close, the jailers in the Lubianka building became almost as hounded as the jailed. Factional fighting had broken out inside the Politburo for the succession to the aging tyrant; and the State Security Ministry, a key bastion in any leadership struggle, took the shock waves. The heaviest of these struck it in July 1951 when the minister himself, General Viktor Abakumov, was dismissed in an order signed by Stalin, imprisoned and later executed. All of his six deputies and many of his senior aides followed him, first into jail, and then, in many cases, to the firing squads. Deriabin seemed in no immediate danger, for he had no personal patrons among the mighty and would not therefore stand or fall simply through this battle of the titans. Nonetheless, it was time for a prudent man to seek cover from all the close fire. So, soon after Abakumov's fall, he again consulted his fixer, who had safely survived all the storms.

It was Deriabin who raised the possibility of a move right across the checkerboard into the Second Chief Directorate, which dealt with foreign intelligence. This department, which often worked under the cover of the Foreign Ministry, was just about as far away as a security officer could place himself from the dangerous domestic infighting at the Kremlin. In theory, the Guard Directorate had a veto on anyone quitting their ranks. However, it was so preoccupied now with its own problems, which included a heavy cutback in staff, that the invaluable Pavel Zuikov was able to set the transfer in motion by a few telephone calls. In May 1952, Captain Deriabin reported for duty to Colonel Eugeny Kravtsov, head of the Austro-German section of the Second Directorate, which was housed in a complex of gray buildings some comforting distance from Dzerzhinsky Square. For Deriabin, it was like emerging from a stifling jungle onto open grassland. The atmosphere was so relaxed that the eighty-one officers who served under Kravtsov would greet him, in English, with "Hello, Boss" instead of the formal "Comrade Colonel" Deriabin was used to.

Casual it may have been; cheery it was not. For the next fifteen months, Deriabin worked in a key section of a directorate which numbered some three thousand foreign intelligence personnel at headquarters, plus another fifteen thousand officers and agents, Soviet and non-Soviet, working for it abroad. In contrast to the Guard Directorate, which, as a general rule, selected men of limited education judged more suitable to a robot role, Second Chief Directorate was staffed by some of the most intelligent and sophisticated people which Soviet society was capable of producing. This was another welcome change for the new recruit, who held a high-school teacher's degree and a diploma certificate, issued in 1951, for a two-year advanced course at Moscow's Marxist-Leninist Institute.[10]

The work was also more challenging, as well as being less hazardous. His main domestic duty now was not to protect Soviet leaders but merely to inform them about what was going on in the world outside. The Second Directorate made four grades of reports. The first had thirteen copies, one for each member of the Central Committee's Presidium. The next had only seven, for the seven most powerful men in that body. Then came an edition with only three copies, one of which went to Stalin. Finally there was a one-copy version which went, as a working paper, only to the secretary of the Central Committee, who, at this time, was Georgi Malenkov. None of the papers was ever marked "Secret," or given any security classification. The recipients, Colonel Kravtsov explained, were presumed to know everything anyway.

Yet congenial though both the duties and the atmosphere were, the dark side of the Second Directorate could never be avoided. The darkest was its "Spetsburo" or "Special Bureau Number One," which dealt with terror operations abroad, notably assassinations and kidnappings of declared Soviet traitors or suspected enemies of the regime of any race or creed. We shall meet up with one of its key operators in the chapter which follows. Though never working for the Spetsburo, Deriabin was himself involved in arranging an operation very much in this field—the kidnapping in West Berlin on July 8, 1952, of Dr. Walter Linse, the acting head of the so-called Association of Free German Jurists, an anti-Communist professional body. It caused a diplomatic storm abroad and, back in Moscow, brought a pat on the back for Captain Deriabin. He claims, nonetheless, to have felt a few pangs of conscience at the time.[11]

Be that as it may, it seems probable that it was fear of being caught up and destroyed in the power-struggle vortex rather than any overwhelming repugnance for Communism which now began to turn the mind of Peter Deriabin toward complete escape. He had an unpleasant scare, for example, in the winter of 1952–53, which he never wrote about in his books, when a former female assistant of his denounced him for "anti-Stalin talk." The woman, Valya Orlik, seems to have acted (according to Deriabin) more out of spite and wounded vanity than out of genuine concern for the reputation of the fading tyrant. She had repeatedly asked Deriabin to visit her at home when her husband was away on official business. He had repeatedly declined. For one thing, he explained later, she was far too heavy for his taste. Moreover, he avoided on principle any "office romances."

Whatever her motives, he was nonetheless vulnerable, especially in the tense and suspicious atmosphere of the time. He had certainly exchanged gossip, though only with his colleagues, about those personal or family scandals, known only to the Moscow inner circle, which the leadership was so anxious to hide from the outside world. Stalin's odious police chief, Lavrenty Beria, was notorious in the service, for example, for his unbridled womanizing and, in particular, for his sexual passion for nymphets, whom, on occasion, he would select from teenagers walking on the pavements as he drove through the city in his bulletproof car. The gossip about Stalin centered mainly on his children, and especially on his worthless son Vasily, who had been made a general in the Soviet air force.

The latest of Vasily's many scandalous exploits had been to get into his plane when drunk on May Day, 1952, fly it low over

the Kremlin—a heinous offense in itself—and then crash-land
it. As a result, he was hauled up before his father, who personally ripped off the lieutenant general's epaulets from his son's
uniform, demoted him to colonel and posted him away to the
Zhukovski Air Academy. Even to mention matters like this,
Valya Orlik maintained, was to indulge in anti-Stalin activities.
She demanded that the security minister, Semen Ignatiev, institute a formal inquiry into Deriabin's behavior. The minister, a
weak and nervous Party functionary who had been put at his
desk as a stopgap, duly ordered one.[12]

Before long, however, this file was swept away, with many
weightier matters, by the storm which struck the Kremlin upon
Stalin's death, which was announced to the Russian people on
March 6, 1953. The struggle for the succession which ensued is
familiar history. Malenkov was the heir apparent, and duly took
over as head of both Party and government. Yet, within a fortnight, he was persuaded (by what pressure or threats is still
unknown) to hand over the key Party role to Nikita Khrushchev. An uneasy phase of collective leadership followed, with
Malenkov, now only premier, Nikolay Bulganin, now head of
the armed forces, and Molotov, the foreign minister, all jockey-
ing for position. But it was Beria, who had been installed as
security supremo, who made the first naked bid for power
through a military coup d'état in Moscow which he had timed
for June 27, 1953, using the special units under his command.
However, he was betrayed by his deputy, Colonel Sergey Kru-
glov, who had been tapping his master's telephone, thus providing convincing evidence of his guilt. Beria's rivals combined
forces to crush the plotter by summoning a regular armored
division answerable to Marshal Bulganin to take over key
points in the capital. On the eve of his intended putsch, Beria
was called to the Presidium offices in the Kremlin and arrested.
The news was not released to the public until July 9. After six
months of continuous interrogations, in the course of which
Beria and his henchmen were at the receiving end of many of
the techniques, physical and psychological, they had perfected
for use on others, the plotters were sentenced to death and shot
on December 23.

As can be imagined, these months of ruthless struggle for mastery over the Kremlin produced a hurricane inside the walls of 2 Dzerzhinsky Square. First, Beria had purged the organization he had taken over, installing his own men in all the crucial posts. Then, his henchmen had been bundled off en bloc, to be replaced by a mixture of faces old and new. The upheaval was somehow more alarming than anything endured in Stalin's time because the threats now came unpredictably and from so many sides.

Like everyone else in the Moscow Center, both Colonel Kravtsov and Captain Deriabin had been constantly mulling over the best way to guard their flanks and preserve their futures. The opportunity came for both in the summer of 1953 when Kravtsov's name was put forward to become "rezident," or chief of intelligence operations, in Vienna. For the head of the whole Austro-German section, this was no promotion; but it was a plum posting nonetheless, not least because it meant a few years abroad in a pleasant capital, close enough to Moscow to watch how the power struggle was developing there, but far enough away not to be caught up in it directly. Kravtsov doubtless jumped at the proposal, which then had to go before his Party committee for approval. And who should be the secretary of this committee but Deriabin, who had already filled this same role in so many different professional settings. A profitable bargain was struck. The captain would praise the colonel before the committee as being in every way suitable for the Vienna post. The colonel would in turn suggest taking the captain to Vienna with him "as a key man in rebuilding an efficient apparatus."[13]

There could easily have been great difficulties in carrying out the second part of the operation. One was the denunciation for "anti-Stalin activities" and the official inquiry it had sparked. However, when it was Deriabin's turn to come before the committee for approval, he was told to forget the whole Valya Orlik incident. Ignatiev had long ceased to be security minister and the denunciation file had anyway gone into the wastepaper basket. A bigger problem, at least on paper, was Deriabin's spell with the Guard Directorate, for there was a supposedly inflexible rule that nobody who had served in this particular section, where he was privy to so many secrets about the Soviet leadership, should ever be allowed outside the country. Deriabin, knowing the mentality of Party committees, was shrewd enough to refer to the ban himself. He was smilingly told to forget that technicality as well.[14] The Austrian appointment was confirmed and, on September 28, 1953, Captain Deriabin, with his wife and small daughter, arrived by train in Vienna.

Deriabin's defection to the West, which took place less than four months afterward, was presented in his memoirs as an impulse decision. In the sense that a match is always needed to light the fuse which in turn leads to the gunpowder barrel and blows it up, this is true. But, as he admitted some thirty years after that book was written, he had half-resolved to jump clear even before leaving Moscow.

> My thoughts when asking for the transfer were "Why not look at the outside world and see what it is like?" Only then could I decide whether to make the move. Of course, there were doubts in my mind. I had no idea how the Americans would treat me. All Soviet propaganda put them in such a bad light. Perhaps I half-believed in our own anti-American stuff.[15]

First impressions of Vienna showed him not only what the "outside world" was like but convinced him that even this curious sample of it was better than anything he had known before. The city was still burdened with four-power occupation, and it still showed many of the scars of the 1944–45 fighting and air bombardment. But the restaurants and wine bars were full; the streets were choked with private cars; and the shop windows underneath the pockmarked facades were bursting with goods whose quality and variety spoke quite simply of a new dimension to life. Astoundingly, there were no queues waiting to purchase all these delights.

On the advice of his colleagues, who had told him to "buy everything there," he had traveled from Moscow with the one suit he stood up in. In the first three days, he outfitted himself with a complete wardrobe of Western clothes. His wife bought up for her entire family back in Moscow, and sent the parcels home via the first Soviet delegation to visit Vienna. The great lie of Communist supremacy, even in material things, was something he had grown suspicious of from the moment the first supplies of Western food, clothing, transport and military equipment had reached the Soviet Union during the war. Now, in peace, that lie grew larger with every stroll around the Austrian capital. Moreover, as head of the SK counterintelligence unit at the Soviet mission, he could take his strolls more or less when and where he pleased. He was comfortably quartered with his wife in the Grand Hotel on the Ringstrasse and the luxury shops and restaurants of the internationally policed First District were only a stone's throw behind him.

The mission which he had joined (its headquarters were in the Imperial Hotel on the opposite side of the Ring) was undergoing a complete transfiguration. Some of the changes, such as the appointment of the Soviet high commissioner, the GRU Lieutenant General Ivan Ivanovich Ilyichev, to a second role as ambassador to the Austrian republic, were familiar enough; his three Western colleagues were also wearing the same two hats. But other things were going on in secret inside the Imperial Hotel which those colleagues and their political masters would have given much to know about at the time. For example, though it did not emerge until the beginning of 1955 that the post-Stalin leadership was at last preparing to withdraw its troops from Austria and give that country its freedom, Captain Deriabin was sure when he arrived in Vienna eighteen months before that the decision had already been made.

The talk in the Soviet mission was all of the neutral Austria which Khrushchev was now ready to accept, and General Ilyichev had been ordered to revamp the entire Soviet intelligence apparatus accordingly. Contact with so-called illegal agents (i.e., those operating without any official cover) was being stepped up, as these would form the main espionage network to be left behind after the evacuation. On the other hand, as the time was approaching when the Soviet High Commission would melt away, leaving only a Soviet embassy in its place, the regular intelligence officers were being given formal diplomatic slots, as though Vienna were already like any other Western capital. As for the reasons behind this 1953 decision in principle, Deriabin assumed that it was partly an attempt by Khrushchev to buy the cheapest entry ticket he could to get the Soviet Union accepted back into the civilized international arena. The Soviet leader's resolve to heal the breach with Yugoslavia (which had broken with the Soviet Union in 1948) was another powerful factor. Marshal Tito, it seemed, had made it clear that, if the Kremlin wanted a reconciliation with Belgrade, it had better remove the Red Army from Austria first.[16] Deriabin soon decided that he was going to leave before it, and in the opposite direction.

Though he wrote nothing of this in his memoirs, his first attempts to contact the American authorities were in fact made before Christmas of 1953, when he had been less than three months in Vienna. He hung around in the Soviet bookshop in the First District, which he knew American diplomats and intelligence officers regularly visited; he frequented restaurants favored by the Western community, hoping to strike up a promising conversation. There was little danger that such behavior would arouse suspicion among his own colleagues: as head of Soviet personnel security, part of his job was to move around the capital and keep an eye on who was where at any given time. It was a particularly disagreeable snooping assignment which finally triggered his decision to get out immediately and take things head-on, at any cost.

Early in the morning of February 13, he was awakened by a telephone call from his chief, Colonel Kravtsov, who ordered him to make immediate investigations into the disappearance of a Soviet official. The missing man, Anatoly Skachkov, had returned home drunk that night from a spree at the well-known strip-tease cabaret Maxim's and, after collecting some clothes, had walked out, telling his wife that he was leaving "for the Americans." The frightened woman had duly informed the Soviet mission.

Deriabin was puzzled, as well as irritated, by the assignment. To begin with, the missing official had gone to the nightclub together with a State Security lieutenant colonel on a visit from Moscow, hardly the company that any would-be defector, drunk or sober, would pick for the eve of his flight. Moreover, Colonel Kravtsov had said something very strange before hanging up: "Don't dig too deep," he had warned. The mystery was solved for Deriabin when he visited the Skachkovs' home. He found more than a hundred American paperbacks scattered, without any attempt at concealment, around the flat. Deriabin took this as proof that the "defector" was in fact a KGB plant, who had been familiarizing himself with the American way of life. He was infuriated at being used as a dummy in a deception game. Unpleasant though many of his surveillance tasks had been through the years (including several he had been obliged to carry out against his fellow citizens in Vienna), he had never been exploited in this fashion before.

It was therefore a very touchy and very irritable Captain Deriabin who, having been up all night, called in at his Grand Hotel apartment around noon on the fourteenth. His wife, with whom he was anyway on poor terms, snapped at him for another of his nocturnal disappearing acts. As he prepared to march out again and avoid another domestic row, she asked when he expected to be back this time. Almost without realizing what he had said, he retorted, as he slammed the door behind him, "Maybe I'll never come back." There was no "maybe" about it. His mind was made up.

At around four in the afternoon, after a final appearance to cover his tracks at the Skachkov flat, he made his way by taxi and on foot to the Stiftskaserne, the main American military headquarters in the Mariahilferstrasse. The fact that it was close to Herzmansky's, a popular modest-priced department store where many of the Soviet colony did their shopping, gave him an alibi until the moment of no return. This was reached as he passed the sentry at the gate and, once inside the building, asked to talk to a Russian-speaking American intelligence officer. When a U.S. Army captain with the right credentials eventually appeared, Deriabin gave his own rank and position in the Soviet mission and applied on the spot for asylum. Once the

American had assured himself that the caller really meant what he said, Deriabin was whisked away into hiding. The end of the story we already know.

Peter Deriabin was interesting as an intelligence defector because of the varied nature of his career. He is interesting as a human case history because of the different factors which caused him to throw up that career. Some of these elements stemmed, as already described, from the circumstances of his birth and background. The independent spirit of the Siberian frontiersman was never quite snuffed out by Communist indoctrination. But that spirit meant, above all, survival, the saving of one's skin. Survival was sought first in the Party network, which he embraced with teenage enthusiasm. Then it was sought, in a different and more desperate context, in Red Army uniform, which, like the red scarf of the Young Pioneers, he also wore with pride and distinction. It was only after Hitler's war, after this double flush of youthful zest and patriotic ardor, that a new factor crept into the equation: the steadily mounting clash between his character and his work. Deriabin gives the strong impression in exile of an honest and decent human being, and there is no reason to believe that he was any different at heart when serving as an intelligence officer in Stalin's Russia. Yet, because of the security branch work he was drafted into after leaving the army, he found himself nearly always engaged in the most unsavory of duties, the surveillance of his fellow citizens. The born snooper has in him a streak of meanness which Deriabin never displayed. We can believe him when he maintained that it was the nature of his work as much as the nature of Communism which slowly turned his gaze westward.

Disillusionment with the system itself doubtless played a role, though probably not as great a one as his Western hosts were waiting to hear (like all defectors, Deriabin found that he had a clamorous gallery to play before in exile). What fed the disillusionment in his case was the material rather than the spiritual contrast between West and East. Deriabin came over less as a crusader than as a man in search of a better life. No one should think less of him for that; such a search is a form of crusade in itself.

Then came the professional and family factors behind his decision. His flight was not prompted, as in the case of other defectors at this time, by fears that the ax would fall on his head if he went back to Moscow. He felt under no immediate threat. On the other hand, he did feel an increasing reluctance to return from this new world of enjoyment and plenty to the old one of tensions and scarcities. Moreover, there was hardly anyone left to go back to, beyond old comrades-in-arms and a few trusted colleagues like Pavel the fixer. His father, the ex-tsarist sergeant, had died in 1936, his mother five years later. His one brother, Vladimir, had been killed in action against the Germans. Only his sister, Valya, remained as a close relative and hostage living in Russia.

There was, of course, the problem of his own wife and infant daughter left behind in the Grand Hotel. This second marriage may have turned sour, but was that enough to expose his wife and child to certain retribution? Asked about this many years afterward, he replied, first, that he had no choice: even if his wife had agreed to make the attempt with him, the odds against all three of them succeeding were overwhelming, and the punishment, if caught in the act of flight, more severe than that which in fact awaited them as a defector's next of kin. He then added something which shows how much previous calculation had gone behind that sudden impulse of February 15, 1954. His wife, he reckoned, might well be banished to Siberia for five years, but the sentence would be no longer and no harsher than that, for the whole retribution process was not as severe as it had been in Stalin's day. Moreover, the law precluded any child under eight years of age being sent to jail. His little girl was only four.[17]

In short, Deriabin at the end of his career, as throughout it, had tried to do as little harm as he could. Above all, he had worked out the odds. This was again consistent. He had always worked out the odds.

7

Frankfurt

WHEN, IN the 1960s, Svetlana Alliluyeva, Stalin's daughter, was busy in the West publishing embarrassing truths about her late father and his regime, the KGB put up a submission to the Kremlin to be allowed to silence her for good. The application was considered and permission was refused. Premier Aleksei N. Kosygin is said to have conveyed the thumbs-up verdict on her life.

It is a macabre but by no means fantastic speculation to wonder whether, had the old tyrant himself been still alive at the time, the decision might have been otherwise. The assassination of anyone who threatened to defame or undermine his Soviet state was a particular feature of Stalin's rule, and the dictator had even set up a special department to carry out these so-called wet jobs abroad. As so often in the workings of tyranny, naked terrorism was clothed in rags of loyalty. Stalin's victims would always be tried in absentia in advance, accused and convicted by Party judges of offenses, either real or invented, and the death sentence handed down to the appropriate "authorities" to execute.

Thus, in 1936, Ignatz Reiss, one of the first Soviet agents to cross over to the West, was murdered by his former colleagues on the shores of Lake Geneva. The following year, Juliet Stuart Poyntz, who had deserted from the Soviet intelligence network in America, was lured into an ambush in New York's Central

Park, bundled by two hatchet men into a car and never seen again. The same year, 1937, saw the kidnapping in Paris of General Eugene Miller, a leader of the White Russian émigré movement about which Stalin had become paranoiac.

Nineteen forty-one was another year when the wet-jobs department had much to do. In February, the former NKVD officer Walter Krivitsky, one of the most damaging of the early defectors, was found shot in his Washington hotel room. The contrived "suicide note" was one of several indications which pointed strongly to murder, though, to this day, there is some puzzlement about how the Russians pulled it off, given the fact that both door and window in the room appeared to have been locked from the inside. There was no riddle over the most famous and infamous of these political assassinations, the murder in Mexico in 1940 of Leon Trotsky, Stalin's old rival. It is believed that the hand that drove the ice pick into Trotsky's skull belonged to a certain Jacques Mornard, a so-called disaffected follower of the murdered man. Few doubted at the time that the hand had been guided from the Kremlin, though final confirmation did not reach the West until after the war.*

Stalin's assassination department survived him for a while and thus it was that he never lived to see its greatest humiliation. At about 7 P.M. on the evening of February 18, 1954—eleven months after the old tyrant's death—its most eccentric but still trusted operator called at an apartment in the Inheiderstrasse in Frankfurt rented by Georgi Sergeyevich Okolovich, an anti-Soviet émigré who was a far bigger thorn in the Kremlin's side than General Miller had been. The business on hand was, of course, murder. But things took a very different turn when Okolovich opened the door. The caller came straight out with it on the threshold: "I am a captain in the Ministry of State Security and I have been sent from Moscow to Frankfurt to organize your assassination. I don't want to carry the order out and I need your help."

For a moment, the two men looked at each other. They made an odd contrast. The intended victim was a shambly, slightly

*See p. 170.

disheveled figure in his fifties, with spectacles perched on his high-bridged nose, looking far more like an unworldly professor than a man who had dedicated most of his adult life to a relentless underground battle against the Soviet regime. His would-be murderer was twenty years younger and his blond hair, blue eyes and neat appearance perfectly fitted (as they were intended to do) his bogus identity as an Austrian businessman. But, for all the differences, it was one Russian looking searchingly at another. The older man acted, as he usually did, on impulse. Slav instincts told him now that he was faced with a compatriot who had, in truth, just joined him as a renegade. His reply, when it came, was disarmingly simple. "Well, in that case," he said, "you had better come in and have a cup of tea." And, as a gesture of trust, he turned and walked ahead of his visitor, presenting his back to him as a target.[1]

Such was the end of the operation, code-named "Rhein," whose origins went back to the heart of the Kremlin the previous summer. What follows is the first full account of this extraordinary episode. The elaborate complexity of its planning, and the vulnerability of human beings which destroyed all those plans, make it a classic episode of espionage and counterespionage in action. They also make it, at times, hard to follow.

The Okolovich assassination project was first discussed in July of 1953 by the First Chief Directorate of the MVD. Beria, the head of that force, who had tried to seize the levers of power after Stalin's death the previous March, had himself been arrested that same month, and the MVD went through a long hot summer of purges and reorganizations. But Operation Rhein emerged from the chaos unaltered. At the end of September 1953, Nikolai Eugenevich Khokhlov, a captain in the Ninth Department of the MVD (which dealt with such "wet affairs"), was told by the department's new chief, Colonel Lev Alexsandrovich Studnikov, that he had been elected for "a very important mission in West Germany." The next day, Khokhlov learned precisely what the mission was. About a fortnight later, Studnikov sent for the captain again and informed him that congratulations were in order. Operation Rhein had been approved (at 1 P.M. that day by the Presidium of the Central Committee) and the go-ahead signed personally by Khrushchev and. Malenkov, the two most powerful men in the uneasy collective which was then ruling the country. The MVD's assassination project had thus become a top-level Party and state priority. Why did it seem so vital to eliminate Okolovich, and how did Captain Khokhlov come to be chosen for the job?

Okolovich was a senior controller of the émigré organization NTS, whose full name translates as the National Alliance of Russian Solidarists. It was founded in 1930 as an anti-Communist movement of exiles dedicated to the overthrow of the Soviet state. It was not monarchist, so received no funds from such tsarist émigrés who had any money to spare. It got no aid from the sworn enemies of Bolshevism, such as Nazi Germany. Because the frontiers were sealed, nothing came from the Russian motherland itself, which had succored all prewar revolutionary movements abroad. Finally, because its members possessed only Nansen passports, travel was difficult. Between 1935 and 1937, its representatives scoured Western and Central Europe to find sponsors; the NTS, by this time, had some dedicated cadres but it lacked an operational base.

At last, in 1938, Poland agreed to provide that base. The only requirement was that NTS operatives supply Polish intelligence with any interesting information they gathered while inside the Soviet Union. By the autumn of 1938, the first small NTS groups were infiltrated across the Polish-Russian border. Each man set off with two complete sets of clothes. One was worn for travel in the frontier region itself and varied from peasant costume to tourist garb, depending on the sector chosen. The other, carried in a rucksack, consisted of genuine Russian garments and equipment (even down to pencils, penknives and razor blades), all smuggled out of the Soviet Union by the Poles for the purpose. They were equipped with genuine Soviet passports or military identity documents in blank, provided by the same sources, and enough Russian money to live for a year inside the Soviet Union. They also carried one pistol per man and several hand grenades. What were they trying to do?

They had drawn up six aims. These were: negative propaganda, or the discrediting of the regime; positive propaganda, that is, preaching the feasibility of revolution; the search for resistance workers inside the country; the arousal of a general fighting spirit; the creation of public-order chaos needed for an uprising to be launched; and, as the glorious apotheosis to all this, the supervision of any transfer of power.

As things turned out, the Polish base itself lasted for only a year. In September of 1939, it was wiped out with much else by the German invasion. The NTS, which had not lost a man during those halcyon twelve months except in skirmishes with Soviet frontier guards, switched its base to Romania (then trying to observe neutrality in the European war). For two years, it claimed successes, especially in encouraging subversion within the Red Army. Its losses were comparatively small: one operative caught and executed and another sentenced to ten years in a labor camp in Kamchatka. But when, in 1941, Hitler invaded Russia and eventually sucked Romania into the conflict, these operations ceased as well.

The huge movements, eastward and westward, of refugees and prisoners of war which followed during and after the defeat of Nazi Germany gave the NTS new recruits and new openings. Nonetheless, the postwar organization, based in Frankfurt under American protection, appears to have lowered its sights somewhat. The new emphasis was on the nonviolent approach, above all the dissemination of propaganda leaflets either with a declared foreign origin or purporting to originate from within the Soviet Union itself. The NTS was now more concerned with hydrogen balloons to float these leaflets across the frontier than with tossing hand grenades inside the Communist fortress. However, its operatives resumed their border crossings into the Soviet Union to try to preach the gospel there, and Okolovich had made several such trips before settling in Frankfurt to direct operations.

One must still ask: why was the liquidation of such an organization, whose postwar weight was no more than nuisance value, given the top priority of a Soviet Central Committee order signed by Khrushchev and Malenkov? Surely, the struggle against the imperialist West was of far greater import? The question was once put to Okolovich himself. He replied: "You must realize that, to the Russians, the Americans are a fly on their nose. But we are a sore on that nose."

What he meant was that anything done by Russians against Russians, even if relatively trivial, was something organic, something in the bloodstream which the Soviet body politic had to get rid of. It had been so under tsarism. The Okhrana of imperialist times was given the same priority of liquidating subversive movements, which, then as in the Communist era, were based almost entirely in Western Europe. The Communists had even more reason than the tsarists to respect the potential of these political exiles. The Bolshevik revolution only happened when and how it did because in 1917 the Germans had allowed Lenin to return, in a sealed military train, from Switzerland to St. Petersburg.

Nikolai Khokhlov makes an interesting case study not only because of the extraordinary existence he had led before and after being recruited into the secret police. He is remarkable also as being the prototype of many later defections: a man who loved Russia and fought hard for it as a wartime patriot but who came to hate the Soviet system which demanded the same sacrifices from him after the war, in order to ensure its own survival and not that of the motherland. That repugnance was what Okolovich had somehow sensed when he offered his would-be assassin a cup of tea. The captain was joining the émigrés, rather than defecting to the West.

Khokhlov's life story reads like a film script, though one whose comic touches and boring interludes are always mixed in with the full-blooded adventures. He was born on June 7, 1922, in the town of Nizhni-Novgorod, now known as Gorki. The baby was of irreproachable proletarian stock. His paternal grandfather had been a shoemaker; his father, a private in the tsarist army, had joined the Bolshevik party in 1917. When he was five years old, however, his parents were divorced (on the grounds of mutual infidelity), and the following year his mother, a local girl called Anna, married Eugeni Mikhailovich Mikhailovski. This was a big step up. Mikhailovski, of Polish origin, was the son of a Warsaw University professor who had

been a well-known painter in his day and was himself a qualified lawyer. In 1930, the family moved to Moscow, where the
new husband was given a good apartment and a relatively high
salary as a defense attorney and member of the Moscow Bar
Association.

It was during his Moscow schooldays that young Khokhlov
gravitated to the theater. In addition to his normal subjects
(which he completed in 1939–40) he took a full course in drama
at the Teatralnaya Studiya Imeni Khmeleva and emerged with
a certificate entitling him to work as a stage director. He seems
to have filled that role only for the one summer of 1940 when,
after graduation, the theatrical school which had trained him
went on tour giving performances at rest homes. He discovered
his real artistic bent, however, as a whistler, a talent which he
had developed as a schoolboy. Somewhat improbably, he was to
whistle his way right into the secret police.

In December 1940, he was given a woman partner, one Ag-
nessa Shur, for his act and, for the next six months, the duo
toured Russia, performing at major cities such as Minsk, Smolensk, Kiev and Sevastopol, and even appearing in May 1941 at
Moscow's Eremitage variety theater. Their act was one of three
to win top awards in a nationwide variety contest and Khokhlov
was even given a part in *The Test,* a propaganda film about
students. On June 22, he and his partner were about to go on-
stage when the news spread that Molotov was about to make an
important speech on the radio. Everybody rushed to the loud-
speakers in the main square. The announcement, of course, was
that the Nazis had invaded the Soviet Union. From now on
Khokhlov was to perform a bewildering variety of roles on a
much larger stage.

He hurried back to Moscow in a mood of patriotic fervor,
wanting to enlist at once. But all three services turned him
down for bad eyesight and gave him the so-called *Bely Bilet* of
exemption. He was determined to get into uniform, however,
and, ignoring recruiting stations, entered the first military
building he saw. It turned out to be a special unit of the NKVD
called the Istrebitelny Batalyon, and the political commissar,
hearing his tale, signed him up at once, myopia or no myopia.[2]

The recruit still had no idea what was in store for him. He got no wiser during the first three months of the war, for, as Hitler's armies moved closer and closer to the capital, Khokhlov had a merry time of it making films at Ulianovsk on a two months' leave of absence from his unit. It was all too good, and too unreal, to last, and on September 23, 1941, he was recalled to Moscow and told that an operational assignment now awaited him. His whistling act, from now on, was to be used as cover for an underground "stay behind" role, which would begin for him when and if the Germans took the capital. He was fully briefed by an NKVD Lieutenant Colonel Maklyarski and accepted eagerly, signing pledges to secrecy and obedience in carrying out any orders "in the fight against the German invaders." It was patriotism and not any Party fervor from his days with the Communist youth organization Komsomol which was still spurring him on.

But Moscow did not fall and, for a while, the good life continued. Throughout the winter of 1941–42, Khokhlov continued to give his variety performances at various sectors of the front while receiving, when in Moscow, further training with his cell of two men and two women. When Maklyarski gave them (apart from a suitcase full of weapons and ammunition) the princely sum of 30,000 rubles for "operational funds," the temptation was too great to resist. They promptly spent half on amusements and black-market luxuries.[3] But by January of 1942 the party was over. Their assignment was called off, first because a German occupation no longer seemed likely, and secondly because the quartet had anyway blown themselves with their extravagant life-style. What happened to the other three members is not known, but the NKVD now decided that Khokhlov's whistling days were over and that it was time to get value for their money out of him. Assassination was the first project they chose for him, as it was to be their last.

In February, Khokhlov was summoned to a house on Moscow's Ulitsa Gorki and received by a top NKVD official, Commissar (later Lieutenant General) Sudoplatov. He was ordered to proceed the next day to Tbilisi in Georgia and from there to the little border town of Luxembourg, where there was a community of ethnic Germans. He was to assume the identity of one of these, slip across the Turkish border and walk to Ankara, where he would receive further orders from Soviet agents. These orders, Khokhlov discovered by pure chance two years later, would have been to murder Franz von Papen, Hitler's onetime vice-chancellor, then serving as the very active and influential German ambassador to Turkey. Khokhlov got as far as Luxembourg, where he came down with typhus. It was three months before he was fit enough to return to Moscow. Missing the von Papen assignment was a stroke of good fortune, for the conspiracy was uncovered and a public trial of the culprits ensued. The important thing, however, was that the onetime variety whistler was now down on the NKVD lists as a hit man.

He was also down, due to his blond looks, as a future operator in German-speaking countries. He was now given German lessons at least twice a week by Tamara Ivanova (who, he eventually discovered, was also a member of the NKVD) and, during the winter of 1942–43, perfected his knowledge of the language by frequent visits to the prisoner-of-war camp at Krasnogorsk, where he chatted with the inmates and studied their mannerisms, both Nazi and Teutonic. His acting experience proved as useful as his good ear for language and by April of 1943 he managed to spend four weeks at another prisoner-of-war camp where he successfully posed as a German army lieutenant. This was precisely what he was destined to become in his next incarnation. His new identity was Oberleutnant Otto Wittgenstein* of the German Army Secret Field Police. Another trainee, an ethnic German named Karl Kleinjung, was to pose as his corporal. The two men, after arduous sessions of firearms instruction, cipher work, radio operating, dynamite techniques and parachute jumps, were finally landed by air, in August 1943, deep behind the German lines in Byelorussia.[4] A truly heroic year in Khokhlov's life—perhaps the only unsullied one—now began.

They had come down in Soviet partisan territory; it was from

---

*An unwise choice of alias by the NKVD. An unusual name, it would be known to any cultured German as that of the famous Austrian philosopher. Khokhlov could have been vulnerable, unless warned, to questions.

the chief of the detachment, Lieutenant Colonel Yuri Max-
imovich Kutsin, that Khokhlov now got his instructions. It was
another assassination, though this time much closer to his heart.
He and his "corporal" were to proceed to the German army
headquarters at Minsk and finalize arrangements for the killing
of the regional gauleiter, Wilhelm Kube. As Kube, a notorious
Nazi butcher, had sent thousands of ordinary people to their
deaths in Byelorussia, setting fire to whole villages and burning
some of the inhabitants alive in their houses, Khokhlov needed
little encouragement. The task would be tricky. The partisans
had themselves made several unsuccessful attempts to kill Kube
in raids on the German garrison and the gauleiter had doubled
his guard. But the NKVD had already made contact with
Galina Mazanik, a local peasant woman who worked in the
Kube household. She was clearly the key to the plot.

Wearing his German uniform (with the ribbons of Iron Cross
Class One and Two plus the 1941–42 Winter Campaign medal on
his chest)) Khokhlov had little problem, with his excellently
forged documents, in moving freely around Minsk, ostensibly
on secret military police business. Galina had already been provided with a limpet mine by an NKVD woman helper called
Nadya Trayan.[5] Khokhlov's task was to persuade her to do the
deed and to give her precise instructions about how it should
be carried out. This was achieved, without much difficulty, in
two sessions at her apartment. At 2 A.M. on the morning of
September 18, 1943, Wilhelm Kube was blown to pieces as he
slept peacefully in his bed by the magnetic bomb attached to the
metal springs underneath him. It was no great loss to humanity
but a tremendous boost to civil morale throughout occupied
Russia. For their part in the exploit, Galina Mazanik, who had
primed and set the bomb, and Nadya Trayan, who had smuggled it to her, were later both made a Hero of the Soviet Union.
"Lieutenant Wittgenstein" and his "corporal" were awarded
the Orden Otechestvennoi Voiny, Pervoi Stepeni medal, in
gold.

The two men had sailed out of Minsk after the assassination
by brazenly hitching a ride on an SS troop carrier, and, even
more brazenly, taking with them two young Russian sisters in

whose house they had been living. They made their excuses to
get off fifteen miles out of town and rejoined the Kutsin partisan
detachment on foot. For the next seven months, Khokhlov himself became a partisan fighter. Until February of 1944 he remained with the Kutsin group, making several forays back into
Minsk, sometimes in his German officer's uniform, sometimes
in civilian clothes. Then, out of the blue, he received orders
from the NKVD headquarters in Moscow to proceed with a
detachment of forty men all the way up to the Lake Naroch area
of Lithuania. The march, a distance of several hundred miles,
most of it through or close to German-occupied territory, took
a hazardous six weeks. After various operations in the Baltic
and central sectors of the fighting, Khokhlov returned again in
the summer of 1944 to Minsk, but this time on a transport of the
advancing Red Army. Here, at a ceremony attended by all the
local guerrilla detachments, he was awarded the Partisano-
Techestvennoi Voiny, the highest decoration that a Soviet partisan fighter could win.

Khokhlov's war record—a mixture of enforced opéra bouffe
and extreme bravery when the call came—is worth recounting
in much more detail than he ever published himself because the
end product was, seemingly, a devoted and well-trained NKVD
field operator who could be relied upon to carry out any task
required of him. To drain away this degree of enthusiasm to the
point where it was replaced by rebellion was no mean feat on
the part of his NKVD masters. They started the process by
consigning him to five years of unemployment at home and
virtual exile abroad.

From September 1944 to March 1945, throughout those stir-
ring six months of the Red Army's triumphant advance toward
Nazi Germany, Khokhlov was given absolutely nothing to do.
He sat at home in his mother's Moscow apartment, drawing his
salary of 1,500 rubles a month and waiting for orders. From
Maklyarski, his immediate NKVD superior, he learned simply
that he was now "earmarked for foreign assignments." It was
during this period that Maklyarski told him something else far
more unpalatable. Khokhlov now learned that his father, who
had joined the revolution in 1917, had perished serving in a penal

battalion in the fight against Hitler. And what had caused the old Bolshevik to be sent to such a unit, a posting which was tantamount to a death sentence in view of the suicide missions the penal battalions were given, had been nothing more than a few incautious remarks about the way the Soviet regime had grown up.[6] Though separated from his father since childhood, Khokhlov had never lost his hero-worship for the old veteran of the First World War. This revelation did not enamor him of the Stalinist police state which he would be expected to serve in peacetime. His first postwar mission thrilled him even less.

On March 20, 1945, he was flown in a military aircraft from Moscow to Bucharest. For the flight he was dressed as a Red Army major. Once on the ground he became Stanislaw Lewandowski, a Polish citizen born in Lvov on June 7, 1923. He carried a genuine Polish passport to this effect and had learned a few phrases in the language to support the legend. He was to remain for four frustrating years in Bucharest, without ever learning why he was there or being given anything of importance to do.* Romanian collaborators of the Russians helped to set him up as cover in a radio and electrical equipment store. They also established him in the Pension Viktoria on the Strada Akademiei. Here Khokhlov (who could never last for long without the solace of a woman's arms) promptly started an affair with the twenty-two-year-old Emilia, one of the Romanian women in the household. She moved into his room and they lived together for a year before finally marrying on April 13, 1946. The move had the advantage of entitling him to apply for Romanian citizenship.

Keeping in touch with Moscow was at times well nigh impossible. From June 1945 until March 1946 he had no contact whatsoever and was driven in desperation to do the unmentionable and write to the center direct. At the turn of the year 1945–46, he addressed two letters asking for help to Room 736 (Secretariat) at the NKVD Headquarters, Ulitsa Dzerzhinskovo 2 in Moscow.[7] One he dropped in the mailbox of the Soviet military

---

*One theory was that his superiors had dumped him well out of Moscow's way to prevent him from being poached and transferred to a rival intelligence organization.

mission in Bucharest; the other he handed to a Red Army senti-
nel he saw on guard outside some military installation. At this,
high-level NKVD officials from the Soviet Union descended on
Bucharest and berated Khokhlov both for his marriage and for
his appalling breach of security. But they could still tell him
nothing firm about his future. There was vague talk of setting
him up in Italy or France, then the venue was switched to
Austria for an unspecified mission. Although, thanks to a good
monthly allowance padded out by constant black-market operations, Khokhlov was living very comfortably, it was hardly
surprising that he had begun to doubt whether, once the patriotic impulses of war had been removed, Soviet intelligence was
really the life for him. Nor did everything he was witnessing
around him in Bucharest—the elimination of the monarchy and
the ruthless suppression of all non-Communist individuals and
organizations—make the police state as such seem any more
attractive. But at this stage personal frustration was probably
stronger than ideological repugnance.

At last, in October of 1949, he was told he could return to
Moscow. The reason, in all probability, was a formal letter he
had written, this time through proper channels, to the head of
his department at the NKVD asking to be released from the
service "to continue my education." Once given the green light,
Khokhlov wound up his private affairs (about which he has said
little in print) by admitting to the long-suffering Emilia that he
had been unfaithful to her on several occasions, that he was
trying to get to the West and did not propose to take her with
him, and that he therefore would like a divorce. A fortnight
later, he was gone for good. The woman who was still his wife
(there was indeed to be no record that the divorce ever took
place) was left with the apartment and a payoff of 100,000 lei
from the NKVD's Romanian cashbox.

Back in Moscow, Khokhlov continued to press for his release,
asking that his salary be stopped. His superiors, right up to
General Sudaplatov, continued to fob him off. That autumn,
however, something happened which was both to quicken and
to deepen his desire to cut loose. Khokhlov's main romantic
interest in Moscow throughout the war had been a singer called

Taissiya Ignatova, who had been one of the winners, alongside himself, in the 1941 eve-of-war national variety contest. His affair with her had lasted throughout the Moscow war years, but he was either unable or unwilling to rekindle the flame now. So, on an impulse, he called at the apartment of Yanina Adamovna Timashkevich, who had sat at the desk next to his for seven years at school. His schoolmate, now twenty-seven and single, happened to be at home and opened the door. That was on November 13, 1949. By Christmas, he had moved in with her and they lived from then on as husband and wife. His superiors finally allowed him to marry her legally two years later to the day, at a drab three-minute ceremony conducted in the offices of Moscow's Registrar of Civilian Status.

First as loving partner and later as wife, Yanina exercised a strong influence on Khokhlov, all of it directed toward persuading him to break his links with the secret police. She was an independent young Soviet technocrat, earning a good salary at the time as a construction engineer. But she was also a devoutly religious Russian woman. She had been baptized and brought up as a Uniate Catholic and when that faith was suppressed she took spiritual refuge in the Russian Orthodox Church, which even Stalin had not dared to ban. She was thus anything but a Communist; indeed she had somehow contrived, even as a schoolgirl, to avoid being drafted, like all the others, into the Komsomol. Her horror at learning of her husband's real work can be imagined; also her determination to help him wriggle free from it. That, as they both should have known, was impossible while on Soviet soil.

For a while, the uneasy coexistence between Khokhlov and his masters continued. They allowed him to "continue his education" by enrolling him at the Scientific Research Institute in Moscow, from where he transferred to the Philological Department of the university. But it was made clear to him that this was nothing but special leave and that he remained on the books of the secret police and was subject to recall at any moment. When he protested, they produced an order, backdated to October 1941, certifying that he was a regular full-time officer of the service and, as such, bound to it for life. It was made clear to him that, if he insisted on backing out, the consequences could be very unpleasant.

His first recall from the university came in March 1951 when General Sudaplatov summoned him to headquarters and proposed that he make a reconnaissance trip through various Western European countries traveling on an Austrian passport, simply to determine how easy it was for Austrian citizens to obtain visas and open foreign bank accounts. It seemed a pleasant enough assignment, especially as he was to be given the then princely sum of 4,000 American dollars as expenses. So, after some weak protests for the record, Khokhlov agreed—to Yanina's fury. It was now that he acquired the last of his many NKVD (by then MGB) identities—Josef Hofbauer, born in St. Poelten, Lower Austria, on December 31, 1925. Though Josef Hofbauer never existed, the passport was a genuine one, properly registered and backed by every conceivable supporting document from all the appropriate Austrian central and local government departments. But though the Russians had succeeded in bribing or browbeating the Austrian police into compliance,* one archive remained beyond their control, the church registry. There was nothing for it but to send an agent into the parish church of St. Poelten and rip out from the records the last page for 1925. The legend was now solid. In all this, Khokhlov was briefed in Moscow by Lieutenant Colonel Sergei Lvovich Okun, who dealt with MGB operations in Austria. The two men had already met in Romania; their paths were to cross once more on Okun's home territory.

The assignment proved every bit as harmless and enjoyable as Khokhlov had imagined. From April until August of 1951, "Josef Hofbauer" traveled around Switzerland, France, Denmark, Belgium and Holland, merrily opening bank accounts and collecting visas as he went. There was, however, a bad snag at the end of the journey when the entertainer (and habitual man-on-the-make) in Khokhlov combined to trip him up. On reentering Austria from Switzerland, he tried to smuggle

---

*Austria was at this time still under four-power occupation (which did not end until 1955) but the Federal Republic issued its own passports. St. Poelten was in the Russian zone.

through the customs at Feldkirch an expensive Hohner accordion. The instrument, and his luggage, were impounded and he was fined 4,500 schillings, which was far more than he had on him. Even when he returned from Vienna, where Okun had provided him with the money, and paid his fine, he was grilled by the local police—Feldkirch was in the French zone of occupation and far removed from Russian influence—and his passport taken away. He only got it back by brazening it out with the local district attorney. It took him a month (and at least one hefty bribe) to sort everything out legally and he did not return to Moscow until September 21, 1951. There, despite the hash he had made of things by his own greed and incompetence (and, still hoping to be sacked, he had deliberately exaggerated the incident), he was given, not a stiff reprimand, but thirty days' leave. Off he and Yanina went to Gagry on the Black Sea, where they holidayed throughout October.

It was in early March of 1952 that the first crisis came. Khokhlov was once more summoned from his university lecture halls to General Sudaplatov's office to be given a new field assignment. It was very different from the previous summer's leisurely tour of the capitalist West. He had been put back on the murder trail. He was to go to Paris (not as Josef Hofbauer but with fake Swiss papers) and contact a veteran Soviet agent operating in the French capital. The agent would lead him to the target, a Russian émigré. Khokhlov would then liquidate the victim with his Parker fountain pen (another trophy from his travels abroad) which would be specially adapted as a small pistol. Later, the agent, who had outlived his usefulness, would also be "taken care of."

Khokhlov asked for time to think it over, a strange enough reaction in itself. But when he returned the next day, after a long overnight discussion with the woman who by now was his wife, his attitude was even more bizarre. He simply could not carry out the assignment, he told an astonished General Sudaplatov, because his nerves were not up to it. There was no point, he pleaded, in sending, on a mission like this, someone "whose hands and legs are trembling."[8] He was dismissed, though more, it seemed, in sorrow than in anger. Despite this mild reaction, the Khokhlov couple spent a very nervous few weeks, jumping whenever a car pulled up in the courtyard of their apartment house. But when the next summons came it was once more to a routine and fairly pleasant task abroad, almost as though his superiors wanted to soothe his frayed nerves with another bloodless staff job before returning to the question of spilling blood again. From May until August of 1952, Khokhlov was in East Berlin doing intelligence evaluations and other administrative work from a desk at the MGB's center there. He managed to get home leave in order to be present at the birth of his child and was back in Moscow in time to see his son, Alexander, born on August 23.

That event seems to have made his mind up. He would stop talking of resignation but instead use his strange career with the organization to get a regular posting abroad with his family, eventual defection to the West being a growing possibility in his mind. Accordingly, he informed his long-suffering general that he was now prepared to take up residence as an agent in some Western country, provided that his wife and child could accompany him. It was not an unreasonable professional request since, even with his family abroad with him, his own mother and his wife's sister would still remain behind as "hostages." At all events, General Sudaplatov fell in with the suggestion and, for the next seven months, Khokhlov happily busied himself with creating a revised Hofbauer legend for use in Switzerland, the country provisionally chosen for his mission. The plan was for him first to travel via Vienna to Switzerland on faked Swiss papers; then return to West (not East) Berlin on his genuine Austrian passport; once there, "marry his wife" (who would have been provided with special documentation); and then, "Herr and Frau Josef Hofbauer" would return to Switzerland as an Austrian business couple to start permanent undercover work. How the infant Alexander was to be explained or included in the plan was not clear. The scheme was anyway abandoned in the chaos which overwhelmed Russia in general, and the secret police headquarters in particular, when Stalin died and the struggle for the Kremlin crown began. Both Sudaplatov and his deputy General Eitingon were arrested and disappeared from sight during the turmoil. Thus it was the new chief of the Ninth Department, General Studnikov, who, in September 1953, informed a somewhat dazed Khokhlov about Operation Rhein.

In the light of everything recounted above about Khokhlov's character and checkered career, it seems incredible that he was chosen. The search case on Okolovich had been started by the then NKVD as far back as January 1939 and had been resumed in earnest after the war. In 1948, when a report was received that the émigré leader was living in the West German town of Limburg, a team of agents was sent to the city to spirit him away into the Russian occupation zone. Okolovich was not there when they called.[9] In 1951 the Russians tried again, this time using a team of three of their German agents equipped with morphine injections to stupefy their victim. Again, the quarry eluded his hunters, two of whom surrendered in panic with all their equipment to the West German police. The quest seemed doomed to end in failure or fiasco. But by 1953 the MVD had firm evidence about Okolovich's new base in Frankfurt, where he was spending most of his time. One of Beria's last orders had been to liquidate the NTS leadership with a broad offensive whose main feature was to be the murder of Okolovich. As we have seen, that decision was later endorsed in the name of the Presidium of the Party's Central Committee over the personal signatures of Comrades Khrushchev and Malenkov. The disaster of the 1951 attempt had to be avoided at all costs. An MVD agent, someone totally ruthless, efficient, leakproof and reliable, would have to be in charge.

Yet how did Captain Nikolai Eugenevich Khokhlov measure up, on his own fully documented track record, to these requirements? Throughout his service, as might have been expected from someone recruited from the variety theater, he had displayed all the tantrums and egotistic flourishes of the artist. Twice, he had perpetrated appalling security lapses—once when preparing for his stay-behind role in Moscow and again, in an even more alarming fashion, with the letters he sent through open channels from Romania. Once, and fairly recently, he had actually refused an assassination mission, on the grounds that his nerves would fail him. To cap it all, for the past nine years he had been trying, at frequent intervals, to resign altogether. Measured against this dismal background, his selection was hazardous in the extreme. There could have been only two reasons for choosing him. The first was the scarcity of operatives with his Teutonic appearance, command of the German language and perfect Austrian legend. That would have been a professional decision. The second motive was far from professional. His masters were still mesmerized by Khokhlov's *annus mirabilis* of 1943–44 when he had instigated the murder of Gauleiter Kube in Minsk and distinguished himself as a partisan fighter. They made the grave mistake of believing that such ardor was automatically transferable to peacetime, and to themselves.

There was also a dual factor at work in Khokhlov's own calculations. As he told his wife, he felt he dare not refuse a second murder mission, especially one authorized from such a high level.[10] But the thought of defecting, using the intended victim as a channel, had also struck him. Somehow, the formidable Okolovich could surely arrange to have Yanina and their son spirited out of Russia to join him in exile. He began to collect material which he thought would be of interest to his Western hosts.

If the MVD had harbored any doubts about his mission, they did their best to allay them by the priority treatment the chosen assassin was now given. Major General Aleksandr Semenovich Panyushkin, the head of the Second Chief Directorate of the MVD, received him half a dozen times that autumn to discuss the plan. At Khokhlov's insistence, two German agents he had recruited in Berlin the previous year—Kurt Weber, known as "Franz," and Hans Kukovich, code-named "Felix"—were the only people allowed to go on the operation with him. At his insistence too he was provided with the very latest murder weapon devised by the MVD's secret arms laboratory at Khozyaistvo Kheleznovo, near Kuchino. This was an electrically operated firing device which would fire poisoned bullets from any innocent-looking container (the outward form chosen on this occasion was that of a pack of twenty cigarettes).[11] What was quite unique about the weapon, at least to the Western armorers who eventually examined it, was its silencing system. The noise was muffled not by a device over the concealed barrel but by a wad inside the cartridge itself which released gas immediately after the bullet was expelled. Despite this modification, the cigarette-pack pistol could penetrate a board two inches thick. When a delay threatened in getting the equipment ready on time, General Panyushkin personally intervened with the heads of the MVD laboratories involved to speed things up.

In October, Khokhlov (traveling, for extra security, as Red Army Captain Egorov) flew to Berlin to bring his German henchmen back to Moscow. Franz and Felix were then taken in hand by Colonel Okun, who had arrived from Vienna to help supervise preparations. They were given a five-week intensive course by the finest trainers in the country. Their judo instructor, for example, was Mikhail Rubak, a Soviet champion; Lieutenant Colonel Godlevski, five times a winner of national pistol tournaments, took over the firearms instruction. In January of 1954 the assassins and their equipment were moved to Austria, separately and by different routes. Franz and Felix went first, each equipped with Austrian passports secured by Okun's obliging local contacts. They were quartered in a safe house at Baden, the Red Army's HQ just south of Vienna, and, soon afterward, Colonel Godlevski arrived with the special weapons, which the two agents were now allowed to handle for the first time.

At this point, one of Okun's best Austrian agents comes into the picture. He was a forty-four-year-old businessman (the representative in Vienna of the Swiss firm Geigy) called Erich Lampel. His main task to date for the Russians had been to use his company, which also operated in Turkey, to provide cover to plant, as his employee, an underground MVD agent called Grigoris Aleksandrovich Bratsikhin. Now Lampel was also sucked up, unfortunately as it turned out, into Operation Rhein. It was decided that he was the man who would transport the murder weapons, concealed in the specially adapted battery of his car, from Austria to West Germany. In all, there were four of these, two small pistols and two starter pistols, each firing cyanide-tipped bullets out of their harmless-looking Camel cigarette packs.*

Khokhlov's itinerary was made extremely complicated. So many traces were to be smothered over by so many journeys that he must have wondered at some moments just where in Western Europe he really was. The program was, from the professional point of view, something of a textbook example of elaborate and probably unnecessary undercover deception.[12] Things had hung fire in January, Colonel Okun having received orders to postpone the operation for a while in order not to prejudice the Soviet position at the Conference of Foreign Ministers being held in Berlin.† Then, on February 8, Khokhlov set off from Vienna.

Frankfurt lay a long and tortuous way ahead. He went first by train to Venice, traveling not as an Austrian but on forged Swiss papers in the name of Walter Gesch. At the station in Venice a Soviet courier awaited him with his regular Josef Hofbauer passport in which an Austrian-Italian border exit stamp had been entered. For recognition signals, the courier asked in German, "Is there a nightclub anywhere near?" and he replied in the same language with "No idea. Anyway I'm married."

As it happened, that particular exchange was to prove rich in irony. For the courier turned out to be a not unattractive twenty-four-year-old Austrian woman agent of Okun's called Rosa Schneider. She had first been recruited by Soviet intelligence as an eighteen-year-old Viennese girl who was involved with a Red Army lieutenant. She now immediately became involved with Captain Khokhlov. Indeed, only one hour later, the pair took a train to Rome, where they spent two nights and a day at the MVD's expense at the Hotel Splendere, leaving for Milan on February 12. There he changed trains for Zurich, arriving in time for a prearranged rendezvous with Franz oppo-

---

*Analysis in the West later showed that each bullet had enough poison to kill ten people through the mouth and enough to kill one hundred people if injected into the bloodstream.

†When the operation was finally blown, and then publicized by the Americans, there was at first some suspicion, not confined to the Russians, that the affair had been manipulated to torpedo the Berlin talks.

site the Hotel Krone on the following day. They were joined there by Felix that afternoon. On the fifteenth, Franz took the train direct to Frankfurt, whereas Khokhlov took Felix with him to Geneva and then Lausanne, depositing money in both places. They then made their separate ways to Frankfurt, where all three met up again, "Herr Hofbauer" registering by himself at the Pension Zeppelin. Lampel, who had been alerted by coded letter that they were assembled and ready, would deliver the murder weapons concealed in his car battery to a rendezvous in Augsburg in about five days' time. Then, with everything arranged, all traces covered and ample escape funds behind them, they could strike at leisure. Such was the enormously expensive and elaborately prepared top-level Soviet conspiracy which Khokhlov proceeded to unmask and destroy in a few seconds when he called at the Okolovich apartment the evening after his arrival.

The aftermath to that evening call on February 18 was almost as complex—and, at times, hilarious—as the long prelude had been. Leaving Okolovich's apartment, Khokhlov to begin with gave no hint to his two German agents that he had just blown the entire operation. Instead he dispatched them, on February 23, to Augsburg to collect the lethal battery from Lampel's car and bring it back to Frankfurt, where it was to be deposited in the baggage-check office of the main railway station. Okolovich, who was naturally on good terms with the Western Allies, had meanwhile got in touch, on Khokhlov's behalf, with American intelligence officials in Frankfurt. These at first refused to believe his story. The assassination tale sounded too fantastic to be taken seriously; so did Khokhlov's plea to defect. A captain in the Soviet secret service had such a good life, they reasoned, why should he want to quit it, leaving his family behind into the bargain? Khokhlov's own superiors were not the only experts who could so misread human nature.

It was the car battery which settled the issue. At noon on February 25, Khokhlov persuaded the skeptical American agents to shadow the meeting he had arranged with Franz and Felix in the Friedrich Eberstrasse to hand over the heavy package. The two Germans were seized on the spot and taken to an

American safe house. Khokhlov joined them there, explained the position to them and urged that they too, being now hopelessly compromised, should elect to stay in the West. Both men agreed, without much argument. Then the battery was dragged in and Khokhlov started chipping away, first at the ebonite cover and then at the lead plates. Glued to the walls inside were two plastic packages which were revealed once the sulfuric acid had been emptied out. The weapons they contained corresponded exactly with Khokhlov's description. The Americans were astounded, delighted and apologetic in equal proportions. Their apathy was now converted into an all-out effort to smash or, better still, to rope in the entire MVD operational network in Austria so far as Khokhlov's story had exposed it.

The start was promising. With Franz and Felix already whisked off to an interrogation center, Khokhlov was instructed to go on sending messages to Colonel Okun's organization via prearranged postbox addresses in Vienna, explaining why the mission was being "delayed." He received back, via the Frankfurt post office, replies which indicated that, up to April 10, the Russians had no inkling that the whole assassination party had been in American hands for the past fortnight.

It was on April 10, a Saturday, that the American military authorities, accompanied by Austrian police, arrested Erich Lampel at his Vienna apartment. Lampel confessed immediately, offered to cooperate, and promptly named as his Soviet controller none other than the Bratsikhin for whom he had arranged cover as an employee in his own firm. This individual was already known to the West as a Russian émigré, settled in Paris since 1920, who had been recruited by Soviet intelligence in 1936, had served with the International Brigade in Spain until 1939, and had then returned to the Soviet Union and regained his Soviet citizenship. Since then, he had used at least ten aliases over the years, including that of Anton Hladik, under which he was operating now. Lampel was told to arrange a meeting with him that same day outside the offices of his company, Gerola, in Vienna's First District, an area under joint control of the four occupation powers. "Herr Hladik" turned up, as requested, at 5 P.M. and Lampel, with an American CIA official disguised as his chauffeur, suggested they drive off to discuss things over a meal. After a few hundred yards, the car was safely in a British sector and three more Western agents duly piled in. Their opening remarks were in such good Russian that Bratsikhin at first believed he was entirely in the company of his own MVD. Indeed, he took some disabusing of this idea and was only convinced by their identification papers. Like Lampel, he promptly accepted the situation and was flown out to Frankfurt.* So far, so good.

But on the following morning things began to go wrong. The Vienna police, who leaked like a sieve, especially on happenings in the sensitive First District, passed the news of Lampel's arrest to the Austrian Sunday papers. They came out with headlines such as: WHAT DOES AMERICAN INTELLIGENCE WANT WITH ENGINEER L?† Khokhlov had blown Operation Rhein. Now the Vienna press had blown the Western counterattack.

Lieutenant Colonel Okun, known to be a top figure in the MVD operational group in Austria, if not the head of it, was the big prize. Bratsikhin revealed that he had a prearranged meeting with his chief at 11 A.M. on April 13. The site was a path running alongside the Wienfluss,‡ a stream which trickles through Vienna's Stadtpark, close to the city center. Bratsikhin would enter the path from one end, Okun from the other, and they would meet in the middle. Perhaps unwisely, the Anglo-American intelligence team working on the case decided to preempt this by an immediate approach to the colonel direct. So, in an unprecedented move, a letter in duplicate, each signed as coming from an officer of the American occupation forces, was delivered that same Sunday by Western couriers to Okun's house in Baden. The letter indicated to the Russian that he was in trouble and invited him to come on the following day to one of two alternate meeting places in the international First District. No Okun turned up on April 12, nor on the thirteenth, to

*He was ultimately resettled, under yet another alias, in the United States.

†"Herr Ingeniur" is an academic title awarded in German-speaking countries to those with academic qualifications in science or engineering.

‡This dismal little brown stream is the only "river" to flow through Vienna. The course of the Danube is just east of the capital.

keep the appointment, but, in a *mise-en-scène* worthy of spy fiction, there were plenty of other people on hand as Bratsikhin started to walk up the appointed path. Fifteen armed Americans stood by. A party of agents from the rival MVD was also lurking behind the trees, just, it seemed, to watch what was going on. By now Lieutenant Colonel Okun, who had been exposed several times over through some rather unprofessional overkill, was probably already back in Moscow.

However, one more Russian fish, a strange one, did land in the Western net. His name was Anatoly Alexevich Shmelov, who had arrived in Vienna at the beginning of 1954 to work in a lowly civilian capacity at the Soviet headquarters. He had other things on his mind and eventually succeeded in making contact with a genuine NTS émigré member working in Austria, claiming he had messages from the organization inside Russia to deliver personally to Okolovich. Khokhlov had declared the man to be a plant, but something in Okolovich's instincts told him otherwise. So, in the middle of the drama, he made a very dangerous trip to Vienna to find out for himself. There was a meeting at which Shmelov produced offerings of vodka and caviar and American cigarettes. Okolovich did not flinch at the cigarette packs, though he knew by now what they might contain, and consumed some of the vodka and caviar— which might well have been lethal also—as a gesture of good faith.

Neither Okolovich nor the Americans ever made this curious case out. Shmelov, who always stoutly denied that he was anything but a loyal NTS Russian, was eventually persuaded to defect. But he was never completely accepted in the West, and he sensed it. After some six months spent in an American safe house in Germany, one day he simply returned to Russia. His fate there remained as obscure as his real identity had been.

The fate of Khokhlov, on the other hand, was relatively clearcut. It was only a matter of time before the West would make propaganda capital out of his defection and the brutal murder mission which had sparked it off. The time came earlier than expected. On the same day, April 13, that Colonel Okun had eluded Western intelligence in Vienna, the Russians, in an action originally planned to run parallel with Khokhlov's mission, had kidnapped the NTS leader in West Berlin, Dr. Trushnovich, and taken him into the Soviet zone. As a counterblow, the Americans urged Khokhlov to appear as soon as possible before the Western press.

He was aghast. Already it was becoming clear to him that the prospects of getting his wife and child out to the West were fading. Okolovich, on whom he had pinned his faith, had to confess that his own NTS network was not up to the task. That left the Americans, who had promised him nothing in advance because they had not known of him in advance. They put forward a strange-sounding plan to Khokhlov that, the moment his broadcast press conference began in Bonn at 2 P.M. on April 22, Western journalists would flock to his wife's Moscow apartment for an "interview" which would, in fact, be a device to rush her and the child to the American embassy. Once there, Khokhlov was assured, they would be safe and as good as on their way to the West. Whether the plan was a bogus inducement from the start or whether it was seriously considered in Washington remains unclear. The fact is, however, that on that April 22, Khokhlov appeared, as arranged, before the world press in Bonn, whereas nobody appeared at the door of his wife's apartment in Moscow. Soon afterward other callers appeared: the secret police, who took both the woman and her child into custody. They disappeared for good into the gray gloom inhabited by the "nonpersons" of the Soviet state.

A fortnight later, on May 6, Khokhlov agreed to be flown out to the United States. He had been persuaded that, from there, he could best conduct a campaign for the release of his family. That campaign predictably led nowhere. Nonetheless, over the next few years, Khokhlov did become a very effective public propagandist for the anti-Soviet cause, so effective indeed that his onetime masters tried to silence him. After publishing his articles and touring all over the United States on lecture tours which excoriated the Soviet Union—an activity which, he professed to believe, would somehow help the cause of his captive wife and child—he was drawn by the tragic drama of the 1956 Hungarian revolution to return to Europe. He joined forces

with the NTS, whose leader it had once been his job to liquidate, and in his words, "it was this activity which brought me
to the brink of a horrible death in September 1957."[13]

He was back in Frankfurt that month, seeing Okolovich and
other familiar NTS figures, and on Sunday the fifteenth addressed the closing session at a conference of international anti-
Communist groups which had convened in the city's botanical
gardens. It was inviting trouble, and trouble soon arrived.

He ordered some coffee afterward on the terrace. It tasted less
agreeable than usual and, after sipping, he left it undrunk in the
cup. That certainly saved his life, for even the two sips were
nearly lethal. He collapsed and spent the next month first in a
German hospital and then, when poisoning was suspected (the
original diagnosis had been acute gastritis), in the American
military hospital, under twenty-four-hour guard. After a nightmare illness, during which his body broke out in brown stripes
and his hair came away in tufts, the American doctors finally
managed to pull him through with massive blood transfusions
and a variety of injections, some of them still experimental.

Khokhlov had no doubts now about who had tried to kill him,
but he was curious about the method his former colleagues had
employed. The final analysis was only given him by a toxicolo-
gist when he was convalescing back in America. He had been
poisoned with something totally new—radioactive thallium,
fragments of deadly metal which gradually disintegrated inside
his system. One presumes that the former highly trained Soviet
assassin, who had insisted on the most up-to-date gadgetry for
his own use, was, despite everything, somewhat impressed.

8

Canberra

THESE DEFECTION dramas of the winter of 1954 ended with a unique double act. Ten years before, Igor Gouzenko had fled the Soviet embassy in Ottawa with his wife at his side and she had sustained him throughout the personal ordeal which followed. Anna, however, had been an ordinary Soviet citizen, as were the wives of the defectors who followed Gouzenko's example a decade later, whether their husbands had left them behind willingly, resignedly or sorrowfully. With Vladimir and Evdokia Petrov, on the other hand, we are dealing not simply with husband and wife but with professional colleagues: at the time of their defection, he was a lieutenant colonel in the MVD, as Soviet political intelligence was styled in his day, while she held the rank of captain in the same service. The fact that, to begin with, they could not get their double act together—with a delay of more than a fortnight before the hysterical wife was forced from her Soviet bodyguards to join her husband in freedom and safety—only gave an added and very spectacular impact to their flight. The case of the Petrovs' defection is unique in another sense too. It was the only one, before or since, whose climax was played out in the full glare of Western publicity, with newspaper photographers and reporters and a large and enthusiastic audience of spectators in attendance. Neither of the Petrovs could have dreamt of such scenes, or such circumstances, when their careers in Soviet intelligence began.

137

Even before they came together by marriage ("Dusya," as she was always known, was his second wife) their lives had run along somewhat parallel courses. He had been born, on February 15, 1907, to a peasant family called Shorokhov, who had worked on the land for generations at Larikha in Central Siberia and, like his forefathers, the new Shorokhov had been duly christened in the Russian Orthodox village church. She came into the world, seven years before him, also in a primitive village of tsarist Russia, and, like her future husband, had been christened in her village church at Lipky. But Lipky, in Ryazan Province, was not far from Moscow, and it was to the Soviet capital that the girl moved with her family when only ten years old. As she later wrote, this was to leave a different stamp on their characters throughout life, despite all that they came to share. He lived and worked in the countryside until his mid-twenties, enjoying the outdoor life, and especially the hunting, which even the peasants could indulge in. "My greatest prize," he wrote of his youth in later years, "was a gun of my own."[1] She grew up in a great city which, for all its shortcomings, was the hub of the Soviet world. Oddly enough, when their turn came to reject this world, each was helped by these very different personal surroundings. He found in the Australian outback something of the primitive countryside freedoms of his native Siberia; she, essentially *une femme d'asphalte,* found, even in Sydney's social life, a whiff of the cosmopolitan excitement she had begun to yearn for in Moscow.

In their early years, both went through the familiar Communist hatchery of the Young Pioneers and the Komsomol youth movement. Vladimir gradually became such an ardent Communist that, in 1929, two years after becoming a full member of the Party, he changed his name to Proletarsky to demonstrate his ardor for the cause.* Both Vladimir and his future wife faced, and survived, some awkward challenges to their youthful ardor. There was the extinction of the kulak peasantry in the late 1920s, for example, when both of them swallowed the official line

---

*The name Petrov, by which he finally came to be known, was wished on him by his intelligence service.

despite the fact that the victims included peasants from their own native villages. Both were shocked and troubled by Stalin's ruthless political purges of the 1930s, and especially by the mysterious murder of the old Bolshevik hero Sergei Kirov, whom Vladimir, in particular, had venerated. But both, at the time, once again accepted the official line. Looking back on those traumatic years, she wrote:

> What did we say? What the newspapers told us. Or better still, nothing at all. How could we arrive at any worthwhile opinions? For the younger generation like myself there was no alternative voice, no background of expression against which we could test the truth of what we read every day. These matters of high politics were far above my head. . . .[2]

One good reason for keeping quiet was that, by now, both were members of Stalin's principal machine of oppression, the secret police itself. He had volunteered for the service in 1933 after three and a half years' service with the Red Navy's Baltic fleet, during which he had been trained as a cipher specialist.[3] On one of his last shore leaves he had entered into what turned out to be a typical sailor's marriage to a flighty young girl, who separated from him five years later. But as a new bridegroom he had felt new responsibilities. He is refreshingly honest about his reasons for joining the intelligence service:

> I was married. I wanted a job and I wanted enough to eat. . . . When I finished my years of naval service and came to Moscow, I was glad to be issued that warm uniform jacket with its mauve shoulder tabs. . . . And I was very glad to possess a pass to the excellent restaurant.[4]

The future Mrs. Petrov first swam into the OGPU (the Soviet secret police) net in a much odder way. Aged twelve, she was walking one day along Moscow's Lubianka Street and passed the huge building which, unknown to her, housed Stalin's secret police headquarters. She wandered in, attracted by a lively crowd of children in the hall. These latter turned out to be

Communist Young Pioneers. Could she join too? she asked the adult in charge. Well, that depended, came the reply. These were OGPU pioneers; what did her father do? By a freak coincidence, her father had in fact just got a job as a truck driver in the OGPU's Transport Section. It was enough to give her the proper credentials; the newcomer was accepted into the fold. Seven years later, after completing her secondary education and finishing a two-year foreign-language course, she also opted, when aged only nineteen, for a career in intelligence. Like Vladimir, she was assigned to cipher work, first with military intelligence and then with the main political branch in Dzerzhinsky Square. Like Vladimir, she was always frank about her motives. She wrote later: "I took this step . . . because at the time it seemed the most normal and obvious thing in the world to do." To her, the secret police were purely and simply "the body set up by Lenin . . . to protect the Revolution from its political enemies."[5] As a keen young cipher clerk engaged in foreign intelligence, she knew little, and probably at first cared less, about the methods used against Soviet citizens to preserve that revolution at home. Awkward reminders came before long. Two of her chiefs, a certain Gusev and Gleb Boki, an old Bolshevik and onetime friend of Lenin himself, were swept away and executed in the violent purge waves of 1937.[6]

A far more immediate shock was to hit her in her own home in July of that year. She had fallen in love with a colleague in the Dzerzhinsky Square headquarters, a certain Roman Krivosh, a controversial figure with potentially dangerous ancestry and potentially dangerous tastes. He was a Serb by origin, and his father had served as a senior official in the tsarist Okhrana; after the revolution, he had alternately been employed by Moscow Center for his linguistic talents or locked up by them for his political lineage. The son was also something of an oddity as a Communist intelligence officer, as much interested in writing novels and poetry as in the serious business of fighting imperialist subversion. It was this artistic quality and the cosmopolitan world it conjured up which Dusya found so attractive. At all events, in 1936, after he had divorced his variety actress wife, she moved into his apartment and they lived as a married couple. In June of 1937 a daughter was born and their domestic bliss (there was no need, in those days, for unions to be formally registered as marriages) seemed complete. It was shattered when she was halfway through the forty-five days of statutory leave granted to Soviet mothers after the birth of a child. At two o'clock in the morning, two uniformed security officers from their own intelligence service knocked on the door, arrested Roman on no specified charges and turned the flat upside down before leading him away. Dawn found her sitting on the bed alone with her infant daughter, incredulously surveying the wreckage of her home and, seemingly, her life.*

Her own account of this traumatic episode[7] is, again, refreshingly frank. If it opened her eyes to the tyranny she was serving, she does not say so. Far from revulsion, her sole thought was survival, on her own account and that of her child. She fought like a tigress at the inevitable Party inquisitions which followed over her own future and eventually escaped with a "severe reprimand and serious warning" for the offense of not having read the character of her common-law husband correctly. Even this lunatic verdict does not seem to have shaken her faith in the system at the time. Indeed, her only thought was to hang on to her privileged position inside that system, and this she succeeded in doing. She remained a member of the Komsomol and she returned to her desk in Dzerzhinsky Square.

It was there that she met Volodya Proletarsky, as the future Vladimir Petrov was calling himself. He was by now deputy chief of the Cipher Section at the center, having returned to Moscow in February 1938 after a spell with a special cipher unit operating in the occupied Sinkiang Province of Western China.[8] He pursued her stolidly and persistently. Unlike the first courtship, which had been strewn with flowers, boxes of her favorite brand of chocolates and endless compliments, this was a bureaucrat's plodding process; his most conspicuous display of affection was to check up on all her movements. It was

---

*Roman survived Stalin's purges and Hitler's war. Dusya ran into him once again in Moscow ten years later. She noted that he was shabbily dressed and had several front teeth missing, presumably the result of "interrogation."

the death of her daughter from meningitis in April 1940 which decided her to accept him. He had become a cherished "Uncle Volodya" to the child. She had died calling for him, and he came to keep the death vigil over the body with the stricken mother. But there was more than shared emotion in her decision to marry him. Following the shock of Roman's arrest, she was, above all else, in pursuit of respectability and security within the privileged core of the system. As she herself wrote of her choice:

> Not only by name but also by origin and background he was a man of the people. He was of peasant stock; he was on the Committee of the Communist Party unit in our Department and led a study circle on the history of the Communist party. Here, if anywhere, was surely a man with his foot set firmly on the stairway of solid progress and safe orthodoxy within the framework of the Soviet Service. After the experience of my earlier marriage, there was a particular appeal for me in that.[9]

Alone, bereaved and still politically vulnerable, she sought safety with a seemingly archetypal apparatchiki. It was, from the first, a marriage made in the office and not in heaven. When they went to record their marriage at the Moscow Registry, she kept her maiden name in order, as she put it, to "retain something of my independence." She felt anyway that "Proletarsky" sounded too artificial. What she probably felt in addition, though without admitting it at the time, was that it was also too vulgar. At all events, the problem was happily resolved when, two years later, in July 1942, they were posted together, as a married couple and as intelligence colleagues, to Stockholm. Their new foreign passports described them as "Mr. and Mrs. Petrov." The authorities had decided that "Proletarsky" sounded altogether too militant for a neutral capital and had chosen instead the name by which the couple was eventually to go down in espionage history.

The new Mrs. Petrov set off for Sweden determined, as she put it even when in exile years later, "to prove myself in every way a worthy daughter of my Soviet homeland."[10] It was a nightmare voyage which began with a fruitless journey up to Archangel in the hope of catching a convoy bound for London. This was abandoned after ten weeks and there followed a round-the-globe approach by plane and ship to Teheran, Cairo and Durban (their ship was torpedoed en route on the Red Sea) and then by passenger liner to Britain, from where they finally reached Stockholm by a night flight from Aberdeen. More than one thing happened during this seven-month odyssey to make the "worthy daughter of my Soviet homeland" draw uncomfortable parallels: the abundance of food in the Cairo markets; the kindness of the crew on the British destroyer which picked them up in the Red Sea in their lifeboat; and the rapturous hospitality to the "torpedoed Russians" everywhere in South Africa. But what strikes the reader most of all in her account of this first journey into the Western world are two incidents which stuck in her mind from her brief stay in London.

In Westminster Abbey, she was impressed but also disturbed by the tomb of the Unknown Warrior. What a profound reverence for the dead this showed, and what a contrast with Soviet attitudes, where funerals were held without dignity and cemeteries were left to rot. The second incident was trivial by comparison but almost equal in impact. Their hotel was near Hyde Park, and when she and her husband walked around the Serpentine they were amazed to watch the ducks and swans coming so tamely to the banks to be fed by hand: "We had never seen such a thing before. In the Soviet Union it is unknown. There the birds (like the people) are much too frightened."[11]

Their four years in Sweden provided them with many more examples of Western freedom and plenty. There was the predictable astonishment at the Stockholm shops, bursting like a fairyland with glittering goods—luxuries in their eyes, everyday consumer goods to the natives. Mrs. Petrov's eye was taken in particular by all the well-dressed women in the streets. Back in Moscow, a foreign woman walking about the city instantly stood out from the crowd "like a parrot among crows," as the Russian saying went. Here, they were all parrots. The newcomer from Russia began to put on some plumage as well. A fateful fondness for Western feminine chic was taking root.

Yet none of this had shaken the Communist loyalty of the Petrovs. One reason was their work, which was congenial to them and evidently appreciated in Moscow. Vladimir, though officially on the diplomatic staff, had a second secret function as cipher officer to the intelligence section and security officer for all Soviet personnel in the Swedish capital. The latter function seems to have caused him no misgivings, despite the fact that this so-called SK work included a special investigation, on orders, of the ambassadress herself, Madame Aleksandra Kollontai, a much respected heroine of the revolution and a figure of worldwide reputation. There were apparently those in Moscow who feared that this frail old living legend of Communism, by now paralyzed and confined to a wheelchair, somehow constituted a threat.*

Dusya was also happy in her work, first as a secretary doing office duties in the embassy's intelligence section, and then as a "case officer" cultivating a potential woman agent in the Swedish Ministry of Foreign Affairs. The fact that the woman in question, code-named "Maria," finally refused to cooperate did not trouble her pursuer unduly. For Mrs. Petrov, the important thing was that the Moscow Center had given her the assignment in the first place. That signaled rehabilitation in the system, which was all that she was interested in at the time.

Perhaps the main reason for the Petrovs' contentment in Stockholm was not so much the professional success (he was promoted to lieutenant colonel and she to captain) as the happy atmosphere in the embassy under the courteous and considerate Madame Kollontai, who took a personal human interest in everybody working in the building. They felt part of a harmonious Russian enclave doing useful work in exceptionally pleasant surroundings, which, though often seductive, were never really corrupting. They had seen many things which troubled them when contrasted with Soviet practice—the way, for example, in which the Swedish authorities, paid only modest salaries, would travel to work by train or bus as compared with those

---

*In the event, Petrov's investigation proved negative and when Madame Kollontai died in Moscow in March 1952 she was buried with full state honors.

fleets of speeding armored cars used by the Kremlin bosses, with their limitless and unquestioned privileges. But nothing had yet happened inside either of the Petrovs to cause them to repudiate the Communist cause. Vladimir doubtless spoke for them both when he wrote of their recall to Moscow in October of 1947:

My four years' service in Sweden left an abiding impression in my mind of the prosperity and truly democratic atmosphere of this small capitalist country. It brought home to me in a hundred ways the falsehood and futility of Soviet propaganda and the stupidity and inhumanity of the system it served. I pondered over these things. But the same system had opened for me a career in which I was successful, privileged and trusted. I had no personal grievance to goad me into action. That was to be provided later, under very different circumstances, in our embassy at Canberra.[12]

Indeed it was. They arrived there on February 5, 1951, after Vladimir had done an uneventful three-year stint as a Moscow security snooper, monitoring the loyalty of Soviet crews on vessels sailing to Anglo-American countries and members of Soviet delegations visiting the West.[13] His new post had a much broader base. He retained SK responsibilities, to watch over all Soviet personnel in the embassy, including, as in Stockholm, a close surveillance of the ambassador himself. He also had a commission from the so-called EM Department of Moscow Center to investigate suspected anti-Soviet elements among the émigré Balts or displaced Russian citizens who had settled in Australia. But there were other, more pleasant duties. He was made official representative in Australia of VOKS, the Soviet cultural organization, which gave him the enviable privilege of traveling, more or less at will, throughout the continent, distributing propaganda films and literature to friendship societies in the various Australian states.

Most challenging of all, he was eventually given the tricky task of organizing an "illegal" Soviet spy organization in Australia, that is, a network of agents operating underground without official cover. By the time he got this additional responsibility, Vladimir Petrov had been appointed acting rezident, that is, chief of all intelligence operations in his theater. Though the appointment, made in February of 1952, was technically only temporary, he in fact remained in sole charge until his defection three years later. These substantial intelligence duties all went under the modest diplomatic cloak of an embassy third secretary. His wife, whose official post was embassy accountant and secretary to the ambassador, also continued with the same sort of special espionage operations she had been given in Sweden. Mainly because of Vladimir's work, they were not required to live in the embassy compound but occupied an agreeable little modern bungalow in a fashionable suburb of Canberra. As the only embassy couple who spoke good English, they were instantly in social demand. It was not surprising that the Petrovs came to be envied by their colleagues. Their money alone would have been enough. With both in good posts and no children to support, they were the most prosperous pair in the entire mission.

It was this jealousy, leading first to spiteful personal campaigns against them and finally to dangerous and open office feuds, which drove the Petrovs, more than any other single factor, toward the break. In this, their defection is once again unique. Had there been a serene, fair-minded and kindly figure of authority like Madame Kollontai in charge, they would, in all probability, have stayed at their posts, as they had firmly intended to do when coming to Australia. As it was, trouble started brewing within months of their arrival. One of the embassy documents which Petrov brought with him on his flight was a telegram from Moscow Center dated June 6, 1952, showing that the clouds were already gathering over his wife's head. The communiqué was addressed to the husband.

According to information in our possession [its final paragraph ran], Mrs. Petrov occasionally shows a lack of tact in her relations with the employees of the Embassy, including the Ambassador, which cannot fail to have an adverse effect on her work.

In this connection, we request you to administer an appropriate reprimand to her.[14]

What Petrov would have passed on to his wife was an alarm signal for them both. In any case, as both of them knew, this particular problem stemmed not so much from the ambassador, Lifanov, who had already served for nine years in Canberra and had become quite popular there, as from his wife. Madame Lifanov was his second wife and evidently a poor replacement for the first, a beautiful woman who had walked out on him. Though herself plain and skinny, the poor creature did her best to accommodate her husband's liking for plump women by wearing endless petticoats, even in hot weather. She only attracted ridicule.

> Her clothes [Mrs. Petrov recalled] were the laughing stock of the embassy. Even doorkeepers' wives, on a quarter the salary, dressed better. . . . In her nine years in Australia she bought one pair of nylons; after that, declaring them too expensive, she wore patched cotton ones. . . .[15]

This emphasis on dress sense is significant, for the younger woman who was acting as the ambassador's secretary was rapidly becoming as smartly turned out as any Western diplomat's wife. This did not help her cause. Her predecessor, a single woman, was rumored to have been on extremely close terms with the ambassador, and Madame Lifanov became automatically suspicious of any female, especially such a well-dressed one, occupying the same post.

The luckless Dusya Petrov also ran into trouble with her second official job, that of embassy accountant. She was determined to go by the Moscow rule book, and that meant, for example, insisting that all the embassy staff, including the ambassador, pay the regulation fee for renting their state-property furniture. There were furious protests, for this was one of the many regulations which the whole mission had been bending or evading for years, in order to pocket some extra money, in good capitalist style. No less a person than the Moscow auditor himself, on a visit to Canberra, backed the embassy accountant, and that was the end of the wrangle. But from then on, she had both the ambassador and his wife as enemies.

The sniping attacks were soon launched. First came accusations of poking fun at the great Stalin. The "evidence" was that, under her glass-topped worktable, which bore a picture of the dictator, Mrs. Petrov had inserted two magazine pictures, one of a Hollywood actress and the other of a dog playing the piano. This led to the solemn charge being produced at an embassy Party members' meeting that Comrade Petrova was deliberately ridiculing the great leader. She knew the tense and suspicion-laden mood in Moscow too well to treat the matter lightly: careers were being blighted and heads sent rolling for such trivial denunciations. Her defense was a formal letter of denial, addressed to the Central Committee of the Party with a sketch demonstrating the harmless nature of her desktop.

A dog, in this case her husband's beloved Jack, also figured in the next formal complaint, which accused the animal of running wild up and down the corridors of the embassy. They hoped for better things when the Lifanovs were recalled late in 1953 to Moscow (Madame Lifanov flaunting her execrable taste to the very last by boarding the aircraft with a silver fox fur draped over a raincoat). But the new ambassador, Generalov, did not even bother to look at the files before continuing to apply the pressure. He had brought his instructions with him. One of his first acts was to summon Petrov and solemnly announce, "Vladimir Mikhailovich, the Central Committee of the Communist Party of the Soviet Union has ordered that you are not to bring your dog into the precincts of our embassy."[16]

The persecution had gained momentum ever since Stalin's death in March of 1953 if only because, envy in Canberra apart, it reflected the deep-seated hostility in Moscow between the Soviet foreign service and the intelligence world, which was now plunged into a long phase of weakness and upheaval. But it was only after the fall of Beria in July of that year that the anti-Petrov campaign in the Canberra embassy took a deadly turn, with their own Moscow Center either unable or unwilling to support them. The Petrovs were now accused of plotting to form a pro-Beria faction within the mission itself. Moreover, they learned through one of their few friends in the embassy, the cipher clerk Prudnikov, that this accusation had been relayed in separate signals to Moscow—one from the ambassador to the Foreign Ministry and the other from the Party secretary of the mission to the Central Committee. In the fraught summer of 1953, this was tantamount to a charge of treachery. It seemed certain to lead to a recall, followed at best by demotion and at worst by arrest and death. If embassy spite and intrigue had nudged the Petrovs toward the edge of the abyss, it was, as Vladimir, at least for his part, freely admitted, naked fear which prodded him into crossing over it.

Fortunately, by now, a ladder was moving into position. The first moves toward putting it there had been taken, very quietly, from the Australian side, only a few months after the Petrovs' arrival in Canberra. The unusual freedom of "Third Secretary" Petrov's movements had soon aroused the interest of the Australian Security Service, who had held him under surveillance from time to time. For this task, initially only a protective counterintelligence one, they employed a certain Dr. Michael Bialoguski.[17] He had been born in Kiev, capital of the Russian Ukraine, on March 19, 1917, but both his parents were Polish, and in 1920, since Poland had become an independent state, the family escaped across the border to settle at Vilna in its northeastern provinces. This area again became Russian in September 1939 when the Red Army moved in at the outbreak of Hitler's war. However, it was ceded within a few weeks to the neighboring Baltic Republic of Lithuania, which was under strong German influence. The Polish doctor (he had secured a medical certificate in 1935) decided to flee again, and his final escape was as bizarre as his history to date. He secured an exit permit from the British consul to visit a fictitious aunt in Curaçao. Then, in the guise of an out-of-work musician, he traveled by the Trans-Siberian train to Vladivostok, from where he made his way to Japan and finally to Australia, where he landed on June 24, 1941, a few days after the German invasion of Russia. The hospitable Australians made him an orderly in their army medical corps and gave him a grant to complete his full doctor's degree at Sydney University.

This extraordinary background, which included flights from both the Soviet and the Nazi tyrannies, enabled him to fit perfectly into the Petrov puzzle. In addition to practicing his profession, he worked in secret for Australian intelligence, partly for the money (he was always squabbling over his expenses) and partly out of gratitude for what the country had done for him. In public, he presented himself as strongly pro-Russian and equally strongly pro-Communist. He thus became a natural target for the spy-recruiter Petrov, whom in fact he was targeting himself. The two men first met at the Russian Social Club in Sydney in July 1951, and a complicated game of double deception began. Petrov thought he was onto a local recruit for Soviet intelligence. Bialoguski eventually realized that he was onto a major Soviet defector.[18]

It was, of course, a gradual process, with Petrov's office problems leading him to complain more and more bitterly about his discontent with life as a Soviet diplomat (it was not until the end that he admitted his true role), and Bialoguski expatiating more and more about the delights of life under the Australian sun. Early in 1953, more than a year before Petrov finally decided to defect, his complaints to his doctor friend about the intolerable friction inside the Soviet mission became so bitter that Bialoguski was authorized to offer some tempting capitalist bait. The men were by now on first-name terms and met whenever Petrov came down to Sydney. One of their favorite eating places there was the Adria Café in King's Cross, a restaurant run by George Chomentowski, a Pole who was also a professional chef. Having prepared the ground with the owner, Bialoguski proposed to Petrov that they each put up 500 pounds to buy a share in the Adria. In fact, the scheme came to nothing. The encouraging thing had been Petrov's reaction. This was enthusiastic (subject, of course, to a check on the proprietor's background) and it was clear that the Russian had been more interested in a good investment for himself than in finding a new base for his official operations. "Anyway, if not with

George, we must find some other money-making business," he had declared.[19]

Petrov edged a little closer to the brink in May 1953, when he and his wife were summoned back for a long spell of "leave" in the Soviet Union, a recall which, they both feared, might turn out to be permanent. Providentially, before they could leave, Petrov developed a perfectly genuine case of eye trouble. His friend the Polish doctor recommended him to a Dr. Beckett, a Sydney eye surgeon who also operated for Australian intelligence. The eye complaint (which necessitated a spell in a Canberra hospital) led to the postponement and, finally, the cancellation of the dreaded home-leave summons, but by then Petrov's jitters had been aggravated by the news of Beria's arrest. When, on July 23, he went again to Beckett's office for an examination, the eye specialist started probing his patient's nonmedical problems as well. If he was unhappy, why not stay in Australia for good? And if he should make that decision, then Dr. Beckett could provide all the official contacts necessary to make a new life safe and pleasant. Petrov returned to Canberra with his mind in a whirl. At this stage, he did not even tell his wife what had happened. This was not only because her sense of loyalty was stronger than his. Unlike him, she had a large family back in Russia. When any Soviet defector, in any post in any place, wanted to jump, each close relative at home was a ball and chain around the legs.

By the end of the year, however, her own defenses had weakened. The new ambassador, Generalov, sacked her as embassy secretary. One of the main reasons given was her "discourtesy" toward the ambassador's wife. Part of the "evidence" was a ludicrous tale that she had thrown a pie at Madame Generalov. This was now black comedy indeed, though all the Petrovs could see was the blackness. Vladimir's fury, when he unburdened himself to Bialoguski, was now verging on hysteria. The Australian authorities began to move in for the kill.

On January 31, 1954, Bialoguski visited the Petrov home in Canberra and tried outright to persuade Dusya to join her husband if and when he decided to come over to the West. The approach failed. She responded at first with an attack on the "imperialistic capitalist system" straight out of the Marxist handbook, but later indicated that her real concern was for her family, especially her mother and sister, back in Moscow.[20] Whatever hesitations she still had, Vladimir was by now getting in too deep to turn back. He started deceiving his wife to prepare for his own flight.

In February 1954 both of them were required, as MVD officials, to sign declarations that all the 1952 letters sent to them in Canberra from Moscow Center had been burned. Petrov assured his wife that the documents had indeed been destroyed, thus securing her signature on the joint certificate. In fact, he had hidden them away as part of his intelligence "dowry." The ingenious part of the scheme was that their removal would not be traced because, officially, they no longer existed.

In the coming weeks, Petrov and Australia came steadily closer as partners for life. Petrov, having expressed an interest in chicken farming, was shown by Bialoguski a suitable little property, Dream Acres, at Parramatta. For 3,800 pounds, the doctor said, they could buy it outright between them. Australian government officials and Australian government money now entered the scene. On February 27, Petrov made his first official contact with Australian intelligence when he was introduced, at Bialoguski's Sydney apartment, to a Mr. Richards, the deputy director of security. Richards immediately assured the Russian that, once he had formally applied for asylum, he would be looked after in all aspects and that special funds would be drawn on to finance him. (The down payment was later fixed at 5,000 pounds, more than enough to buy Dream Acres by himself.) Still Petrov kept up the pretense that he was merely a third secretary at the Soviet mission. Still he hesitated.

The first of April 1954, far from being a harmless April Fools' Day for Petrov, brought about the decision. On his arrival at the embassy, he was summoned, first to the chief cipher clerk and then to the ambassador, over a serious breach of security. A spot check had been carried out the previous evening on the embassy safes and the one which was supposed to hold only Petrov's routine consular papers was found to contain secret documents which should have been locked up elsewhere. His relief that the precious envelope with the "destroyed" 1952 letters had not been unearthed (that had been hidden away in his intelligence office) evaporated when a smug Generalov informed him that a report on such laxity would be sent to Moscow. Petrov knew that this single offense could get him ten years in a labor camp. That evening, at a rendezvous with Richards, he announced that he would defect on the following day.

The cover was simple. Petrov had to fly down to Sydney anyway on April 2 to meet new arrivals for the Soviet mission off their ship and arrange for their onward flight to Canberra. One of the newcomers, Comrade Kovalenok of the MVD, who had been posted as his eventual successor, brought him greetings from their Moscow Center and earnest assurances that all would be well on his return there. Had Petrov's mind not already been made up, that blatant exercise in deception would have resolved the issue for him. He saw his comrades onto the Canberra plane and then, without even waiting for it to take off, stepped into the backseat of Richards's car and drove off to begin his life as a political refugee in Australia. He had signed the paper requesting asylum at a hurried meeting that afternoon. The embassy documents, which he had stowed in his travel bag, wrapped in a copy of *Pravda*, were handed over at the safe house in Sydney where he spent his first night as a defector. He was handed in return 5,000 pounds in cash. It was all over, for him at any rate.

For his wife, the drama was only now beginning. He had left her in Canberra that morning without giving the slightest inkling of what he intended to do in Sydney in a few hours' time. The less she knew, the better for her. The less she was involved, the easier for him. It was a blend of panic and concern. But, as soon as he was safe, remorse took over. He pleaded with his Australian guards that they should organize a kidnap operation to bring her to his side. In the event, force was needed to bring them together, but in a setting much more favorable to the West.

The Soviet ambassador was no more than irritated when

Petrov failed to appear on Monday morning, putting it down to his multifarious intelligence duties in Sydney. But when the whole of Monday and Tuesday passed without even a message, the alarm bells started ringing. The missing man had either had an accident, had been abducted or, unmentionable thought, had defected. The first priority was to find out, the second to secure, in the meantime, his wife. Mrs. Petrov was bundled out of their private house and moved to the embassy, where she was held as a virtual prisoner. After two days, newspapers were taken away from her and the radio removed from her room. Madame Generalova led the other women of the mission in a display of icy hostility. At one point she became so desperate—fearing the worst but knowing nothing—that she tried to hang herself with the cord of an electric iron doubled over the hooks of a built-in cupboard. Fortunately for her, the hooks gave way.

On April 13, the uncertainty, at least, was ended. Australian radio broadcast a statement by the prime minister, Robert Menzies, that "one Vladimir Mikhailovich Petrov, third secretary of the Soviet embassy in Canberra, had requested and been granted political asylum." Nothing showed more clearly his wife's psychological captivity within the Communist system than her instinctive distrust of the announcement. All her training urged her to believe that the capitalists were lying and that Vladimir had been taken against his will. Whatever the facts, from now on Mrs. Petrov was not merely a captive, but an embarrassment which had to be got rid of and returned to Moscow as soon as possible for treatment, or destruction. A fortnight after it had been written, a letter from her husband was now put in her hands, pleading for a meeting. Her reply was dictated for her. "I cannot meet you because I am afraid of falling into a trap."[21] She probably half-believed it. In any case when, on April 19, the day for her return to Moscow arrived, she was still ready at heart to go back. Vladimir, for all she knew, might well be dead. Her family in Moscow, on the other hand, were alive and their well-being depended on her rejoining them. Not that she had much choice. Two "diplomatic couriers," "Jarkov" and "Karpinsky,"* had been detailed to guard her on the flight from Sydney up to Darwin and then homeward bound via Singapore. They would accompany her, she was assured, even to the toilet. In addition, Kislystin, a second secretary at the embassy, would also travel with the party to give it some semblance of diplomatic status. They were all to play cards together in the airport lounge at Singapore during the overnight stop there, and she was ordered to laugh at intervals so that they would look like happy tourists. Her superiors in Moscow had thought of everything, except for the factors they could not comprehend: the pressures which public opinion and an uninhibited press can exert in a free country.

There was a foretaste of this in the crowd of sympathetic Canberra bystanders and eager reporters which had gathered outside the gates of the embassy to watch their departure. At this point, she witnessed something which spoke volumes for the contrast in the two worlds between which she was now suspended. The ambassador ordered two of his officials to go and disperse the crowds *by photographing them.* [22] In this, he had simply followed Soviet police practice, for in Russia the crowd, fearing anything which might go in a file against them, would have melted away at the very sight of a camera. Here, in Canberra, the people just waved back, and it seemed that they were not waving for Ambassador Generalov.

When the party reached Sydney's airport after a four-hour drive, there could be no doubt what the Australian people, alerted by radio to every stage of the operation, really felt. A large crowd had gathered, surging around the car. One man stuck his head inside, asking in English, "Mrs. Petrov, will you make a statement? Do you wish to return to Russia or do you want to stay here?" Still she made no attempt to escape. She was even afraid she might be torn to pieces by the mob for working as a Soviet spy in Australia. It was a dazed and half-demented woman who was dragged bodily across the tarmac and up the

---

*The reader will recall "Baiko" and "Danilov," the two "couriers" who took Volkov out of Istanbul nine years before.

gangway into the airliner, shouts of "Don't go back, it's death or a labor camp for you!" ringing in her ears. As the plane took off and circled over the lights of Sydney, she bade a mental farewell to her husband, wondering where he might be. Ironically, he was right underneath her. He had been brought by Australian security police to the airport in case the chance presented itself to speak to her.

The authorities had taken other steps as well. The captain of the plane had been instructed to reassure her and find out what was in her mind. A sympathetic air hostess managed to question her two or three times about the future. Still dodging the issue of asylum, she kept repeating that she wished to see her husband and warned that the couriers were armed. What neither she nor any other of the passengers—least of all her Soviet escorts—realized was that this information was being radioed direct from the cockpit to Colonel Spry, the director general of Australian Security, who, from Canberra, had kept in touch with the plane on its northward flight throughout the night.

The denouement came just before dawn on April 20, when the airliner landed at Darwin, its last stop on Australian soil. There was no crowd waiting for them here, and no battery of photographers; only what she glimpsed as "a small group of gray figures" clustered under the airport lights on the tarmac. One of them came up to her and introduced himself as "Mr. Leydin, representative of the Australian government."* He asked her outright, in the name of that government, whether she wanted political asylum. The overwrought woman still avoided a direct answer, moaning in one breath about the danger to her family in Russia and in another asking for poison to kill herself on the spot. She stopped talking of suicide when Mr. Leydin, who remained impressively calm, assured her that her husband was alive and well, but she was still in a dither of indecision when the party was escorted into the airport buildings while the plane was refueling for the flight to Singapore.

Only now did she learn from the glum-looking couriers that, while she had been agonizing with Mr. Leydin, they had been

*He was in fact the acting administrator of the Northern Territory.

surrounded by Australian police a few yards away and relieved of all their arms and ammunition. Dawn had now come and Kislystin, as the only regular diplomat of the Soviet party, got through to his mission in Canberra to report and ask for instructions. He returned to announce to her that, at this hour, he could only raise the embassy cleaner. Throughout, she made no attempt to contact Mr. Leydin again but just sat woodenly with her escort, so drained as to be incapable of making any decision. When, just before 7 A.M., she saw the flight crew returning to the aircraft for takeoff, it was actually Mrs. Petrov, the prisoner, who suggested to her guards that they should all reboard the plane and be done with it. At that moment an airport official ran up to announce that her husband was on the phone from Sydney. She took the call surrounded by her escorts. After two minutes of agitated exchanges, there was no doubt left in her mind that this was indeed Vladimir, nor that he had fled of his own accord and wanted her to join him. The prisoner, the wife and the intelligence professional all snapped into life again inside her at once. To fool her guards, she banged down the receiver shouting, "No, you are not my husband, good-bye!" To indicate to Mr. Leydin, waiting outside the office, that she had made up her mind at last, she gave him an emphatic wink. He got rid of the other Russians and they returned alone to the room where she had taken the call. Her final decision was announced in pragmatic style rather than in ringing ideological terms: "Mr. Leydin, I have decided to stay because there is no other way out."[23] It was not exactly enthusiastic, but it was enough. A few minutes later she was on her way to Government House in Darwin and, a day or two afterward, was reunited with her husband in the safe house in Sydney. It was still some weeks before she came to trust her new hosts completely and realize what madness it would have been to reboard the plane at Darwin. Evdokia Alexeevna Petrov, to give her her full name, was, ironically, the most hesitant as well as the most public of all Soviet defectors.

* * *

The debriefing began and, later, the testimony which the Petrovs gave to the Australian Royal Commission on Espionage,
which sat continuously from October 18 to November 11, 1954,
hearing a total of 119 witnesses. The commission's 483-page report concerns itself entirely with the threat, now exposed in
full, posed by Soviet espionage and subversive activities to the
security of Australia. That was indeed the prime thrust of Petrov's revelations, both in the envelope of Moscow instructions
he had brought over with him and in the mass of oral information about Soviet operations which he and his wife could provide between them. They explained, for example, that, though
Moscow was at pains to give substantial secret support to the
Australian Communist party (Petrov had direct knowledge of
one payment of 25,000 American dollars in cash to the Party's
general secretary, Mr. Sharkey), it was Communist sympathizers rather than Party members whom the Russians had targeted. A copious list of such target individuals could now be
drawn up, together with their code names and their Soviet
operators. They included hopeful contacts (by no means all of
them recruited agents) in all walks of Australian life: public
servants, Members of Parliament, businessmen, scientists, journalists and, above all, Russian and East European émigrés.

Petrov's interrogators were particularly interested in his
claim, made in a statement written on the day of his defection,
that "between 1945 and 1948, there was a very serious situation
in Australia in the Dept. of External Affairs." Indeed there was.
An Anglo-American cryptoanalytic team had managed, early in
1948, to decipher MVD traffic passing between the Soviet station in Canberra and Moscow Center. The material sent to
Moscow included a top secret report prepared for the British
chiefs of staff on "Security in the Western Mediterranean and
the Eastern Atlantic," which outlined Britain's strategic interests in these areas in the postwar era. A copy had been sent to
the Australian government.

A powerful MI5 team, led by one of its eventual chiefs, the
controversial Roger Hollis, descended on Canberra to convince

the Australians that they had been penetrated.* Two officials in the Department of External Affairs, Ian Milner and Jim Hill, were pinpointed as suspects. The result of this scare was not only a thorough counterespionage overhaul in Canberra but the setting up of an Australian security service, the ASIO, based on the MI5 model, to deal with the problem permanently. Now, the Petrovs were able to provide much new information to confirm the diagnosis, especially as regards Milner, who, by then, had more or less convicted himself by settling with his wife in Prague. The Petrovs also helped to identify Walter Clayton as the External Affairs official who, under the code name "Klod," had masterminded much of this early postwar leakage.[24]

In addition, of course, the entire "legal" apparatus of Soviet espionage was exposed and thus destroyed by the Petrovs, while the establishment of a more dangerous "illegal" apparatus had been prevented in the nick of time. One of Vladimir Petrov's more alarming disclosures was that his successor, Kovalenok, had come from the Fourth Directorate of Moscow Center, which specialized in setting up and operating such underground networks.

Petrov's years at the Moscow headquarters produced some useful information on a wider field. He claimed, for example, that Soviet intelligence agents in Yugoslavia had predicted Marshal Tito's resolve to break with the Soviet Union long before the event, only to have their warnings ignored. And, because he had actually seen the assassination file on Leon Trotsky in the secret Registry, he could confirm, in detail, how the deed to dispose of Stalin's exiled rival in Mexico had been meticulously planned by the Kremlin.

Tidbits like these embellished the Petrovs' revelations about Australia. But, all things considered, perhaps the most important thing about their defection was not what it produced, partly in secret, afterward, but something displayed in full public glare at the time—the ordeal of the Petrovs' escape. Only a

---

*To protect the highly sensitive fact that the proof came from deciphered intercepts, the British presented their evidence as having been provided by agents.

handful of people were aware at the time of how deeply and genuinely torn Dusya had been between staying and leaving until, in the end, a mixture of Soviet stick and Australian carrot made up her mind.

What remained most vividly in the Australian, and Western, imagination for years afterward were those press photographs of the agonized woman being hustled across the tarmac of Sydney airport in the grip of two of the gorillalike figures detailed to escort her. She is smartly dressed as usual, but her left shoe, from a new black pair, has been lost in the melee. One of her white-gloved hands clutches a black leather bag to match the remaining shoe; the other is pressed against her heart. Her face bears an expression of unendurable agony, in contrast with the flinty countenances of the men gripping her arms. These pictures form a permanent record of something far wider than the sufferings of one Russian woman on an Australian airfield in the spring of 1954.

A picture which in 1954 opened millions of eyes in the West to the reality of Stalin's police state. Evdokia Petrov, whose husband Vladimir had just defected to the Australian authorities, is dragged by Soviet security men to a Moscow-bound plane at Sydney airport. Happily, the couple were reunited in freedom a few hours later.

Dr. Alan Nunn May, the KGB's scientific mole, helped speed up the production of the Russian atom bomb by passing on secrets of Western technology. He was unmasked in 1946 by Gouzenko and sentenced to ten years in prison.

Nikolai Khokhlov, a highly trained and trusted Soviet political assassin who, in February 1954, surrendered to his intended victim—an anti-Soviet Russian émigré leader—instead of shooting him.

The KGB headquarters, Dzerzhinsky Square, Moscow.

H. A. R. ("Kim") Philby, the KGB's master spy inside British intelligence, photographed before the walls of the Kremlin he had served so faithfully since the thirties. Up to his death in 1988, he was never allowed to boast about his supreme service to Stalin.

The handsome Oleg Lyalin whose defection to London in 1971 was partly motivated by a love affair. The first Soviet agent to defect to the British since the war, his importance has been overestimated in some ways, underestimated in others.

Colonel Penkovsky, whose double life the KGB stumbled onto by accident, was sentenced to death and executed in May 1964. The prosecution had little difficulty, after Penkovsky had been driven to confess by severe torture, in proving guilt. They had more problems in explaining how he had been able to pass the West nearly 5,500 top secret documents, covering everything from the Soviet Union's newest tanks to its programs for space war.

It was through Colonel Oleg Penkovsky, a supremely important Western mole operating inside Soviet military headquarters, that the Americans realized what these excavations on the Cuban mainland meant. The lay-out models he had passed on revealed them as sites for offensive Soviet missiles.

James Angleton, a key figure in America's postwar intelligence. A brilliant but deeply pessimistic officer, he became convinced that the Russians had penetrated almost every aspect of Western operations. This picture shows him as a young officer in wartime Italy.

Did the KGB have a hand in the killing? A controversial Soviet defector has given the fullest account yet published of how the Kremlin reacted to the assassination crisis.

Soviet Speznaz forces in training. The wartime role of these Soviet terrorist units includes the assassination of political leaders, and industrial and religious figures in the target NATO countries. This and much else was revealed to the West in 1978 by the military defector Vladimir Rezun.

Arkady Shevchenko, Soviet Under Secretary-General of the United Nations, was the most senior political figure ever to defect. He had formerly served as secretary to the veteran Soviet Foreign Minister Andrei Gromyko, and was able to provide the West with a unique insight into the Kremlin's workings.

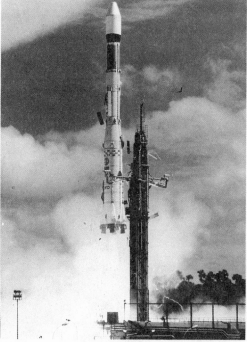

The ebullient Soviet leader Nikita Khrushchev behaving at his worst during the United Nations General Assembly meeting in October 1960. His behavior so embarrassed his Kremlin colleagues that he was, in fact, hammering a nail in his own political coffin. Shevchenko was one of his chief advisers at the time.

This pride of French technology was one of the hundreds of Western scientific secrets which the KGB sought to pilfer, as revealed by "Farewell," France's top-level agent in the Kremlin. His disclosures largely accounted for President Mitterrand's cool attitude toward Moscow.

Mikhail Gorbachev with the British prime minister on his famous visit to London in 1984. Then only a Politburo member, he succeeded Chernenko as Party Leader three months later. Ironically, one of his advisers during the visit was KGB Colonel Gordievski.

A giant among the West's postwar intelligence prizes, Oleg Gordievski opened the eyes of Western leaders to the dangerous paranoias of the Kremlin. He had been working for the British for more than a decade when, as head of the KGB's London office, he was finally forced to defect in 1985.

PART THREE

Crisis and Confusion

9

Penkovsky—Contact

WITH THE enigmatic figure of Colonel Oleg Vladimirovich Penkovsky, the East-West espionage struggle entered a new dimension. For the first and, so far, the only recorded time in postwar history, human intelligence, supplied directly to the enemy, helped to tilt the course of world events. The Cuban missile crisis, though far from being the only example of Penkovsky's far-reaching influence, was certainly the most spectacular. In the late summer of 1962, some fifteen months after the GRU colonel had started operating for British intelligence, Western experts were studying one of his many offerings. It was a photocopy of a top secret document prepared at the headquarters of Missile and Ground Artillery of the Soviet armed forces. Penkovsky had no authorized access to the building. He had got in "for study purposes" because he was well known to the staff as a long-standing personal friend and protégé of the commanding officer, Chief Marshal Sergey Sergeyevich Varentsov.

The theme of the paper, which was entitled "Methods of Protecting and Defending Strategic Rocket Sites," seemed fairly mundane. It dealt with layout, camouflage policy, ways of "hardening" sites and the preparation of alternatives if the primary ones were damaged or destroyed. But the illustrations, especially those of the camouflage outlines, made the American experts sit up. They showed distinctly different concealment profiles for Soviet surface-to-surface as compared with surface-

to-air weapons, in other words, for offensive as opposed to defensive missiles. For some time, there had been reports of Soviet
engineers working on major construction sites in Cuba, and on
August 29 these had been photographed by American U-2 spy
planes. It had been assumed that the sites were simply expan-
sions of Cuba's antiaircraft armory following the CIA's notorious Bay of Pigs invasion of 1961—a fiasco which nonetheless
carried with it the threat of more serious attacks. Now, thanks
to this document from Marshal Varentsov's safes, a more positive identification was possible. The U-2s were sent out over
Cuba to take more detailed pictures. What they brought back
was an electric shock. The site layout and camouflage outlines
they now filmed were found to match exactly those of Russian
medium-range surface-to-surface weapons as reproduced in
the purloined Soviet report. There could be no doubt about it.
The ebullient Soviet leader Nikita Khrushchev, who had
spoken so loudly of coexistence, was preparing to place the
American mainland under the immediate threat of nuclear attack. Thanks to Penkovsky, President John F. Kennedy, who
had gone through a baffling and nonproductive first encounter
with Khrushchev in Vienna only a few weeks before, now knew
where he stood. That was not the only service the GRU colonel
was able to render the White House in the Cuban missile crisis
which now opened.

Just before the crisis ended, on October 27, 1962, with Khrushchev's missile-carrying convoys retreating in the face of a
formidable American naval blockade, Penkovsky himself had
been arrested in Moscow, after nearly nine months of mounting
surveillance by the KGB, which will be detailed below. But
before he was swept abruptly from the scene, Penkovsky had
presented the West with a whole cupboardful of other Soviet
missile treasures. Thanks to him, the West now knew one of the
most crucial enemy secrets of all: the various "Alert" stages to
be ordered for the Kremlin's Strategic Rocket Forces to match
any deepening international crisis, together with the times required to prepare the missiles for firing from the start of each
of the Alert stages. This gave the West the Russian countdown
plan for doomsday.

Penkovsky had also passed on the detailed drill for setting up missiles on their launchpads, all the checks (including electronic controls) before firing, and the firing sequences themselves. He had photographs of the full technical details of the formidable surface-to-air SAM Guidelines missile, in which NATO was very interested, as well as numerous graphs and formulae calculating how many kilotons or megatons of warhead yield would be required to eliminate different targets in battle. These ranged from troops out in the open to enemy tank formations and atomic warhead dumps. His graphs, showing the estimated damage or radiation caused by the different missiles, enabled the West to work out the actual weight and yield of warheads which had been standardized to support the Red Army in battle.

But how reliable were these missiles, and how many of them were there? These had always been key questions for the Western alliance. They were of overriding importance to the White House as the Cuban missile crisis developed in the summer and autumn of 1962 and, with it, the awesome prospect of the first East-West nuclear duel. Here again, the material passed on by Penkovsky over the preceding fifteen months proved of supreme value. It was by no means all heartening reading. The documents he had photographed on new Soviet tactical cruise missiles showed, for example, that these were likely to prove very dangerous against pinpointed targets such as NATO's missile sites. The bulk of the information he had provided about the Soviet nuclear armory was, however, more reassuring.

To begin with, he had given an authoritative and up-to-date survey of the Soviet Union's stock of intercontinental ballistic missiles (ICBMs) for 1961, the year before the Cuban crisis. This was lower by several hundred than the American estimate, despite the fact that, at the same time, Penkovsky revealed the sites of dozens of ICBMs all over the Soviet Union which were unknown to Washington in an era when "look-down cover" from satellites was still undeveloped. So much for the strategic picture. Other material which he produced revealed certain weaknesses—logistical rather than technical—in the tactical missile system which would be employed to clear the ground for a Red Army offensive. The range of these weapons evidently far exceeded the ability of the troops on the ground to reconnoiter fresh targets for attack in any swiftly moving battle. Could television or guided course missiles with cameras be used to overcome the difficulty? This was a question the Russians were debating. Then there were the formidable problems of resupplying those short-range missile batteries with their warheads and delicate electronic gear along communication lines already jammed with ordinary reinforcement traffic. No solutions had yet been reached. Other top secret inspection reports revealed deficiencies in all Soviet liquid-fueled missiles, giving details of construction defects and listing the percentages of misfires and inaccuracies in targeting.

Now it is possible that Khrushchev had been bluffing from the very start of the Cuban missile affair. Arkady Shevchenko, the onetime under secretary-general at the United Nations and the most senior Soviet political figure ever to defect to the West,* has told the author that though Khrushchev had launched the crisis as a personal adventure (even sometimes bypassing the Presidium in his messages to President Kennedy), he never had the slightest intention of actually pressing the button, in Cuba or anywhere else.[1] But this, Shevchenko admitted, was hearsay evidence, collected much later. At the time, the White House had to reckon, and did reckon, with the possibility that the world might be faced with a nuclear exchange. Thus, either Khrushchev's nerve would have to be broken, if he were in deadly earnest; or, if he were not, then his bluff would have to be called and exposed. For either option, Penkovsky's authentic blueprint of the Soviet missile arsenal, both strategic and tactical, as it existed on the eve of the crisis, was a vital factor in American decision making.†

Yet his cardinal role in the Cuban affair must not be allowed to overshadow Penkovsky's huge intelligence contributions to the West in other fields which did not hit the headlines. In all,

---

*See chapter 14.

†So vital that the extravagant armchair theory has been aired that Penkovsky was in fact a pawn, advanced and controlled by the doves of the Kremlin to unmask Khrushchev as a mere blusterer. This is dealt with in the analysis which follows.

the colonel is known to have produced 110 cassettes with the Minox camera which he had been given and trained to use by British intelligence.[2] The British received 103 of them, mostly handed over in the West. The other seven, the last to be delivered, went straight to the Americans in Moscow in the summer of 1962. As his camera work was almost 100 percent successful and the cassettes averaged 50 exposures, this gave a grand total over the months of nearly 5,500 items.[3] It eventually provided the material for some 370 Western intelligence studies totaling 7,650 pages. All the assessments were made jointly. At peak periods, a special section of some twenty CIA staff was working in Washington on the Penkovsky gold seam, while about half that number of British officials were examining the material simultaneously in London.

Penkovsky's rare (and possibly unique) quality in the annals of twentieth-century espionage lay in this sheer mass, in the breadth, weight and continuity of the highly classified material he provided. A top-level "agent in place" (to give him his correct Western label) would normally only surface and deliver at intervals, thus rendering any overall judgment on his material very difficult to make. Penkovsky provided a steady and solid flood of information, collected over a period of more than two years, and backed up, during his visits abroad, by many hours of intensive personal interrogation by Western experts. All of the defense publications he photocopied and passed on were highly classified.

Four of the series—"Special Collection of Military Thoughts," "Information Bulletin of Missile Troops," "Artillery Information Collection" and "Information Collection of Missile Units and Artillery"—were not merely top secret in grade but were issued to "Special List personnel" only, meaning the top brass of the armed forces from major generals upward and the highest echelons of the Party. They contained, apart from sensitive technical information, details of the even more sensitive debate raging between the generals and the Party over Khrushchev's plan to recast the entire mold of Soviet military planning to take into account the nuclear age, with a cutback in conventional forces to be balanced against increased reliance on missiles. The impact of all this information must be weighed quite separately from the rapid upsurge and equally rapid subsidence of the Cuban crisis. It led, quite simply, to a complete rethinking of NATO's strategy and tactics. Even when the Soviet leaders learned that these secrets had been betrayed, they were powerless to change most of the long-term doctrines and production schedules, already set in train, which Penkovsky's information had exposed. It is not too much to say that, over a broad front of military planning, the policy of the Western alliance was to be shaped by Penkovsky's revelations for a decade to come.*

In some cases, for more than a decade; right down, in fact, to the present day. NATO's decision, made in the early 1960s, to prepare to face chemical warfare as a major weapon in any war with the Soviet Union stems directly, for example, from the chilling disclosures Penkovsky had produced. Some of these disclosures have already been published, such as his revelation that there was a special Seventh Directorate of the Soviet General Staff working on chemical and bacteriological weapons, with testing grounds and storage depots spread throughout the country.[4] But what really alarmed Western military experts in 1961–62 about Penkovsky's information was not the existence of a Soviet chemical warfare program (which they had taken for granted) but the massive scale of Red Army preparations to use these weapons in missile form in battle. Penkovsky had gone on to disclose that, in one recent exercise on a Soviet army front, the artillery and missile units of all formations had actually been issued *more* chemical than atomic warheads at the start of the maneuvers. Moreover, he had photographed, from the top secret "Information Collection of Missile Units," all the graphs and formulae for these weapons as well as the normal nuclear ones. The data showed the optimum height of burst for chemical warheads and the varying areas of contamination to be expected in different wind conditions, with the resulting esti-

---

*Early in 1964, for example, NATO's Military Committee drew up a new assessment of Soviet strategic (ICBM) missile redeployment, based largely on a study of Penkovsky's material.

mates of casualties which enemy troops would suffer. From this, NATO concluded not only that the Soviet Union had a chemical warfare agent, probably a mixture of two gases, which was at least as deadly as anything which its own secret arsenals possessed, but also that the Kremlin was prepared to make extensive use of it as a first-strike (not retaliatory) weapon. An overhaul of NATO's defensive measures and a rethinking about its own chemical warfare program followed. The insistence that the Soviet Union must agree to chemical weapons disarmament has lasted to this day.

There was a similar rethinking about the development and strategic use of Western armored forces. This resulted from what Penkovsky passed on, not only about the general philosophy of the Soviet General Staff but on the equipment they had available. He provided NATO with all the essential details of three new Red Army tanks of which Western intelligence had been totally unaware. One was an amphibious model which could "swim" right up to periscope depth.

Finally (for the list must be drawn to a close)* the colonel had lifted the lid, back in 1961, on Soviet plans for the military use of outer space. He passed on the texts of essays and staff papers written by the top brass of the Soviet armed forces in which projects such as global rockets, photoreconnaissance by orbiting satellites and the setting up of manned space military command posts were discussed. Obligingly, these papers also included Soviet estimates of what the Americans might be planning, and able to achieve, in these same fields. In this, Penkovsky helped to guide and propel the United States down those immense space trails which, twenty-five years later, led to President Ronald Reagan's Star Wars program.

Such was the vast and far-reaching impact of Penkovsky's information, and it seems proper to start with this survey since the historic importance of the man lies in what he revealed to the adversaries of his own motherland. But why did he do it?

---

*Among his more mundane, but nonetheless very valuable, offerings were the Soviet code designations used in signals traffic for hundreds of military items, the Red Army's complete order of battle, and the Kremlin telephone directory.

What prompted Colonel Penkovsky to betray the regime which had trained him in the Communist mold from boyhood onward and had promoted him to be one of its own elite? What drew him to the West, and how did he behave there? What picture of him was left behind in the minds and memoirs of the various British and American officials with whom he came into secret contact? Finally, how was that secret broken? When and by what methods did the KGB close in on what was probably the most serious military treachery they had ever had to face? It is time to look at Penkovsky not as a mine of information, but as a complex and, ultimately, a tragic human being. As we shall see, the picture which has been drawn of him—that of the honest soldier disgusted with the corruption and cynicism of the Communist regime and the idealist prepared to betray his country to save the world from a nuclear holocaust—is both incomplete and false.

He was born in the dawn of the Bolshevik era on April 23, 1919, in the Caucasian town of Ordzhonikidze. He came from an upper-middle-class professional family which had prospered in the service of the tsar. His grandfather, who died before the 1917 revolution, had been a judge at Stavropol. His great-uncle, Valentin Atonevich Penkovsky, not only survived the revolution but rose high in the Communist regime, ending up a lieutenant general in the Red Army. However, by far the most important member of the family from the point of view of Oleg's later career was the only one he never set eyes on: his own father, Vladimir Florianovich, an engineer by profession who disappeared in the Civil War maelstrom of 1919–21 while fighting as an officer in the royalist White Army.* This inconvenient fact had been hidden from the son, who was a four-month-old baby when the family separated. His father's past rose up from the archives to compromise him only when he was already in mid-career as an intelligence officer. There is an exact parallel here with, among others, the case of Yuri Rastvorov.†

---

*It was assumed that he had been killed in the fighting, though it is not impossible that he had escaped abroad.

†See pp. 80–81.

To begin with, young Penkovsky's military career was a model of Communist orthodoxy. He joined the army and the Komsomol youth movement in the same year, 1937, and became a Communist party member three years later. In the Great Patriotic War against Hitler, he served for four years as political officer to various units and also distinguished himself in battle. In 1943–44 he took over an artillery regiment in the First Ukrainian Army Front (which, according to him, made him the youngest field commander of his day). More important for his later life (and for his eventual services to the West), he also became a personal friend and protégé of his chief of artillery, the then Colonel General Varentsov. This crucial friendship was cemented by an impulsive act of kindness, perhaps mixed with a little calculation, on Penkovsky's part. In the summer of 1944, he visited his chief in a Moscow hospital, where the general was recovering from a broken hip sustained in a car accident at the front. Varentsov was worried about reports of a tragedy which had befallen his family, then living in Lvov, and asked his aide to investigate.

When Penkovsky arrived in Lvov, he found a tragedy indeed. The general's son-in-law, Major Loshak, who was Jewish, had been executed, together with two brother officers, for "stealing socialist property." His widow Nina (the general's daughter from his first marriage) found herself shunned by everyone in the hospital where she worked. Unable to bear this treatment, she had one day snatched out of its holster the pistol of a lieutenant passing her in the corridor and shot herself. Still, nobody wanted to help her, dead or alive, and no arrangements were being made for a proper burial. Penkovsky, who had arrived just in time, sold his watch, bought a coffin and a black dress for the dead woman and organized a decent funeral for her. When he reported all this to his chief on his return to Moscow, the general embraced him and declared, "You are now like my own son."[5] It was this "son" who, seventeen years later, was able to trade on their relationship by walking in and out of Marshal Varentsov's Missile Headquarters unchallenged with a Minox camera in his pocket.

All he was thinking about when the war ended, however, was

promotion within the system, not defection from it. His marriage, in 1945, to the seventeen-year-old Vera Dmitriyeva Gapanovich was prompted not only by the girl's good looks but by the fact that her father was a Red Army general with excellent Party contacts. (He rose to be a member of the Military Council and the chief political officer for the Moscow Military District.) For the first ten years of their marriage it looked as though Penkovsky was heading for similar heights. From 1945 to 1948, he was enrolled at the Frunze Military Academy and duly emerged with the coveted diamond-shaped insignia of a graduate pinned on his chest. In 1949, after twelve months spent in various staff jobs, he entered the Military Diplomatic Academy, which was the acknowledged training school for intelligence officers. On completion, he was posted, like most of the students, to Soviet Military Intelligence, the GRU. He had already been promoted to colonel during his first year at the academy. His future in the Communist world looked both assured and rosy.

It was he who ruined everything. In January of 1955,* he was assigned to Turkey as assistant military attaché and acting head of the local GRU network. For a year when the reins were in his hands, everything went smoothly. Then, in January of 1956, he ceased to be in charge of either office. Major General Savchenko, a sixty-year-old GRU veteran with previous service in Kabul, arrived in Ankara to take over both as military attaché and as GRU rezident. Penkovsky chafed at becoming a subordinate. He chafed even more at the crude personality and (to his eyes) even cruder operational methods of his newly acquired chief. The friction between the two men ended with Penkovsky committing an act of almost unbelievable professional folly: he sent an official cable of complaint to Moscow alleging that the general had violated his instructions. His own organization might conceivably have forgiven him in time had he kept the row within the family by using GRU channels. Instead, he

---

*He had spent the preceding eighteen months working in the Fourth Directorate of the GRU, which dealt with the Near East. A projected assignment to Pakistan collapsed when he was refused a visa.

manifoldly compounded his offense by using the network of the KGB, which was headed in Ankara by General Vavilov. This was a blunder of Himalayan proportions. His colleagues never forgave him for betraying this quarrel to their bitter intelligence rivals. For its part, the KGB, far from being grateful, instantly distrusted this officer who was prepared to tear up the rule book and attack his superior behind his back in order to satisfy some personal vendetta. Penkovsky was sent home in November of 1956, ostensibly on leave, but in reality in semi-disgrace.

He now entered into an ominous limbo. The GRU showed its displeasure by placing him on the reserve list. When he tried to break with intelligence altogether and rejoin the regular army, he found his path blocked there as well. It was only thanks to the efforts of his loyal patron Varentsov, now in charge of Ground Forces Artillery, that, as a temporary face-saver, he was enrolled in September 1958 at yet another prestigious institution, the Dzerzhinsky Academy, for a nine-month course on missiles. It was here, as an embittered forty-year-old student senior officer, seemingly barred from all operational duties (and therefore from promotion), that his betrayal of the regime began.

It is important to fix the starting point accurately. Versions so far published suggest that Penkovsky was already seeking out and finding Western intelligence contacts during his Ankara days. This he is said to have done by sitting alone in sidewalk cafés "not once but on many evenings," with a "faraway expression" on his face.[6] In fact, the GRU colonel did absolutely nothing in Ankara to mark himself down as a possible future defector. It was only in January 1961, under very different circumstances, that British intelligence began to take an interest in Penkovsky when a report, sent by the Canadian embassy in Moscow to their British colleagues there, eventually landed on the right London desk. Penkovsky's own account of his career, as given later on to his Western interrogators, confirms this basically passive version of his Ankara days. He did claim to have indulged in one or two private subversive activities during that period. He alleged, for example, that in 1956 he had made a number of anonymous telephone calls to Turkish intelligence concerning Soviet clandestine operations, as a result of which a Soviet colonel was expelled from the country. Whether this particular denunciation was for personal, professional or ideological motives was not made clear. At any rate, Western intelligence was in the dark about all this at the time. Throughout his twenty-two months in Ankara, Penkovsky did not make contact with any NATO power. He later alleged that he had contemplated approaching the American military attaché in Ankara in the autumn of 1956, when his own recall to Moscow was imminent, but could not get in touch because the American was away at the time. He had ruled out any approach to his British counterpart because he considered the British attaché to be "too stuffy."

The clear decision to work against the Soviet system by collaborating with the West only came during his course at the Dzerzhinsky Academy, which ended in May of 1959. It was at this point that he actually began to collect material for eventual handing over. He copied out, from secret manuals made available to him as a student, technical details on Soviet rockets and tactical missiles then in use with the Red Army, selecting material which he judged to be of particular interest to the West. But, as he later explained to his Western interrogators, he had immediately run into security problems as an embryonic spy. As the documents could not yet be passed on, how could they be concealed? Oleg Penkovsky's first batch of secrets for the West ended up being sewn into the lining of his clothes. He either hung them in the closet or literally carried them around with him for two years, before the chance at last came, in the spring of 1961, to hand them over. Even allowing for the bulkiness of Soviet men's suits at the time, it was a precarious expedient.

Between first preparing to spy against his country and actually being able to do something about it, there was thus a long period of delay. It was a time of successive frustrations during which Penkovsky's resentment against the regime steadily mounted and, with it, his resolve to get his own back. The matter of a canceled posting to India helped, more than anything else, to spur him along his Westward course.

When he returned to GRU headquarters after his missile course, the skies had seemed suddenly to lighten. He was told he would be posted to New Delhi as military attaché and, of course, head of GRU operations throughout India. This meant an operational role again at last, and one which probably carried promotion. Whether the good news caused him to suspend his thoughts of betrayal or whether he now began planning his approach to the West from a nonaligned capital is not clear. What is clear is that it was the KGB, who had the ultimate say in clearance for foreign postings, who vetoed the assignment. They had been digging away into his background ever since that disastrous fiasco in Ankara and had now unearthed the file on Vladimir Florianovich Penkovsky, onetime lieutenant in the White Army. Why, he was now asked by his personnel chief, Major General Shumsky, had he never declared the truth about his father on any of the dozens of forms he had filled in over the years about his background? Penkovsky produced a statement from his mother describing the turbulent events of 1919 and the family's ignorance of what had befallen her husband. This explanation was noted and filed away, but with it were placed back on the shelf any hopes of a worthwhile career. It was the disappearance of his father which worried the interrogators most. The possibility that Penkovsky senior might still be alive as an émigré in the West was, for the KGB, the blackest of all black question marks in his family dossier. Add to that the blunder entered in his personal file from Turkey, and the stairway to the top was barred for good.

Penkovsky was made to feel this more and more in the months which followed. After another spell on the reserve list, he was again given a desk in the GRU's Near East directorate at the end of February 1960. In June of that year, he was assigned to training duties, first as a member of the selection board for the Military and Diplomatic Academy and then as designated head of the incoming class for the 1960–63 course. For a moment, things looked somewhat brighter again: a top instructor's post normally carried with it a major general's rank. The KGB intervened once more. In August he was told that the senior appointment was no longer his. He was offered instead a job as plain instructor (one of seven) at the academy or a transfer to the information directorate. Either option implied a step sideways, if not a step downward. He refused both offers and returned again to the GRU reserves.

It was a very bitter Colonel Penkovsky who, in November of 1960, was posted to work with a group of fifty-eight GRU officers attached to the various overt Soviet organizations which dealt with Western countries. His particular assignment was the State Committee for Science and Technology, later renamed the State Committee for the Coordination of Scientific-Technical Matters for the Soviet Council of Ministers. Whatever the resounding title of the organization, the job itself was not prestigious. It had, however, one supreme attraction for the man now determined at all costs to desert and sabotage his own regime: it offered both bona fide travel abroad and the chance to meet officially with Western representatives in the Soviet Union. Indeed, one of Penkovsky's first duties in his new post was to receive, in Moscow, a delegation of British industrialists. It was headed by Greville Wynne, an engineer from Shropshire who conducted an import-export enterprise specializing in the sale of heavy industrial products to the Soviet bloc.

A lot of misapprehensions need undoing about Wynne and his relationship with the Russian colonel who was now set to become one of the master spies of the century. Some of them arose out of the account—understandably subjective—which Wynne himself gave of the affair. They have been compounded in a recent wide-ranging treatise on espionage[7] dedicated to the proposition that the role of spies throughout history has been greatly exaggerated, that of Colonel Penkovsky very much included. Versions such as these not only distort the role of the major figures in the East-West espionage struggle, but also the parts played by lesser figures who operated in their wake.

Thus, although during the November 1960 visit Wynne made contact with the Foreign Department of Penkovsky's committee, which was chaired by one Dzherman Mikhailovich Gvishiani, at this stage he had absolutely no brief to cultivate Penkovsky, with whom, to begin with, he had only official commercial dealings. (It later transpired that the colonel had in fact made approaches to two other members of the British delegation, approaches of which Wynne was unaware.) However, Wynne's potential importance had already been noted. His travels behind the Iron Curtain as a businessman had certainly been marked down and encouraged by British intelligence as being of possible future use, but he had not been brought into play yet as a conduit. The link was established on Wynne's subsequent visit to Moscow in April of 1961 (to find out why a reciprocal Soviet trade visit to London, scheduled for the beginning of that year, had still not materialized); and it was set up in topsy-turvy fashion. It was not Wynne, acting as a recruiting officer for London, who approached Penkovsky. It was the restless colonel, still seeking his coveted opening to the West, who approached the businessman, wrongly convinced that he was a full-fledged member of British intelligence moving under commercial camouflage.

That the colonel had by now got so restless was understandable. It is not true that, in Moscow, he "haunted diplomatic functions, cornered CIA, SIS* and military officers and breathlessly offered them his knowledge of Soviet plans for the Middle East."[8] He made only one approach to a Western mission, a melodramatic plunge which seemingly led to nothing but, in the end, led to everything. In the first days of January 1961, at an encounter with the commercial attaché at the Canadian embassy, he baldly handed over, as a "first installment" of what he could produce for the West, the documents from the Dzerzhinsky missile course, which he had been concealing for more than eighteen months. Those papers were not, as has been written, forwarded to Western capitals, to be examined there with excitement and anticipation of more to come. Far from it. The hapless commercial attaché, out of his depth in such a situation, accepted the package, carried it around with him for twenty-four hours but then, at another official reception the following

*MI6.

day, actually handed it back to the flabbergasted colonel. The
Canadian had not opened the envelope, nor given it to any of
his political or intelligence colleagues to examine. There can be
few parallels for such naïveté.

Penkovsky's feelings can be imagined: was there *nobody* in
NATO prepared to look at his treasures? This was, in fact, his
fourth attempt to make contact. The first, made the previous
August, had been to American students studying in Moscow,*
and had led to nothing. The two approaches to British scientists
in Wynne's delegation the following November had been
equally fruitless. Now, a Canadian diplomat was actually rejecting his precious wares. However, this apparent dead end was
to bring him fairly swiftly to his destination at last. The commercial attaché, who had been too scared to do anything at the
time, afterward became doubly scared that he had failed to act.
He told his own ambassador about the episode and the Canadian embassy, which was not equipped to handle a problem of
this magnitude, informed the Americans and the British. What
now followed was typical of the peculiar relationship, cordially
entwined yet coolly separated, between these two major Western intelligence services.

When, in January 1961, the British approached their "cousins"
over this extraordinary Canadian lead, they were asked, for the
time being, to hold off, as the CIA was already preparing to
launch its own agent to contact Penkovsky in Moscow. This it
did, and British intelligence, which had not been aware of Penkovsky's first approach to the American students, kept purely
a watching brief while their colleagues made their approach in
February. There was a mix-up over communications and the
CIA's move proved abortive. Still, the British side, having by
now learned that Penkovsky was due to visit London in April,
made no move whatsoever in Moscow, and persuaded the
Americans to refrain as well.

---

*This timing disposes, incidentally, of another canard concerning the Penkovsky case,
namely that one of its aims was to secure a British agent (Wynne) for a trade-off with the
Soviet spy Conon Molody ("Gordon Lonsdale"). Though this exchange ultimately took
place, on April 22, 1964, the Russians could not possibly have known that Lonsdale might
be arrested in London when Penkovsky was making his first moves to the West.

There was thus at this time no perusal of Penkovsky's material by "Ministry of Defence experts in the SIS" (because nothing was yet in London); no top-level requests for more, overriding so-called American reservations about Penkovsky; no "summary of Penkovsky's first offerings" being sent to the CIA; and no appointment of Wynne as official go-between.[9] (There were three months to go before Penkovsky himself recruited the Englishman.) There is even some confusion as to how Penkovsky's first precious package of missile secrets reached London in April of 1961, when the colonel arrived with the Soviet delegation. In his account, Wynne states that he brought the material over himself.[10]

There are two points where all accounts, imaginative or authoritative, of what followed are in agreement. The first is the phenomenal energy which Penkovsky now displayed; the second is the chameleonlike facility with which he flitted from role to role in his trips to the West. Penkovsky had to wear three different masks and lead three different existences on these occasions. The first was the formal one of a GRU officer attached to the State Committee for Science and Technology, in which capacity he acted as the general supervisor of the delegates, whose finances were under his control. This involved a great deal of administrative work and still more demands both on his time and on his capacity for playacting at the frequent representative functions. But as he was also a senior GRU officer (even if a professionally frustrated one), his own colleagues at the residency in London looked to him to do a bit of spying on their behalf while he was moving about so freely.* (The British helped to oblige by providing Penkovsky with some pictures of guided-missile sites and military installations which he could plausibly claim to have taken himself on his travels around the country.) Finally, of course, there was the secret life he had just embarked upon, that of a top-level agent for Western intelligence.

---

*The counselor at the Soviet embassy in London, Anatoly Pavlov, who was the committee's representative in Britain and who had arranged the delegation's visit, was himself a colonel in the GRU. The delegation went to factories in Wolverhampton, Sheffield, Leeds, Manchester and Slough as well as London.

This third existence may be said to have been launched at 11 P.M. on April 20, 1961, at the Mount Royal Hotel near Marble Arch in London, where the Soviet party was being put up. Penkovsky had slipped away at the end of the first day's engagements and, instead of retiring to his bed, went up to a specially reserved suite for his first encounter with Western intelligence. This session, and the ones which followed, usually lasted until well into the small hours. The colonel was left with very little chance of sleep before resuming the daily round with his delegation the following morning.

It had already been agreed between London and Washington that the exploitation of Penkovsky in Britain should be on a fifty-fifty basis. Thus it was that he found himself in the company of two SIS case officers and two of their colleagues from the CIA. No names were ever used, though Moscow later invented "Grille" and "Miles" for the British pair and "Alexander" and "Oslaf" for the Americans.[11] Greville Wynne, already very useful as Penkovsky's chosen contact man (and destined, unhappily for him, to become steadily more valuable as a communications link), never met any of those case officers and himself took no part whatsoever in the debriefings, which were professional matters above his head. His story, repeated in several other books, that at one point during that week Penkovsky was also greeted in that hotel room by twenty Soviet defectors "who had been flown from all over the United States and Britain"[12] just to convince the colonel that they were not dead but alive and well in the West and happy to welcome him to the fold, strains credulity.

The truth is that at no point did Penkovsky need the slightest inducement to work as an "agent in place" for the West— something he had been yearning for and preparing to do for two years past, as he himself had promptly shown. At only the second midnight session in the Mount Royal, he, at his own request, signed a solemn "Oath of Allegiance" which his Western hosts drafted for him. In this curious document, the colonel swore his services to the British and American governments and undertook to work on their behalf inside the Soviet Union for as long as they required. In return, he requested that, if need be, he and his family be given political asylum in one of these countries, with "appropriate status" for himself. Henceforth, he declared at the end of the document, he was "a soldier of the free world fighting against Soviet tyranny."

At the end of that first London visit, which lasted until May 6, he departed for Moscow with a Minox camera and a one-way transistor radio receiver concealed, among other tools of the spy trade, in his luggage. He had been given a lightning course in their use and, as regards the camera, told in broad terms the sort of material it ought to focus upon. Penkovsky was to prove a gluttonous and indiscriminating magpie when it came to stealing Soviet secrets. These more or less random methods scarcely mattered because practically everything his camera focused on was, by its nature, of the highest security grades. It was not, incidentally, in the central Registry that he copied the masses of GRU documents but in its secret library. As an active army officer, he was required anyway to keep himself up-to-date with military thinking so, initially at any rate, his assiduous "study sessions" aroused no suspicions.

As a photographer of precious documents he was, as already indicated, a 99 percent success. The only problems for the West, over the sixteen exhilarating months of his espionage career which now followed, were how to restrain and control him, in both his professional and private life. One of his big handicaps on the professional side was that he could add little or nothing by way of personal elucidation to the hive of material he provided. Though a gunner by training (and one who had passed a missile course) he did not have a keen technical brain. Indeed, he had little idea of the enormous significance of the photographs he was handing over because he had never paused—perhaps understandably—to read the originals. As for his political judgments on events in the Kremlin, these soon came to be regarded as very uncertain. It is also worth recording that he did *not* rant on about Khrushchev as a threat to world peace, despite all that has been written on this. He never conveyed any sense of obsession about the Soviet leader's volatility and never expressed strong sentiments against him.

Penkovsky himself was, however, highly volatile, and here

we come to the second difficulty which periodically confronted his Western case officers, namely, how to cope with a sort of Walter Mitty complex in the man. He flabbergasted them on one early occasion, for example, by proposing that he might walk into the Soviet Defense Ministry in Moscow with a miniature atomic bomb in his pocket and blow the building and himself to smithereens. It was firmly pointed out that the West had altogether different ideas about the proper role of agent "Yoga."*

His tendency to fantasize accompanied and boosted his considerable vanity. Thus he told his private "confidant" Wynne that he had been received in Britain by the Queen, and this episode, entirely fictional, was later to figure in a television film about him. In fact, the closest Colonel Penkovsky got to royal preserves was a drive through Richmond Park, which probably gave him the idea for his daydream. Once he did, in fact, ask to see the Queen. She was, however, conveniently absent on a state visit to Rome at the time of his request, which was warded off without offense. All the time, he had to appear supremely important to himself, as well as to his case officers, who needed no persuading. Though this could lead to complications at times, such vanity was also of value to the West. He loved to have the pictures he had brought out of Moscow laid out for his inspection, and gloated over them. This helped to spur him on to even greater efforts with his Minox. He was determined, he told his Western hosts, that the name of Oleg Penkovsky go down as that of the greatest spy in history. This was the obsession which helped to drive him forward into ever greater danger.

Then there was his private life. His extravagance with the State Committee funds he controlled, amply supplemented by his British recompenses, was more that of a tsarist grand duke on holiday on the Riviera than a Soviet colonel on business in London. Though it constantly drew unwelcome attention to

---

*This was one of Penkovsky's official code names. Several were used in order to protect his identity from the great variety of "customers" who saw different parts of his information. "Alex" was an unofficial nickname.

him, it could not be curbed. He would throw 5-pound notes at London taxi drivers for tips, and worse followed when he went on shopping expeditions. These were primarily intended to buy up Western luxuries which he had been commissioned to take back to various higher-ups in Moscow, including General Serov, the head of the KGB, and his wife.* Penkovsky could not resist acting as though these sprees were purely personal indulgences. On one occasion in Harrods, for example, where he was purchasing perfume (the inevitable Chanel No. 5) for Madame Serova, he bought several extra bottles and presented one with a flourish to every girl on the counter staff.

His womanizing, which could only be described as ferocious, could be a problem in itself. Here again, vanity and a certain fantasy element entered into the picture. The grand duke throwing money around behaved like an Ottoman sultan when it came to women. It was clearly advisable for his hosts to steer all this lava along secure channels. These were sometimes too sedate for the amorous colonel. On one occasion, he came up with the imperious demand that he wanted only the services of virgins under eighteen. Every effort was made to accommodate him, at least as regards age.

Penkovsky made his second visit to London in midsummer of 1961. He arrived on July 18—this time to supervise a delegation of technical experts attending the opening of the Soviet Industrial Exhibition—and remained until August 10. During this long spell, he was able to remain for much longer in the capital itself, where he was put up with his delegates at the Kensington Close Hotel and was therefore able to spend much more time with the same quartet of British and American interrogators, who received him at a safe house in Old Brompton Road. His triple life continued as busily as before. Each day, he administered from the Soviet embassy the official program of the delegates. In another room of the embassy, he would hand over to

---

*At one time, Serov's daughter was on a trip to London during Penkovsky's stay and, at the general's request, he kept a friendly eye on her and took her out to restaurants and nightclubs—all at the British taxpayer's expense.

Colonel Pavlov such tidbits of military intelligence as had been specially provided by his hosts for the purpose.* At intervals, he continued his shopping expeditions for all his special Moscow customers.

Most important of all, his secret training as a Western spy made huge strides, for he was sometimes able to spend as much as ten nocturnal hours at a stretch in the South Kensington safe house. He had brought over with him another consignment of Minox cassettes, which he handed over to Wynne in a quick visit to the Englishman's house, and he was now briefed on further requirements and new communication procedures in Moscow. The most important and, as things turned out, the most fateful of them was a meeting to familiarize himself with Mrs. Janet Anne Chisholm, the wife of Roderick Chisholm, a second secretary at the British embassy who had been made Penkovsky's local case officer. She was to be the so-called brush contact, to be bumped into accidentally either at embassy receptions or during her innocent-looking strolls with her young family in Moscow's parks and gardens. For these outdoor occasions, a little box, seemingly containing candy for the children, had been designed instead to hold exactly four cassettes. This, plus a replacement camera, was handed to him later that summer in Moscow by the ubiquitous Wynne, who had now become a most valuable communications channel.

What was to prove Penkovsky's last visit to the West took place in Paris two months later. Again, he came as GRU controller of another Soviet trade delegation to another Soviet Industrial Fair. Again, the colonel brought with him another consignment of precious cassettes, this time fifteen rolls of film containing more than seven hundred copies of top secret documents; again, it was Wynne who took delivery at the airport, Le Bourget, where Penkovsky arrived on September 20. Again, there were long discussions and training sessions held at secret

---

*These were being received with enthusiasm in Moscow, where the GRU's opinion of their erratic officer moved, very temporarily, upward. Penkovsky also earned some valuable Party points by complaining to Comrade Khrushchev that the grave of Karl Marx in Highgate Cemetery was in a disgraceful state of disrepair. Remedial action was ordered instantly from Moscow.

locations with his by now familiar Anglo-American quartet, with Janet Chisholm herself present on one occasion. In particular, the CIA drilled him in a series of "dead drops" to be used in Moscow, a system which was to end in disaster all around.

This visit lasted for four weeks, giving the colonel plenty of time in his leisure hours to sample the culinary delights of Paris restaurants and the titillating joys of Paris cabarets and nightclubs. They combined to strengthen Oleg Penkovsky's conviction that, whatever the Kremlin might, or might not, be up to back home, the West was the place for a man like him. If only, he was heard to sigh more than once, Moscow had anything to compare with all this.

On October 16, the joyride was over and he was obliged to return to Moscow. But before he could leave, something disquieting happened at the airport. There was fog at Le Bourget and the Aeroflot flight was delayed. Was this a hint from whatever patron saint spies may possess that he ought to stay where he was? He seems to have considered it for a moment. Then overconfidence, the sense of so much still to be achieved, and that determination, in achieving it, to become the greatest spy of all time, propelled him through the customs barrier. He was never to tread on Western soil again, and, before long, never to move safely again on his native soil.

10

Penkovsky—Downfall

THE REAL-LIFE story of how the KGB came to suspect, shadow and finally to pounce on the colonel is a complex tale. Penkovsky himself provided the West with one or two bits of the jigsaw before he was rounded up; so, afterward and less consistently, did Greville Wynne. Other pieces are still missing and may well never be filled in. What follows, however, is the fullest reliable account so far available. It is made up of various sequences reconstructed by Western experts after the events. These, in turn, rely partly on accounts given over the past twenty-five years by Soviet intelligence defectors who had access to inside information in Moscow after the scandal broke. The author has taken the opportunity of talks with several of these same defectors to make his own inquiries about the whole Penkovsky affair.

Though nobody knew it then, the first remote threat to his position loomed up in October 1961, the month of his return from Paris. Defectors to the West from East European states have reported that, at this time, Soviet military intelligence officials were asking their counterparts in the Warsaw Pact countries to carry out extra security checks inside their own services. A major leak of information to the West was already suspected in Moscow, but with no indication whatsoever about its origin: could the source be hidden away in one of the satellite armies? (A year later, the Russians had to admit to their allies that it was they who had been harboring the guilty man.)

Penkovsky himself only began to smell what might prove to be a KGB rat early the following year—to be precise, on January 5, 1962, when he was enacting one of his elaborately casual encounters in a Moscow lane with Janet Chisholm, to pass on more film. A small car, which had violated traffic regulations to enter the lane, drove slowly past them. A fortnight later, the same small brown sedan, registration number SHA61–45, appeared again at the same rendezvous. This was disturbing. Penkovsky had carried out his first successful handover to Mrs. Chisholm (the box of "candy") the previous September, before leaving for Paris. Since his return, there had been frequent staged encounters in Moscow with her and other Western agents, and all had passed off smoothly. Moreover, in November and December, he had been granted a month's holiday with his wife in the best resorts of the Caucasus and the Black Sea, normally a sign of full official favor. What had gone wrong?

It was now believed that the KGB was led to Penkovsky by pure coincidence. A so-called blanket surveillance program had been launched by them in the New Year to watch over the movements of all Western diplomats in Moscow and their families, and to pinpoint any strange patterns of behavior. There was seemingly no particular target in mind for this massive security offensive, which was a follow-up to a mildly successful one operated before. But, by January 12, an unlikely but still possible target in the shape of GRU Colonel Penkovsky had presented itself. It so happened that Western brush contacts of the type he was conducting were just what the KGB was particularly looking out for. They had been told all about this technique by their own Lieutenant Colonel Peter Popov, a GRU colleague of Penkovsky's who had offered his services to the CIA in Vienna as far back as 1953 and had spied for them for six years before being caught and arrested with his American case officer on a Moscow bus on October 16, 1959. Between arrest and execution, the luckless Popov had been forced, under savage torture, to reveal all he had learned about the latest in Western

espionage techniques, including "brush contact" methods.
These January encounters of Colonel Penkovsky's seemed exactly to fit the pattern. Yet he was, after all, a senior GRU man,
an officer from the rival organization. Special Party, possibly
even Politburo, approval would be required before launching
an operation against him. Clearance was sought and given and,
for the next nine months, a steadily intensified program of
surveillance was mounted to trap, not simply the colonel, but
all his Western controllers and contacts, as well as other Soviet
traitors assumed for certain to be in the spy ring. (The KGB
refused to believe that he could be acting entirely on his own;
until the end, they remained obsessed with the idea of a major
conspiracy against the state.)

By midsummer, Penkovsky knew from other signs that the
KGB was sharpening its knives against him. Three successive
applications of his to visit the West are known to have been
blocked or refused. In April 1962, he applied through the U.S.
embassy in Moscow for a visa to visit the World's Fair in Seat-
tle. The visa was, of course, promptly issued but the KGB
prevented him from going on the grounds that the Americans
might recognize and identify him as a GRU officer from his
Ankara days. In May, he applied for and received a visa to
Brazil. Again, the trip was vetoed by the KGB, whose formal
permission was necessary for any journey by a Soviet official
abroad. In July, he made a third attempt, this time via his
British friends. He requested and was issued a visa to go to
Cyprus but the KGB stepped in once more and he never turned
up to collect it.

By now, understandably, he was rattled. His Western friends
had already been obliged to switch from open-air meetings to
"dead letter boxes" or handovers on visits to Western embassies
or houses. (One of the most ingenious methods devised for the
latter channel by the British, but never put into use, was a tin
of Harpic lavatory cleanser with a false bottom designed to hold
his Minox cassettes. It was produced as a prime specimen of
evidence at his trial.)

As for Wynne, contrary to what that unfortunate gentleman

thought then and wrote in good faith afterward, it has emerged that the KGB had no suspicions of him at the time. They continued to regard him as a possible recruit rather than as Penkovsky's regular helpmate in espionage. Indeed, it seems likely that the Russians only extracted the full truth about Wynne from the lips of Penkovsky himself. It was the colonel, not his English businessman friend, who was the target of the heavy surveillance Wynne noticed when the pair met for the last time at Moscow's Peking restaurant in early July.

Though Penkovsky's nerves were on edge, he was still in control of himself. He always used his special GRU pass to see Wynne through the controls at Moscow airport, and did the same the following morning. Wynne's own account has the colonel handing over to him another bulky envelope of documents when the flight was called, and also urging him to impress on London the danger he was now in, and the need to organize immediate rescue measures.[1] However, Penkovsky struck a more solid note in the messages he was passing, with other documents, to his Western case officers (the British persevered to the end with handovers at official receptions, where, if things went wrong, nobody could be arrested on the spot). He told them, for example, that he was planning to take a holiday toward the end of September, so there would probably be a break in contact around that time. He also assured them that he was determined to "have it out" with the KGB for cramping his style over travel abroad. No panic yet.

In the event, it was the KGB which had it out with him over the next three months. There was an operational encounter with the CIA in August and a final brush contact on September 5. On September 6, 1962, Penkovsky was seen for the last time by the West. The occasion was a film show at the British embassy. No handover of material took place; none had been planned. His presence had been prearranged so that he and his newly appointed case officer could take a good look at one another. There was no alarm in the Western camp when the rest of September and early October passed with no sign of life from the colonel; he was presumed to be on his holiday. As October dragged on, however, and there was still no contact, anxiety mounted. The uncertainty ended with a rude series of shocks on November 2.

Penkovsky had been given two Moscow numbers to ring for emergency "silent calls"—just to dial and replace the receiver without speaking when an answer came. The Moscow apartment of his new case officer was, obviously, not one of these two numbers. Yet that was the phone which now rang and it was unmistakably Oleg Penkovsky's voice on the line. What he said was just as suspicious as what he had done. To begin with, he asked for his new case officer by his proper name. Then he continued: "You know me. You are my friend. It's essential that we should meet straightaway, outside Moscow Circus."

Everything about this call was wrong, a wild aberration from the security codes laid down by the British. His case officer could only reply that he had not the slightest idea who the caller was and then put down the phone. Clearly, Penkovsky had either gone off the rails with fright or else he was now in KGB hands, and acting under KGB control. Other happenings that same day confirmed the more sinister explanation.

The "marker" agreed upon with his American controllers (a black stripe on the thirty-fifth lamppost along the Kutuzovsky Prospect) had appeared, to indicate there was material to collect in the designated dead letter drops. When the CIA agents hurried there, they walked straight into the hands of the KGB.

Finally came the news, also on that same day, that Greville Wynne had been arrested in Budapest, where he had gone with his new mobile exhibition caravans. This was a trip which Wynne wanted to do himself. Obviously, a journey behind the Iron Curtain at this juncture by anyone connected with the Penkovsky operation was not without its hazards, for all the satellite intelligence organizations worked under the thumb of Moscow. British intelligence had been informed of Wynne's journey and had expressed some misgivings. On balance, however, it had been thought he would be safe in Budapest, where the Russians would be unlikely to strike at him.

That proved a miscalculation. Within hours, the hapless Wynne was whisked off to Moscow and incarcerated in the

Lubianka Prison for interrogation. What had happened between the film show at the British embassy on September 6 and
Penkovsky's phone call to his British controller on November
2? The following sequence of events is, once again, based on
Western reconstructions, relying partly on accounts provided
by later Soviet intelligence defectors.[2]

By midsummer of 1962, KGB surveillance of Penkovsky's
Moscow apartment had begun. It was a long and elaborate
process which started with special cameras which could "bend"
at all angles operating from windows and balconies in the
houses opposite. This showed little more than the colonel writing at his desk and opening and closing various drawers. In
stage two, designed to get a closer outside look at what he was
up to, the flat above his was evacuated (the bemused family
being simply packed off for an indefinite holiday) and an all-
around camera "eye" inserted in the ceiling. This revealed
much more in the way of furtive activities, so that the next
problem which arose was how to get into the flat and search it,
still without alarming the suspected traitor.

It was solved by the dirty tricks department of the KGB,
which supplied a most unusual wax which was to be smeared
lightly on the seat of his desk chair at the State Committee's
offices. The wax was unusual in that it contained a highly corro-
sive substance which, once melted by body heat, worked
through the victim's clothes and turned the whole of his back-
side into a burning sore. By midday, the colonel was duly
removed in agony to a hospital, where the doctors, briefed by
the secret police, insisted that he remain for a few days. His wife
was then kept out of the way by less drastic methods and the
flat was raided and searched. Cameras, cassettes, codebooks,
cipher pads, one-way receivers and most of the other standard
apparatus of espionage were duly unearthed from their various
hiding places and put back. We are now in September. The
KGB had its proof but held back from striking, still convinced
that Penkovsky, if left at large a little longer, would lead them
to a broad ring of traitors.

What made up the hunters' minds for them was a scene which
the overhead camera eye recorded sometime after their secret

raid. It showed Penkovsky taking from a concealed drawer in his desk, which they had missed,* a perfect-looking Soviet passport, with all the official trappings. More ominously, the camera showed that the passport carried his picture but not his name. This could only be an expert Western forgery prepared for his getaway. Moreover, from the way he was fingering it, and apparently filling a name into the blank space, it seemed as though he might well be about to use it. The KGB now had no choice but to seize him at once. The actual arrest, though only known to the West on November 2, is thought to have been carried out at least a week, and possibly a fortnight, before.

The regime thus had at least six months to prepare Penkovsky and Wynne for the roles they were to play at their four-day show trial the following May. Wynne, despite the rough treatment he endured at times, did not cut as abject a figure of apology in court as the prosecutors might have wished. Nonetheless, his case was simple enough to project: he was the honest patriotic businessman suborned by a wicked British intelligence and turned into a willing instrument of their dirty trade. If the pejoratives are left out, this verdict is not very wide of the mark.†

Penkovsky himself, however, who had been driven to confess and comply by the severest torture, still presented enormous problems of stage management. To begin with, the fact that the traitor was a senior member of the GRU had to be hushed up. He was presented as a once-distinguished officer "long since discharged from the army" who had betrayed the trust placed in him as deputy head of the State Committee for Science and Technology. His fall from government grace and his motives for opting out of the system also had to be elaborately distorted. He was described variously as a careerist, a greedy egotist, a

---

*The evidence produced at Penkovsky's trial was doctored to conceal the slipup; the prosecution statement alleged that the forged passport had been found, together with the other incriminating material, by the KGB search party.

†Wynne was duly sentenced to eight years' imprisonment, but after only eleven months he was released on April 22, 1964, and exchanged at the Berlin checkpoint for the Soviet master spy "Gordon Lonsdale," who had been caught in London.

degenerate who had sunk first into moral depravity and then into treachery. As evidence for the depravity, which the accused had been rehearsed to admit in the dock himself, witnesses were produced stating that he had been observed drinking wine out of the slippers of his mistresses, one of the many disgusting habits he had learned in the nightclubs of London and Paris.

But the biggest problem was how to explain the enormity of his crimes. These had to be massive to justify the foam of official wrath welling all over the courtroom, as well as the death sentence which would inevitably be pronounced. Yet that meant admitting to an equally massive lapse of Soviet security and a comparable degree of damage to the state. The trial's stage managers never squared this circle. At one point, he was accused of passing literally thousands of military, political and economic secrets to the West. Yet, after the trial, the chief prosecutor, Lieutenant General A. G. Gorny, felt obliged to play all this down in an official statement. Penkovsky, he said, had only passed on "some technical reports of Soviet specialists who had gone abroad and some scattered data of a military nature that he had pumped out of loose-tongued friends and had taken from classified publications."[3]

A similar struggle against the truth, it must be admitted, has been conducted over the years by Western writers. This would seem the point at which to put the record straight. One version of the Penkovsky case has it that the colonel was eventually "turned" by the KGB and used to feed bogus information to the West. Yet, as has been shown, what Penkovsky provided from first to last was one long stream of top secret documents. Their high quality hardly varied throughout. None of these documents, either on examination at the time or on reevaluation in the years which followed, was held to be anything but authentic and the last batch of such material he handed over was found to be as genuine as the first.

A more ambitious attempt to turn reality upside down is the recent theory that Penkovsky was a KGB plant from the outset. It is suggested that the colonel was merely a pawn advanced by a Kremlin faction opposed to Khrushchev's policies. According to this scenario, his orders were to convince the West that they could safely call Khrushchev's bluff in any showdown because the Soviet nuclear armory which he controlled was in fact too weak to win in an all-out missile exchange. The theory can only be supported by highlighting what Penkovsky told the West about certain deficiencies in Soviet missiles, by ignoring the rest of his nuclear and space warfare information and by dismissing all the rest of his intelligence as trivia. "Western intelligence experts," one recent pronouncement read, "now find it difficult to identify any single piece of military information that Penkovsky brought which proved to be of major value."[4] This statement only needs comparing with the list of Penkovsky's offerings, as set out above, to be reduced to size. The truth is that the NATO alliance still accepts today what it accepted in 1961–62: the colonel's information was so startlingly new, on the conventional as well as the nuclear fronts, as to merit a fundamental rethinking of Western military philosophy.

Nor does the pawn theory stand up when related to the person of Penkovsky himself. It has been demonstrated that his decision to spy for the West stemmed mainly from professional frustration and that he had started collecting his material as early as the spring of 1959, long before he first made contact with Western intelligence. Above all, he would have been the worst possible person for anyone to have selected for the crucially delicate role of a Kremlin pawn. Ever since his Ankara gaffe, he had been regarded as something of an unreliable wild card by both the KGB and the GRU; and the former organization, once onto him, had blocked, not encouraged, every attempt he made to get to the West.

The pawn theory, which may look seductive from an armchair, also flouts everything we know in real life about the Soviet paranoia over secrecy. Soviet defectors who specialized in disinformation have testified to the extreme reluctance of Moscow Center to release even scraps of classified information for them to feed, in suitably modified form, to the West. The unstable GRU colonel had his head full of secrets before he clicked his Minox camera once. To turn him loose and trust him to keep that information to himself would have run straight against all the hardened grain of Communist wood.

The same argument of security obsession would apply fortissimo against the release of thousands of top secret documents on Soviet nuclear and conventional warfare, as well as the most damaging disclosures about the Soviet intelligence services themselves. The information provided by Penkovsky on the purely professional front is known to have led to the identification of more than six hundred Soviet intelligence officers, all but fifty of them in his own GRU.* He also brought over six bulky GRU treatises on various undercover techniques, including criticisms of shortcomings in this fieldwork and many smaller gems of information such as the internal layout of the Soviet embassies in London and Paris. It is hard to conceive that anything could have justified to anyone in the Kremlin the throwing away of this huge and varied hoard of secrets.

But, it is suggested, this enormous risk and this whole desperate adventure could have been undertaken in 1961–62 because of the importance of Cuba in Soviet strategy and the eventual threat of the missile crisis itself (unknown, incidentally, when the colonel made his first moves to the West). Moreover, the stratagem could be launched because such a powerful ring of Khrushchev's opponents was behind the conspiracy. The simple answer to this theory is that if any Kremlin clique had been able in 1961–62 to hatch such a plot, open up all the archives of the GRU and the Missile Headquarters to the colonel (needing the connivance of most of the top brass of the armed forces and the intelligence community), and then control the entire operation unchallenged and untroubled for nearly two years, right down to selecting the ideal time to announce the arrest of their pawn (the height of the missile affair), then this ring of united and powerful manipulators would not have been a Kremlin

*The major overhaul of the GRU, following directly on the Penkovsky affair, also brought about the fall of its boss, General Serov, known to be the colonel's friend. Serov's replacement in 1962, General Petr Ivanovich Ivashutin, is thought to have filled that post until 1987.

clique. They would have been the government of the Soviet Union itself. Given the monolithic nature of a police state, no other construction is possible.

It ought also to be recorded that no Soviet intelligence defector (with one bizarre exception, whose case is discussed in the following chapter) has ever crossed to the West who doubts the reality of Penkovsky's treachery, or his fate. The pawn theory would, presumably, have him, not executed, but living in privileged comfort somewhere in the Soviet Union.

There is, finally, one specifically British aspect to the Penkovsky affair. If it is accepted, on the arguments and the evidence set out above, that Oleg Penkovsky was not a Soviet plant, it must follow, as night must follow day, that Roger Hollis, the then head of MI5, was not a Soviet agent. Any spy operating at that level would obviously go to extreme lengths to protect his identity, even if it meant sacrificing many intelligence assets, as well as many colleagues, in the process. But when Sir Roger became one of the handful of people* in London who, early in 1961, were told Penkovsky's real name and function as well as his code name, when he then read in the following months the flood of Soviet material which began to appear after the colonel's visits and saw, from the evaluation reports, that the Ministry of Defense and the NATO planners, as well as Western intelligence services, were redoing their sums as a result, there is simply no way that he would not have tipped off Moscow to the peril. If he had been serving the Soviet Union, this was damage to the Kremlin on a scale he could not have allowed to continue. The hemorrhage would have to be stopped, even if he risked his own blood in the process, and, with so many in the know, the risk would have seemed acceptable.

The bona fides of Penkovsky are thus central to the whole controversy over Soviet high-level penetration of the West in the postwar era. He *was* genuine, but in a strange way. He did

---

*Six people in MI5 were given the full story by MI6 even before the colonel's first appearance in Britain. They included, apart from Hollis, his deputy, Graham Mitchell, and the head of counterespionage, Martin Furnival Jones. As the persons responsible for the special security arrangements, they were automatically involved. In all, nearly fifty officials in London were brought in on the secret.

heroic things, yet without being himself a hero. He served what the West would call a noble cause, yet he served it without nobility. For all that, he was no pawn, pushed out from behind onto the intelligence chessboard. He ventured out himself and nearly made it all the way to the far end, only to be cut down by his own overconfidence.

11

The Dark Messenger

ON DECEMBER 22, 1961, when Penkovsky's breathtaking exploits were at their height, another Soviet intelligence officer—quite unconnected with Penkovsky and totally ignorant of the secret role he was playing—offered his services to the West. The newcomer's name was Lieutenant Colonel Anatoly Mikhailovich Golitsyn and he had turned up unheralded on the doorstep of Frank Friberg, the CIA station chief in Helsinki, where, under the alias of "Klimov," the colonel was working on KGB counter-intelligence against NATO countries in Finland. He was "exfiltrated," not without complications,* by air to Frankfurt in the American zone of Germany, and thence to the United States. The Americans had bought themselves one of the most intriguing, troublesome and, ultimately, the most damaging of packages ever to change hands in the East-West espionage game.

Unlike most of his colleagues who had sought asylum before him across the Atlantic, Golitsyn was never to testify before Congress; nor was he ever to appear in print before his political testament, *New Lies for Old*,[1] appeared in 1984, twenty-three years after his defection. The obsessive thesis of this book—that what the West regards as world history over the past thirty

---

*He was recalled to Moscow for a brief period after making his offer and could only be got at again when he returned to Helsinki, under yet another alias.

years is nothing more than a giant conjuror's trick of KGB disinformation—will be dealt with later. All that need be noted here is that the work tells us absolutely nothing about the life, character and career of the author himself. Nor has any biography ever been written about him, though he would make an admirable Kafkaesque study. To present even the bare bones of Golitsyn the man we must therefore draw on what he told his Western interrogators about himself, on their opinions of him and, wherever possible, on the verdicts of his onetime colleagues who also defected to the West.

Golitsyn was thirty-five at the time of his defection, a step which, he claimed, he had long been contemplating out of disillusionment with the corruption and ineptitude of the Soviet system. This is the usual cry of the defector and, in Golitsyn's case, it needs to be taken with a larger than usual grain of salt. The basic truth of the matter seems to be that, by 1961, Golitsyn, like Penkovsky, had come to feel himself frustrated in his career. Quite unlike Penkovsky, however, who never bothered his head about the theory of intelligence, Golitsyn suffered from a restless itch to reform and reorganize the service he worked for. It was only when his blueprints failed to get anywhere in the Soviet Union (despite claims he later made of top-level encouragement) that he took some even more ambitious theories with him to the West. There, after a slow start, he was to make staggering progress.

Counterintelligence, that is, spying on the potentially subversive activities either of his own countrymen or Westerners, had made up almost all of Golitsyn's adult life. To be a KGB man had, apparently, been one of his boyhood dreams. In 1944, when a young soldier aged only eighteen, he had transferred at his own request from the Soviet army to a counterintelligence school. When he had completed a one-year course there, he joined the KGB and worked for the next three years with a section responsible for the security of Soviet nationals abroad, an area which had been given high priority after the defection of Gouzenko in Ottawa and the near defection of Volkov in Istanbul. From 1948 to 1950, he took an advanced two-year course, again in counterintelligence, and it was in that capacity that he returned to KGB headquarters in 1951, as a case officer in the First Chief Directorate's Anglo-American Department. From 1953 to 1955, he had his first posting abroad. This was to Vienna, working, to begin with, on the surveillance of Soviet émigrés in an Austria still under four-power occupation, and then against the British authorities. Yet another course in counterintelligence awaited him on his return to Moscow and this one, at the KGB's Higher Intelligence School, lasted for four years, until 1959. In 1960, after a short spell in headquarters, working once more on American and NATO targets, he was posted to Finland, inevitably to take over Western counterintelligence there.

Such is the dull outline of a dreary monotone career, and one would imagine the end product to be a stolid and unimaginative Soviet police agent. But Anatoly Golitsyn was nothing of the sort. He had attended far too many study courses for his own good; they had left an already busy brain seething with ideas to put the world right, beginning with the world immediately around him. Many years later, this description of Golitsyn when in his twenties was given by Peter Deriabin, a KGB colleague who had preceded him to the West in 1954:*

I first met Golitsyn in Moscow in 1952, when he was working in the American Department of Moscow Center, and then again a year later in Vienna, where we were both working at the residency. He kept himself to himself and was not popular; in fact, I was one of his few friends and managed to get a room at the Grand Hotel for him and his wife, whom he had married just before the posting.

What struck me above all about Golitsyn was that he seemed to be the perpetual student rather than the practical operator he was supposed to be. He had a big mouth and tended to invent stories which would make him look important. He spread it about, for example, that in 1951, he had been with Stalin at Sochi. This couldn't have been true, because Stalin didn't go there that year! And he was always full of plans, plans to reorganize everything.[2]

*See chapter 6.

One of these plans, we know from his Western interrogators, had been for nothing less than a complete restructuring of the KGB's First Directorate, which he had devised together with a colleague, Major Kashcheyev, while both were serving at the Moscow Center in 1952. The authors took their draft to a Politburo meeting and were told that it had been approved, though in fact no reorganization took place as a result. (The episode was later dressed up by Golitsyn to suggest that Stalin had given the plan his personal blessing, though it is not clear whether the Soviet dictator was actually at the meeting himself.)

This was the somewhat arrogant theorist who arrived in Finland in 1960, and, before long, he was trying to run things there. He had a row with the rezident, Colonel Zhennikov, over how the station should be operated, and, in 1961, he made the same blunder, though on a lesser scale, that the impatient Penkovsky had fallen into while serving in Istanbul five years previously— namely, a complaint to Moscow Center about the behavior of his chief. Though Golitsyn, unlike the colonel, had at least dispatched his protest through the channels of his own service, the result, so far as his own career prospects were concerned, was not very different. He was told to mind his own business, and it seems clear that, from now on, Anatoly Golitsyn, never a comfortable colleague, was marked down by Moscow Center as a conspiring troublemaker. In that situation, a medium-grade KGB officer like himself needed at least one highly placed official either in the intelligence or Party hierarchy to pull him up the promotion ladder. Golitsyn had no such powerful patron. It was not surprising that his ambitions sought their outlet in the West instead.

There was little left in his marriage to hold him back: colleagues had noted that this was going on the rocks even in the early stages of the Vienna posting.[3] There was, on the other hand, plenty to tempt him forward. Golitsyn cannot have been indifferent to the material benefits of life in the capitalist world, of which he had seen some samples in two Western-style capitals. But, in his case, the intellectual enticement may well have been stronger. As a privileged student, he had been able to immerse himself over the years in American newspapers and

literature and to take stock of the American mentality. He probably sensed that the big audience for which he craved lay across
the Atlantic, and in this he was to prove correct. A purely moral
repugnance against Communism may have stirred in his breast
to some degree. But what really drove him on was a desire to
spill the beans and to feel that he was changing the thinking of
governments in the process. It was an impulse of exhibitionism
rather than ideology.

In appraising the beans that he actually spilled after arriving
in the West, we must distinguish between the purely professional assets he brought with him as an intelligence officer and
the value of his cosmic theories about the postwar world as put
forward in his one and only publication. To begin at the fieldwork end, what he told his interrogators about Finland, his
recent post, was disappointingly meager. Western contemporaries of his in that capital reckon that he provided them with
only one operational lead: a Soviet penetration of the British
consulate in Helsinki in the person of a Finnish woman member of the staff, Elsa Mai Evans. This was useful but essentially
low-grade information. At the other extreme, Golitsyn went on
to name five highly placed Finns who, he alleged, were Soviet
"agents of influence." With one possible exception (who was
himself now new to the West) the list was considered to be
dubious. It included, for example, the name of the Finnish head
of state, President Urho Kaleva Kekkonnen himself. The general view at the time was that Kekkonnen was, in fact, a good
Finn who used the Russians more than they were ever able to
use him.[4] In the eyes of the KGB, however, he was one of the
rezident's most important contacts.

On the NATO front, however, Golitsyn undoubtedly provided some very valuable leads. His last job in Moscow before
his Helsinki posting had been to write up NATO intelligence
reports from abroad in digest form for his superiors. This
meant that, though he was never senior enough to know the
true identity of KGB agents in NATO countries, he was familiar with much of the material they had sent and where it had
come from. When presented with a selection of original documents, this guided him, and ultimately his interrogators, to

identify at least one major Soviet spy in NATO's headquarters—George Pâques, deputy chief of the French Section of the organization's Press and Information Department.* As a result of leads given by Golitsyn to a French counterintelligence officer in 1962 (the meeting was arranged by courtesy of the CIA, on the island of Martinique), Pâques was put under surveillance in Paris early the following year and was observed holding regular meetings with Vladimir Khrenov, a Soviet agent masquerading, like dozens of his colleagues, as an official at UNESCO. After his arrest on August 10 (carrying classified documents in his briefcase), Pâques confessed to having worked for the KGB since the early 1950s. Among the major secrets he had passed on to Moscow during those twenty years was the operational plan for the Anglo-French attack on Suez in 1956 and, in the year of his arrest, details of NATO's latest strategy to combat a lightning Soviet strike against Western Europe.[5]

Golitsyn's leads were also partially responsible for the identification—which came much later in the day—of the Canadian professor Hugh Hambleton as another Soviet mole in the heart of the Western alliance. Hambleton, a picaresque individual who had fallen in love with espionage for its own sake, was another KGB recruit from the early 1950s, who had rendered by far his greatest services for Moscow after securing an appointment as an economic analyst to NATO in 1956. Before leaving the job in 1961, when he attempted vainly to sever all contact with the KGB, he had passed over hundreds of NATO documents for his Soviet controllers to photocopy. Though he never had access to the very highest-grade information, the material he supplied included secret papers on NATO nuclear strategy, prospective weapons systems, estimates of the East-West military balance and political stresses inside the rival blocs, as well as future projections on the missile conflict, the space race and the long-term impact of new microchip and laser technology. Hambleton was not finally run to earth until 1979, at the end of a long spell of espionage activities based in Canada. Even then,

---

*At the time of Pâques's activities, NATO's HQ was still in Paris, and France was still a full military member of the alliance.

the Canadians decided to forgo prosecution in return for his cooperation in exhaustive debriefings and on the technical grounds that it was NATO's secrets, not Canada's, which he had betrayed. It was not until he rashly flew to London in June of 1982 that he fell afoul of another country's less accommodating Official Secrets Act. He was arrested and put on trial in Britain (though born in Ottawa, Hambleton had an English father and so held dual nationality and owed dual allegiance). On December 6 of that year, this most amicable and eccentric of spies, then aged sixty, began a ten-year prison sentence.[6]

Once removed from the NATO context, Golitsyn's professional offerings were less tangible. One basic difficulty, revealed later by his interrogators, was that, for more than ten years, he stolidly refused to speak Russian. His paranoia that the KGB had penetrated every nook and cranny of the Western intelligence edifice was so intense that he suspected any CIA or MI6 official who spoke his own language to be working for his own service. He thus conversed only in the fractured English he had learned at school and this led to much confusion as well as much delay. Frequently, he would use the wrong English words, either because his vocabulary was deficient or because he was thinking in Russian, and his interrogators often had to play over the tapes of his debriefings again and again to make out what he really meant. Then, quite apart from the obstacle of his own arrogance, the vagueness of his leads caused many problems. He had brought no documents over with him. This, and his imprecise presentation of the facts, was hardly consistent with his claim to have carefully prepared for his defection ever since 1956. He always insisted on seeing Western documents before commenting on the questions they raised; in this way, he was provided with a firm foundation on which to build.

On the Philby case, where everyone at the time was still treading on wobbly ground, Golitsyn certainly pointed the West further along the road to positive identification. He did not, as has often been stated, provide the final proof of Philby's guilt. His interrogators recall that he had never heard the name of Philby when first questioned about him in 1962. What he did produce for them to help unravel the mystery was one word, at least that was how it came out in Russian when his English was translated. The Russian word was "Pyatyorka," the equivalent of what Golitsyn called "The Ring of Five" to describe the KGB's prime nest of agents perched high up in the British establishment. When pressed on this, Golitsyn admitted that he had heard the phrase from only one source, his friend Kashcheyev, in Moscow in 1955. Kashcheyev had served in the KGB residency in London in 1953–54, only to be returned smartly home after he had been found by British police drunk while driving his car. On a "need to know" basis, Kashcheyev was aware of the phrase, but if he had any detailed information, which is doubtful, he did not pass it on to his friend. Golitsyn was unaware even of the code names.

As for identification, Burgess and Maclean had already long since been revealed. They made two. Hugh Cairncross, who had served in Signals Intelligence during the war and had later been privy, as a senior civil servant, to nuclear secrets, had already been eased out of Whitehall on security grounds and allowed to depart for the UN's Food and Agricultural Organization in Rome. That made three. All that Golitsyn could provide about the remaining couple in the "Ring" was that one was "a senior officer in British intelligence" (a less precise lead than that given by the hapless Volkov nearly twenty years before). Blunt, who fitted that description, at least in the past tense, was revealed, by other means, in 1964. Philby, already under suspicion, finally unmasked himself by his flight to Moscow in January 1963. Nonetheless, it was Golitsyn's talk of the sinister-sounding Ring of Five which had strengthened that suspicion in 1962. Indeed, it led to a further indecisive confrontation between Philby and his investigators.

One oddity needs recording in this connection. When Golitsyn first mentioned to his CIA interrogators the existence of Soviet moles in British intelligence, he was asked by them whether this could be passed on to London. "Yes," he replied, "provided it is at the top level. It's the lower grades I'm worried about." Such was the Golitsyn of 1962. He was to sing a very different tune as time went by.

One of the most significant new leads which he provided for

the British concerned Soviet penetration of the Admiralty. There were, he claimed, at least two KGB agents installed in this Whitehall holy of holies. One, relatively junior, had been recruited in Moscow in 1955 while serving on the British naval attaché's staff and was now operating back in London. (This led to a shortlist of four suspects being drawn up by MI5, of whom John Vassall, the guilty party, was one.) But Golitsyn was certain that a much more senior British officer had to be involved as well. He based his insistence on the high-grade nature of the naval documents, photocopies of which he had seen when drawing up his intelligence summary reports for the First Chief Directorate at Moscow Center. These documents dealt with top secret matters such as the establishment of a Scottish base for the Polaris missile submarine fleet, and he unhesitatingly identified the originals when they were drawn out of the London files for his inspection. Vassall, he insisted, was too junior, a KGB "throwaway" to protect someone higher up.

If Golitsyn's thesis was correct, then there were several graying heads in the Admiralty on which the cap of Soviet superspy might conceivably fit. It is quite untrue to suggest that the then head of MI5, Sir Roger Hollis, personally intervened to protect the officers under suspicion from interrogation and even ordered the files on them to be destroyed. (The allegation is part of the case put together by those serving under Sir Roger who were convinced that their master was a long-serving Soviet agent.) It was, in fact, the case officer dealing with the investigation who decided against interrogation and destroyed the papers because no evidence against any individual could be put forward. However, the search for Golitsyn's second Admiralty spy went on, though it was never to lead anywhere.

As things turned out, the firm identification of Vassall as the culprit (made possible by the evidence of another Soviet defector, with whom, as we shall see, Golitsyn was to engage in a bitter feud) explained the high grade of the material leaked. His post as a clerk in the office of the Civil Lord of the Admiralty, though a humble one, gave him almost unlimited access to secret papers. After his arrest and conviction, the search for Golitsyn's second spy was gradually wound down.

In March 1963, Golitsyn, who was anyway growing dissatisfied with his conditions in America, went to London for a thorough on-the-spot debriefing by MI5. He instantly galvanized the world of high politics as well as intelligence. Hugh Gaitskell, leader of the Labour Opposition and therefore the putative next prime minister of Britain, had recently died of a mystery disease eventually diagnosed as lupus erythematosus. It was a virus, extremely rare in temperate climates, which wasted the victim's system and, in Gaitskell's case, had led ultimately to heart and kidney failure. This appeared to Golitsyn to be a sinister match with a story he had heard two years before in Moscow. His informant, a colleague in the KGB's First Directorate, had told him then that there were plans afoot in the center to assassinate "a Western leader." The information was never made more precise than that, but as the officer concerned had previously served in the KGB residency in London, Golitsyn inferred that the unnamed target might be British. Some six weeks before his death, Gaitskell had called in at the Soviet embassy about his visa for a visit to Moscow as the personal guest of Khrushchev. Moreover, he had been offered and had drunk a cup of coffee in the consul's office there. When Golitsyn heard this, he put one and one together and made five. Gaitskell had been murdered by the Russians, he suggested, in order to clear the path to 10 Downing Street for Harold Wilson, regarded in Moscow as the socialist politician most sympathetic to the Soviet cause.

The medical arguments against this could not be conclusive as so little was known about the disease; nonetheless, on the available evidence, they were weighty. Clinical projections seemed to prove that, whatever had been in that first cup of coffee, further doses of the poison would have had to be administered at regular intervals over long periods to be fatal. Yet Gaitskell had been under close British medical supervision for weeks before his death. The countervailing political arguments were even stronger.

East-West détente was still in the air diplomatically and the "wet jobs" squad of the KGB was already in decline professionally. The assassination of a future British prime minister went against the grain of both these trends. Above all, in 1962, when the act was supposed to have been committed, it was George Brown, even more than Harold Wilson, who was being touted as a likely successor to the Labour crown. To exchange Gaitskell for the rambunctiously anti-Communist Brown would have been a poor bargain indeed for the Kremlin.* Incidentally, in view of what was to follow, it is interesting and perhaps important to note that at no time during this 1963 stay in Britain did Golitsyn raise the slightest security suspicions about Harold Wilson himself or his circle of friends. This would have been the natural time and place to spell out why the Kremlin favored Wilson as Labour leader so strongly as to commit murder on his behalf. Yet not a word was said about this in London.

It is the wildest of exaggerations to claim that Golitsyn provided the British with "two thousand leads"[7] about Soviet agents in their midst. His so-called penetration leads, apart from the phrase Ring of Five and his help over the Admiralty case, were numbered only in dozens and it was his bad luck that London knew of most of them already. Nine months before Golitsyn's defection, the MI6 officer George Blake had been unmasked as a Soviet agent. He made a full confession on arrest and told all when interrogated in jail after being sentenced. Much of what he told dealt, in far greater detail, with the same cases later mentioned by Golitsyn, whose information under these headings therefore became superfluous.

Some of the other "disclosures" attributed to Golitsyn were, on the other hand, not so much superfluous as totally inaccurate. One notable example was his claim that, exceptionally, the KGB residency in London had no SK department to watch over the security of all Soviet nationals in the country. The departure this represented from standard practice, Golitsyn explained, was made possible by the fact that the Kremlin possessed an agent of its own high up in British counterintelligence. All the information it needed on security matters would thus be provided anyway through that channel. This

---

*It should be noted that no subsequent Soviet intelligence or political defector to the West lent any credence to the Gaitskell murder theory.

story, which has been put forward in Western writings,[8] seems hard put to match the actual facts. The KGB residency in London was never without its SK staff, for the simple reason that they, and only they, could identify and watch over Soviet citizens who *might* be thinking of defection. George Blake, who, in the late 1950s, was the most valuable Soviet agent operating in Whitehall, could only tip the local KGB off about Russians who had actually made contact with British intelligence (and at least one such case is known to have happened).

It seems extraordinary that the whole scenario put forward by Golitsyn could have been taken seriously by any professional. First, by leaving the SK slot so conspicuously empty, the KGB would only run the danger of drawing attention to its having British assets in the security field. Moreover, the Russians would in any event always double-bank, always over-insure, when it came to surveillance over their own nationals. Someone in the Soviet embassy would always have this task, if only to check reports and suspicions with any top British agent the Kremlin possessed. After all, that agent might at any time turn cautious, go cold altogether, get transferred or even get caught. The SK network was not likely to have been dismantled as though it had become completely and permanently superfluous thanks to the existence of some omniscient guardian angel in Whitehall.

Golitsyn's sojourn in Britain ended in July of 1963 after only four months, and it ended in abrupt and muddled fashion. The right-wing *Daily Telegraph* heard via Washington that an important KGB defector was in Britain and the editor, Colin Coote, started using his considerable personal influence with the Conservative government of the day to get the actual name. This the intelligence community, busy milking Golitsyn, was desperate to prevent and, in their desperation, they resorted to an extraordinary ruse. They "released" the name of Anatoly Dolnytsin, a Soviet official who had served in London some years before, in the hope that the rough confusion over identities would get them off the hook both with their political masters and with the defector himself. In fact, the only satisfaction they got was to

deprive the *Telegraph* of its exclusive story by putting the false
name out over the agency tapes for everyone to pick up. Golitsyn, furious at the exposure of his whereabouts, left by the first
available plane to Washington. There were inevitably suspicions that the original leak over his presence in Britain had been
put out by the Americans precisely to make him catch that
plane back.

If the CIA had engineered his return (for which there is no
proof), they were to live to regret it. Once back in his own safe
house in the suburbs of Washington (where he had been installed with a false identity and a monthly paycheck), Golitsyn
changed into another and higher gear over his allegations. Indeed, as time went by, it seemed as though he had switched to
another and more rasping engine. The allegations themselves,
however, were maddeningly vague, except as regards other Soviet defectors or FBI informants. They were all Kremlin plants,
Golitsyn insisted, whose sole purpose was to discredit him and
so muffle the great message he had for the Western world. The
cat's cradle which these changes produced will be examined
below. But as regards the worlds of American intelligence and
politics, Golitsyn never produced anything comparable with
the leads he had provided in London: no serials pointing to
individual suspects high up in the Pentagon, no Ring of Five–
type phrases hinting at a parallel band of top Soviet moles
operating in Washington and, above all, no allegations that
assassination was being plotted in or around the White House
or that the White House itself was under a powerful KGB siege.

It was this last scenario, however, which Golitsyn now proceeded to sketch out for London. Again, Golitsyn produced no
concrete evidence and no detailed allegations. His "case" was
based entirely on deductions drawn from the matrix of his
philosophy—namely, that the KGB had penetrated every nook
and cranny of the Western alliance. Harold Wilson had made
frequent trips to Moscow during the 1950s, in the service of the
timber business he worked for during his years in opposition.
That was quite enough for Golitsyn. Wilson, he argued, must
have been at least propositioned by the KGB during these visits

and might well have been recruited. A future prime minister was, after all, the supreme prize and this all dovetailed with Golitsyn's other story about the Gaitskell murder plot. But it was pure supposition. Any hard accusations against members of the Wilson circle had to wait for another Soviet defector who only appeared on the London scene in 1971.

Golitsyn obviously needed a powerful sponsor within the CIA to get his theories launched, and he had found the man he needed in the person of James Angleton, head of the agency's counterintelligence division. It would be something of an insult to the intellectual distinction and the great professional experience which Angleton possessed to suggest that it was Anatoly Golitsyn who alone convinced him of the omnipresent hand of the KGB's penetration of the West. (The same observation applies to Angleton's deputy, Ramond Rocca, who supported his chief wholeheartedly in the matter.) Angleton, half-American by birth but wholly American by assimilation and loyalties, was one of the agency's most brilliant and respected figures, a man who, back in 1944, had been the head of U.S. counterintelligence operations* in Italy when aged only twenty-seven. By the time Golitsyn floated into his world, he was still only forty-five. Yet much had happened in the meantime to disillusion him long before this dogmatic, evangelical crusader from Moscow appeared on the scene.

Angleton, like everyone in Western intelligence, had been shaken by the defection of Burgess and Maclean in 1951. But it was, his contemporaries recall, the later revelation that Kim Philby was also a long-serving Soviet agent which really shattered the American's faith in the world around him. Angleton had himself worked with Philby on and off for twenty years before the Englishman's flight to Moscow in January 1963. They had first met in wartime Britain in 1943, when Angleton was a brand-new recruit to the OSS and Philby the head of MI6's Iberian Department. During the years Philby had served in Washington, the two men had been in close and constant con-

*Then still the OSS.

tact, both professionally and personally. And, just like Philby's own British colleagues, Angleton had been completely deceived by this plausible charmer with a head and heart of ice. It seems Angleton was particularly disturbed by the revelation that it was Philby who had blocked Volkov's path to the West in 1945 (and, in the process, had signed the man's death warrant). If a would-be defector of this significance could be swept away by the KGB like a fly from a tablecloth on a high-level tip-off received from the West, then who was safe and who was genuine? Thus, Angleton's doubt loomed large in his own mind before this Soviet prophet of doom landed in Washington. What now took place was a systematic inflation of those doubts. Golitsyn played Iago to Angleton's Othello. The fires which the Russian fed were not of jealousy, as with the Shakespearean Moor, but of despondent suspicion.

Part of the havoc which resulted came from the mole trails laid by Golitsyn into the CIA itself, shaky and imprecise though they were. Thus the defector was able to launch an all-out search for spies among CIA officers who had served or were still serving in Germany by alleging that the KGB had planted a source named "Sasha" in the middle of these operations. Though he could not recall the agent's real name, he was sure it began with K. All that the subsequent exhaustive mole hunt uncovered was one officer who was found to have been misappropriating CIA funds. It was a meager trawl. Of spies among the agency's German operations there was no sign then, nor has any evidence emerged of one since.*

Golitsyn started an even more frantic search for traitors in Washington itself by talking of a trip made to the American capital in 1957 by V. M. Kovshuk, head of the section in the KGB's Second Chief Directorate which handled the American embassy in Moscow. Such a trip by such a senior official, he argued, could only have been made in order to contact some high-level agent serving in CIA headquarters.[9] In fact, plain

---

*There had been a CIA staff officer in the German theater actually nicknamed Sasha, which added to the general mayhem until he was cleared.

logic suggested that the visit could have had one of a dozen different explanations (and at least one other was to emerge in due course). But such was Angleton's zeal and Golitsyn's persuasiveness that the CIA began to turn itself inside out in the quest for a Philby of its own. Again, none was found of that stature, then or since.

Ironically, Golitsyn's greatest havoc was created in the one field where he had begun by making a genuine and important contribution to Western knowledge. This was in the field of Soviet disinformation. His real message, he declared, was not in the mundane operational sphere of spy versus counterspy but concerned the supreme political strategy of the Kremlin's battle against the West. This message only reached the wider world after more than twenty years of gestation and considerable editing of his million-word manuscript by four of his Western supporters.* But over those same years he had advanced its main thesis ad nauseam in private. The core of his case was that in 1957, in the light of "fissiparous tendencies in Hungary and elsewhere in Eastern Europe," the Soviet Union had decided to embark on a totally new policy. It would, from now on, pretend that it was weak so that the West would be less inclined to take it so seriously. That is the message in plain English. It is worth quoting how it comes out in Golitsyn's presentation (even after devoted editing) to give a sample of the labyrinthine workings of the man's mind:

> If the factors that had previously served to forge a degree of Western cohesion—that is Communist ideological militancy and monolithic unity—were to be perceived by the West, respectively, as moderating and disintegrating and if, despite an actual increase in the bloc's strength, an image was to be successfully projected of a bloc weakened by economic, political and economic disarray, then the Western response to Communist policy would be fuller and less co-ordinated; actual Western tendencies

*Stephen de Mowbray and Arthur Martin of MI5 and Vasia C. Gmirkin and Scott Miler of the CIA, all of them Golitsyn converts who commended the work in a jointly signed foreword.

towards disintegration might be promoted and encouraged, thereby creating conditions for a change in the balance of power in favour of the Communist bloc.[10]

The following year, according to Golitsyn, practical steps were taken to implement the policy. New Foreign Policy and Active Operations Measures departments were set up in the Soviet Central Committee, and a news agency, Novosti, was founded to serve their needs abroad. Above all, thanks largely to the efforts of Aleksandr Shelepin (who became chairman of the KGB in December 1958), a special disinformation agency, Department D, was established to coordinate the global process of pulling the wool over Western eyes. Its first head was Colonel Agayants from the KGB's Higher Intelligence School, and he started off with a staff of more than fifty officers who were specialists on all countries from Japan to Israel and all subjects from rocketry to Latin American labor problems.[11]

So far so good: this was valuable material to have had as early as 1962, always assuming that it was produced then and not in response to subsequent Western discoveries. Golitsyn had, as usual, provided no documentary evidence, no precision about dates and practically no firsthand evidence. But he had been the first to alert the West to the Kremlin's new emphasis on "active measures," an exponent of which will be examined in a later chapter. His appalling, self-destructive error was to assume that, from 1958 onward, Colonel Agayants and his merry men had pulled off nothing but disinformation triumphs over every major issue arising anywhere on the globe.

Thus, under the "New Methodology," not only was Tito's quarrel with Moscow, which began before the colonel's time, bogus from start to finish, but so was the Sino-Soviet split and the invasion of Czechoslovakia to suppress the "Prague Spring." Alexander Dubček's peaceful revolution is presented as "a controlled operation planned and conducted by the [Czech] party apparatus itself" (in which case it is hard to fathom why control had to be established by Warsaw Pact armies). Nobody who actually witnessed any of these happenings on the ground, as opposed to from the comfort of a Washington armchair,[12] could credit Golitsyn's case, though up to this point, 1968, it remains just remotely arguable. But the thesis dissolves into farce when it is extended to portray events such as the Solidarity upheaval in Poland as being just another of Colonel Agayants' little conjuring tricks. Thankfully for what he leaves behind of his academic reputation at the end of his book, even Golitsyn does not go on to present the Soviet invasion of Afghanistan as another exercise in disinformation, though one feels that he is nibbling for an opening even here.

The Golitsyn syndrome did damage enough in Britain, through the long-running debate over the Wilson circle and the equally durable controversy over Sir Roger Hollis and other candidates for a London archtraitor's chair. But while it divided the British intelligence community, it decimated the CIA, dozens of whose most capable officers had their careers ended and their reputations tarnished by ending up on the losing side of the debate. As we shall shortly see, it was the search for the truth about Moscow's involvement in President Kennedy's assassination which gave the issue a particular desperate urgency in Washington. Yet it is not fanciful to look for broader reasons behind the much greater impact which Golitsyn's dark meteor had when it landed on American soil.

To begin with, the average Briton is, by nature, more of a pragmatist than his American cousin. He is thus inoculated from birth with a dose of skepticism which renders him more immune from the fevers of euphoria on the one hand or despair on the other. He instinctively distrusts theories which explain everything, just as the American instinctively embraces them. And, from the mid-1960s onward, there were special reasons why some of the best brains in that nation, always prone to accepting all or nothing, black or white, should have swallowed wholesale Golitsyn's message of gloom and doom. These were the years of the Vietnam trauma, when America's masochism and self-doubt were at their height. Only the deeply disillusioned Angleton speaking in the 1960s could have credited the Soviet bloc with creating "a kind of wilderness of mirrors" so that, all over the globe, the West was rendered simply incapable of separating fact from illusion.

Looking back, we can now see the truth to be very different. Communist power politics, whether played out in Belgrade, Warsaw or Peking, have had their own proven national impulses and are not Punch and Judy shows whose wires are all manipulated from Moscow. No operator and no organization could lay claim, even on the law of averages, to that degree of manifold and universal success. In fact, like anyone else in the East-West deception game, Colonel Agayants has won some and lost some, the minuses including, in particular, his clumsy and occasionally counterproductive attempts at Western document forgeries. But this is to view it all from the end of the 1980s when the West in general, and America in particular, find themselves in a more robust mood than a generation ago.

Twenty-five years later, the prophet of this despair himself cuts a sorry figure, whose self-centeredness has come to match the obsessiveness of his theories. The comings and goings across the Atlantic of Stalin's restless daughter Svetlana provided Golitsyn's American hosts with an alarming insight into his paranoia. When she first arrived in the United States, he informed them that she had only been allowed to make the journey so that he, Golitsyn, would contact her, out of plain curiosity, and thus deliver himself into the arms of KGB killers. When, after several years of residence in the West, she returned to Moscow, his only comment was that the Kremlin had evidently abandoned the plot. He was even undismayed when she returned again to America as Mrs. Lana Peters in 1986. This meant, he said, that the murder plot was now being resumed. That the woman, her daughter Olga, attending a Quaker school in England, and the bemused authorities in Moscow were acting on their own behalf could not be countenanced by Golitsyn. Like Lech Walesa in Poland, they were unwelcome disturbances of his vision, wavelets which presumed to undermine the sand castle of his beliefs.

Mikhail Gorbachev is the latest such wavelet. To be consistent, Golitsyn has to be convinced that glasnost is just another manifestation of Department D's "active measures." He is, in fact, so convinced and, from the isolation of his safe house, he has bombarded the White House with lengthy memoranda of warning. He keeps a pistol by his side because he believes that, since he is the only person in the West who is qualified to deliver such warnings, he is therefore the one voice the Kremlin is most determined to silence. If there is any truth in the saying that "the medium is the message," then this sad personal decline throws a poor light on the entire Golitsyn syndrome. The only time he was in any danger of extermination by his former colleagues was, surely, in 1961–63, when he was providing intelligence leads of real if sometimes elusive significance to the West. Since then, in view of all the havoc he has created, knowingly albeit not willfully, in the Western intelligence community, the KGB would be more likely to give him not a bullet, but a medal.

12

The "Bone in the Throat"

ON JUNE 3, 1962, less than six months after Comrade "Klimov" had turned up on the CIA's doorstep in Helsinki, another KGB officer, who was serving as a security watchdog to the Soviet disarmament delegation in Geneva, took an American aside during an interval between sessions and said he would like to arrange a private meeting. Thus began the saga of Yuri Nosenko, who was destined to become, if that were possible, an even more controversial figure than Golitsyn. The cases of the two men, and their depositions, soon became liberally entwined in contradictions. Unlike Golitsyn, Nosenko was to suffer harsh treatment at the hands of his hosts; but, again unlike his fellow defector, he enjoyed, in the end, a spectacular vindication. This vindication has always, however, been edged with controversy. To this day, the argument rumbles on over which of the two men was on the side of the angels and which was a Soviet devil in disguise.

Nosenko's defection began in characteristically ambivalent style. When his secret meetings with the Americans took place in Geneva (first with Peter Bagley, a CIA officer based in Berne who was later joined by the Russian-born George Kiesevalter from the Soviet department at the CIA's headquarters at Langley), Nosenko described himself as a lieutenant colonel, though it later emerged that he was only a captain. His opening gambit hardly matched his advertised rank. In fact, he began by demanding only 800 Swiss francs as a down payment for his services as a spy. The sum seemed, at first sight, absurdly small. Nosenko explained that he had been putting his hand in the till after overspending and this was the amount he needed immediately to put back into the KGB's running Geneva cash account before the next monthly audit. The CIA had, in fact, known other cases of Communist officials in similar plights, desperately searching around for relatively modest sums of money to balance their books, so his explanation did not sound too farfetched. However, as Nosenko admitted many years later, it was not so much farfetched as plain untrue:

> The story that I needed the 800 francs was a deliberate falsehood, and this is why. I reasoned that if I approached the CIA and told them I wanted to work for them for purely ideological reasons, nobody would believe me. So I invented the story of the debt.[1]

There was another muddle, from the very first, over his future intentions. The interrogators, who were initially convinced that this new KGB walk-in was both genuine and valuable, were left with the firm impression, when Nosenko returned to Moscow, that though he was prepared to spy for them he was not prepared to defect. Nosenko denied this in later years:

> I neither said at these first meetings in 1962 that I would defect one day or that I would not. I left it open. All I said was that I hoped to meet them again in Geneva when the disarmament talks resumed there next year. In the meantime, I forbade all contacts in Moscow because I knew too much about our improved surveillance techniques as a result of the Popov case.*[2]

As Nosenko, like Golitsyn, never wrote anything about his own life (and there is hardly anything on the subject in his June 1978 hearings before Congress), it seems essential, before look-

---

*See p. 200, in connection with the unmasking of Penkovsky.

ing at the enigma of the defector, to say something about the
personal background of Yuri Nosenko the man. It is impossible
to judge one without examining the other.

Yuri Ivanovich Nosenko, who was born in the city of Nickolaev, near Odessa, in 1927, may have grown up as a child of the
Soviet elite, but the family did not start life that way.[3] His
grandfather had been an ordinary laborer who had worked in
the Odessa shipyards until he was seventy-five. His father had
followed on in the same simple fashion, but, through years of
studying in the evenings, had just qualified as an engineer by
the time of Yuri's birth. The mother, daughter of a Nickolaev
architect and a member, therefore, of the town's upper classes,
was the formative influence on both her husband and her son.
"She polished both him and me" was how her son put it, revealing how his mother brought culture and manners into the
household, encouraging the father to better himself and giving
the boy Western classics to read. The father's career progressed
steadily. In 1934, he moved with his family to Leningrad, where
he worked for the next five years as a chief engineer in the
shipbuilding plants. In 1939, he was transferred to Moscow,
where he remained for the rest of his life, dying in 1956 as
minister of shipping. A shipyard in Nickolaev was named after
him and his ashes were buried in the Kremlin wall. When, eight
years later, the son publicly broke with the regime and fled to
the West, the shipyard was renamed, though the ashes remained
where they were.

It was inevitable that such a father should try to point his son
toward the sea. In 1942, when Yuri was still only fourteen, he
was sent to the Naval Preparatory School to be trained for the
Naval Academy. But the boy had other ideas. In 1945, aged
seventeen and a half, he persuaded his father that what he
wanted was a career on dry land—but abroad. Perhaps encouraged by his cultured mother, he already had ideas of becoming
a diplomat. As he freely admitted, even at that tender age what
had attracted him about the foreign service was "the life-style
which it offered." There was precious little ideology here. Indeed, when, thanks to his father's position, he was duly enrolled

at Moscow's elite State Institute of International Relations, Marxism-Leninism became his bête noire as a student. He failed it the first time around but managed a grade 3 (the top grade being 5) at the second attempt. He was much better at English, which he took as a major subject, and for his thesis had chosen "Diplomatic Immunity," despite the fact that many of the standard works in that field were in French, which he needed to have laboriously translated for him.

The course lasted two years, and he gives an interesting account of how, in the year before graduation, the state authorities descended on the institute to assess the senior students, like so much expensively reared livestock, for marketing within the system. He and his classmates were summoned one by one before a selection committee of about twenty-five officials representing all major departments and ministries, notably Foreign Affairs, Trade, the Trade Unions, the Tass news agency and, of course, the KGB and the GRU. It was this last body which chose Yuri Nosenko. Mindful probably of his family background and the training he had already received as a naval cadet, they gave him a telephone number to ring. It turned out to be the headquarters (then a separate body) of the GRU's Naval Intelligence. It was—and probably still is—characteristic of the system that he was neither consulted about the decision nor informed about it. He was simply drafted, and drafted, without written instructions, in the most anonymous way possible.

Nosenko served with Naval Intelligence for the next three years.[4] Part of that service (he says the posting was at his own request) was done with the Seventh (Far Eastern) Fleet in the Vladivostok region. There, because of his English-language qualifications, he worked on the analysis of American signals intercepts and on military items appearing in the American newspapers and magazines. They gave him, apart from a wealth of gratuitous technical information, a good long look at the capitalist world as it was presented in print, and he was intrigued by what he saw. From the intercepts, he claims that he and his superiors in Naval Intelligence knew everything about the American aircraft which were operating from the Atsugi air base in Japan—everything, that is, except for the technical details of the top secret U-2 spy plane.

Nineteen fifty-three was a big year in his life. To begin with, after returning from Moscow, he married. His wife, Ludmilla, was from a top Communist family, which would do his career no harm. That career also now took a new turn. At a Moscow New Year's party at the end of 1952, he had got into conversation with a general and first deputy minister in the KGB called Bogdan Kubulov, with whom he had discussed his future. Soon afterward, he was again told to "ring this number," which, on this occasion, turned out to be the KGB's Moscow Center. When, as instructed, he reported there in March of 1953, everything had been fixed up by his powerful New Year's Eve acquaintance. Once again, he was shown nothing on paper. He was merely informed that he was now working in the KGB's Second Chief Directorate (which dealt with foreign intelligence), where a desk was waiting for him.

For the next ten years, he zigzagged* between the First Department of that directorate, which dealt with the Americans, and the Seventh Department, specially created in 1955 to recruit agents from among the Western tourists visiting the Soviet Union. It seems that 1959 was a vintage year for the latter department. "We had quite a few recruitments in 1959," he testified later, "a very big amount of them, very interesting, professors and teachers. . . ."[5] Among the Americans who arrived in Moscow in the autumn of that year was a young man who was to play a fateful role in world history as well as in the small personal world of Yuri Nosenko. This was Lee Harvey Oswald, at that time merely a mixed-up ex-marine who had decided he wanted to live in the Soviet Union but who was to end up, after his return to the United States, as the assassin of President Kennedy.

Before coming to Nosenko's role in that drama, however, we must trace his steady drift toward defection. According to his

---

*These frequent switches, four of them between June 1955 and January 1962, led later to some confusion over what his real job was at any given moment.

account given in later years,[6] this had begun during his first trip abroad, when, under the alias of Nicholaev, a Ministry of Culture official, he was sent to England in 1957 as a security officer accompanying a team of Soviet athletes. He recalls the dual impact—familiar from the cases of almost every defector dealt with above—of the abundance in Western shops and the evidently superior living standards of the workingman. He had formed his images of all this through reading Western books and newspapers. Here was the reality, and for someone who, as a teenager, had dreamed of a diplomatic career abroad "because of the life-style," it was an intoxicating reality. Equally intoxicating was the air of freedom which he began to breathe for the first time. He had read countless surveillance files back in Moscow Center and had been appalled to discover that the KGB held one on his own father, the loyalest of the loyal, who had found his resting place in the Kremlin wall. England seemed on a different planet.

A trip he took on a London bus when he had a couple of hours to spare led to an encounter which made a deep impression on him. He rode along to the end of the line, where he got off at the depot and started chatting with the driver. The man convinced him that he and his family actually lived in an entire house and not in one room sharing facilities with five other families. Moreover, the wife of this humble bus driver did not have to work. His earnings were enough.

Though Nosenko was not yet ready to defect on this 1957 trip, he decided to try to make noncommittal contact. The local KGB had identified a "Mr. Sutton," who turned up at most of the official receptions, as a probable MI5 officer. Nosenko approached him and asked him if he could show him a typical London pub. The Englishman was happy to oblige and the two men spent a pleasant couple of hours drinking and chatting, Nosenko presenting his guide with a jar of caviar when they parted. On the eve of the delegation's return to Moscow, "Mr. Sutton" contacted Nosenko again to thank him for the caviar but also to hand over a parcel. The KGB man excitedly carried it back to his hotel room, half-hoping to find some secret message inside. But all the parcel contained was a London beer mug, by way of a return present. If "Mr. Sutton" was from British intelligence, he had, for some reason, held off. On the other hand, Nosenko's colleagues could have got it wrong: his friend in the pub could really have been plain Mr. Sutton.

Nosenko claims that he made another attempt to interest Western intelligence services in him in 1960, on his return journey from a trip to Cuba. On a stopover in Amsterdam, he left a bundle of classified documents with a letter lying around at the airport, in the hope that someone would pick it up. Nobody did, which helps to explain why, on his third bid to contact, in Geneva two years later, he made a direct approach to an American whom he had picked off the diplomatic list as one to contact. He did not return to Switzerland as he had planned, in twelve months' time, for the simple reason that no East-West talks involving him were held in Geneva in 1963. But he was back with the Soviet delegation in January of 1964 and, on a prearranged signal, met up with Bagley again.

Things now took on a very lively and, to the Americans, very unexpected turn. Bagley has testified that already, toward the end of 1962, he had begun to have serious doubts about Nosenko's reliability and that was entirely due to being shown, when back in Washington, the information that Golitsyn was providing. The young CIA man was not merely shown the discrepancies, for example, over the Admiralty mole hunt in London, or over the number and location of secret microphones said to exist in the American embassy in Moscow. The case for Golitsyn was also being argued by Bagley's powerful and persuasive superior, James Angleton. As Bagley was to tell Congress:

> Alone, Nosenko looked good to me. . . . Seen alongside "x" [Golitsyn] whose reporting I had not seen before coming to headquarters after the 1962 meetings with Nosenko, he looked very odd indeed. . . . Nosenko's information tended to negate or deflect leads from "x."[7]

Thus in 1964 Nosenko was, quite unknown to him, dealing with a case officer who, for professional reasons, already suspected him of being a KGB plant, dispatched to the West to discredit an earlier defector. Much graver suspicions were to crop up later. There is, as mentioned in connection with Penkovsky, always a prima facie reason to doubt any such theory: the Russians' phobia over security which, in this case, makes it unlikely that they would risk letting anyone who knew as much as Nosenko about the KGB's crucial anti-American operations float around freely in the West on a deception mission. Nevertheless, Bagley did have his doubts, and these were strengthened by what happened when they met. "Peter," he was told straightaway, "I'm not going home."[8]

Bagley, to whom this appeared as a complete about-turn, tried to talk Nosenko into returning to Moscow, even if contact continued to be forbidden there, and to remain as an agent in place. A tense period of stalemate followed during which Nosenko's nerves began to fray. He later cited two reasons for his crash decision. First, an overall tightening up of security had just been launched by the KGB in Geneva: Soviet officials of all types were being moved out of their hotels and into the mission's compound. Were they suspecting anyone in particular? Would this complicate his ability to maintain clandestine contact? Second, Nosenko had heard that General Oleg Gribanov, who was still head of the KGB's Second Chief Directorate and therefore his boss, might pass through Geneva at any time during the course of his European tour. At the end of a week, Nosenko stopped arguing and simply jumped into the CIA's lap. He turned up at its Geneva safe house with his bags packed, claiming that his bridges were already burned behind him. When the CIA still tried to talk him out of it, he told what he later admitted was another lie. He had, he said, received an ominous telegram of recall from Moscow Center. "I invented the story to put pressure on the Americans to act, and they did. That same night they moved me on to Frankfurt."*[9]

There seems in fact to have been nothing specific happening on any personal front which had made Nosenko arrive in Ge-

*The Americans soon established that no such telegram had been dispatched to Geneva, by methods they did not reveal to Nosenko: they were monitoring KGB traffic.

neva quite determined to defect at the beginning of 1964. Though regarded in the KGB as something of a wild man, susceptible above the average to vodka and women, his career prospects, if not brilliant, were not blocked, as with Penkovsky. He had not been given a repugnant murder task to perform, like Khokhlov. He was not openly feuding with his immediate superiors, like Petrov or Golitsyn. He had not, after progressive disenchantment, been overtaken by sudden fury, like Deriabin. He was not genuinely staring arrest in the face, like Lieutenant Gouzenko. He did not loathe his wife and love the capitalist game of tennis, like Rastvorov. Had he then simply decided that the time had come to opt permanently for the life-style abroad which had attracted him in his youth?

That would be the innocent and straightforward explanation. So far as his family was concerned, he would have felt both regret and pangs of conscience; but, in this scenario, they could not be part of his journey, and that was that. He had tried, he said later, to arrange a posting to Ethiopia, where both his wife and their two young daughters (born in 1954 and 1958) could have accompanied him. But the attempt had failed and, from then on, he realized he would have to leave them behind.[10] Also left back in Moscow would be one brother and the mother to whom he owed so much. Both wife and mother signed letters which were forwarded to him a few weeks later via the American embassy in Moscow. The texts, full of indignant reproaches and appeals, had clearly been dictated. He never discovered what happened to any of his relatives but, as a KGB man, he must have known that, if he defected, they would all become, in varying degrees, nonpersons in the Soviet world.

But another, very different construction could explain his flight. For Nosenko had come up with something which had made the CIA sit bolt upright and listen. In what was the most startling piece of political intelligence ever produced by a defector, he claimed to have been the case officer in Moscow of Lee Harvey Oswald, and to have seen all the KGB files on President Kennedy's assassin. The KGB, he could assure the Americans, was in the clear; the Kremlin had had nothing to do with the shootings in Dallas two weeks earlier. With this statement,

Nosenko propelled himself out of the ordinary intelligence world, with its Byzantine debates about throwaways, walk-ins, serials and dummy leads, and had entered the stratosphere of East-West power politics. If the Russians had been involved in the murder of an American president, then this would signal, at the minimum, the breaking off of diplomatic relations with Moscow, not to mention the abandonment of all hopes of détente. If they were not involved, then the logical thing to do— on the commonsense principle of *Qui s'excuse, s'accuse*—would be to stick to earnest messages of condolence and do nothing to raise even a mention of the KGB. But statesmen are not always logical, especially statesmen in a panic (and plenty of evidence was to emerge later that the Kremlin really was in a panic over the news from Dallas). So the second construction regarding Nosenko's 1964 bid for asylum emerged, and he had helped to point the crooked finger at himself. Might he not have been planted on the Americans with the express purpose of convincing them of Khrushchev's innocence in the matter? Such a crucial purpose would, surely, override any professional reluctance to let a KGB officer, and all his secrets, out of the bag.

Before weighing the alternatives, let us see what the assassin himself had been up to before he blasted his way into the history books. The twenty-year-old ex-marine had lost little time, after arriving in Moscow from Helsinki in the autumn of 1959, in breaking off his American ties, and doing it in the most formal military fashion. On October 31, he approached the United States embassy and handed over to Richard Snyder, of the consulate staff, a note stating that he wished his American citizenship to be revoked as he had already applied for Soviet nationality. In a manner described as "arrogant and aggressive" he added that he had "offered the Soviets any information he had acquired as an enlisted radar operator."[11] This last passage got underlined when the text of the embassy telegram went around the State Department. Not surprisingly: Oswald had at one time been stationed at a U.S. air base in Japan which was also used by the ultrasecret U-2 spy planes, though he never had access to the U-2s or to U-2-related information.

There is no argument about the sequence of events which

preceded or followed Oswald's call on the embassy, whatever
the debate about the right explanations. In his "Historic
Diary," the original of which has survived, he describes how,
having been told by his Intourist official on October 21 that his
visa could not be extended, he "decided to end it" in his hotel
room by slashing his wrists five times. But the "sweet death" he
had promised himself was not to be. He was hauled unconscious
out of his bloodred bathwater and rushed to Moscow's Botkin
Hospital, where he was stitched up, put back on his feet and
returned to another hotel. On October 28, he was summoned to
Moscow's Passport Registration Office, to be interviewed by a
panel of four officials. He repeated his demand for Soviet citizenship and, most significantly in view of the later controversy,
he then handed over his discharge papers from the Marine
Corps to a body which, by its very nature, had the closest links
with the secret police.

There followed a long wait during which he made two calls
on the American embassy (the second to leave behind a written
note of protest at their inaction) and started giving interviews
to the Western press. Christmas and New Year's went by without any word from the Russians. Then, on January 4, he was
summoned to the Passport Office again and issued a residence
permit; no Soviet citizenship but, at least, permission to stay.[12]
He was told that the Soviet Red Cross would pay all his bills
and provide him with funds to start his new life (and, the next
day, he duly collected the large sum of 4,000 rubles from the
Red Cross office). He was also told that he would be settled in
Minsk. "Is that in Siberia?" he asked. The passport officer
laughed.[13]

Oswald remained in Minsk for the rest of his sojourn in the
Soviet Union. He was given work at a radio factory and provided almost rent-free a one-room flat five minutes' walk from
his work, with a bath and two balconies. ("It is a Russian
dream," he writes in his diary.) Every month he receives a Red
Cross check for 700 rubles. As he earns roughly the same sum
again at the factory, that gives him a total salary equal to that
of the manager himself. Nonetheless, by the beginning of 1961,
disillusionment is setting in. On January 4 he confides to his

"Historic Diary": "I am starting to reconsider my desire about staying. The work is drab, the money I get has nowhere to be spent, no nightclubs or bowling alleys, no places of recreation except the Trade Union dances. I have had enough." Then, soon after he has mailed his first letter of reconsideration to the American embassy in Moscow, he becomes entranced, at one of those maligned Trade Union dances, by "a girl with a French hair-do and white slippers" called Marina. A fortnight later, he proposes to the Russian girl and is accepted. For a few months, the rapture of a newlywed stills the ache for home. Then, in June 1961, he tells his "slightly startled" wife that he wants to take them back to America. By the following February, when a baby girl is born, there are three of them. The Russians raise no objections, and the Americans restore his passport and add his family to it. Finally, in June 1962, he leaves the Soviet Union with them to go and live with his mother in Vernon, Texas. The Russians never saw him again, but they had not quite heard the last of him. In September 1963, a "Lee Henry Oswald" turned up at the Soviet consulate in New Mexico, reportedly to inquire about a reply to a telegram he had sent to Moscow. That information was entered in Oswald's CIA dossier in Washington on October 11. The next entry about him, a month later, concerned Dallas, Texas.

Such is the bald outline of Oswald's Russian odyssey. It needs to be set out in order to compare the two rival constructions which were fiercely argued in the wake of President Kennedy's assassination. On the face of things, it seemed inconceivable that the Kremlin, which by now was beginning to wind down even on the elimination of its own defectors to the West, would plot the murder of the leader of the whole Western world, a deed which would carry the gravest and most unpredictable consequences. (Moscow, be it noted in parenthesis, being always concerned above all about unpredictability.) Assuming it had been hatching such a dastardly scheme, it seemed even more inconceivable that the KGB, which would be given the job, would select Oswald to carry out the killing. He had proved himself, by almost everything he had done during his sojourn in the Soviet Union, to be the most impulsive, unstable and unreliable of creatures, all qualities which would have ruled him out as even a low-level political assassin.

Yet it also seemed impossible to believe that the regime had not made some use of Oswald and that the KGB, as the agency involved, had not given him special treatment throughout. That would explain, so this construction ran, the saving of his life; the granting of the residence permit; all the money, disguised as Red Cross payments, handed over to him; the "dream flat" in Minsk; the fact that no objections were raised to his marrying a reputable local girl (Marina was the niece of a colonel in the Minsk militia); and, most interesting of all, the fact that no obstacles were put in the way of his returning to America with his family. In flat opposition to all this was Nosenko's assertion that the KGB was "clean" in the Oswald affair and indeed had never adopted any "active policy" toward him. The credibility of Nosenko had thus become something far more than an exercise in intelligence esoterics. As Richard Helms,* then deputy director of the CIA responsible for among other things the agency's covert operations, put it:

> It is difficult to overstate the significance that Yuri Nosenko's defection assumed in the investigation of President Kennedy's assassination. If Mr. Nosenko turned out to be a *bona fide* defector and his information were to be believed, then we could conclude that the KGB and the Soviet Union had nothing to do with Lee Harvey Oswald in 1963 and therefore nothing to do with President Kennedy's murder.
>
> If, on the other hand, Mr. Nosenko had been programmed in advance by the KGB to minimize KGB connections with Oswald, if Mr. Nosenko was giving us false information about Oswald's contacts with the KGB in 1959 to 1962, it was fair for us to suppose that there may have been a KGB-Oswald connection in November 1963, more specifically that Oswald was acting as a Soviet agent when he shot down President Kennedy.[14]

As there was only Nosenko's word to go on at the time, uncorroborated by hard evidence and unsubstantiated by a sin-

*Helms headed the CIA from 1966 to 1973 and then served as American ambassador to Iran.

gle document, it was not surprising that his interrogation stretched over years rather than months and that it grew increasingly hostile. It was equally understandable that Golitsyn, true to his passionate belief that the Kremlin was bamboozling the entire globe with its deception games, promptly leaped onto the stage like some pantomime demon against Nosenko. Golitsyn's gospel had already received a boost with the entry on the New York scene of a KGB agent, working under United Nations cover, who in March of 1962 had started volunteering information to the FBI. Code-named "Fedora" (various sorts of headgear were currently being used for naming Soviet agents), he was soon joined by a colleague from Soviet military intelligence, who also approached Hoover's bureau with offers of help and was duly christened "Tophat." Some believe both men to have been probable Moscow plants, whose function was to spread false tales about Russia's nuclear deficiencies while culling all they could about the true state of America's missile arsenal. But this was not the initial view of the FBI. However, the mere fact that there had been two mysterious walk-ins, whatever their story might be, only strengthened Angleton's conviction that Golitsyn was right, and his mood was not sweetened by the fact that Hoover insisted on keeping both the volunteers firmly under his own wing and out of contact with the rival CIA.

But it was Yuri Nosenko whom Golitsyn hailed as the supreme walk-in, a Kremlin agent, aimed, moreover, directly at him. Golitsyn did not know Nosenko's identity until 1964, although he was aware that a KGB officer had defected soon after his own arrival in the United States. He was in New York at the time and immediately rushed straight to Washington and into Angleton's office. "This," he declared, "is the one I warned you about. This is the man who has come to discredit me." Angleton needed little convincing, in view of his own gloomy philosophy and the existing doubts about Nosenko's information. In an unprecedented move, he actually showed Golitsyn the file on his ex-colleague. Once again, Golitsyn had some hard documentary meat provided by the West to chew on.

In Nosenko's case, he spat it all out as disinformation. It was

partly, at least, due to Golitsyn that Nosenko was to be held by
the CIA for a total of 1,277 days* and was interrogated on 292 of
these days,[15] at times under harsh conditions of confinement.

So what was Nosenko telling his interrogators about the Oswald case during those endless sessions of cross-questioning
between March 1962 and October 1967 when, to quote the official
version, "his case passed through various stages of phased nor-
malization as he was given an increased degree of freedom and
independence"?[16] What did the other innocent construction
about the KGB connection amount to? Though the debate on
this one issue covers more than six hundred pages of congressional hearings, there remained large gaps in the published
record which Nosenko himself filled in privately some years
later.

Two obvious puzzles which needed further explanation
were, first, why, as the KGB officer whose express task at that
time was to look for potential agents among Westerners in
Moscow, Nosenko had not tried to recruit Oswald; and, second,
if Oswald was not under the KGB's wing during his sojourn in
the Soviet Union, how was his special treatment to be explained? Nosenko's explanation on the first point runs as follows:

> Oswald's file was passed to me straightaway from Intourist in
> October 1959 after he had told them, immediately on arriving in
> Moscow, that he wanted to stay. Our business in the Seventh
> Section obviously covered any Western walks-ins as well as the
> active penetration of Western visitors. But a scale of priorities
> had been laid down by the KGB. The top targets, especially as
> regards Americans, were any employees of the Federal Govern-
> ment. Next in line were academics in general and Sovietologists
> in particular. Then came students, and finally, people who had
> ethnic links with the Soviet Union. Oswald didn't fall into any
> one of these categories and both my section head and his boss

---

*It needs recording that some of Angleton's colleagues have maintained that he had abso-
lutely no part in the decision, made later in 1964, to intensify the "hostile interrogation"
and transfer Nosenko to a specially constructed "bank vault" for this purpose.

[the chief of the Second Directorate] agreed that he was of no interest to us.

After the wrist-slashing episode, the case was returned to us again. You must remember this was the beginning of détente and though we still didn't want to deal with him, we felt it would send the right signal if he were allowed to remain. So it was agreed that Intourist should approach the government via the Ministry of Foreign Trade, under whom they worked.[17]

There is, it should be noted, some independent confirmation, admittedly indirect and secondhand, of the claim that Oswald's case was transferred at some time from the KGB to ordinary government channels. According to the report passed to the State Department from an American press correspondent, Madame Furtseva, minister of culture and a member of the Presidium of the Party's Central Committee, had interceded on Oswald's behalf after he had been "inspected by another Soviet agency." She had argued that the Soviet Union would only get adverse publicity and set a discouraging example if an American who was prepared to die in the attempt to seek asylum were turned away.[18] Oswald's own account in his "Historic Diary" of being handled by a completely different set of officials also indicates a switch of channels.

This does not, of course, mean that the KGB washed its hands of Oswald: once in its books, always in its books. But there are those the KGB seeks to recruit and those on whom it just keeps surveillance. According to Nosenko, Oswald was now placed in the latter category:

The city of Minsk was picked more or less out of the hat as his place of residence. The fact that it was fairly modern and would make a good impression certainly had something to do with it. But the KGB in Minsk, having been given all the particulars on Oswald's case so far, were instructed by Moscow Center just to keep him under routine security supervision—tap his phone, control his mail and, from time to time, watch his movements. Specific orders were issued not to approach him for any operational contact. I myself saw this letter which the Second Chief

Directorate sent down and these instructions were never coun-
termanded. If they had been, it would have come from the highest levels. All moves to recruit foreigners as agents have to be
approved by both the head of the KGB and the party's secretary-
general in person.[19]

As we have seen, Oswald duly tired of Minsk and the Soviet
way of life and returned to America with his young Russian
family in the summer of 1962. If the Nosenko version of his case
is to be believed, the KGB would then have closed its books on
this troublesome young American with a sigh of relief, never
expecting to open them again. Then, in November of the following year, came Kennedy's assassination, and the Oswald file
suddenly became the hottest one in the Moscow records.

Nosenko later described how, the moment the news from
Dallas reached Moscow, his Second Directorate boss, General
Oleg Gribanov, called him in and ordered the papers on Oswald
to be rushed up by military plane from Minsk. They arrived one
and a half hours later, delivered by hand by an officer who had
traveled in a bomber plane. The general had been perturbed by
the final sentence of a summary of the case as given over the
telephone from Minsk. The local KGB had concluded by saying
that it had "endeavored to influence Oswald in the right direction."[20] This ran flatly against its instructions.

So what was in the famous Oswald file? Considering its crucial information, the résumé of its contents, as given in the
congressional hearings, is somewhat skimpy. Asked later to describe the papers as fully as he could remember, Nosenko replied as follows:

> The file was in fact several folders. What the officers from Minsk
> handed over was a suitcase full of papers, perhaps six or seven
> folders in all. I had it in my hands to read for about thirty
> minutes. It began with a serial of 20–30 pages formally opening
> the file on Moscow's orders. This was largely familiar as it re-
> peated the instructions we had sent down to Minsk five years
> earlier. Had there been any decision to approach Oswald for
> operational purposes, that is, active contact, it would have been

recorded here. But there was nothing out of the ordinary—just a program, going into enormous bureaucratic detail, of his surveillance over an initial six-month period at his house and in the factory. There was only a brief mention of his wife's family and of Marina herself, who was described as "uninteresting." There were a few comments on his social life, including a report of him being taken out to shoot rabbits by some of the other factory workers. Ironically, in view of what happened later, it seemed he was a poor shot and didn't hit one.[21]

After about half an hour, Nosenko had to hand the file over to Colonel Mateev from the American Department of the Second Chief Directorate. General Gribanov needed everything available on Oswald, in order to make an urgent report to the Party secretary, Khrushchev. The need now was to show a pair of lily-white Soviet hands to Washington. As already stated, the dangerous instability of Oswald was, in itself, a powerful a priori argument against any Russian involvement in the affair. Further indicators that the Kremlin was innocent were given by the horrified shock which the assassination caused among top Soviet officers in the United States. The then United Nation's under secretary-general, Arkady Shevchenko, remembers how everybody at the Soviet mission (including its powerful KGB components, who would presumably have been aware of any murder plot) was appalled by the news:

> To begin with, we put our mission premises on full security alert, in case we might be stormed. It was clear from the talks we had had about the affair—and, later, in Moscow, with those in charge of American affairs—that they had been just as surprised and apprehensive. But, as so often, we had no directives as to how we should act. We proposed our own policy line of expressing sorrow and sympathy, and this was approved. Had there really been a plot we would surely, on this occasion, have had special guidance.[22]

By determining that Oswald had acted alone, that there had been no conspiracy with anyone else, the Warren Commission on the assassination did, in effect, exonerate the Soviet Union of blame. But this, of course, did not clear Nosenko of the suspicion that he had been floated out into the West to provide such exoneration in advance. We are back to the credibility of Nosenko's own story, which, as even his detractors had to admit, could not be questioned by any contradictory evidence from Intourist, the Moscow Passport Office, the Soviet Foreign Ministry or the KGB either in Moscow or Minsk, because not a shred of such evidence ever became available. It was the impossibility of contradiction which, in the end, weighed in his favor. Also in the same scales were the dogged persistence with which Nosenko stuck to his tale during hundreds of interrogation sessions, as well as a general CIA weariness with the entire wrangle. The upshot was his formal clearance and the payment of substantial compensation.

Yet one question mark has never been erased from his file and it looms so large that it is worth treating by itself in conclusion. The KGB knew that Oswald had served in the U.S. Marines, an elite corps. Why then did they not give him even the routine military interrogation which must surely have been standard procedure for any Western ex-serviceman who fell into their hands? Bagley, Nosenko's very capable Geneva case officer, who later swung against him, blasted this discrepancy in his account, quoting Oswald's own threat to the American consul that he intended to pass on to the Russians all the military information he possessed, including radar operations. For Oswald not to have been interrogated ran slap against everything the West took for gospel as Soviet practice. "Oswald's experience, as Nosenko tells it, cannot have happened."[23] Richard Helms, the deputy director of the CIA, was more circumspect. But even he, speaking five years after the event, admitted that the whole Nosenko version of Oswald's relations with the KGB continued to lack credibility. "I do not know how one resolves this bone in the throat."[24]

Nosenko tries to get the bone swallowed by insisting that neither he nor anyone else in Moscow had the slightest idea that Oswald had worked on air bases used by U-2s when the ex-marine turned up out of the blue as a tourist in October 1959:

He never mentioned this to Intourist and we never heard it from him or from anyone else. We knew all about spy flights and, even before the U-2s came into operation, every flight was being registered in and out of Korea, when I was serving in the Far East in 1951–52. But we just couldn't reach the U-2 planes, and had we known there was an American here who might just have a scrap of information to help with technical data, of course we would have sent someone to question him. But we didn't know and, just as a troublesome tourist, we were glad to get him off our hands.[25]

Thus Nosenko; the answer which not only opponents but also many neutral parties would give to this is that, spy planes or no spy planes, any NATO ex-serviceman in Soviet hands (especially one who placed himself there so eagerly) would automatically get a military debriefing, if only at the basic level of his personal weaponry and tactical training.

The one thing which has helped to dissolve Nosenko's "bone in the throat" is the steady drip-drip of time. Since he produced his controversial story, about a dozen major Soviet intelligence defectors, and one or two minor ones, have come over to the West. All of them who ever served in Moscow Center, more particularly those involved, even tangentially, in American operations, have been quizzed, at some point, on the Oswald-KGB connection. None has produced evidence or claims which contradict Nosenko's version. It can be argued, therefore, that it stands by default. There is, however, one explanation which might square the circle of the missing debriefing and which the disputants in the argument left out.

The Soviet Union is a grossly inefficient country, and we know of extraordinary lapses by the KGB over the years. This could have been one of them. The ex-marine should have been professionally debriefed; but in the mayhem of his suicide attempt and the transfer of his case to government hands, it is not inconceivable that the matter was lost sight of. As for Oswald, who is revealed by his own extraordinary "Historic Diary" to have been a young man of fantasy, boastfulness and contradictory impulses, his threat at the American embassy to "reveal all" to the Russians might very well have been no more than a display of peacock's feathers. The truth is that we shall never know the truth.

Yuri Nosenko himself, after three years of what was legally called "parole and exclusion"[26] in the United States, ending with his long spell of intensive grilling under Spartan conditions, was finally cleared of suspicion and "resettled on the economy"[27] in April of 1969. As from that month, he not only started to receive a regular salary as a contract adviser to the CIA but, over the years, received a series of lump-sum payments.

There were some, drawn not entirely from the ranks of his departed opponents, who felt that, leaving the money aside, for the CIA to employ this controversial figure as a consultant and lecturer was overegging the pudding of repentance. If there is one answer to that, it lies again in the passage of time. Throughout the twenty years of his professional services as a contract adviser, Nosenko was deemed to have earned his keep, albeit many of the CIA's Old Guard will die still feeling that 1964 bone pricking their throats.

PART FOUR

The Wheel Turns

13

Pluses and Minuses

WHEN WE move into the 1970s and 1980s, we enter a time of harvest for the Western intelligence services, a harvest where the quality of the crop is much more significant than the quantity. The count begins with a curious but important plus and several equally curious but relatively unimportant cases who are both plus and minus.

The plus was Oleg Lyalin, a member of the large Soviet Trade Mission in London, who used his post there, in common with several other colleagues, as cover for his KGB work in Britain. Though he held an official Soviet passport, he did not have diplomatic status, and this led to problems of all sorts when, in the early hours of August 31, 1971, the London police stopped him, seemingly drunk at the wheel of his car, which was steering a distinctly erratic course down Tottenham Court Road. He gave them his name and official status but refused either to submit to an on-the-spot Breathalyzer test or to provide a blood or urine sample at the local police station, where he was taken for the night. Having clearly broken the law by rejecting all the prescribed tests, he was duly charged and remanded on bail when brought up before the Marlborough Street magistrate the following morning. The bail, of 50 pounds, was provided by an official of the Soviet embassy, Aleksandr Abramov. Like Lyalin, he was a KGB man. Unlike Lyalin, he had full diplomatic cover for his job. As Soviet security officer, his worry now was that his colleague, who could not claim immunity, would inevitably be tried in open court and possibly given a short spell in a British prison. It was imperative, therefore, either to silence Lyalin or get him out of the country.

But though Comrade Abramov had no inkling of it at the time, his concern was shared, for very different reasons, by the British counterintelligence service MI5. In February 1971, Lyalin had been recruited by them as an agent in place, mainly because of a passionate love affair he was having with his secretary at the Highgate trade mission, one Irina Teplyakova. Lyalin's immediate demand, in return for his cooperation, had been for safe houses in London which he and Irina could use as love nests; his longer-term demand was that, if and when the time came, they could be launched on a new life together in Britain. (Each was married, though both his wife and her husband were living in the Soviet Union.) Now the time had come, much sooner than any of the partners to the bargain had expected. As Lyalin was in British custody when the alarm bells first rang, it was not difficult for MI5 to beat the KGB to the post. He formally defected, virtually from his remand cell, and the case against him was discreetly dropped.

His importance has been both underestimated and overplayed. Oleg Lyalin has a distinct historical significance in that he was the first Soviet intelligence agent to defect to the British since the war; the first to have been recruited by MI5, as opposed to its intelligence-gathering counterpart, MI6; and the first agent to be run by either service from inside the KGB.

One aspect of his professional importance has also been overlooked. His main job in London was to scout around for terrorist targets which Soviet special forces would be required to destroy or neutralize throughout Britain in the event of war. One of the projects he had been working on was how to make the trains in Britain run late or, perhaps one should say, even later. A more bizarre KGB scheme of his was to strew small glass balls containing nerve gas along the carpets and corridors of the Foreign Office, to be crushed under the feet of British diplomats, who would thus knock themselves out.

In this weird capacity, he worked for the KGB First Chief Directorate's Department V, Sabotage and Assassination, and he provided the West with the first proof that the Kremlin had an institutional framework for such activities. This particular department was, in fact, wound up as a result of his defection. Despite the fact that it was to reemerge some years later as Department Eight of the KGB's Illegals Directorate, the short- and medium-term damage to Soviet intelligence operations had been considerable.

On the other hand, though Lyalin named dozens of names, it is misleading to regard him as the sole explanation for the mass expulsion of ninety Soviet agents from Britain (and the exclusion of fifteen more who were abroad at the time) which followed in September of that year. Lyalin had revealed several cases which were new, including the particularly intriguing one of Sirioj Husein Abdoolcader, a young civil servant of distinguished Malaysian origin who, at the relevant time, had been working as a clerk in the Motor Licensing Department of the Greater London Council. At first sight, few official posts would appear to have been of less interest to the KGB. In fact, Abdoolcader's knowledge was of prime importance: all vehicles used by MI5 or Special Branch officers were on a classified protection list to prevent any ordinary police inquiries about their movements being followed up and exposed. If any one of these vehicles were to be observed speeding or illegally parked, steps would be immediately taken to warn the Metropolitan Police off any further action. Abdoolcader had access to this special screening list and was thus able to provide his KGB masters with the complete "order of battle" of the security services' mobile surveillance force. It was an example of a tiny cog which helped to turn a weighty intelligence wheel.

At the time of his arrest, in County Hall on September 17, 1971, Abdoolcader had been under Lyalin's direct control as Soviet case officer for more than two years. Few agents have been caught more clumsily red-handed. When he was searched, a postcard was found in his wallet addressed to Lyalin with a further list of MI5 vehicle registration numbers on the back. It was not surprising that the GLC file clerk pleaded guilty when his case came up at the Old Bailey on February 8, 1972. He was jailed for three years.*

However, Lyalin was only partly responsible for the 105 Soviet victims in the purge which followed his defection. The majority of these—one authoritative estimate puts it as high as 80 percent—were already known to the British authorities without his help or confirmation. But even when he was not the source, he was the pretext for the greatest-known mass expulsion of agents in the history of modern intelligence. As later Soviet defectors were to confirm, the British government's bold stroke was to hit Moscow Center like a tidal wave.

The other respect in which Lyalin's influence has been overplayed concerns the allegations of pro-Soviet sympathies, amounting to outright security risks, which swirled around the head of Harold Wilson and his government. It will be remembered that, ten years before, it was the Cassandralike defector Anatoly Golitsyn who had first raised this scare, though his imprecise misgivings were based on little more than suspicion over the frequent visits which the socialist leader had paid to Moscow as a bona fide businessman when out of office. To Golitsyn, there was simply no such thing as a bona fide stay in the Soviet capital for any Westerner at any time.

Now, in the early 1970s, Lyalin raised the specter again, during his first months as an agent in place for MI5. He was completely "freestanding" in that his information was not linked with anything that previous defectors had said. Though not as vague as Golitsyn, he produced only one hard lead. One of the KGB colleagues he named as working, like himself, under cover

---

*Two months before, on December 7, 1971, two of Lyalin's other agents, the Greek Cypriots Constantinos Martianon and Kyriacos Costi, had been sentenced to four and six years' imprisonment respectively. Nigel West gave the first full account of Abdoolcader's case in his *A Matter of Trust* (London, 1982), pp. 170 et seq.

of the Soviet Trade Mission was a Lithuanian called Richardas Vaygaukus. This agent, he said, kept close contact with the wealthy British raincoat manufacturer Joseph Kagan (also of Lithuanian origin) and Kagan, in turn, was the friend and financial backer of Harold Wilson. That was all, but the rumors which the story set off in Westminster and Whitehall were enough to prod Wilson himself into action. In 1972, out of office, he asked to be briefed personally by MI5 on the allegations. When told the bald facts, the former and future prime minister merely thanked the officer concerned and informed him that, as a purely social friend, Kagan had been given no sensitive information. However, Wilson added that steps would be taken in the future to ensure that this state of affairs would continue.* In the event, after Harold Wilson moved into Downing Street, there were said, at one time, to be half a dozen members of his government (though none of them in the Cabinet itself) to whom particularly sensitive papers were, on security grounds, never shown. But this is another story, and one to which Oleg Lyalin contributed nothing except, perhaps, some of the atmospherics.

The other curiosity of those early 1970s was an unprecedented cluster of redefections to the Soviet Union of intelligence officers who had fled, for only brief periods, to the West. The series began, and began in the oddest fashion, with Anatoliy Kuzmich Chebotarev, a thirty-seven-year-old major in the Technical Directorate of the GRU, working in Brussels under cover of a member of the Soviet Trade Delegation there. On October 2, 1971, he suddenly appeared at the British embassy in Brussels and asked for asylum, only to be told by a member of the staff that, as the weekend had begun and there was nobody to deal with him, he had better "come back on Monday." At this, Major Chebotarev decided to leave the British to their weekend and

---

*This did not stop Wilson from making Kagan one of his controversial life peers—an especially unhappy choice, in view of the businessman's later conviction for theft.

went the same night to the American embassy, which promptly accepted his defection. Five days later, he was in the United States, where, over the ensuing weeks, he identified to the CIA thirty-three Soviet intelligence officers working under a variety of covers in the Belgian capital. (Most were subsequently expelled by the Belgian government.)

Throughout the autumn, the Soviet embassy in Washington had been pressing the American authorities to allow them at least the opportunity of a face-to-face meeting with their defector, under proper safeguards. Eventually, with CIA agreement and a CIA presence, a somewhat reluctant Chebotarev was brought together with the Soviet chargé d'affaires. That was on December 21, 1971. Three days later, on Christmas Eve, Chebotarev's reluctance had vanished to the point where he went to the Soviet embassy by himself and asked for repatriation. Two days after that, he was flown back to Moscow, seemingly of his own free will. His later fate is not known, nor is it clear what, if any, were the special arguments or pressures which the Soviet authorities had applied to induce his return. What does seem evident is that he was not, from the very beginning, a plant. It defies logic, as well as all precedent, to imagine that the Russians would have organized the defection of a senior technical official who, having exposed a large part of their intelligence operations in Belgium, would then return to Moscow by prior arrangement to get a pat on the back, instead of being left where he was.

The same considerations apply to the others in this group. On June 12, 1972, for example, Nikolai Grigorievich Petrov, a thirty-two-year-old GRU captain working as an interpreter in the Soviet naval attaché's office in Jakarta, crashed his car when drunk close to the American embassy and decided to make a real night of it by walking up and defecting. (A smashed-up official car spelled, as he well knew, serious trouble with his own authorities.) However, life in the United States simply did not match up to what had been basically a panic decision, made under the influence of alcohol. Petrov finally redefected at the Soviet embassy in Washington on November 12, 1973.

The case that had immediately followed him was even more

extraordinary. In July 1972, a young KGB lieutenant called Artush Sergeyevich Organesyan walked across from Soviet Armenia into Turkey, accompanied by his wife and child. There was no doubt that this was not an impulse defection like that of Petrov, for the lieutenant had arranged a fishing holiday with his family close to the border in order to facilitate his escape. After a month's debriefing by the Turks, he was flown to America, where, over the best part of a year, he provided the CIA with much valuable information, including the names of over two hundred KGB men, several of whom were working in the United States. A more unusual "gift" which he had brought with him was one of the latest issues of the KGB's Watch List. This was the annually revised catalog of Soviet citizens of all sorts—ballet dancers, opera singers, musicians, writers, scientists, seamen and even circus clowns, as well as officials and intelligence personnel—who had failed to return from visits to the West, many of whom were known to have applied for asylum there.* The list, containing thousands of names with brief biographical details of each subject, was issued to, among other people, all Soviet border guards. The genuineness of Organesyan's defection (mainly motivated, he stated, by his disgust at the corruption within the KGB) can therefore scarcely be questioned.

Yet, as the first months of asylum in a strange and bewildering land went by, nostalgia for his Russian homeland overcame his revulsion against the regime which ruled it. The decisive emotional crisis arose in the spring of 1973, when his wife told him that she was carrying their second child. Both of them decided that, whatever the consequences for themselves, the baby would have to be born in their homeland. They had left things very late. The infant was, in fact, delivered on board the Aeroflot plane which was flying them back to Moscow in September of 1973. The airliner had to make a scheduled refueling stop at Heathrow, where British officials made a point of interviewing the couple to make sure that they really were acting of

---

*The criminal code of the Soviet Union, as amended on September 1, 1943, declared all such nonreturnees as traitors, to be executed by shooting within twenty-four hours of being apprehended and identified.

their own free will. That was the last trace the West had of them.

The last of this early-1970s bunch was almost a carbon copy of Nikolai Petrov. On September 10, 1972, Yevgeniy Georgiyevich Sorokin, a GRU lieutenant listed as a secretary to the Soviet military attaché in Vientiane, Laos, crashed his car into a tree in the Laotian capital and soon afterward walked into the American embassy to defect. Like Petrov, he was a heavy drinker and, like Petrov again, he found it hard to settle in the United States, where he produced some unexciting but nonetheless useful items of information. He proved altogether too moody and unstable to settle down. The end of an unhappy year came in October of 1973 when a shotgun he had purchased accidentally went off and smashed a television set. The next day he went to the Soviet embassy in Washington and asked for repatriation. He was flown back on October 26. The following day, his former chief in Vientiane, Colonel Vladimir Petrovich Grechanin, was recalled to Moscow. Sorokin is the only one of this group whose fate is known: he was later mentioned in a samizdat underground chronicle as having been sentenced to twelve years' imprisonment.

Four KGB or GRU men defecting to the United States within a year of each other, and all redefecting to the Soviet Union a few months after that. Was there a pattern, and could it have been sinister? It is very doubtful. Not even the most fanatical of the Golitsyn faction has been able to show that any one of the four—let alone all of them—was planted in the West. If one was, the purpose is obscure in the extreme. Between them, they inflicted damage on Soviet intelligence operations ranging from moderate to substantial. Their data, in all cases, proved basically accurate. They left no false trails, planted no confusion and spread no disinformation. In each case, their request for repatriation appeared unforced and seemed to spring naturally from family reasons (in the case of Organesyan) or problems of temperament and character (in the case of the other three). It is possible that more sensitive and sympathetic treatment on the part of their American hosts would have kept some of them in the West; that, however, only underlines the genuineness of their original defection. This quartet who crossed and then recrossed in the early 1970s is a statistical aberration, but nothing more. The rest of the epoch they ushered in was to be much more straightforward.

14

The Under Secretary-General

ONE OF the more bizarre scenes in postwar espionage features a senior Soviet official staring aghast at the bathroom shelf in his Havana luxury hotel on a spring evening of 1976. His horror is caused, not by something he sees there but by something he does not see, an old-fashioned twist-grip razor with numbers on the handle to adjust the setting of the flat blade inside. And the cause for concern is that before leaving New York, his regular base abroad, to attend a conference in Cuba, he was provided by the CIA with two identical-looking razors of that design. The difference lay hidden inside the cylinder of one of them. This had been specially adapted to conceal a microfilm giving the Russian all the emergency escape details he would need if he ended up in Moscow and in fear for his life. Now the hotel maid appeared to have stolen, along with his shirts, the razor he had left, without checking which, in the bathroom. Was it the incriminating one, or not?

In a cold sweat, he searches his luggage and retrieves its twin. There is a wave of panic when he twists the handle and the cylinder does not move. The maid is a security agent and his secret is out! Then he tries again, more deliberately, and the hidden chamber snaps open to reveal the roll of microfilm still inside. The man is safe after all, and resumes his duties with the Soviet delegation to the Havana apartheid meeting, trying hard to look unconcerned.

Had he really been betrayed by a Communist agent that day, the Cuban and Soviet intelligence services would have had the shock of their lives. For the Russian with the two razors was Arkady Nikolaevich Shevchenko, under secretary-general at the United Nations, who, for months past, had been working for the Americans "in place," and who was eventually to become the highest-ranking Soviet official ever to defect to the West. Shevchenko was never a Soviet intelligence officer, though the KGB did try to persuade him to join them very early on, and the CIA, as we have just seen, succeeded in recruiting him as one of their agents toward the end of his career. But, quite apart from these contacts at opposing tangents of his official service, he could and did disclose as much about the inner workings of the Soviet police state as any defector from the KGB itself. That is why this study would be incomplete without him, especially as he has greatly enlarged upon his published material for this purpose.

A career abroad as a Soviet diplomat always seemed the natural destiny for the young Shevchenko.[1] He was born in 1930, at Gorlovka in the eastern Ukraine, into a relatively sophisticated family. His father was the local doctor in a practice in which his mother, also of middle-class background, acted as nurse. When the child was five, the family moved to the congenial surroundings of the Crimean Black Sea coast, where the doctor had been appointed administrator of the tuberculosis sanatorium at Yevpatoriya (being obliged, whether he liked it or not, to put on a lieutenant colonel's uniform and join the Communist party). The Crimea had a relaxed, almost cosmopolitan air about it, at least compared with the countryside of the Ukraine, or indeed with any city of the industrial heartland. Living on a coast which looked toward Europe turned the eyes and the imagination outward and young Arkady's interest in this world outside was increased by his favorite hobby, which was stamp collecting.

School, the Young Pioneers and the Komsomol all did their best to nail his feelings down. Hitler's war (which cost his brother his life in the Red Air Force) inevitably fired his patriotism. But there was something in the boy's makeup which re-

belled at tunnel vision and yearned for wider horizons, especially after an exciting incident in February 1945 which drew
his own father, if only for a few hours, onto the fringes of
highest diplomacy. It was the time of the Yalta summit meeting,
when Stalin played host to the ailing President Roosevelt and
Prime Minister Churchill. Dr. Shevchenko found himself summoned to attend the welcoming ceremony at Simferopol airport
as one of a team of medical men ordered to observe and report
on the American leader's state of health. Arkady's father returned to describe how he had actually shaken the hand of the
great Stalin and had been presented to the two Western statesmen. He even brought back snippets of Yalta summit gossip.
Some new international organization was apparently being
planned by these giants to keep the peace in the postwar world.
His son wrote many years later: "I believe that my interest in
the UN dates from that time."[2] In 1949, when he left high
school, he took the first step in that direction. Resisting parental
attempts to steer him into the family profession of medicine, he
applied instead, and was accepted, to Moscow's State Institute
of International Relations, which supplied the Ministry of Foreign Affairs with most of its recruits. "The idea of being a
diplomat appealed to me and I also liked the notion of traveling
abroad," he wrote in his memoirs.[3]

He was not the only one. The institute was becoming very
popular with the nation's *jeunesse dorée*, which meant, for the
most part, the children of ministers or senior Party officials.
They had tasted all the high life which the Soviet Union had
to offer and wanted to move on to the far greater delights which
they knew, from the tales of privileged friends or relatives,
existed abroad. Arkady got into the institute partly by his own
family credentials, acceptable though modest, and partly on
scholastic merit. As soon as he entered the four-story building
near Moscow's Krynsky Bridge, he set his course for a foreign-
service career, choosing international law and French-language
studies with the aim of becoming a diplomat in Paris. Yet, after
finishing the grueling five-year course in 1954, he flirted for a
while with the idea of an academic career. It was his choice of
one particular subject for his postgraduate dissertation and a

meeting it produced with a famous figure in the Kremlin which put him back on his original course.

One of his fellow graduates at the institute was Anatoly Gromyko, the son of the Soviet foreign minister, who proposed that they write a joint article for the journal *International Life* on the role of parliaments (whatever that meant in the Communist scheme of things) in the struggle for disarmament. In the spring of that year, 1955, Shevchenko had already published a paper of his own on "Problems of Atomic Energy and Peaceful Coexistence," but this new project was on a different plane. *International Life* was the semiofficial journal of the Ministry of Foreign Affairs, and the minister himself was its editor in chief. Anatoly took both his friend and their joint article to be inspected by his father. The great man received them cordially in his somber Moscow apartment, approved the manuscript with a few additional points and then asked Shevchenko what he intended to do with his life. The young man replied that he was torn between academic research and a diplomatic career. The two could be combined, observed the minister. Matters were left at that, but not for long. A few months later, Shevchenko was summoned to the Ministry of Foreign Affairs and offered an attaché's post in a new department for United Nations and disarmament affairs headed by Semyon Tsarapkin.

There were two new reasons why Shevchenko accepted, two additional attractions about the career which had been his first love. To begin with, he was by now a married man, with an infant son. He had fallen in love at first sight with his pretty blond Lena at a skating party in Gorki Park in the winter of 1951 and they were wed in June of that year. She was an extraordinary mixture of Polish, Latvian, Belorussian and Lithuanian stock, and many of her relations, who spoke different languages, had no love for the Soviet police state. Lena's own urge to experience something better had been fired by descriptions of life in the Russian-occupied zone of Austria. Her mother was living there with her stepfather, who was working as an engineer on industrial plants seized by the Red Army as war reparations. The clothes she brought back at intervals from Vienna told their own story of vastly superior living standards, even in

a country under four-power occupation. The Shevchenkos did
not need much persuading that the poorest Austrian peasant
was better housed than they were: their first married home in
Moscow had been her stepfather's single room in a three-room
communal apartment in which fifteen people shared one
kitchen, toilet and sink. They went to the nearby public bath-
house to bathe. If occupied Austria was anything to go by, a
posting anywhere abroad would get them far away from that.

The second reason why young Arkady looked with added
favor on a foreign-service career was that his specialty—disarmament—now seemed to be coming in vogue at the Kremlin at
last. As a student at the institute, he had been nothing more
than a fascinated observer of the power struggle which had
followed Stalin's death in March of 1953. For him, the emergence of Nikita Khrushchev at the top of the Kremlin's very
greasy pole meant, above all, détente—a new opening to the
West and a new impetus to disarmament. It was this which had
inspired the last years of his academic studies. Now he was
being given the chance to put some of those ideas into practice.
It was thus a happy and eager Arkady Shevchenko who reported for duty at the ornate twenty-three-story building on
Smolensk Square which was to rule his life from now on.

He soon became a rather puzzled young man as well. He
joined in mid-October of 1956. On the twenty-third of that
month, a revolution against both Communism and the Russian
occupation broke out in Hungary, only to be crushed by Soviet
tanks ten days later, and thereafter held down by police-state
repression reminiscent of the worst excesses of Stalin. Perhaps
the Hungarians had gone too far in trying to break with the
Warsaw Pact; still, how could Khrushchev, who had publicly
broken with Stalinism, endorse such brutality? Trying to find
the answer was not the least of the young recruit's worries.

Years later, he described his bewildered ignorance,[4] sitting at
what he had imagined to be the hub of activity and information.
Despite repeated requests for guidance, there was never, from
first to last in the Hungarian crisis, a ministry briefing on the
situation. The staff had to be content with reading the ordinary
Tass messages from Budapest, which gave only a general out-

line of events. Even the classified Tass service, which was made available to senior officials, presented at best a sketchy and obviously slanted picture. Senior and junior staff alike looked in vain to see what Soviet missions were reporting back about reaction in Western, neutral and Third World countries. The cables from these capitals were never generally circulated in the ministry. This was an early taste of that starvation diet over official guidance and information which Shevchenko was to complain about for the rest of his career.

His physical comforts, on the other hand, began to be amply catered to from the moment he joined. He had entered the steel doors which opened into that hidden world of the privileged Soviet castes. The Ministry of Foreign Affairs had its own restaurant, its own medical facilities, its own holiday and convalescent centers and even its own special clothing stores. Shevchenko would never be an ordinary Soviet citizen again. At the highest levels of power, the separation was almost comic. The foreign minister, Andrei Gromyko, had not set foot on the sidewalks of Moscow for twenty-five years, according to his own daughter, Emilia.[5] This was the remote, ice-cold and dedicated Communist with whom Shevchenko's career was to be so closely bound.

In September 1958, after two years of back-room work on the Soviet arms-reduction proposals to be presented to the Western powers, he realized his childhood dream: a trip abroad, and to America at that. He was to go to New York, working for three months as a disarmament specialist with the Soviet delegation to the United Nations General Assembly meeting. Shortly before, he had become a member of the Communist party. He wrote quite frankly about his motive:

> I joined the Party in 1958 for very practical reasons: without the right political credentials I would not get Party and KGB approval for promotions or assignments abroad.[6]

Now the coveted *komandirovka,* or business trip, had arrived, years before a junior recruit to the service could normally have expected one. New York more than lived up to his imaginings.

In most cases where this first impact of capitalist plenty has been described, the Russian newcomers were people who had sprung from primitive peasant or worker backgrounds and had themselves known only a narrow intelligence training. That their eyes would widen, and jaws drop, at the first glimpse of "decadent imperialism" was natural enough. But Arkady Shevchenko was from a relatively sophisticated background; his education at the institute had been on a far wider basis, which included access, for study purposes, to much Western material. For two years past, he had been dealing with the West, if only on paper, and at several removes. The reaction of a privileged twenty-eight-year-old Russian of his stamp on landing in America is therefore doubly revealing:

> I had seen photographs of New York but nothing had prepared me for the impact of the towering city on the horizon. On our way from the airport to Glen Cove, Long Island, where we were staying, I saw comfortable-looking houses with neatly kept lawns, the endless stream of automobiles snaking along the wide highways, and countless abundantly stocked stores. The dozens of small food shops with all kinds of fruit and vegetables piled in boxes and baskets along the sidewalks made the strongest impression of all. I had never seen such displays in the Soviet Union, where everything was scarce or unavailable. If a store had dared to set a box of fruits outside its door, the box would have been snatched away instantly.[7]

When it is remembered that Shevchenko as a child had always been fascinated by this other world, and that, as a young man, he had joined the Communist party and the Ministry of Foreign Affairs with the prime objective of seeing this world, those feelings were prophetic. It was recognition, rather than discovery. Arkady Shevchenko seemed destined from the beginning not just to work in the West but, finally, to embrace it. The security officers watching over the Soviet delegation had done their best to dispel any "illusions" by organizing special tours of the worst slums in Harlem and the Bowery. In vain; even there, Shevchenko saw more fruit stalls, newsstands and bookshops where everything was freely on sale, as well as a five-and-ten-cent store whose range of merchandise would have been an Aladdin's Cave of luxury to ordinary Moscow shoppers.

Fortunately for him, this young man who had become privately captivated with New York became officially designated by his ministry for a career there. In September of 1960, he returned, this time as a full member of the Soviet delegation to the UN General Assembly, a delegation which was headed by Nikita Khrushchev himself. Moreover, he traveled to America in the company of the Soviet leader (and the Party secretaries of Hungary, Romania and Bulgaria) on a small Russian passenger liner, the *Baltika*. For the ten days the journey took, he had his first taste of life with, and conversation with, the rulers of the Communist world. Khrushchev, "a plain man, almost bald, with small piggish eyes and several large warts on his round, typically Russian face," was then at the unchallenged zenith of his power. He appeared to young Shevchenko as a figure of boundless, invincible energy. This impression was only strengthened when, as the Atlantic gales laid low most of the passengers and even half of the crew with seasickness, the Kremlin's ruler went on eating and drinking quite unconcernedly in the liner's deserted restaurant, scoffing at the sufferers for being weaklings. Occasionally, however, the guard would drop and he would give a hint of his own vulnerability. He was often seen reading, but rarely Western literature and never in foreign languages, which he did not know and had no intention of learning. "It would be better for me to master Russian properly," he confessed.

Shevchenko saw a lot of the great man during the voyage, for Khrushchev was writing and rewriting his speech to the General Assembly, where he intended to float the idea of general and complete disarmament. When the young expert cautiously suggested that such an approach was surely no substitute for practical East-West discussions, Khrushchev replied that, in the Soviet scheme of things, propaganda and real negotiation were not contradictory but complementary. He continued with a little lecture whose relevance was long to outlast his heyday:

Never forget the appeal the idea of disarmament has in the outside world. All you have to do is say "I'm in favor of it," and that pays big dividends. . . . A seductive slogan is a most powerful political instrument. The Americans don't understand that.[8]

A week or two later, on October 1, 1960, Shevchenko and the rest of the Soviet delegation were to sit in the UN General Assembly in stunned confusion as their leader started behaving at his worst before a world audience. This was the famous occasion where Khrushchev began by getting so carried away in a virulent onslaught against the Spanish dictator General Francisco Franco that he had to be rebuked by the Irish president of the Assembly, Frederick Boland, for attacking the head of state of a member country. It was but a mild overture to the scene which followed when the Spanish foreign minister, Fernando Castiella, took the floor to respond. After pounding the desk with his fists in protest, the ham actor and hot-blooded peasant in Nikita Khrushchev took over as he removed a shoe and started banging away with that to reduce the speaker to silence. Finally, when Castiella walked past Khrushchev's desk on his way back to his seat, the Russian lunged at him, brandishing his fists. Security guards had to rush forward to protect the frail Spaniard. Khrushchev was in high spirits afterward. The rest of the delegation were acutely embarrassed; Gromyko was white in the face with anger. Though he did not realize it at the time, Shevchenko had witnessed Khrushchev driving the first nail with his own shoe into his own political coffin.

The fiasco of the Cuban missile affair was to drive home another and far bigger nail two years later. Some of Shevchenko's observations on this upheaval have already been quoted in the Penkovsky context.* He had watched the autumn drama of 1962 from the tranquil shores of Lake Geneva, as part of the Soviet delegation to the Disarmament Committee. For the thirteen days of the crisis, he and his colleagues there held their breath with the rest of the world. They had been told nothing of Khrushchev's plans in advance. They learned noth-

*See p. 177.

ing of the struggle as it unfolded between the Kremlin and the White House, beyond what they were told by the Western media. Not a scrap of information or instruction was sent to Geneva from Moscow during the entire period. The chief Soviet delegate, Ambassador Semyon Tsarapkin, was not even given guidance on whether he should continue or suspend his negotiations with America and Britain on a nuclear test ban in view of the full-blown missile crisis which had erupted between the two superpowers. It was another staggering example of the way in which the Soviet leadership, out of a blend of arrogance and secrecy mania, would simply ignore the entire official network in a matter deemed to be the Politburo's own. For Shevchenko, Cuba had been a bitter, baffling experience which destroyed his initial illusions about Khrushchev. The Soviet New World had lost its glitter.

It was a relief when, the following summer, he was able to escape far away from the political battles of the postmortem in Moscow. In June 1963, he was posted to the UN in New York again, this time not only as a disarmament expert but as head of the Soviet mission's key division for Security Council and political affairs, with a staff of twenty-eight diplomats working under him. Only seven of these were Foreign Ministry officials. The others were all professionals from the two Soviet intelligence services, the KGB and the GRU.

He later described the problems of shouldering this heavy, poorly camouflaged burden. To begin with, as he was constantly complaining to one of his juniors, the KGB chief in New York, Major General Ivan Glazkov, these bogus diplomats only exposed themselves by refusing to take any part in the formal activities of the mission. But he was ignored. The general had his espionage slots in the mission, allotted to him by Moscow, and nothing but the Politburo could remove them. In any case, the KGB ignored the mission's work and, for that matter, were indifferent to the UN itself. For these cuckoos in the diplomatic nest, the world body was purely a platform for intelligence operations against the Americans. They never interfered in Shevchenko's policy decisions because these were of no interest to them.[9]

However, this overpowering physical presence of the intelligence community within the mission did have one advantage: the KGB knew far more about the prevailing mood in Moscow than did the diplomats, and could therefore predict, better than anyone else in New York, what changes in Soviet foreign policy might be in the offing. They went back and forth to the Soviet capital and brought back the nearest thing to inside information which Shevchenko and his professional colleagues could hope to glean.[10] Their own cables from the Ministry of Foreign Affairs gave them, as usual, little or no help, even over a major diplomatic crisis which profoundly concerned the United Nations such as the Six-Day War between Israel and the Arab states in 1967. Only when it was clear beyond doubt that the Israelis had triumphed did Moscow issue instructions and then, by an extraordinary procedure, over an open telephone line, order the Soviet mission to follow the American line and get an immediate cease-fire at all costs.[11] The Kremlin, of course, had a strategic aim throughout the Middle East and the Arab world: to widen its power in the region, undermine Western strength there and so build up a staging area for further expansion into the Mediterranean and the Indian Ocean. But it had no coherent or consistent policy toward achieving that aim. Decisions were made pragmatically. Grand operational theories were distrusted by the members of the Politburo. It was dangerous to advance initiatives there. The ideas might so easily go wrong, and then the luckless sponsor would be labeled with their failure. The result was that, in Shevchenko's time, Moscow tended to react to events on the world scene rather than anticipate them.*

It was when Shevchenko returned to Moscow in the spring of 1970, which marked the time limit for his tour abroad, that he moved, for the first and only time in his life, to be within touching distance of the hub of Soviet power. Andrei Gromyko, his sponsor since the beginnings of his career and still minister

---

*Decisions made within the Soviet power orbit, such as the 1968 invasion of Czechoslovakia which put a permanent frost on Dubček's Prague Spring, were, of course, a different matter. This was not diplomacy, it was self-preservation.

of foreign affairs, had offered him the post of personal adviser; he had jumped at the opportunity, despite rival bids by the Central Committee to recruit him for a job there. At forty, Arkady Shevchenko, as can be seen, was a man in great demand, in both government and Party circles. His status and salary in New York (where he had ended up as minister plenipotentiary) had already enabled him to buy first a large Moscow apartment for Lena and their two children and then a dacha in the woods outside the city. These were the material symbols of the Nomenklatura, the top Soviet elite, to which he now belonged. He moved among that elite until returning to New York for his most prestigious and most fateful posting three years later, and it is this Moscow period, April 1970 to April 1973, which proved most revealing for him, and therefore for anyone writing about him. His link to the Kremlin's main power circuit was, of course, through his minister, who in turn had close contact, and considerable influence, with Leonid Brezhnev, the stolid Party infighter who had taken over the leadership in 1964. He had been shrewdly cultivated by Gromyko even in Khrushchev's day.

The portrait Shevchenko gives of his master does not differ in outline from that asbestoslike image which the foreign minister displayed to the outside world: calm, persistent, patient, indefatigable, humorless, above all the supreme professional, a robot version of Talleyrand in his mastery of the diplomatic craft. Yet Shevchenko was able to shed some new light on the familiar figure. Whereas, to the West, Gromyko was "Mr. Nyet," the seeming embodiment of Soviet hostility and intransigence, Shevchenko claims that, in reality, his chief was always so obsessed with American-Soviet relations, and with the need to keep them on an even keel, that the Politburo hard-liners would openly criticize him for being too keen on realpolitik. The criticism was dampened when, in 1973, Gromyko was himself elevated to the Politburo. From then on until his gradual demise in the Gorbachev era, Gromyko had an institutional base from which to operate—indeed, the supreme one—though he never possessed, and never sought, any broader power base in the Party itself. One of the secrets of his survival was that he was uniquely valuable in his own chosen sphere yet never tried to step beyond it. Every Kremlin leader from Khrushchev to Yuri Andropov relied on him both to suggest and then to execute Soviet foreign policy. None of them had the slightest grounds to fear him as a rival. Indeed, he consistently and deliberately isolated himself, not only from Party feuding but from Russia's domestic problems as a whole. Perhaps it was partly because he realized that these were even more insoluble than the trickiest of international questions.

Shevchenko was fortunate enough to work with Gromyko—with broad authority "to review and comment on sensitive proposals and to report personally to him"[12]—at a time when the foreign minister, basking in Brezhnev's favor, was at the peak of his influence. Indeed, during the three years Shevchenko served him as adviser, there was not a single occasion when any of Gromyko's submissions on foreign affairs was rejected or even substantially reversed by the leadership. If the minister sniffed any opposition floating in the air, he would have it blown away by going straight to Brezhnev behind the Politburo's back. The reason why this behavior aroused so little enmity was, again, because everyone knew that Andrei Gromyko was pleading the cause of his problems and not of his ambitions.

There were, of course, plenty of other hands who wanted to mold those policies for him. The three most powerful pairs belonged to the KGB, the military and the International Department of the Central Committee. His links with the KGB inevitably increased after his promotion to the Politburo. The so-called Secretariat, which was in fact his private office, was expanded to include KGB guards, advisers who read all KGB and GRU code cables from abroad, and liaison personnel with the KGB Moscow Center. Gromyko gave the intelligence services all they demanded in the way of diplomatic cover abroad but he distanced himself from them as much as possible. They dealt primarily with individuals, mostly in a callous or brutal fashion. He was concerned throughout with ideas which, for him, transcended the tragedy of individual human lives. Thus, he was always irritated when caught up in the diplomatic backlash of KGB domestic repression against, for example, dissidents and refuseniks. They were none of his business. It was typical of him that whereas his predecessors had from time to time called on the KGB headquarters to discuss problems of mutual interest, Gromyko never set foot in the place but held the discussions in his own office. One of his blind spots as a devoted and, ultimately, a desiccated servant of the Party was his failure to realize how important an international issue the whole question of human rights had become.

With the military, on the other hand, Gromyko was consciously—and constantly—locked in conflict. His principal antagonist here was the hard-line minister of defense, Marshal Grechko, a bitter opponent of détente in general and of disarmament talks in particular. As a specialist in this field, Shevchenko saw plenty of their rivalry in action. When, for example, the first Strategic Arms Limitation Treaty (or SALT) talks were started up (over Grechko's apoplectically twitching body), a dispute broke out over who was to head the Soviet delegation. Gromyko wanted a soldier as the chief delegate; Grechko insisted on a civilian. Each was preparing the ground for the strong possibility of failure, which, if it came, would not be laid against his own departmental door. According to Shevchenko, Grechko's stand had another explanation: the obsession with secrecy. He was afraid that a soldier, untrained in the subtle arts of diplomacy, might be drawn out beyond his brief by cunning American negotiators and so let slip sensitive details about the true Soviet situation in the nuclear field.[13] The marshal won that particular round. In the end, it was a civilian, Simirov, who was appointed.

Wherever geopolitics entered into Soviet diplomacy (which was not infrequently), Gromyko and Grechko would again often find themselves at cross-purposes. This was above all true of the Third World, where Soviet military supplies formed the main pillar of Soviet influence and where the two ministers, or their deputies, negotiated together with the recipient country and put their joint signatures on any agreement. The arguments in Moscow often began afterward, as Shevchenko has described in the crucial example of the arms-to-Egypt affair.

Once the initial transfer of weapons had been made, the Ministry of Defense, presumably with Politburo approval, began to squeeze the independent-minded Egyptian president, Anwar Sadat, by holding back on deliveries of the vital spare parts for the armadas of old Soviet planes and tanks they had equipped his armed forces with. Gromyko, though not well served by the advice from his ambassador in Cairo, Vinogradov, was nonetheless concerned that Sadat might call Moscow's bluff and wipe out the political and strategic stronghold which the Russians had managed to build up in Egypt.[14] He proved correct. In July of 1972, Sadat's patience snapped over the delays. He abruptly closed down all Russian military facilities in the country, including their burgeoning naval base at Alexandria, and threw out the hundreds of Soviet advisers who had been working with his armed forces. To this day, the Soviet Union has not regained a comparable stronghold in the Mediterranean, though it can, of course, be argued that, with each advance in missile technology, such conventional land bases have become less important.

By the time the Kremlin made its most costly postwar mistake, the invasion of Afghanistan at the end of 1979, Arkady Shevchenko was not only out of the mainstream of Soviet diplomacy, he had cut ties with his homeland altogether. But he is convinced that, if anyone voiced reservations in the Politburo about the decision—because of the formidable damage it would do to the Soviet Union's standing abroad, and especially in the Third World—that man would have been his former mentor and master, Foreign Minister Gromyko.[15]

The third force which was always trying to get its hands on Soviet foreign policy was, of course, the Communist party itself, and, specifically, the International Department of the Central Committee. Indeed, the view has often been expressed in the West that this body in fact controls Soviet diplomacy and that the Ministry of Foreign Affairs in Moscow is purely its tool. Shevchenko has put forward a corrective to this theory, at least as regards any period, like his own time in Gromyko's office, when the minister is an authoritative figure who enjoys some clout in the Politburo, and especially among the Moscow-based members who compose that body's inner core.

There are, he says, no rules governing relations between the Foreign Ministry and the International Department, and in his time the ministry never had to submit any proposal to its rival. Yet there was always a basic clash of policy between the ministry, which under Gromyko (and even more under his successor) had worked for peaceful coexistence, and the department, which strove for the expansion of Soviet influence abroad through local Communist parties or armed "liberation movements." This is part of the deep-rooted conflict in Soviet history between pragmatism and ideology, and on the diplomatic front it was particularly sharp so long as the International Department was run by Boris Ponomarev, a convinced hard-liner and instinctive opponent of détente.

There were occasions, Shevchenko recalls, when the rival elements were compelled to act together; any decision affecting the Palestine Liberation Organization, for example, was always made jointly because the PLO spanned both their worlds. But on Middle Eastern policy in general (on which Shevchenko, through his duties at the UN, became something of an expert) the clash was often quite open. Thus, after Israel had routed her Arab neighbors in the Six-Day War of 1967, Gromyko realized that it was simply impracticable to expect the victor to retreat to her old frontiers. Ponomarev, on the other hand, was for pressuring the Israelis to hand back all the territories they had conquered, in order to help Soviet relations with the Arab world as a whole.[16] The final decision was, as always, up to the Politburo, which itself had no rules of procedure, kept no verbatim records and was subject to the constant fluxes of personal rivalries. In all, the picture of the Soviet power system which Shevchenko painted for Western experts left them wondering how, in the period between the fall of Khrushchev and the rise of Gorbachev, the Kremlin managed to decide anything at all.

It is time to recount how Shevchenko came to be in a Havana hotel, equipped with two razors specially made for him by the CIA, and how, two years later, he finally made the open break with his career, Party and motherland and crossed over for good into the West.[17] The same blend of motives is discernible as with the defectors from the intelligence world. As in their cases, the problem is to see through any distortion or self-deception and weigh the true balance between those motives.

Shevchenko himself, and those who advised and helped with his memoirs, put an overwhelming emphasis on the ideological factor: disillusionment with the hypocrisy, venality, oppressiveness, inefficiency and institutionalized inequality of the Soviet system. Yet the truth, as we have seen, is that Shevchenko never had much ideology to jettison in the first place. He was a pragmatic, even a reluctant Communist who had only joined the Party to make sure of both promotion and perks in his diplomatic career—above all, the supreme perk of a foreign posting. Even nostalgia for Rodina, the Russian motherland, proved in his case relatively easy to suppress. In the total span of more than ten years he spent at the United Nations, America, as he himself admitted, had gradually become a second and substitute home. Of all the defections studied so far, his was the longest in preparation and the most likely in outcome.

On the other hand, that outcome meant in his case that he also had the most to lose. As a United Nations under secretary-general when only in his mid-forties, Shevchenko had a glittering career ahead of him, with one of the major Soviet ambassadorships or the rank of deputy foreign minister as a natural climax. Already in 1970, when appointed one of Gromyko's personal advisers, he had commanded the privileges of the top government elite. Even if required to serve again in Moscow, therefore, life for himself and his family could only grow lusher and lusher by Communist standards. The trouble, as he had come gradually to realize, was that those standards were simply not enough, as regards both a freer and a fuller life. Shevchenko was not so much spurning a system he had come to loathe (though that element certainly entered into it) as reaching out for something more congenial and—given the fact that he was defecting to the land of unlimited opportunity— potentially just as rewarding. As with so many of the intelligence defectors, disagreements with his colleagues and marital considerations also played their part in weakening further the Soviet hold over him. And, as with nearly all of the others, fear for his life was what propelled him into the final leap.

There seems to have been no single incident which prompted his first approach to the Americans. Though he was on the worst of terms with Yakov Malik, the vituperative Cold War warrior who was his country's ambassador to the UN, there was no last straw of argument at the office which drove him to turn his back on all his colleagues. Moreover, though on his own admission his marriage was by now failing, there was no row at home with his wife to trigger his actions, like the domestic flare-up which snapped the patience of Major Peter Deriabin in Vienna twenty years before. The under secretary-general just decided, sitting in his office on the thirty-fifth floor of the slab-like UN Secretariat building one Friday in 1975, that enough was enough and the time for the long-meditated move had come.

It was for him a hazardous decision. This was the heyday of détente, which the Americans might well be reluctant to damage; there were, in any case, no precedents for handling a defector of his rank and international status. Having had no intelligence experience, he, in turn, was a child in the art of covering his tracks from the eyes of his own security services. Even greater danger loomed up when he finally made contact, through an American diplomatic colleague, with an agent of the CIA, the meeting having been arranged through slips of paper pressed into his hands, first at the UN Library and then in a New York bookstore. For when he finally met up, in a brownstone on the Upper East Side of New York, with "Bert Johnson," the man who had come up from Washington to see him, he found that what the Americans wanted him to do for the time being was to stay on at his key post in the UN and feed them from there with information. To defect in one bound as a diplomat was one thing. To remain in place as a spy was quite another. He was not the type. He did not have the training for it, nor did he have the stomach for it. Open defiance was honorable; spying smelled of deceit and treachery. Like career diplomats all over the world, he regarded espionage as a somewhat dubious business.

Above all, it was a perilous business. The trial in Moscow in 1963 of Colonel Oleg Penkovsky flashed across his mind, along with other disturbing images. He also recalled the controversy, still raging in American official circles, over the KGB defector Yuri Nosenko. Once he himself started dabbling in this complex intelligence game, might he not fall under suspicion with his new spy masters? Yet in the end, he accepted. He felt in any case trapped by the mere fact of having applied for asylum. If the KGB regularly practiced blackmail, surely the CIA would not be above it? He began to reason out the potential gains. He would win time to persuade his wife Lena (who knew nothing of his plans and would probably oppose them) that his decision was the right one. More precious to him than Lena was his daughter Anna. Gennady, their son, was happily established in Moscow starting on a career in the Foreign Ministry. There was no hope of extracting him, even had he been willing. But the girl, who was his favorite child, was with them in New York and would be allowed to go on studying at the Soviet school there until she reached the senior grades, when she would have to return home. It ought to be possible to take her with him into exile. So, for more than two years, the Soviet under secretary-general at the United Nations worked from his office as an American agent.

He appears never to have photographed secret Soviet documents for the CIA. The "Referentura," Ambassador Malik's special cipher and communications unit, was guarded like a fortress, with electronic surveillance over every visitor. What Shevchenko could, and did, do from now on was to memorize as much as possible from any cables he read and keep the Americans up-to-date on general policy discussions inside the Soviet mission. In this way, they learned, for example, as much as that mission ever knew itself about the Kremlin's calculated views on détente; Russia's aims in the Middle East; her relations with Cuba; Cuba's involvement in Africa; and, of course, any behind-the-scenes developments in Shevchenko's specialty of disarmament. Moreover, as the official the KGB relied upon to sponsor and help its agents, disguised as diplomats, in the United Nations, he could provide the Americans with a complete picture of Soviet intelligence penetration of the world body.

Apart from one or two scares, which turned out to be false

alarms, at the beginning of his time as a CIA agent, Shevchenko found the business of discreet espionage less difficult and perilous than he had imagined. Indeed, he was growing almost confident about his ability to sustain this deadly double game until the first serious check on his activities cropped up in the spring of 1977. Oleg Troyanovsky, who had replaced Malik at the turn of the year, summoned all senior Soviet officials from both the Soviet mission and the Secretariat to hear a statement by the KGB chief inside the UN, Yuri Drozdov. This turned out to be a call for increased vigilance against "imperialist provocations," spelled out at great length and couched in familiar Party propaganda language. But it was followed by an order tightening up on all contacts with foreigners in New York and with detailed restrictions on movements in the city applying equally to Soviet citizens in the Secretariat. Shevchenko did not feel, as yet, personally threatened by all this. However, as under secretary-general, he knew that he would be responsible, in the Kremlin's eyes, for seeing that these curbs were observed. He would also, as a matter of course, be the top target himself for extra routine surveillance.

It was while he was on home leave to visit his mother in the Crimea the following summer that he first began to suspect that the surveillance was not simply routine. A man who was patently a security agent boarded the southbound express train at Kursk with him and kept watch in the corridor outside his sleeping compartment. On the return journey from the family home at Yevpatoriya, he found his berth had been changed without explanation by the stationmaster to a relatively empty compartment where another KGB man was able to keep a close watch on him throughout the trip. He later wrote:

> Andrei Gromyko and everyone below him in the Foreign Ministry had treated me completely normally. But the secret police, it seemed, took another and possibly ominous attitude.[18]

These unwelcome attentions continued when he joined his wife for a three-week stay at the Caucasian spa of Kislovodsk, where a suite had been reserved for them in the resort's finest hotel, an establishment reserved exclusively for the Soviet elite. Here, their privacy was constantly disturbed by two male fellow guests who persistently engaged them in conversation and stuck to them like glue on their walks and picnics. Shevchenko's final taste of Nomenklatura luxury left him with a distinctly bitter feeling in his mouth. Nor was his mood helped by having to leave his daughter behind him in Moscow to attend high school. If he was to take Anna with him one day to the West, it would have to be during one of her holidays in America. That meant further problems and further delays.

He spent an uneasy winter in New York. There were disagreements with his colleagues. Gossip murmurs arose among the Soviet wives that the Shevchenkos had been at the UN long enough. One Saturday night early in 1978, after he had pleaded illness to escape the regular Party committee meeting, there was a pounding on the door of his apartment. He refused to answer but discovered the next morning that his callers had been the Soviet doctor and Yuri Shcherbakov, the mission's security officer. They had been "concerned about him." He could feel the net closing. The question was: how fast? After pleading from his CIA contacts, he agreed to hang on until the summer, when his daughter would be back in New York. All the hints he had dropped to his wife about starting a new existence together in America had fallen on stony ground; perhaps the child would help to change her mother's mood. Then, on Friday, March 31, 1978, the blow came which squashed all hopes of playing for a bit more time. His masters had decided for him that his time was up. A telegram had arrived from the Foreign Ministry recalling him "for several days of consultations in connection with the forthcoming special session of the U.N. General Assembly on disarmament, as well as for discussion of certain other questions."[19] He was instructed to advise Moscow of his flight plans.

The weekend gave him two days to play with. He used part of it to make emergency contact with his American spy masters. On Monday morning he found Ambassador Troyanovsky anxious to bundle him on the first Moscow-bound flight. That was ominous enough. But the alarm signal flashed bright red when, over lunch that day, he pumped a close friend in the Soviet mission over the Foreign Ministry's interest in the UN's special Disarmament Committee. The big boys in Moscow, he was told, were just not interested. They had decided on their policy in advance of its debates and wanted only a retrospective report when the committee had wound up its work. The summons home had clearly not been inspired by Gromyko. It was a KGB deception. He phoned his CIA contact from the restaurant. At a meeting with them the same evening, Thursday of that week, three days before he was booked on his Moscow plane, was fixed as the time for him to jump clear. Once again, as with so many defectors who had preceded him from the Soviet intelligence world, it was the dire threat of a recall telegram which had provided the ultimate impulse.

Compared with so many of their cases, however, the mechanics of extracting Shevchenko from Soviet security control were child's play. He was a top UN official living in a private New York apartment and working in the most famous, and most public, international building in the world. On the agreed day, he stayed late at his office, packing personal files and other mementos into his briefcase. He also took from his safe a long pleading letter, addressed to his wife, whose main purpose was to make it clear to the KGB that she had not been his accomplice. He was abandoning her to her fate with decent concern rather than with loving anguish. As he wrote later of this moment: "We had grown apart."[20]

Sentiment apart, the practical side of things—which looms very large in a defector's eyes when the moment of truth arrives—ruled out any direct approach to her. She would never have consented to come with him, leaving the schoolgirl daughter stranded in Moscow. Moreover, being a woman with a hot temper, she might even have exposed him. So he slid out of her life as quietly as he had slipped away from his career. Returning home after midnight, he took one last look at his sleeping wife, left his farewell letter with some money in an envelope by the door, packed an overnight bag and walked down twenty flights of the fire escape to the ground. Fifty yards away on Sixty-fourth Street, the CIA car was waiting as arranged. They were holding the back door open for him as he ran up. A few seconds later they were on their way to Pennsylvania, and a safe house in the Poconos, two hours outside the city.

Shevchenko's status at the United Nations had aided his escape. Now he set about using it as a springboard to launch him into his new life. Though Moscow had recalled him as a Soviet citizen, he still had a two-year contract to run as an international civil servant. His master in this capacity was not Andrei Gromyko but Kurt Waldheim, the UN secretary-general, at that moment abroad. Shevchenko would approach him on his return. The United Nations operated openly, not secretly. It knew only resignation, not defection. The next few weeks passed in a curious blend of ugly KGB pressure and bland, reassuring UN bureaucracy.

The pressure followed predictable lines. His wife had been packed off home by the Soviet mission soon after his defection. He now received letters both from her and from his son Gennady,* urging him to return. Both were artificially phrased and had clearly been concocted. The message from Gennady, which was typed, did not even carry a signature. Similar routine attempts to get him to change his mind were made by Troyanovsky and Anatoly Dobrynin, the Soviet ambassador to Washington, at a face-to-face meeting arranged in the New York office of Ernest Gross, the American lawyer he had engaged to represent him, at the CIA's suggestion. Both his former colleagues affected ignorance of a letter Shevchenko had left behind addressed to Leonid Brezhev. In this, the defector had formally renounced his Communist party membership and had proposed a bargain with Moscow: he would resign from his UN position (and thus spare the Soviet regime further embarrassment) only when "certain questions regarding my family are resolved."[21] Needless to say, no reply ever came from the Party leader in Moscow. Instead, the Kremlin brought all the pressure it could exert on Waldheim, at every stage of his foreign

---

*Gennady, who was serving with the Soviet mission in Geneva at the time of his father's defection, was bundled back to Moscow under guard in a Soviet airliner within hours of the news becoming known.

tour, to sack his fugitive aide back in New York and announce the dismissal publicly.

To his credit, Waldheim was to refuse to the end.[22] Yet some announcement about the under secretary-general had to be made. By now, ten days had passed; his absence was becoming impossible to conceal and difficult to explain. On Monday, April 11, the United Nations spokesman came out with it at his regular noon briefing, which, for once, provided spectacular copy:

> Mr. Shevchenko has informed the Secretary-General that he is absenting himself from the office and, in this connection, he mentioned differences with his government. Efforts are being made to clarify the matter and, for the time being, therefore, Mr. Shevchenko is considered to be on leave.[23]

This was precisely what Shevchenko had been hoping for, indeed suggesting, in his contacts with the Secretariat. He was still under secretary-general of the world body, answerable to it, and not to the Kremlin. At the same time, it was being made plain, without being stated, that he had broken with the Soviet regime and was seeking political asylum.

The final act was played out, on the thirty-eighth floor of the UN building on the night of April 25, immediately after the secretary-general's return from Europe. The United Nations flag was wrapped around Shevchenko to the last. Though armed American guards accompanied him to the basement entrance of the building, the UN's own security men took him up to Waldheim's office, a venue which both recognized his status and guaranteed his safety. Once Waldheim was assured that his aide was acting of his own free will and did not intend to make difficulties, the formalities were rapidly and amicably concluded. All went according to the UN rule book. Waldheim and his Soviet aide signed the formal separation papers and the agreed financial settlement. This came to just over 72,000 dollars and was made up of accrued pension, early retirement pay, unused annual leave allowance and so on. Like the bereaved who are obliged in their grief to talk business with the undertaker, Shevchenko doubtless found this bureaucratic rigmarole useful in controlling his emotions. A handshake with Wald-heim, an elevator ride down to the underground garage and he was back again with his American guards in the New York street—but now a private citizen, without status or even nation-ality.

There was a bitter beginning to this new existence. Early on May 11, just as he was settling down to his long debriefing sessions in a Washington safe house, a Western newspaper re-port was handed to him saying that his wife Lena was dead. This was no mere press speculation. It bore the byline of Victor Louis, a Soviet citizen who operated as the Moscow correspon-dent of the London *Evening News*. He was a notorious KGB conduit, and had been chosen, for example, in 1964, to break the news of Khrushchev's fall from power. According to Louis, Lena Shevchenko had committed suicide. Her husband, shocked and remorseful rather than grief-stricken, found this hard to believe. But the alternative, that she had been executed, was even harder to stomach. He never discovered the truth; nor, despite repeated letters and telegrams to his children, did he ever find out what had happened to them. There was a further low point in his life when, complaining of loneliness, he was introduced through the CIA to one Judy Chavez, with whom he embarked on a disastrous affair. After living with him for some weeks, this Mexican lady moved out and sold her story of life with the famous defector to the media, revealing his address in the process.

From that low point, however, Shevchenko's path as an exile went steadily upward. In December 1978, he married an intelli-gent and attractive southerner and acquired an all-American family as well as an all-American wife to settle him in his new world. His earnings as a lecturer and the author of a best-selling book soon started to top his old salary as a senior Soviet official. After a brief period disguising himself with dark glasses and a false mustache, he dropped any pretense at hiding and assumed a high profile. This was common sense, not bravado. The KGB was primarily concerned with tracking down defectors from their own ranks. They would hardly risk the outcry which the murder of a former UN under secretary-general would provoke.

The American government made regular use of him as a policy consultant. One of the principal questions they must surely have put to him after the arrival to power in Moscow of Mikhail Gorbachev was whether the changes which followed in the Soviet world were cosmetic or fundamental. The following comment would give a good indication of his verdict:

> The process Gorbachev has started is irreversible. A reversion to terror is unthinkable. So is a reversal to the old isolation. The new information technology will guarantee this by itself. Dish antennae (which can be home produced) will gradually link the Soviet Union to the television programs of the entire globe, for example.
>
> Yet politically Gorbachev is himself a transitional figure, because he still believes his glasnost, even when extended to the full, is compatible with a Leninist Socialist society. It is not. What will be the political shape of Russia in the next century I cannot judge. But, within a generation, Communism there as a system is doomed.[24]

15

The Ideal Soldier

ON SEPTEMBER 13, 1985, the largest military home defense exercise to be held in Britain since the Second World War ended with a mass drop of paratroops at Thetford in East Anglia. "Brave Defender," as the exercise was named, had lasted eight days and had involved a total of 65,000 personnel. The emphasis throughout was to defend from saboteurs the country's key installations in the Third World War: its missile sites, air bases, radar stations, power plants, fuel storage depots, ports, broadcasting transmitters and so on. The scale of these defensive measures was remarkable; so was the pinpointing of the threat, which had been precisely defined in the British media weeks in advance.

Brave Defender was not to be just another routine mock battle against unnamed "hostile forces." It was specifically designated as an exercise to combat the landing of the so-called Speznaz forces of the Soviet army, the Kremlin's specially trained terrorist units whose prime function in wartime is to paralyze the resistance capacity of NATO countries as a prelude or accompaniment to full-scale attack.

There was a further burst of publicity when the exercise was over and the referees declared themselves well satisfied, from NATO's point of view, with the outcome. Two less satisfying aspects of the operation were neither made public by the directing staff nor unearthed by the swarms of newspaper and television reporters invited to cover these maneuvers. One was that the British general selected to command part of the invading Speznaz forces had managed to "eliminate" an entire American air base by ordering his men to ignore the heavily guarded fighter-bombers. Instead, they succeeded in "gassing" all the pilots as they slept by laying a dummy chemical warfare cylinder alongside the air-conditioning of the officers' quarters. Had the contest, and the gas cylinder, been real, that would have spelled total success for the invaders.

The second, and more significant, happening took place after the communiqués had been issued and the reporters had departed. The senior officers of both sides were called together, told to forget mock warfare and combine in an authentic operation. They were to search the thickly wooded Norfolk countryside for *real* arms and supply dumps presumed to have been already hidden there by Soviet underground agents as contingency measures for genuine Speznaz landings. Nothing, it seems, was unearthed, though the matter is unlikely to have been neglected since.[1]

The fact that Brave Defender was staged at all, let alone with such (albeit selective) publicity, had much to do with the defection to Britain, seven years earlier, of a young Red Army intelligence officer whose varied career had included firsthand experience of Speznaz itself. Vladimir Bogdanovich Rezun,[2] who put himself in the hands of the British authorities in June 1978 and was promptly transported to England, proved a very important source of information on the Red Army as a whole. He also gave the most complete picture of its military intelligence organization, the GRU, to be provided for the West since the heady but short-lived months of Penkovsky's services almost twenty years before. But his particular contribution was to describe in detail the training, organization and, above all, the massive development of the Soviet "Spetsialnoye Nashacheniye," or "Special Purpose Forces," to give Speznaz its full title.[3] The West knew of the existence of these forces, just as, in the early 1960s, it had known of the existence of Soviet chemical warfare weapons. Rezun's revelations about Speznaz were comparable with Penkovsky's disclosures about poison gas (among many other military items): they laid bare not only the true nature but also the sheer scale of the threat.

The charts Rezun drew up[4] showed that these special sabotage and terrorist units had been integrated into every layer of the Soviet military, naval and intelligence network. In wartime, each of the forty-one Soviet armies would have a Speznaz company of 115 men, commanded by a major, as part of its regular strength, though separate from all other units and reporting directly to the intelligence staff.* The peacetime structure of the armed forces Rezun described as divided up between sixteen military districts which cover the entire territory of the Soviet Union and would become huge army fronts in wartime, plus four groups of forces stationed in Eastern Europe and the four naval fleets. Each district, group and fleet is allotted one whole Speznaz brigade, and at this level, in addition to the parachute battalions, there is a special headquarters company whose duties are described succinctly as "anti-VIP." This relates to another prime task of the Speznaz at war. In addition to destroying the body and the nervous system of the NATO country under attack (by which is meant all those installations Brave Defender was organized to defend), Speznaz has been programmed and trained to destroy the nation's "brain." This means the elimination of its leading politicians of all parties, along with the religious leaders, military commanders, police chiefs and trade union bosses—anyone, in fact, to whom the target country might turn for guidance in the hour of peril.

Just as Speznaz has its equivalent in Britain's much more modestly scaled SAS and other NATO special units, so, one must assume, is there a similarity in many of the allotted tasks. What seems peculiar to Speznaz, apart from its sheer size, is the recruitment pattern. As with all the special areas which support the Soviet power structure, its members are selected and drafted with scant, if any, regard for the wishes of the individual. Rezun gives a chilling description of the finished product:

---

*There used to be a full battalion for each army, and these larger units may well be reinstated, in which case each battalion, with 360 men, could put forty-five small groups of saboteurs behind enemy lines.

The typical Speznaz soldier is a sceptic, a cynic and a pessimist. He believes profoundly in the depravity of human nature and knows (from his own experience) that in extreme conditions a man becomes a beast. . . . In the Speznaz soldier's opinion the most dangerous thing he can do is to put faith in his comrade, who may at the most critical moment turn out to be a beast. . . . Better that he regards all his fellow men as beasts than to make that discovery in an utterly hopeless situation.

The training is all geared to this end:

All the beatings, all the insults and humiliations he has suffered are steps on the path to a brilliant, suicidal feat of heroism. . . . Only someone who has been driven barefoot into the mud and snow, who has had even his bread taken away from him and has proved every day with his fists his right to existence—only this kind of man is capable of showing one day that he is the best.[5]

It is a grim picture of a murderous, moronic army of robots, put together and programmed for the sole purpose of terrorism, each member driven by such single-minded savagery as to exclude even that great saving grace of the normal man-at-arms, comradeship. There is, however, a more rarefied and much more interesting specimen, who sits at the top of the Speznaz operational pyramid. He is the professional athlete, groomed for the dual purpose of bringing international glory to the Soviet Union in peacetime and assassinating its opponents in wartime. That headquarters company attached to every active-service Soviet army with the anti-VIP assignment is drawn almost exclusively from the elite of the nation's athletes, who, in uniform, become the elite of its Speznaz soldiers. The recruiting ground here is the Central Army Sports Unit (whose initials in Russian are ZSKA). Rezun describes it as "the most successful, richest and largest sports organization in the Soviet Union, whose members had included, even in 1979 statistics, 850 European champions, 625 world champions and 182 Olympic gold medalists."[6] The army club attracts such men into its fold by giving them noncommissioned or even officer's rank, the level being determined solely by their prowess.

Once in the army, the professional athlete can become an "amateur," and compete accordingly, with a basic pay which continues long after his days of competition are over and ends with a pension for life. Throughout their active careers, in or out of sports, all those recruited into Speznaz lead an existence which is a blend of sports, espionage and preparation for armed terrorism. It is a daunting thought that some of the Soviet athletes who are warmly applauded by Western spectators when they step onto the victor's rostrum in an Olympic stadium are being trained in their other, secret life to murder the leaders of the nations cheering them.

At this point, the reader needs to be made aware that Rezun himself belonged to neither chilling category of the Homo Sovieticus we have been examining. As he explains in another of his books,[7] his knowledge of Speznaz dates from the time when, in 1970, as a GRU lieutenant, he was posted to the Intelligence Department of the Volga Military District. During the year he spent there, he was given basic Speznaz instruction (though without any of the ordeals undergone by the ordinary recruit) before being sent, as an inspector and intelligence officer, on parachute training exercises with a Speznaz group of the 296th Independent Reconnaissance Battalion. Though the twenty-three-day exercise was extremely rough going, he had, as he admitted, the easiest role:

> My job was to put questions to the troops, to the commanding officer or his deputy just when they least expected them. . . . I had with me a list of a hundred questions, many of which I didn't know the right answer to myself. My job was to put the question and record the reply.

Lieutenant Rezun was simply helping Big Brother to watch over a tiny group of thirteen Soviet soldiers practicing their sabotage in subzero winter temperatures somewhere in the Volga Basin. But how did he get there in the first place?

It is curious that, in none of his publications to date, does

"Viktor Suvorov" say anything about himself, his family background, or his childhood and adolescence, presumably because he is writing as another and semifictitious person. To understand the real man, and the real defector, these early years have had to be reconstructed[8] from his own lips.

What springs to light at once is that, from birth, he was almost predestined to wear a military uniform. Vladimir Bogdanovich Rezun* was born in 1947 at the army headquarters garrison in Barabasch near Vladivostok, where his father was stationed. His father, a Ukrainian, had joined up as a career soldier in 1939 and was then a major (later lieutenant colonel) of an antiaircraft regiment. But the military tradition did not begin there. All of the father's five brothers had served in the Red Army, one rising to be a corps commander. His paternal grandfather had also been a military man. He too had had five brothers and they also had all worn a uniform—four of them fighting with the anti-Bolshevik White Army, duly emigrating when that fight was lost. But, White or Red, it was army, right back to grandfather and five great-uncles as well as father and five uncles. Even Vladimir's mother, though without the same lineage, had come into the Rezun family in true martial fashion. A Russian by extraction, she met her future husband while working as a trainee doctor in 1943 at the Stara Russa military hospital, where he was a patient, wounded with a severe concussion. When they were married, the following year, the brief ceremony was conducted at the front by the regimental commander. After the war, the Rezuns led the usual career officer's life of postings from garrison to garrison, with the mother sometimes resuming her medical work and sometimes concentrating on her family. (A first son had been born in 1945; Vladimir was the second child.)

Both sons duly went into the army but, at least in the case of the younger boy, it was his own enthusiasm rather than any pressure from his father which dictated the choice. As he later explained:

---

*Ironically, in view of his later entanglement with Speznaz, the name means "Throat Slitter" in Russian.

The army was my ambition from boyhood. All our games as
children were war games. In the Far East garrisons our world
was nothing but tanks and planes, especially during the Korean
War. In fact, the first time in my life that I saw a man without
shoulder epaulets was when I was ten years old. All the talk of
the other boys was army, army: "What rank is your father?"
"What job is he doing?" I simply had no other scale of judgment.[9]

Vladimir Rezun began early, and he began well. In 1958, when
only eleven, he was accepted at the famous Suvorov military
cadet school, and there he spent the next seven years, the formative ones of his young life. For the first five of these, the school
was at Voronzh, moving to Kalinin for the last two. He thus
grew up as a soldier, for the pupils were on the army's strength
from the first day of their training. Moreover, he grew up as one
of the young military elite. Nearly all his fellow cadets were
from army families, the sons of officers killed in battle having
the automatic right to apply. To be a *Suvorovski,* and to wear the
special cadet uniform, black with a red trouser stripe, was a
badge of pride. The school also brought other benefits. The food
was first-rate and there was food for the brain too. The library
was, by Soviet standards, magnificently eclectic, and included
a wide variety of "acceptable" Western classics, ranging from
Dickens to Victor Hugo. The curriculum also made him something of a linguist, particularly in German, the foreign language
which continued to obsess the Soviet authorities long after the
war. He recalls that, throughout his five years at Voronezh, he
had German-language instruction every single day. Mathemat-
ics was actually taught in German and, on two days each
month, the whole school spoke nothing but German. Only toward the end, in the Kalinin period, did he start learning English, which began to take priority after the image of Russia's
principal enemy changed.

In 1965, Cadet Rezun graduated from the Suvorov Academy.
There followed three years of more advanced instruction at the
All-Army Higher Military Counterintelligence School. This
started off briefly at Odessa (where, in a special camp linked to
the school, he saw black African terrorists being trained) and

then transferred to Kiev. During these years, he and his fellow pupils were constantly under the eye of the GRU, for it was to the Higher Military Counterintelligence School that Soviet army intelligence looked for its recruits. However, no approach was made to him as yet, though, as a matter of course with the young military elite, he had become a candidate member of the Communist party in 1967 and a full member the following February.

Nineteen sixty-eight was to be one of his years of destiny, all because of one sudden and profound shock to his faith. It was a shock which, even when smothered, could never afterward be eliminated from his system: the Soviet invasion of Czechoslovakia. Rezun became involved almost by accident. As he had graduated with distinction from Kiev, he was allowed to pick which of the sixteen military districts he wished to serve in (a rare instance in the Soviet system where one of its young acolytes was asked to choose anything for himself). He opted for the Carpathian Military District because its commander at the time had the reputation of being a lively and open-minded general. In August of 1968, the Carpathian District was transformed into the Carpathian Front for its battle role, the invasion of Czechoslovakia across the common border from the east. Vladimir Rezun, now a lieutenant, duly took part in that invasion as a tiny cog in the Warsaw Pact military machine which lumbered forward to squash flat that "human face" which Comrade Dubček was trying to put on Czech Communism. To be precise, Rezun was a company commander of the 2d Battalion of the 274th Regiment of the crack 24th "Iron" Motor Rifle Division of the 38th Army. It was because he was a tiny cog, operating at ground level, that he saw the reality and the obscenity of the Kremlin's action. In the last section of one of his books on the Soviet army,[10] he gives an episodic and dramatized account of his experiences, a flashback story which left several gaps to be filled in by him afterward. This, for example, was how he learned that the action had been started:

I joined the battalion at the end of July 1968. Together with the other troops of the division it had already been going full blast for weeks on joint Warsaw Pact maneuvers. Then, on August 17, came the boots. Thousands and thousands of new pairs were suddenly unloaded from lorries. The ground was full of them and they were all of real leather, instead of the plastic ones we normally wore. I knew then that we were about to move over the frontier. Soviet "liberators" would have to march in real leather boots. They could not be seen by the "liberated" in shoddy footwear.[11]

Despite the leather boots and the extremely good food and provisions (most of it of Western origin) which had been pre-positioned for the invaders all the way to Prague, every soldier in the force could not help but notice the enormously superior living standards, in both the towns and villages en route, which the Czech city dweller and peasant enjoyed over his Soviet counterparts. That was one disturbing factor. Another was the attitude of the people themselves. As he wrote:

In the early days in Czechoslovakia, everything went according to plan: they threw tomatoes at us and we fired shots in the air.* But very soon everything changed. I don't know whether it was a special tactic or whether it was a spontaneous phenomenon but the people took a different attitude towards us. They became kinder and this was exactly what our army, created in the hot house of isolation from the world at large, was not prepared for. ... The absence of hostility towards the ordinary soldiers created among them a distrust of our official propaganda, because something did not fit. Theory contradicted practice. On the other hand, in the soldiers' minds, the idea appeared, and began to develop with unprecedented speed, that a counter-revolution is a positive event which raises the people's standard of living. The soldiers could not understand why such a beautiful country had to be driven by force into the same state of poverty in which we lived.[12]

*Even this, of course, was no substitute for the real battles which the Red Army had had to fight in Hungary twelve years before. The so-called liberation of Hungary in 1956 had been bought with much Russian blood, and soldiers who are fired at do not think twice about firing back.

Dangerous, sacrilegious thoughts indeed; and it was no wonder that, after this 1968 operation, as after Hungary, the bulk of the invading troops were transferred either to rehabilitation centers or straight to the Far Eastern front after withdrawal, so that their Western "contamination" might evaporate. Even less wonder that any Soviet soldier who tried to stay behind with the "liberated" or make a dash for the West was shot without trial as a deserter. (Rezun himself witnessed one such summary execution, carried out publicly before a full parade of the regiment after its return to the Western Ukraine.)

Rezun's account of his unit's advance into eastern Czechoslovakia in August and withdrawal across the Carpathians in September (by which time the threat of Dubček-style "liberalism" had been quashed) is militarily significant for one thing above all: the proof he provides of long-standing Soviet preparation for the invasion. He reveals, for example, that Major Zhurlavlev, commander of the 508th Reconnaissance Battalion of the 6th Guards Motor Rifle Division, whose troops were the first to set foot in Prague, knew all the streets of the capital by heart. For four months, his whole battalion had been familiarizing themselves with every nook and cranny of the city from maps, models and photographs. Before Operation Danube (as the invasion was code-named) began, all twenty officers of the battalion had visited Prague and traveled as innocent tourists by bus along the routes they were later to traverse as invaders in armored cars. Rezun even refers to Soviet staff plans for Operation Danube being worked out eight months in advance, that is, from January of 1968, when all was polite, if somewhat forced, smiles between Dubček's Prague and Brezhnev's Moscow.[13] This lengthy preparation had not spared the troops much muddle and confusion on the day. For example, all "friendly," that is, invading, armored vehicles were to be identified to each other by a white stripe; any tank without that redeeming mark was to be immediately engaged as hostile. But, on the great day, supplies of white paint simply ran out, which resulted in dangerous mayhem at some points along the advance.

Lieutenant Rezun himself was judged to be immune from

any danger of contamination, let alone any ideas of deserting to the West. He, after all, was a full Party member and, as a soldier, could point to a perfect military record right back to his cadet days as a *Suvorovski* (with, if one ignored those four great-uncles who had fought with the White Army, an impeccable family background before that). So, though he was sent east, it was not to the Far East. Indeed, the years 1968–70 were among the most pleasurable of his career. He was given a company of the 66th Guards Rifle Division at Chernovtsy on the Romanian border. It was lovely countryside, and there he found wine, women and song in abundance. Yet, quite unbeknown to his fellow officers, this model soldier, enjoying an idyllic garrison posting, was a deeply troubled man inside. As he related, nearly twenty years later:

> Czechoslovakia was for me a turning point. All my training had been to protect my own people. But now we were actually suppressing people, ordinary people like ourselves. It was a humble experience to hear the Czechs, and especially the older ones, say to us, "What are you doing here? We remember the *real* liberators of 1944." I felt so disgusted that, had I been operating in the west of the country and not in the extreme eastern half, I might well have tried to escape then and there.[14]

As it was, he was back in the Soviet Union and, whatever his hidden revulsions, he allowed his career to take him forward. It was while he was on the Romanian border and not, as he has written, in the Carpathian Military District[15] that he distinguished himself on exercises by flattening a wall to clear a path for his tanks (though the obstruction was, in fact, of wood and not of bricks). It was this dashing flourish which brought him to the notice of the GRU. On the lookout for bright young officers of initiative, a senior military observer at the exercises offered him, more or less on the spot, a job on the military intelligence staff of the Volga Military District. It was a dazzling opening. Looking back, Rezun was quite frank about his feelings:

There were two opposite currents in me. Deep down, disillusionment was still there. Nonetheless I was proud at having been selected for the GRU. I would still be a military man and, moreover, though only a lieutenant, I would be in a lieutenant colonel's slot in the new job. Had I stayed in the Soviet Union all my life, I would have just gone on and up, to end, no doubt, as a top army officer. As things turned out, it was through the GRU that I was posted abroad and so was brought into direct contact with the West.[16]

That direct contact was not long in coming. After a year at the Volga Military District (where, as explained, his intelligence department controlled the 13th Army's Speznaz activities) and the usual three-year course at the Military and Diplomatic Academy in Moscow, he was posted almost straightaway to the GRU station in Geneva, with the rank of captain. It was a coveted appointment. Geneva, the most luxurious and cosmopolitan of cities, was also, because of its neutral Swiss status and proliferation of international bodies, a key European center for intelligence operations by both East and West.

He was, by now, a family man. Before going to the academy, he had felt some slight pressure from his superiors to get married (the GRU always wanted any of their officers likely to be posted abroad to have an anchor, and a potential hostage, in the Soviet Union). He had no difficulty in finding an eminently suitable bride: Tatiana, the eighteen-year-old daughter of an air force officer, who was working in the ultrasensitive Intelligence Department of the Volga Military District. Anyone who could be trusted with GRU ciphers could certainly, in the organization's eyes, be relied upon to resist the temptations of capitalist affluence. The Rezuns, cleared for a foreign posting, arrived in Geneva with a baby girl; a second child, a boy, was born during their time there.

This would normally have been for three years. He extended this to four and, with the enthusiastic agreement of his wife, had already applied for an exceptional fifth year when he decided to make his final break with Moscow. Why and where did he take this momentous step? The version he gave in his books was intentionally fictional.[17] This paints an imaginative Austrian background to the story, with Rezun himself being stationed in Vienna and defecting to the British embassy there, seemingly motivated by GRU office intrigues and purges and a fear for his own safety. In fact, apart from transit stops, Rezun was never in Vienna; nor was his career, let alone his life, ever in jeopardy there. The real story unfolds entirely in Geneva, and it unfolds in slow and rather confused fashion. He tells it thus:

> Of course, the purely material contrast with life in the Soviet Union played a role. Even from the first moments of arriving at Geneva airport, we realized that we had landed in a different world of unheard-of luxury. It was our first sight of life anywhere outside the Soviet Union and it came as an unbelievable shock. Moreover, as a recruiting officer whose job was to win people over into working for us, I was soon able to sample this life-style all over Geneva and even further afield, for I was able to move around quite freely, like a fighter-bomber ranging the skies.
>
> But there was something else disturbing and quite apart from the contrast in living standards. The reports on me were, I knew, excellent and my prospects in the service looked rosy. Yet all the time I felt I was standing, not on granite, but on quicksands. Despite the shock of Czechoslovakia, which was always deep down inside me, Khrushchev had remained my hero and I couldn't believe it when he was suddenly declared an outcast. What made it worse was his replacement by Brezhnev, who became a positive embarrassment.[18]

What is now clear is that, though he only made his jump in 1978, Captain Vladimir Rezun began putting out his feelers to the West from the start of his Geneva posting, and that he began by using Brezhnev as a signal. At a United Nations cocktail party which he attended during his first week in Geneva, he cornered a likely-looking American diplomat and started up a conversation about the Soviet leader. Brezhnev, he observed, was "not a very clever man." To anyone with the right hearing, that, from a Soviet official, was a clear invitation to the espionage waltz. But Rezun had picked the wrong man. The American simply agreed with him, and that was that.[19]

For the next three years, Rezun pursued, at intervals, this seemingly fruitless courtship. It was a repetition of Penkovsky's initial overtures to the West fifteen years before, though made doubly frustrating by being enacted over years rather than months and conducted in a free city rather than in Moscow. Rezun recalls:

> Later on, I started talking about collecting coins, including gold coins, to Americans I met. This would have been an easy opening. Any professional would have taken the hint and invited me to his house to compare collectors' notes, even if he had to provide himself with a collection for the purpose. On one occasion, I remember, I even bought from a Geneva bank out of my own money a valuable ruble tsarist gold coin and presented it to an American enthusiast. There was still no reaction.[20]

Rezun eventually gave up and turned elsewhere. In July 1977, he managed to establish contact with British intelligence. It was a fruitful partnership from the start and, eleven months later, he was taken at his own request to Britain. He cannot fully explain his abrupt decision to ask for asylum, which he describes as "both instant and long-standing." There was no recall telegram to strike sudden panic. However, in April of 1978 he had seen something very disturbing taking place in the heart of the Soviet mission. That was the month, it will be recalled, when the defection of Arkady Shevchenko, under secretary-general of the United Nations, was announced to the world in New York.* Shevchenko's son, Gennady, had followed his father to become a career officer in the foreign service, and he happened to be serving on a regular diplomatic posting to Geneva at the time. Within hours of the news being broken about his father, the son had been bundled aboard an Aeroflot plane

*See p. 290.

and taken back to Moscow, there to enter into the limbo of the close relatives of the damned. He had been tranquilized to make certain he gave no trouble to his escorts at the busy international airport. Rezun heard all about it from a colleague, one of the KGB men who operated in Geneva under the cover of an Aeroflot employee.[21] It was he who had had to supervise the abduction. As Rezun commented later, it was a very unsettling experience and one which helped to concentrate his mind on his own future. He had realized, in fact, that his own life was in danger. On June 6, 1978, he was safely flown out (with his wife and two children) to London. A new and rewarding life began of writing books about his experiences and periodically advising on military intelligence questions.

Rezun was still only a captain when he reached the West, but the variety of his career and the sharpness of his observations more than made up for his junior rank. Thus, apart from his revelations about Speznaz, he was able to describe in detail the layout and organization of the nine-story rectangular building on the site of Moscow's old Khodinka airfield which is the GRU headquarters, the so-called Aquarium. As with his Speznaz information, he was able to reconstruct from memory a complete functional chart of all its twelve chief directorates and many of their subdepartments.[22] He gave a general description of the GRU's technical espionage work for the mighty Military Industrial Commission (VPK in the Russian initials); he brought the West up-to-date both on the structure of GRU residencies within foreign embassies and on the networks of agents and undercover illegals working for them. He had much of interest to say about GRU "field craft"—its methods of controlling and communicating with these networks.[23] He also produced a breakdown of the Soviet Union's operational intelligence system, which is charged with the conventional task of aiding its country's military operations in war.

His account of life in the Red Army was of almost equal interest. There is a certain parallel here with the dual value to the West which Peter Deriabin, also a career officer before becoming an intelligence man, had incorporated a generation before.* Rezun was, of course, far too young to have fought in battle. Indeed he was only five years old when Deriabin was lying wounded in the rubble of Stalingrad. But his experiences of the postwar Red Army were every bit as valuable (because much harder to come by) as anything Deriabin related about the Great Patriotic War. Again, it was the variety of his experience which was so illuminating. He could relate what the lot of an army private, an army sergeant or an army officer looked like, felt like and smelled like from the barracks room to the tank turret. He had been through it all. Before the Czechoslovakia experience and his transfer to military intelligence, he had seen, as a cadet trainee, life from the inside in some of the most famous Soviet divisions—the 120th Guards Rogachevsky Motor Rifles, the 2d Guards Taman, the 41st Guards Berlin, for example.[24] To talk to him is still to talk to a Red Army professional fighter and clearly a first-rate one at that.

It is here that we touch on what is, in some ways, the most significant aspect of his defection. Vladimir Rezun was the ideal soldier, the product of two generations of military forebears, with discipline, loyalty, obedience and patriotism drilled into his very bones. Yet this ideal soldier was no machine. He had a heart and a conscience. They were first stirred into revulsion against the powers to whom he owed allegiance by the shattering experiences of 1968. Ten years later, that revulsion combined with material factors to make him break that allegiance forever. Quite apart from his value to Western intelligence, a man like Rezun is living proof that, after seventy years of regimentation, the Communist system is still unable to produce a society of robots devoid of decent feelings.

*See pp. 115–16.

16

"Active Measures"

AKTIVNYTYE MEROPRIYATIYA, the KGB term, which translates as "active measures," covers a multitude of sins, as complex as the name. It transcends the world of espionage and counterintelligence altogether to become the offensive arm of Soviet diplomacy. Here, the KGB seeks not to inform or protect the Kremlin but to help execute its grand strategy by penetrating foreign governments, undermining confidence in their systems, discrediting their leaders and, if their countries are in alliance, dividing them from each other. To these ends, it seeks, for example, to control or manipulate the media, above all of Western nations; to muddle their powers of judgment by spreading disinformation or by distributing forged "official documents"; to influence mass opinion through Communist-controlled international "front organizations"; and even to overthrow governments by force through military support for "liberation movements." This goes far beyond the so-called covert actions of the CIA and other Western intelligence systems. These latter are both selective and sporadic. They are usually applied to specific targets for specific purposes and are always subject to cancellation or reactivation at the whim of changing, democratically elected leadership. The KGB active measures, on the other hand, go both broader and deeper; above all, they are constant. Here, we are confronting an ever-running engine of destruction, burrowing ceaselessly away at the foundations of Western society, like some giant mechanical excavator which the Kremlin never switches off.

Some of the techniques applied have been known about for decades: the use of political forgeries, for example, which is not confined to the Soviet Union. The Communist front organizations have been familiar threats (and recognized as such, at least by most Western governments) ever since the first and central web of the matrix was spun in 1950 with the founding of the World Peace Council. But it was not until 1968 that the first inside picture of the Communist active measures organization emerged. It was provided by Ladislav Bittman, whose fourteen years in the Czechoslovak intelligence service culminated in a two-year stint as deputy chief of its Disinformation Department, and whose defection from the Communist world was triggered by the Soviet invasion of his country.[1] He described how his department, formed in 1964 on the Soviet model, carried out a variety of active measures on Czech territory. Instances included building bogus missile ramps to deceive Western intelligence about the nuclear-strike capacity of the Soviet bloc, or pretending that secret lists of Nazi agents had been discovered at the bottom of a Bohemian lake, and then feeding a nervous Bonn government with genuine, very compromising files provided for the purpose from Moscow archives.[2]

He also recounted the services his department had undertaken abroad for the Soviet Union: running a propaganda campaign against the right-wing Senator Barry Goldwater in 1964, when the senator was a presidential candidate, for example, or trying to turn Western journalists and even Western politicians into so-called agents of influence for Moscow's cause. This evidence was impressive enough in itself. It also served as a pretext for the CIA to publish a massive study disclosing Soviet forgeries planted throughout the globe and specific propaganda campaigns, such as that launched against the American neutron bomb in the late 1970s.[3] This campaign, estimated to have cost the Russians over a hundred million dollars, was an expensive but resounding success. The weapon was abandoned as a concession to what was interpreted by President Jimmy Carter as a largely spontaneous wave of global repugnance for the device, which would have destroyed human beings, rather than buildings.*

Yet this picture of Soviet active measures, whether painted by Bittman or by hundreds of lesser sources, had been seen from the outside, through windows which gave views onto the Kremlin. For a picture drawn from the inside, the West had to wait until one evening in October 1979, when a Russian walked uninvited into a Western cocktail party at Tokyo's Sanno Hotel, picked out of the hat an American naval commander and asked to be taken to American intelligence. He promptly was. The gate-crasher turned out to be Major Stanislav Levchenko, the first, and so far the only, expert on active measures to defect to the West from the KGB itself.

Levchenko, then aged thirty-eight, had been trained through nearly all of his professional life to fulfill one task in one area of the world. He was thus a laboratory specimen of system-bred specialization, the product of many years of KGB investment which, in turn, reflected the long-term and unchanging strategic aims of the KGB's political masters. He had never applied for the work; it was the organization which sought him out. Active measures in Western countries demanded officers with intelligence, fluency, good appearance and as much sophistication and good manners as the Soviet system was capable of producing. The young Levchenko fitted this bill. To begin with, he was not of that rough proletarian stock which provided the KGB with so many of its stolid and unquestioning foot soldiers. His father was a research chemist who rose to be chairman of the chemistry department at a military institute, thus acquiring army officer's rank and ending up, just before he died of cancer, with special promotion to major general. His stepmother (his mother, who was Jewish, had died in childbirth when Stanislav was three years old) was a pediatric surgeon.

He was thus reared as a member of the professional classes, the sub-elite of the Soviet Union; and had his father not been

---

*Crudely put, it was a battlefield weapon designed to knock out Soviet-bloc tank crews by enhanced but short-lived radiation, thus neutralizing the huge superiority the Warsaw Pact armies enjoyed over NATO in their armored forces.

a man of strict principles who refused to seek favors, they could certainly have done better than their one-room Moscow dwelling which shared a communal kitchen and bath with seven other families. The father possessed a rare intellectual outlook as well as rare scruples, and it was from him that Stanislav learned much of Russia's great achievements in culture and science before the revolution. The boy's interest was also stirred in the world outside the Soviet Union and it was this interest which was to set young Levchenko's course in life. On leaving high school in 1958, he joined the Institute of Asian and African Studies, attached to Moscow University, and it was he who selected his special subject. He said later:

> I chose Japanese because I had already read a lot of Japanese books in Russian translation and the culture interested me. I was one of a group of six or seven Japanese students in my intake of about sixty at the institute. But I had no thoughts then of the KGB. Like most of the others, I was more interested in becoming a trade delegate or a diplomat.[4]

For the next six years, he immersed himself in the language, literature, history and economics of Japan and emerged with the reputation of a keen worker and an even keener ladies' man. He embarked on two marriages while still at the institute. The first was to an eighteen-year-old fellow student called Yelena. This lasted only two years and was significant in his life mainly for the horror stories of secret-police brutality recounted to him by his wife's grandfather, a onetime landowner who had been incarcerated in the notorious Lubianka Prison during the Stalinist terror.[5] After Yelena came a voluptuous architectural student named Natalia. This second marriage, which was to endure after a fashion until the end, kept Levchenko in the swim of Moscow's intellectual society. His new father-in-law was a member of the Soviet Academy of Sciences. It also continued to keep him well informed about the excesses of the Stalin era, for, during the great purges, many of Natalia's relatives, including some of the Party faithful, had also been swept away into prison camps. This dual exposure, from successive sets of in-

laws, to the seamy side of Soviet Communism was to play a
strong subsidiary role in his ultimate abandonment of the system.

For fifteen years after his graduation in 1964, however, he
served that system energetically in a variety of functions,
though always with Japanese affairs a dominant theme. During
his last year at the institute, he had volunteered for his first
fieldwork—sailing for three months with a Soviet patrol boat in
the Sea of Japan to interrogate any Japanese fishermen who
came their way. This landed him, after graduation, with a mundane post in the Ministry of Fisheries, from which he was
rescued a year later. In 1965, the International Department of
the Party's Central Committee (which dealt, among other
things, with Communist activities abroad) offered him a job as
a Japanese interpreter with the Soviet Peace Committee. This
was the controlling body of the World Peace Council. A year
later, he started to work full-time for the Afro-Asian Solidarity
Committee, a body which sought to manipulate Third World
opinion against the West, again under the direct orders of the
International Department in Moscow. One of his prime tasks
was to help in the worldwide anti-Vietnam War campaign,
targeted, of course, against the Americans. He later described
how, as part of this campaign, American soldiers were persuaded (usually when they were recuperating from wounds in
Japanese base hospitals) to desert and were then spirited away
by hired Japanese fishing vessels to Soviet territorial waters.[6]
Levchenko had been launched on his eventful career in Soviet
propaganda and subversion.

It was only a matter of time before the intelligence services
swept him into their net. Already in 1966, when called up for
his regular period of Red Army conscript service, he had found
himself assigned to a special course in wartime espionage, with
the English port of Liverpool allotted as his particular study
target. But this episode, supervised by the GRU, was an aberration from his prescribed career. In 1971 (by which time he had
become one of the official spokesmen of the Afro-Asian Committee) the KGB recruited him directly into its most prestigious
department, the First Chief Directorate, which supervised all

operations abroad. After a year's training in everything from cipher craft to hand-to-hand combat, carried out at the Foreign Intelligence School at Yurlovo, in the forests surrounding the capital, he was commissioned as a senior KGB lieutenant, and sent to work in the Moscow Center. Inevitably, he was put on the Japanese desk, handling, to begin with, twenty-odd files on agents from all strata of Japanese society who were working for the Soviet Union.[7] He had entered the seductively corrupting world of the privileged. His pay and allowances, at over 300 rubles a month, were nearly twice the average salary of a Soviet scientist, teacher or engineer. On top of this came Natalia's earnings of 120 rubles a month as an architect, while from her parents they had now inherited a two-room apartment with the luxury of a private kitchen and bath.[8]

By now, however, Levchenko had had plenty of opportunity to see for himself what the world outside the Soviet Union had to offer in the way of relaxing and prosperous living. His work with the Afro-Asian Committee had taken him on conferences to several Third World capitals, including, in 1971, cosmopolitan Cairo. Between 1966 and 1974, when he embarked on his first KGB posting abroad, he had also paid no fewer than twelve visits to Japan, always with Soviet delegations discharging propaganda or subversion missions for the Party's International Department in Moscow.[9] When these regular assignments came up, Lieutenant Stanislav Levchenko of the KGB became Mr. Levchenko, journalist and Tokyo correspondent for the Moscow journal *Novoye Vremya*, or *New Times*. It had been founded as far back as 1943 (at a time when its targets included the country's wartime allies) with the prime purpose of providing cover for Soviet intelligence agents abroad. By Politburo orders, twelve of its fourteen foreign bureaus were earmarked for KGB personnel.[10] In February of 1975, he was posted to Tokyo to fill one of those slots.

His first taste of life as an agent abroad was a sour one. Instead of being able to relax, after a long flight through seven time zones, in one of Tokyo's many luxury hotels, he found that he and his wife had been booked into a cheap and seedy establishment which rented most of its rooms by the hour to couples without luggage. His first call on the KGB residency on the tenth floor of the huge Soviet compound did little to raise his spirits. The rezident, Major General Dimitri Yerokhin, dismissed him after three sentences of welcome, making it clear that outstanding results were expected—as much a warning as a greeting. His immediate superior, the chief of "Line PR" (political espionage, and also responsible for active measures), was expansive, yet somehow far more menacing. This was Lieutenant Colonel Vladimir Alexseyevich Pronnikov, a squat peasant's son who lived like a Spartan and worked like a demon. He was eaten up by ambition and had already attracted the Politburo's notice by suborning a Japanese Cabinet minister, Hirohide Ishida. Pronnikov went out of his way to reveal that he already knew every detail about the private life of his new subordinate, ranging from his prizewinning poodle to his beautiful wife. In the KGB world, this was the language of suspicion and blackmail. Levchenko's instinctive uneasiness was to be borne out. Pronnikov was to prove his deadliest enemy.

His immediate priority, however, was to secure accommodations, which apart from providing privacy and comfort, would match those of other leading foreign journalists in the capital and so justify his cover. Naumov, the KGB officer who functioned as the local *Novoye Vremya* editor, saw the point at once. As a result the Levchenkos' life-style was quickly transformed. They were allowed to buy and furnish, at the magazine's expense, a three-bedroom apartment in the fashionable Udagawa district of Tokyo and purchase a new Japanese car, also out of office funds. Stanislav fitted himself out with well-tailored suits and Natalia bought herself a wardrobe of the latest Western fashions. All these perquisites could be justified as operational necessities. Together with the complete freedom of movement the couple enjoyed, they led a privileged existence which was the envy of their colleagues cloistered under close surveillance in the embassy compound. This, despite its swimming pool, sauna, tennis court, commissary shop and cinema, was little better than a comfortable prison.

Levchenko had to achieve results to justify his privileges. The

Soviet colony in Japan numbered then about three hundred people, of whom half (including those placed in the Trade Mission, the state airline Aeroflot and the Soviet media offices) were KGB or GRU officials. This vast intelligence network had managed, by Levchenko's time, to gather in some two hundred assorted Japanese "assets." Only a few of these were motivated by Marxist ideology. A handful had been talked into cooperation on the basis of genuine friendships struck up with Soviet agents (the Japanese were considered to be very vulnerable to this approach). The majority had been delicately bought.[11] This was how Levchenko scored his first major success.

Among the dozen or so contacts handed over to him to develop was an influential figure in the Japanese Socialist party and member of the Japanese Diet, code-named "King." Levchenko enticed him into the net by patiently exploiting all three main approaches. The man was a former Communist, which provided an ideological platform, though not necessarily a pro-Soviet one. He was by nature both kindly and susceptible to flattery, and this enabled Levchenko to gain his personal goodwill by treating him as a valued source of wisdom on Japanese politics who, without fear of being quoted, could help the *Novoye Vremya* correspondent with background material for his articles. King felt even more flattered when Levchenko told him "in strict confidence" that his magazine was in fact an organ of the powerful International Department of the Soviet Communist party and that the information which its correspondents sent to Moscow could help shape Kremlin policy. This "confession" served two ends. It made the journalist rather more than a journalist, though without yet appearing as a spy. At the same time, it made his Japanese friend believe that, in a small and strictly private way, he was influencing world events. Ironically, at this stage, it was King who felt in Levchenko's debt.

But it was hard cash which cemented the union, though the cement was nicely camouflaged until the moment it had set hard. One day, over a nine-course lunch served in a private room of one of Tokyo's best restaurants, King confided to his host that he had long cherished the ambition of publishing a political newsletter of his own. The problem was money. Though he was setting something aside from his comfortable salary, his savings alone would never meet the launching costs, which he put at one million yen. The active measures man, having seen the door opening, was careful not to jam his foot in it at once. Indeed, he changed the subject, and only returned to it a month later, after he had received approval from Moscow Center to advance the money. The next time his Japanese friend admitted sadly that he was getting nowhere with his fund-raising, Levchenko offered "fraternal support" and laid an envelope fat with bank notes on the restaurant table. When King, without much hesitation, took the envelope, Levchenko apologetically asked for some sort of receipt, just to show, he explained, that he had not pocketed the cash himself. King promptly scribbled a receipt on the back of his business card.

The cement had now set. When the victim, realizing what he had done, tried two days later to get the incriminating card back, he was told, in firm tones, that it had already been flown by special courier to Moscow, where it was now "locked in a vault for permanent safekeeping." From now on, it was Levchenko who issued the instructions. When, a few weeks later, he drove to King's apartment with a further installment of three million yen "for your campaign," King calmly counted out the money and wrote out a receipt without even being asked. This was in December of 1975 and, for the next four years, until he was blown, together with the KGB's other local assets, by Levchenko's defection, King played his part in the Kremlin's grand design for Japan.[12]

The first priority of this program was to prevent the formation of any alliance between the United States, Japan and Communist China. Levchenko said later:

> The Kremlin was absolutely paranoid about the so-called "military triangle" between Washington, Tokyo and Peking. They really believed it might happen, and went on believing it until the Andropov era despite the fact that the KGB was assuring them that it was simply not feasible. They would not listen. They were the victims of their own paranoia and propaganda.[13]

As part of the campaign to rout this imaginary specter, Levchenko and his KGB colleagues had been instructed to do all in their power to sow distrust between Japan and America, and to prevent any rapprochement between Japan and China. At the same time, they were to penetrate the Japanese press, public opinion and opposition parties and create pro-Soviet lobbies, though without causing political mayhem, for Moscow wanted a stable Japan in which it could wield increased influence.[14] King's Socialist party was a key element in this process and, before being unmasked, he seems to have earned his millions of yen by, for example, blocking the election to parliament of any pro-Chinese candidates and promoting Marxist domination over the party in general. King's greatest single service to his Kremlin masters was in organizing a Japanese-Soviet parliamentary association. This served as an umbrella under which frequent exchanges of delegations took place between members of the Japanese Diet and the Supreme Soviet of the USSR. It also provided a solid and respectable recruiting platform for the KGB. By the end of the 1970s, nine other influential members of the Japanese Socialist party had joined King in the Moscow net.[15]

The biggest crisis which the Tokyo residency had to face in Levchenko's time broke early in the afternoon of September 6, 1976, when the Soviet air force pilot Senior Lieutenant Viktor Belenko landed his MiG-25 interceptor plane on the Japanese island of Hokkaido and asked for American asylum. Immediately, the residency was flooded with priority cables from Moscow Center demanding reports on what the truant pilot had revealed and what the Japanese authorities were doing with the aircraft, whose ultrasecret electronic devices would be of immense interest to the Americans. Had these been destroyed, Moscow inquired, with the demolition devices provided? The next day, the residency was obliged glumly to report that all the top secret equipment remained intact, and was already being examined by American specialists.

At this, the Active Measures Department in Moscow swung into action. A special courier was dispatched to Tokyo, bearing a tearful letter written in the name of Lieutenant Belenko's

wife, in which she appealed to her errant husband to return
home and spare his family further suffering. Levchenko was
ordered to surface this blatant KGB concoction somehow in the
Japanese press, and so underpin the strenuous Soviet diplomatic efforts being made to persuade the Japanese to hand
Belenko over. Levchenko managed it by feeding the story,
which he freely admitted was nonsense, to a young American
news agency stringer who was hungry for any scoop which
might get him a job on the regular staff. This part of the operation flopped. At an icy confrontation with a Soviet security
officer held under Japanese police auspices, Belenko rejected all
Soviet enticements, which, as he well knew, were simply death
sentences tied up with ribbons. He repeated his request for
American asylum, and the Japanese let the CIA have him.

Having lost the pilot, Moscow Center now concentrated on
trying to get back the plane. The entire KGB network in Japan
was put onto the job and every Soviet "agent of influence" in
Tokyo, starting at the top with Hirohide Ishida, was mobilized
to try to persuade the government that it was humiliating itself
by acting as Washington's pawn and, at the same time, endan-
gering the entire future of Japanese-Soviet relations. In the end,
the Japanese allowed the Americans to strip the MiG-25 and
examine it piece by piece, though they refused repeated American requests to fly and test the plane. Active measures in Tokyo
had achieved only a modest success. Levchenko had, however,
done his part well and, with the odious Pronnikov posted back
to Moscow, more and more assignments began to come his way.
The most important was the further handling of agent "Ares,"
a Japanese journalist recruited some ten years back, who possessed invaluable sources of information inside Japanese counterintelligence. He was probably the most precious purely professional asset which the residency possessed. Outwardly,
Levchenko's career seemed to be prospering happily in propor-
tion to his increased workload. At the beginning of 1979, congratulations were in order as he was promoted to major. The
real picture was somewhat different.

He had started to think seriously about defection after a spell

of home leave in Russia six months before. This has been presented as being entirely a moral decision, born out of growing
repugnance for the cynicism of the Soviet Union, a disillusionment which was driving a tormented Levchenko to seek solace
in the Church. (On trapping King in the KGB net, he is said to
have gone to the only Russian Orthodox church in Tokyo, there
to have prayed for forgiveness and for the souls of both himself
and his victim.)[16] However, Levchenko later played down this
religious aspect, saying that "it was never a dominant factor,"[17]
and it seems prudent to subtract a little emphasis from the
moral aspect as a whole. As with so many other defectors, this
doubtless played a genuine role, and Levchenko certainly had
a particular cause for revulsion in the fate of so many of his
wife's relatives during the Stalin terror. But that had not
stopped him from joining the KGB and working very hard in
its cause. As with most of those who had preceded him to the
West, other, more mundane factors than ideological distaste
must be considered.

To begin with, his career in the KGB was neither as rosy nor
as assured as the formal record would suggest. His archenemy
Pronnikov, whom he had openly attacked on more than one
occasion, was now a full colonel and deputy director of the
Active Measures Department at Moscow Center. The colonel
had already blocked one or two of Levchenko's Japanese initiatives, and, despite the condescendingly friendly air Pronnikov
adopted when receiving his subordinate at headquarters, Levchenko knew full well that he would always have this foe in his
path if he carried on with the same job. There was, of course,
the possibility of transfer to another department, but he was
beginning to get sick and tired of the life of intrigue which a
career anywhere in the KGB involved. Its main attraction for
him had always been the overseas postings and these could not
go on forever: indeed, he knew that in the autumn of 1979 he was
due for recall to do a spell of service at the oppressive Moscow
Center. Why not make his overseas stay permanent? He might
face an uncertain future in the Western world, but of one thing
he was sure: only there could he continue with the life-style to

which his long spell in Tokyo had accustomed him. He felt no urge to take Natalia with him, even had she wished.* Their marriage had gradually gone sour, and Levchenko was never the man to be without female company for long. There was thus plenty to urge him forward, and little to hold him back.

As for the timing, this nominated itself when, in September of 1979, he was instructed to hand over all his principal Japanese contacts to other officers in the residency prior to his own departure for Moscow, scheduled for the end of October. It was an impressive list. Apart from the political agents of influence, headed by Ishida and other Socialist party leaders, there were men like Takuji Yamane, assistant managing editor of the conservative mass-circulation newspaper *Sankei;* a Professor Yamomoto, who headed the group of intellectual agents; and a number of "friendly contacts," like the television executive Kaneji Miura.[18] Active Measures had got its claws into the Japanese media and the academic world as well as into the Diet.

But Ares, the journalist with the counterintelligence contacts, remained the most valuable source for technical, as opposed to propaganda, purposes, and when Levchenko told his friend that he might soon be leaving, Ares provided him with a farewell present. It was a handsome gift: the seven-hundred-page secret directory which listed the names, addresses and telephone numbers of all Japanese security officers. Levchenko decided to make it, in turn, his farewell present to the KGB. Ares could only get hold of it and let it out of his hands for two hours during the night. They chose 1 A.M. to 3 A.M. on October 24. It was duly handed over in a so-called brush pass outside the Japanese-French Cultural Center, rushed by Levchenko and a chain of colleagues to the residency and there furiously photocopied in time to be handed back to Ares at 2:40 A.M. Emotion got the better of security discipline as the two men said an affectionate good-bye to one another. Later that morning, after eating the last breakfast Natalia would ever prepare for him, Levchenko set out on what might seem a normal day's rou-

---

*Their only child, a son, was in Moscow, attending high school.

tine—a call at the Press Club, a visit to the Diet and then a long progression through bookshops and department stores to make quite sure that he was not being followed. As already described, Levchenko's "routine day" ended, in far from routine fashion, with him buttonholing an unknown American naval commander at the Sanno Hotel.

The last Soviet intelligence defection to the West from Tokyo had been that of the MGB Lieutenant Colonel Yuri Rastvorov over twenty-five years before.* Like Rastvorov, Major Levchenko was to have an anxious time at a Japanese airport before his plane took off for the West and freedom. The naval commander at the cocktail party had acted swiftly. Levchenko was led unobtrusively to an empty room in the hotel. Two American military policemen emerged from nowhere to close and guard the door from the inside while the commander hurried to the nearby American embassy to report. He returned in less than half an hour with a senior intelligence officer who satisfied himself, in five rapid-fire questions about Soviet residency personnel, that Levchenko was genuine. The CIA man disappeared, to return again in only twenty minutes with a second embassy official. Levchenko was now informed that he had been granted political asylum and could leave for America immediately. The whole business had taken just under an hour, a vast improvement on the leisurely time schedules which some of the early postwar defectors had had to endure.

In the event, the departure itself was to prove far from immediate. The CIA had hoped to fly him out by military aircraft from Atsugi air base, but Washington denied permission. At dawn on October 25, after a night in an American safe house, Levchenko was told that, instead, he would be departing that day on the normal Pan American flight from Tokyo's Narita airport. He was handed a first-class ticket; and his passport, which had been taken away overnight, was returned, stamped with a U.S. visa. At the airport, as Levchenko had feared, trouble began.

Accompanied by his senior CIA protector and another Amer-

*See chapter 5.

ican agent, he had cleared immigration and customs, only to be recognized by two Japanese counterintelligence officers while on his way to the first-class Pan Am lounge. They notified both police headquarters and their Foreign Ministry and, before long, the lounge was swarming with Japanese officials demanding to know why the correspondent of the Moscow *Novoye Vremya* (whom they probably suspected of working for Soviet intelligence) was leaving for Washington with an American escort. Their agitation increased when Levchenko informed them that he had sought and been given political asylum in the United States. One of the Foreign Ministry officials who was a Russian expert pointed out, in Russian, that under his government's consular agreement with Moscow, a Soviet embassy official had the right to see Levchenko before he left. Levchenko refused and embarked upon one final burst of active measures, this time to save his own skin. Surely, he taunted his interrogators, Japan, "the second greatest capitalist country in the world," had no need to bow and tremble before the Soviets on such a minor problem.[19] As a further touch of bravado, he ordered some champagne just for himself, knowing that the Japanese officials would not drink on duty.

His insouciance masked a clammy and growing fear inside. A second and then a third America-bound flight had left while this long argument was going on and, all the while, his CIA escorts had been forced to move to the other end of the lounge, separated from their charge by a phalanx of Japanese security men. But, in the end, the escorts' exertions on the telephone to their embassy proved enough. When advised of the position, the American minister got onto the Japanese foreign minister in person, protesting this unwarranted detention of a traveler booked to the United States with a valid passport and entry visa. Though General Douglas MacArthur's military occupation of a vanquished Japan had long since ended, American political pressure in Tokyo still carried far more clout than anything the Soviet Union could bring to bear. The senior Foreign Ministry emissary in the lounge was himself summoned to the telephone. He returned red-faced to announce: "You are free to leave the soil of Japan."

Another Pan Am airliner was now waiting for takeoff and he was taken immediately to it. He and his CIA escorts had cleared the lounge just in time to avoid what might well have turned into a physical skirmish. The Soviet mission, alerted by the Japanese as to what was going on, had rushed three carloads of security men out to Narita and these men were now fanning out inside the terminal building. By the time they reached the gates, Pan Am Flight 2 was airborne.

Levchenko had got in his last blow against his former employers a few seconds before takeoff. Among the score of Japanese officials who had ushered him across the tarmac was a tiny officer in counterintelligence who kept pleading for the name of the top KGB officer working against Japan, the man in Moscow against whom they had to be most on their guard. "Pronnikov," he replied as he reached the stairway, "Vladimir Pronnikov." And he repeated the name, to make sure they had got it right.

PART FIVE

Full Circle

17

"Farewell" — A French Connection

"THE END is where we start from." T. S. Eliot's line fits the story of one of the greatest secret agents the French—or, for that matter, the West as a whole—have ever run against the Soviet Union, and run, moreover, from the heart of Moscow itself. The man, who was prophetically code-named "Farewell," was exceptional not merely for the unique information he supplied over a brief but dazzling sunburst of activity. He was rare also in the contrasts of his temperament and character. His mind had developed an intellectual contempt for the regime he served which was as cold and hard as a glacier. Yet the heart was a furnace and, in his outbursts of emotion, violence and excess, he was a figure straight out of the pages of a Russian novel. These passions never weakened his resolve, nor the courage which went with that resolve. But it was, nonetheless, one of those unbridled outbursts which swept him, and his one-man crusade, to destruction. It happened thus.

On a night in February 1982, Farewell was having a very intimate champagne session in his car, which he had driven to a quiet spot in a Moscow park. His drinking partner was his mistress, a secretary in the KGB headquarters called Ludmilla. Suddenly, their revels were interrupted by a knock on the car window. Farewell jumped out to find a man, whom he may or may not have recognized as a KGB colleague, standing along-side in the snow. Whether he knew the man or not, his immediate reaction was that he was under surveillance, that his secret was out and that he was about to be seized as a Western spy. A calmer person in a calmer state of mind would hardly have panicked, noting, for example, that the newcomer seemed to be quite alone. But, as indicated, Farewell was far from calm by temperament and, even when sober, was beginning to be ravaged by the tensions of his double life. On that particular night he was, into the bargain, tipsy if not drunk. Violence took over from reason. He pulled out a knife and stabbed the inter-loper, who fell dead on the spot. At this, the terrified Ludmilla leaped out of the car herself and, by making for the trees, tried to escape her lover, who now appeared to have become a raving lunatic. Farewell chased and overtook the woman, and stabbed her too, leaving her for dead in the snow. He then drove off.

About an hour later—again behaving like a character from some classic tragedy—he, the criminal, felt drawn back to re-visit the scene of his crime. By now, the police were on the scene, but that was not the worst shock awaiting Farewell. Ludmilla, whom he thought he had disposed of as a witness, was still alive, and she immediately pointed to him as the attacker. He identified himself; and the police then discovered that the murderer they had arrested, in what appeared to be a common brawl over a woman, was, in fact, a KGB colonel serving at the Moscow Center. Their initial impression of a jealous quarrel was strengthened when it was established that the murder vic-tim, who indeed had been on his own, lived in a Moscow apart-ment six miles from the scene of his death. A likely explanation for the tragedy was that he, too, was involved with, or enamored of, Ludmilla and had followed the couple that night in order to have it out with his rival. Once sobered up, Farewell realized to his chagrin that he was not under the slightest suspicion of being a Western agent. He indisputably was, however, a mur-derer. For that, he was duly tried, and, in a clear-cut crime such as this, his KGB rank could afford no protection. In the late autumn of 1982, Farewell began a twelve-year sentence in Ir-kutsk Prison. It was only now that the authorities began to suspect him of things far worse in their eyes than murder, and it was the condemned man who betrayed himself as a master spy. From such a strange end, we must return to the beginning. This was almost as bizarre.

Farewell had started adult life with a degree in engineering, specializing in the automobile industry. The Technical Department of the KGB's First Chief Directorate (which controlled the service's foreign espionage activities) was always on the lookout for such specialists to post abroad as one of its "Line X officers." Their task was to gather, by any means, every scrap of scientific and technological information which could be picked up in the West and fed back into the design and construction of the Soviet war machine. Farewell, the young Soviet agent, was posted to Paris as one of Department T's agents in 1965.

He stayed there, under the cover of a Soviet diplomat, for five years and, as part of his job, cultivated all the French scientists and industrialists he could seek out in order to tap them for information and, if possible, for examples of actual hardware. One such potential contact was a businessman who held a senior position in France's advanced electronics industry—a key field for Soviet burrowing. Farewell duly registered him with Moscow as a promising source but, professional matters apart, also got on good personal terms with his "recruit." This relationship became intimate after Farewell, drunk at the wheel of his car, smashed it up one night in the Paris streets. It was an official vehicle and he knew he faced serious trouble if it were ever seen in that state by his local KGB masters. He turned in desperation to the businessman. The latter, whether out of kindness or calculation, duly paid for a complete repair and, moreover, arranged for it to be done within hours. When he saw his resuscitated car, Farewell's Russian soul got the better of his Communist indoctrination. The businessman later described how his friend had dissolved into tears of gratitude and literally thrown himself on his knees to thank his benefactor. His career as a Western spy, though still some years ahead, can, in essence, be dated from that moment.

In 1970, Farewell left his Paris posting, with much regret and many affectionate memories, to return to Moscow. His friend and savior (who was to visit Russia on business trips no less than a hundred times over the years) had a natural working relationship with French intelligence, which had marked the Russian down as a possible long-term prospect. Farewell, for his part, may well have assumed that the Frenchman worked in some way for his country's secret service, despite the fact that he himself had entered the businessman in the KGB's books as an important source of technical information for Moscow. It appears a complicated equation but was, in fact, a very common one in the algebra of espionage. The overriding factor was the human one, the bond of friendship which had developed between the two men, cemented, at Farewell's end, by his deep debt of gratitude.

For the next decade, the French intelligence authorities, showing exemplary professional restraint, used this link simply to keep in touch. On his visits to Moscow, the businessman would periodically look up his Soviet friend but those contacts were always kept on the personal level, without any attempt at an operational approach. They had decided in Paris to play it long, hoping that, one day, Farewell himself would make a move. At the end of 1980, their waiting game was rewarded. The businessman received in Paris a letter from Farewell, backed up by an oral message. Neither the letter nor the message contained anything so compromising as an outright offer to work for France. They merely pressed urgently for another meeting in Moscow. That was a sufficient hint to the French authorities, who were immediately informed. From this point onward, Farewell, assigned that code name, begins as an active case.

The operation was a curious one in that it was run throughout its life by the DST (Direction de la Surveillance du Territoire), whose responsibility was to look after security within France. The Russian had automatically fallen under the DST's surveillance from his five years in Paris as a Soviet agent in search of French technical and scientific secrets. Now, however, he had to be run from Moscow, a task which would normally fall to the DST's sister service (and fierce rival) SEDEC.

The director of the DST, Marcel Chalet, and the new minister of the interior, Gaston Deferre, put the problem to President Mitterrand soon after he had succeeded Valéry Giscard d'Estaing in the summer of 1981. "It is going well, so carry on as you are" was Mitterrand's crisp reply. In this way the newly arrived Socialist political authorities showed how quickly they had understood the potential importance of the case for France's interests and those of the West as a whole.

By the summer of 1981, Farewell was doing rather more than well; he was doing spectacularly. But Commissaire Divisionnaire Raymond Nart, who, as head of the DST's Soviet branch, was called on to mastermind the operation, had had some very tricky problems of "field craft" to surmount in what was, for him, an unfamiliar area. The operation needed improvisation to begin with and constant adaptation afterward. It produced, alongside the magnificent results, hair-raising challenges which were only surmounted by a combination of cool nerves and Gallic panache.

The first question was how Farewell's pressing invitation should be met. The businessman was unable to make an immediate trip to Moscow himself but, by now, his firm had set up a permanent office in the Soviet capital, with another Frenchman in charge as the local representative. It was decided to make the first moves through him. The representative already held the Légion d'Honneur and, when recalled to Paris and presented with the problem, lived up to his reputation as a sound patriot. He immediately agreed to take on the task despite the obvious danger, especially in view of his vulnerability as a person without diplomatic immunity should anything go wrong. He was briefed about Farewell, given some basic training in espionage techniques and, after his crash course of less than a week, sent back to Moscow to start work. Seldom has such a vast intelligence operation been pulled into position by such an exiguous thread.

What simplified matters was that Farewell, who was to make all the procedural decisions in the months ahead, had already worked everything out. When the representative rang him, he promptly suggested a rendezvous in the heart of Moscow and there, almost under the Kremlin walls, handed over his first batch of documents. Some were originals which had to be copied in the firm's office and handed back at another rendezvous without delay. Others, Farewell had already photocopied himself. Ironically, most of these carried the KGB stamp "Photocopying forbidden!"

It was when this first batch of documents arrived in Paris (the representative had sent them by commercial package in the French diplomatic pouch—a normal usage) that Raymond Nart was able to see for himself, and disclose to his superiors, the dimensions of the treasure. Farewell had by now risen to be a senior officer of Department T, the second largest of the three subdivisions of the KGB's First Chief Directorate, and the one specifically charged with the collection of "special information" abroad, notably anything connected with Western nuclear research, missile and space programs and computer technology. Moreover, he was actually supervising the evaluation of the material Department T had gathered from all over the world and its distribution to interested parties within the Soviet Union. He thus had a complete, up-to-the-minute and detailed oversight of what the Kremlin was seeking in the way of military-industrial secrets and how far the KGB had helped toward satisfying those needs.

It was now clear to Raymond Nart and his colleagues that the operation of such a priceless source had to be transferred to more solid ground, and that meant moving it to some extraterritorial patch within the French embassy. The Moscow business representative was risking his freedom, and possibly his neck, with each handover of material. Marcel Chalet, profiting from his relations with General Jeanou Lacaze, chief of staff of the French armed forces, selected an officer from the military attaché's office, who happened to be a friend of Raymond Nart's. This officer was briefed in Paris on his mission, which was to be concealed, he was warned, even from his ambassador. By the early summer of 1981, the attaché had taken over as the contact. It was an arrangement which seemed to have nothing

but advantages. The officer, though not an intelligence specialist, was a professional. The photocopying could now be done in
the security of his embassy office. Above all, he had diplomatic
protection.

But there were also snags, most of them arising from the fact
that he remained a military attaché and had to continue with his
formal duties in that role. On one occasion, for example, he was
obliged to leave for an official lunch at his ambassador's dacha
immediately after receiving one of Farewell's packets (the handover was usually done by car). What to do with this precious
merchandise, which could hardly be carried into the luncheon
and was too bulky to be pocketed in his uniform? On the other
hand, if it remained outside, he would have to reckon with the
Red Army security men who guarded, and maintained surveillance over, this and all other foreign diplomatic properties.

L'audace! Toujours l'audace! The French officer approached one
of the soldiers and told him firmly not to let anyone near his
vehicle. Inside, he explained, was a case of whisky, and he did
not intend having that stolen while he was eating his lunch. To
ensure the man's goodwill, he gave him a bottle of spirits which
he happened to have with him. The sentry accepted the instructions with alacrity. In this way a few hundred Soviet documents
on their way to the West were safeguarded for two hours in a
French embassy car by Soviet soldiers.

It must be added that, by now, the purely physical side of the
operation had been simplified. At Farewell's request, he had
been provided with a special high-performance camera for his
work and, from the late summer of 1981, his deliveries came in
the much more manageable form of small film cassettes. This
method continued to be used to the end of the Farewell saga.

What was the importance of all his documents and cassettes
and how should Farewell be ranked among the roll of postwar
Soviet defectors and agents in place? To begin with, he gave the
Western powers their first complete picture of the scientific and
technological espionage network which had been built up
against them.[1] At the center of the web stands the so-called
Military Industrial Commission (VPK by its Russian initials) of

the Soviet Presidium, a body headed by Leonid Vassilievich Smirnov, himself one of the vice presidents of the Presidium. The West had known of the VPK's existence but had presumed that its function was a purely internal one, namely to coordinate arms production within the Soviet Union, iron out its faults and avoid duplication. Farewell disclosed a second and parallel task: to determine what technical information the Soviet military-industrial machine needed from abroad to fill the gaps in its own knowledge, to establish the priorities among them, and then to set about filling those gaps.

For this purpose, the ministers of all the key departments of Soviet war production sit as representatives at its conference tables: aeronautics, heavy and medium mechanical construction, defense industry, general construction, telecommunications, radio, naval construction and the departments for electronics, chemicals and petrochemicals. In the last analysis, the Soviet armed forces have the last word over the lot, acting on an overriding authority which goes up through the Presidium of the Council of Ministers to the Central Committee and, finally, to the Politburo itself. The priority of the regime, and of the entire industrial output of the Soviet Union which it controls, is thus the preparation for war. Aided by a technical center, the so-called National Institute of Information, or VIMI, which acts as the administrative arm, the needs of the various military industries are put forward each year, converted into two- or five-year "collection programs" and farmed out to the gathering agencies abroad.

Farewell identified no fewer than six bodies responsible for this task. They were his own KGB, with its special Department T; the GRU, or military intelligence network; the State Committee for Science and Technology (GKNT); the Soviet Academy of Sciences; the Ministry of Foreign Trade; and the so-called State Committee for External Economic Relations (GKES), responsible mainly for Third World countries. The last three operate largely on straightforward legal lines. The GKNT uses a mixture of open and secret channels with KGB officers mixed in among its bona fide professors and scientists. The two intelligence services work under their own separate clandestine blankets. For the purpose of information gathering on the VPK's behalf, all those collection agencies are given equal status. Taken together, Farewell explained, they serve a crucial objective of overall Soviet Five-Year Plans, namely not to miss the fast-moving train of worldwide technical innovation. To get on that train in time, they are prepared to spend millions of rubles to purchase Western tickets. When the tickets cannot be bought,* they must be stolen. Farewell emphasized the important and growing assistance rendered to Moscow in all this by the intelligence services of the East European countries. Over one annual accounting period, for example, the Poles and East Germans were credited with providing, by their own efforts, most of the basic information gathered on basic Western nuclear technology, 40 percent of all intelligence gathered by the VPK on Western space-war defenses, valuable information about NATO's chemical and biological weapons, as well as material on its conventional armaments, such as the Leopard tank. The Federal Republic of Germany and Vienna, seat of the International Atomic Energy Authority, were, and continue to be, prime targets for these East European services.

The results yielded by this global vacuum-cleaner operation are revealed in two top secret VPK reports for 1979 and 1980, also passed on by Farewell. During the first year, 58,516 documents and 5,824 industrial samples were logged as having been obtained from abroad.[2] Thanks to these acquisitions, the report claimed, 164 new research and development projects were started up in the Soviet Union while work on 1,262 existing projects could be accelerated or shortened. For the following year, the haul of secrets was down in quantity but seemingly up in quality since it enabled 200 R and D programs to be launched and work saved on 1,458 others. Over a four-year period, Farewell gave a grand total of 30,000 pieces of hardware and some 400,000 technical documents procured in the West.

*Farewell's own Department T report for 1980 revealed that, over the previous twelve months, the KGB alone had spent 850,000 rubles for unspecified Western industrial samples and a further 1.5 million for "measuring and recording equipment, radio receivers and transmitters signals protection" and other items. This single financial account gives some idea of the VPK's massive annual outlay as a whole.

Such statistics, prepared by the VPK for its Politburo masters, may well have been inflated by the presenters. But the Western powers did not need Farewell's information to learn about the major examples of Soviet scientific pillaging, since most of these were visible to the naked eye. Thus, the principal radar-scanning plane of the Soviet air force is a direct copy of the American AWAC; the Russian Blackjack bomber is modeled on the American B-1B; the Antonov-72 short-takeoff transport plane is a twin of the Boeing YC-14; the latest Soviet submarine torpedoes are based on the MK-48 of the U.S. Navy; while, according to another Soviet defector, the theft by the VPK of all the technical blueprints of the American submarine *George Washington* enabled the Russians to build their own copy, ironically nicknamed *Small George*. [3] As these examples indicate, the United States provides the bulk of the gold dust which is sucked up by the VPK's vacuum cleaner. Farewell's documents showed that, in 1980, for example, 61.5 percent of the information collected came from American sources, followed by 10.5 percent from West Germany, 8 percent from France, 7.5 percent from Britain and 3 percent from Japan.[*4]

Most of the details given above of VPK operations and the inroads they have made on Western technology have been published at one time or another as part of an information campaign to alert the free world to the constant espionage offensive which confronts it and which it tends, all too passively, to accept. But there has been no publicity about two other aspects of the dividends which Farewell's disclosures brought to the West. The first was the services they rendered in the purely professional East-West intelligence sphere. The second was the insight they gave, through an analysis of the secrets the Russians were after, into many hitherto unknown, or only partially known, projects of the Soviet war industry. In this respect, Farewell held up a two-way mirror which, when looked

---

*American calculations made on Farewell's disclosures put the VPK's "theft budget" for 1980 at 1.4 billion dollars. It was a good investment. The Russians were reckoned to have saved themselves over 55 million dollars in research and development just by the documents they acquired on the F-18 fighter.

through from behind, showed what those various VPK ministers were up to themselves.

Among the three thousand-plus secret and top secret intelligence documents which Farewell passed to the West were two personnel lists which he had been able to photograph straight from the card indexes locked up in his own office safes.* The first was a roll call of 250 Line X officers operating under legal cover throughout the world as Department T's *spetsinformatsiya* or "special information" collectors. Possession of that list effectively destroyed or neutralized, at least in the short term, the KGB's entire operational activities in this field. But Farewell was also able to do significant damage to the network of local contacts, informants and hardware suppliers which these Line X officers had managed to set up all over the globe. He gave the West slightly under a hundred case leads involving a slightly greater number of individuals, each of whom could be classed as an industrial spy, operating in at least sixteen NATO or neutral countries. Some were arrested, tried and sentenced. Others were scared off or quietly rendered harmless. Others became the object of counteroperations designed, at least in some cases, to feed false reports back to Moscow.

Like the rest of Farewell's disclosures, this was information which vitally affected all of France's NATO partners. Those partners were fully briefed, above all the United States, which, as the KGB statistics showed, was the prime target. There is a story whereby the newly elected President Mitterrand takes President Reagan aside at the ten-power Ottawa summit in July of 1981 and shows him the Farewell dossier, thus, so this version goes, converting American suspicions of the Socialist head of state into instant and wholehearted cordiality.[5] In fact, this exchange took place, not at Ottawa itself, but at a private rendezvous between the two leaders on their way to the summit. And the presentation, though it earned Reagan's gratitude (especially later on, after the information had been evaluated and

---

*In quantity and to some extent in quality, this rich haul from a Western agent in place is surpassed only by Penkovsky's contributions.

acted upon), did not transform American political attitudes overnight. Nonetheless, the Farewell dossier undoubtedly helped to draw France, at times something of a voluntary outsider, much closer into the NATO intelligence fold. Moreover, the revelations made to the White House about the depth and scope of Soviet industrial and scientific espionage led to what was perhaps the principal political impact of the Farewell case. This was a lasting awareness, in the United States and throughout the Western world, of the reality of the threat and the launching of certain countermeasures to meet it. A new offensive was started against the "technobandits," those Western businessmen prepared, for handsome fees, to assist in the smuggling of embargoed goods to the Soviet Union. There was a tightening-up through the COCOM organization* of the embargo itself, especially on the more sophisticated items such as advanced computers and robotics. With strong French support, COCOM itself developed a special advisory body to control the sale of any technological equipment likely to be of specific military value to Moscow.

What all these measures have to face is the built-in openness of Western, and especially American, society. This has enabled the KGB to derive nearly 40 percent of its "special information" from perfectly overt and legitimate sources, such as articles in technical journals, study papers and discussion documents at international scientific gatherings and so on. Even in this inherently porous field of security, there have been determined attempts, thanks to Farewell's warnings, to reduce the seepage.

This is one part of his strategic importance as a spy, a dimension which he shares with only two other of these postwar agents and defectors. Another part is the Soviet Union's own military secrets, which he revealed, almost unconsciously, along with his lists of the Kremlin's information targets. Thus, Moscow's persistent quarrying for data on Western vertical-takeoff planes led to the discovery that the Soviet Union was

---

*The Coordinating Committee of the NATO member countries plus Japan, which lays down restrictions on the sale of high-technology products to the Soviet bloc.

producing its own new and hitherto unreported aircraft of this type, the YAK-44. The airborne radar of the latest Soviet MiG-29 fighter planes could be more easily "read" once it was established that it had been built partly on Western models. Similarly, the famous SS-20 medium-range Soviet nuclear missile held few secrets for NATO, since much of its technology had come from the West in the first place.

As for land warfare, NATO first learned that the Red Army would be confronting it with an entirely new battle tank in the 1990s only after Farewell had passed back the pilfered Western blueprints which were being used to build it. Significant gaps were revealed even in Soviet missile propulsion, one of the relatively few areas where the Russians were commonly held to have a commanding lead over the West. Despite Soviet boasts that they had nothing to learn in this field, Farewell revealed that Moscow was, in fact, very anxious to discover the secret of "Cryogenie," a special pressurized mixture of oxygen and nitrogen which is used as the propellant of France's Ariane rocket. It was the knowledge that key French projects such as this were among the Kremlin's targets (plus, of course, the fact that Farewell had himself chosen to work for France) which led President Mitterrand to take a distinctly hard-nosed attitude toward the Russians—another example of Farewell's impact on the broader political scene.

But it is time to return to the Soviet Union in the winter of 1982 and see how Farewell finally closed his own epic espionage dossier on himself. We need to begin by recounting what little became known about the man himself and his family, for this was the key to his downfall. As he declined all opportunities to meet his Paris controllers face-to-face,* such sketchy information as they got was gathered by the two French contact men who dealt with him in Moscow.

Farewell was born in 1928 and was apparently descended from a former landed family, probably of Russian minor nobil-

---

*Suggestions that Farewell was permanently barred from leaving the Soviet Union because of his special knowledge are incorrect. There were opportunities for meetings abroad, even in Paris, but it was Farewell himself who always declined to take them up.

ity; in any event, he described himself as a *ci-devant*. He was clearly well educated and well read, with a collection of antique furniture and classical art and, in general, a taste for the good life with a traditional stamp. He came to hate the Communist regime above all for its vulgarity, self-seeking and lies, rather in the way that many a Prussian Junker officer disdained the uncouth Nazi system he was obliged to serve. In his eyes, the Communists had forfeited respect and loyalty because they had never seriously attempted to discharge the primary responsibility of any government, to serve the nation. He once pulled out his wallet: "Look what we get for pay," he exclaimed. "All the money goes on arms. There is nothing for the people." Money played no part in his decision to work against the regime. He never tried to bargain for the invaluable material he was handing over, and would only accept small sums of cash to cover his expenses.

His wife was also far removed from the proletariat. This remarkable woman, about whom, unfortunately, even less is known, was the daughter of an admiral and seems to have been a cultured person herself.

Farewell's undoing came after he had been sentenced for murder, when he began to open his own mouth just a fraction. Despite his affairs with women like Ludmilla, his marriage seems to have been a happy one, *à la mode russe*. So, from his cell in Irkutsk Prison, the condemned murderer, in his letters to his wife, could not resist dropping nostalgic hints about "something big" which he had now been forced to abandon. The references, though vague, were disturbing enough to the official eye. As Farewell should have realized, and may have realized, everything he wrote was being read by the prison authorities. The KGB became automatically involved and so, during the winter of 1982–83, Farewell was confronted by security officers from his old organization, who now suspected for the first time that he might be a traitor as well as a murderer.

Owing to an extraordinary stroke of coincidence, the West learned about this interrogation and, indeed, about the gory incident which had led to Farewell's arrest in the first place. The officer sent to do the questioning was Colonel Vitaly Sergeiyvich Yurchenko, who, from September 1980 to March 1985, served as chief of the Fifth Department of Directorate K of the KGB's First Chief Directorate, responsible among other things for the investigation of suspected espionage involving KGB staff personnel. And in August 1985, five months after being transferred to operational work against the United States and Canada, Yurchenko made an "impulse defection" to the American embassy in Rome.[6] Though he made an equally impulsive redefection to the Soviet embassy in Washington only three months later, his bona fides as an informant have been confirmed by other defectors; and one of the things he told the Americans during his regrettably brief time in their hands was that the trauma of the Farewell case had been one of the causes of his initial leap to the West.

This is not surprising for, according to him, Farewell not only promptly admitted to having spied for France but turned his admission into a blistering condemnation of the regime he had disavowed and a paean of praise for the West. He wrote out a long document entitled "The Confession of a Traitor," which, for its well-reasoned invective, puts one in mind of Emile Zola's "J'accuse." His bitterest criticism was leveled against the department in which he had served. The KGB's First Chief Directorate, he declared, was "totally rotten, dominated by alcoholism, corruption and nepotism." His tirade ended with the words: "My only regret is that I was not able to cause more damage to the Soviet Union and render more service to France."

Farewell knew he was doomed anyway; but it is not every condemned man who writes out his own death sentence, and does so gladly, because it is the last round of his fight. In his "Confession," those two contrary aspects of his character noted at the beginning—the calm intellectual disdain and the Slavic passion—merge and form one. Not the least important lesson of Farewell's life was the way he ended it.

He would have smiled at some of the things which happened after his execution. Thus, on April 5, 1983, the French government expelled, in one swoop, forty-seven Soviet intelligence agents operating in France under various forms of diplomatic cover. The bulk were Line X officers taken from the list of 250 VPK operatives which Farewell had handed over to the DST the year before, along with the identities of other KGB officers. This mass expulsion naturally created a great stir and was directly linked in the Western press at the time with the discovery of an intelligence coup of the Russians. Three months earlier the French embassy in Moscow had been obliged, red-faced, to admit that, for the past six years, the KGB had been monitoring all its messages to and from Paris through electronic bugs which tapped the embassy's telex machines before the texts they were transmitting had been converted into cipher or, in the case of incoming traffic, after they had been decoded. The expulsions appeared to be an appropriate riposte to such a humiliation and they were allowed to pass as such. In fact, the two events were totally unconnected. The Soviet agents were expelled in early April of 1983 because, the month before, Raymond Nart and his colleagues had received firm confirmation of Farewell's death. Only now could the French network he had named be destroyed without damaging him. It is believed that President Mitterrand himself, acting on the advice of the new DST Director Yves Bonnet, selected Farewell's victims from the list which the DST presented to him. (In all, nearly 150 Line X officers were expelled worldwide.)

Though the Kremlin refrained from taking any retaliatory measures (aware that the French had a great deal more information up their sleeves), the KGB continued to burrow away at what for them was an incomprehensible defeat, long after Farewell's death. In the summer of 1984, for example, it tried to get its hands on the French businessman who had started the affair rolling by restoring the Russian's smashed car back in the 1960s. A letter was sent to him in the handwriting of Farewell's wife suggesting a meeting in Moscow. It was an obvious trap and he ignored it.

The businessman's name would have appeared on Farewell's official reports as one of his operational contacts from his own time in Paris. It does not appear that his identity, or that of other Frenchmen involved, was extracted from Farewell during interrogation before his death. Both the French commercial representative in Moscow, who had started the hazardous contact, and the military attaché officer who had taken over, finished their prescribed spell of duty in Moscow and returned home, unmolested, a year or two later. Farewell had continued to serve France even after he could no longer serve the West.

18

The "Rezident"

Oleg Gordievski is the third giant in the long list of Soviet intelligence officers who, since 1945, have rejected the Communist system to serve the West. He is also the only one of the trio to survive. Penkovsky in the early 1960s and Farewell in the early 1980s were both trapped, tortured and executed by the regime they had betrayed. Gordievski only escaped the same fate by the skin of his teeth, thanks to his own superb professionalism and, we may assume, the support of the British, for whom he had been working steadily for more than a decade before his secret was suddenly rumbled in Moscow.

All of the defectors, would-be defectors and agents in place described in this book have been far from pygmies in stature. The giants among them are those whose importance can be measured outside a purely professional dimension. The 5,500 top secret documents which Colonel Penkovsky passed to the West altered the military thinking of the NATO powers as well as unraveling the mystery of those Cuban missiles. Farewell's 3,000 documents, mostly of similar top-grade quality, brought France closer to the Western alliance as well as alerting the whole world to the scale of Soviet technological pilfering and espionage. Gordievski brought no sheaves of documents with him when he had to cut and run. He hardly needed to. By the time he was forced to flee, he was KGB rezident-designate in Britain, head of all operations in the country second only to the

United States as a Soviet priority target and second to none in the professional esteem in which it was held. It was a key post, which would normally have carried the rank of major general, and it made Gordievski in some ways the most influential of all Soviet intelligence officers ever to cross over to the West.

Where his two predecessors brought documents, Gordievski brought a unique inside knowledge of the Kremlin, both through his senior rank and through the Moscow posts he had held earlier in his career. Like Penkovsky and Farewell, he was a man with a mission. In his case, the broader contribution to East-West relations sprang not from military or scientific information but from political guidance and his insight into what was going on in the minds of the Soviet leaders. Some of his disclosures were startling. Taken together, they helped produce a transformation of Western understanding of the Soviet regime which still endures today.

When Gordievski was finally plucked from Moscow, he had given Britain and her allies a priceless flow of information as well as a chilling example of how paranoia in the Kremlin almost brought the world to war in the autumn of 1983. The stopgap Soviet leader Yuri Andropov was dying and, in that closed and highly suspicious atmosphere, the leadership was more nervous than usual.

At that moment NATO launched a top secret exercise codenamed "Able Archer," which was to run between November 2 and 11. It was a command-post drill, staged to enable the alliance to practice its own nuclear release procedures in the event of all-out war. As a matter of routine, Warsaw Pact intelligence began to monitor the exercise. In equally routine fashion, Western intelligence began to monitor the monitors.

It soon became clear to both the British and the American listening centers that something was going badly wrong. Instead of the monitoring normally to be expected from across the Iron Curtain, a sharp increase was registered in both the volume and the urgency of the Eastern bloc traffic. The incredible seemed to be happening, namely, that the Warsaw Pact suspected it might really be facing nuclear attack at any moment.

Gordievski was later to explain to the West that this was, in fact, far from incredible. The classic Soviet plan for an offensive against the West envisages that maneuvers will be used as a combined camouflage screen and springboard for the real attack. The Russians naturally assume that their adversaries would do the same. It was for this reason, he said, that KGB headquarters at Moscow Center had always given the highest priority to intelligence on NATO exercises and alert procedures.

This much the West might have assumed. What it was totally unaware of at the time was how far it had really passed through a war danger zone in those early November days of 1983. It was on November 8–9, Gordievski revealed, that the Kremlin had pressed what came close to a panic button. Having noted what appeared to be significant changes in the Able Archer message formats, Moscow Center sent an urgent information order to all its KGB residencies abroad. This was not a surge of Soviet aggression but a spasm of Soviet panic. Moreover, the war jitters which finally produced this spasm had been building up in the Kremlin for several years.

Thus, the information order itself was nothing improvised. It was sent out under the long-standing "Operation Ryan," a code name of the Center's own. And the initials stood for the Russian words *Raketno Yadernoye Napadeniye,* or "Nuclear Missile Attack."

It was at the end of November 1981, two years before the Able Archer scare, that the first of these Ryan circular telegrams was dispatched from Moscow to KGB residencies in the capitals of all NATO states and other major or influential powers outside the alliance, like Japan, Sweden and Switzerland, as well as certain Latin American countries. The recipients were ordered to watch out for anything which might indicate that the West was preparing to launch a lightning nuclear strike against the Soviet Union. The list of headings under which information was demanded varied somewhat according to the political conditions of the target country. It was Gordievski, who had managed to get himself put in charge of the British desk at Moscow Center, who sent the Ryan order to London.

It required the KGB in Britain, for example, to watch carefully the pattern of work at 10 Downing Street, the Ministry of Defense and the Foreign Office (reporting on whether the lights were burning at night); to maintain a similar watch over the American embassy in Grosvenor Square and on the headquarter buildings of MI5 and MI6; to monitor the movements of liaison officers or couriers between any and all of these establishments; to keep the closest scrutiny over the comings and goings of ministers, noting whether Prime Minister Margaret Thatcher was driving more often than usual to Buckingham Palace; to look out for any unusual movement of troops or increased activity at air bases and ports; to watch for any signs of official stockpiling of food, the building up of emergency blood banks and any other civil defense measures which might indicate preparations for a Soviet nuclear counterstrike. Regular reports were demanded every fortnight, but "Flash" telegrams were to be sent in case of any information which smacked of an emergency.

The circular should have been dispatched from Moscow much earlier, but months had been lost because the combined KGB/GRU team of sixty officers detailed to draw up the schedule had not, at first, been able to take it too seriously. (This was the time when the short-lived Soviet leader Yuri Andropov was still head of the KGB. He was thought to have been somewhat skeptical about the exercise himself but was persuaded to join forces with GRU military intelligence by the hawkish Soviet defense minister, Marshal Ustinov.)*

The Ryan concept dated from May 1981 when, for the first time in their histories, the two rival agencies had been ordered by the Politburo to cooperate in a global intelligence-gathering operation. The GRU was tasked to monitor all purely military indications that a nuclear first strike was being planned by the West, while the KGB was ordered to concentrate on any evidence that the political decision had actually been made—either by the United States or by NATO as a whole—to launch nuclear weapons against the Soviet Union. According to Gordiev-

---

*Andropov was anyway believed to be keen on forging closer ties with the military in order to strengthen his chances of succeeding the ailing Brezhnev.

ski, Moscow's view was that this crucial decision would have to
be made by the West a week to ten days before the actual attack.
This, the Kremlin reasoned, was the minimum time needed to
allow for all the massive secret preparations to be made, not just
on the missile front itself but over wide fields of governmental
administration, inter-Allied liaison, economic planning and
civil defense. It was the detection of these various indicators in
advance of the strike that was needed to enable the Soviet High
Command itself, and all its military and missile forces, to move
up to a higher level of alert.

As far as the KGB's First Chief Directorate for espionage
abroad (in which Gordievski was serving) was concerned, all
doubts about the gravity of the operation had been removed by
an address given by the head of this directorate, General Vladimir Kryuchkov, to his senior officers. He told them that the
instruction to make a "special military-strategic assessment"
had come straight from the Politburo (then operating in the last,
decadent phase of the Brezhnev era). "Belligerent imperialist
circles in the U.S.A.," so the guidance went, "are getting ready
for war and are preparing new weapons systems which could
render a sudden attack feasible." The Soviet leadership had thus
decided to mobilize all its intelligence services for a global campaign of special vigilance. Their slogan was to be "Don't Miss
It!" *(Ne Prozerot!)*

The question arose in some Soviet minds then (and in some
Western minds later, when Gordievski's information was made
available) whether this was a genuine political scare or a complex intelligence war game. Gordievski believed it was the former. He argued that, though the fear was self-engendered and
self-developed, it was based on a seemingly plausible view of the
situation in Washington. Soviet hysteria that the world could
be on the brink of a nuclear war had been sparked off in the late
1970s by the Teheran hostages crisis and President Carter's ambitious plans for a large and globally operational U.S. Rapid
Deployment Force. But the fuse began to burn in earnest after
Reagan had been in power for a short while. The KGB thought
that, like Nixon, after a few months of tough talk he would seek
détente. But, no, he simply carried on as he had started.

This disturbing political input had been reinforced by the dangers which Moscow perceived on the missile front itself. It saw the emergence of new and more accurate American missile systems as giving the West a credible second-strike capability against the Soviet nuclear arsenal, thus enabling its first strike to be launched with a reasonable prospect of survival and victory. Among these technical indicators was the development of the MX (Peacekeeper), the Trident II and Pershing II nuclear weapons, as well as cruise missiles for ground, sea or air launching.

There was added alarm in Moscow when NATO adopted its famous "twin-track" decision in 1979, the policy of actually deploying these cruise missiles on the ground in Europe while continuing to seek a negotiated settlement. All that the Kremlin had eyes for was the deployment track. This seemed a clear indication that the entire Western alliance was now behind the American effort to gain decisive superiority over the Soviet Union, despite all Moscow's costly propaganda attempts to pre-empt such solidarity. American talk of a so-called countervailing strategy was interpreted in Moscow as the doctrinal and intellectual blessing for all these new operational postures.

The last public speech Leonid Brezhnev ever made bears out Gordievski's assessment. On October 27, 1982, the failing Soviet leader told the leaders of his armed forces: "The United States is carrying to unprecedented heights the level of its military preparations. . . . We are going through a period when the war readiness of our army and navy must be raised even more. . . . The Soviet army must be at its peak in all areas. . . . Any lagging behind in this conflict cannot be tolerated."

A fortnight later, on November 10, 1982, Brezhnev was dead. However, as Gordievski's revelations were to show, the Kremlin's war jitters did not die with him. As a result of Gordievski's warnings, certain adjustments in Western practices were made, all designed to avoid needless provocation in the future.

On the broader political front, Gordievski's message led to even greater changes. In September and October 1985, British officials passed Gordievski's information on the Ryan exercise to the Americans, including his detailed analysis not merely of the Kremlin's strategy but of the Kremlin's psychology as it affected that strategy. The paper, entitled "Soviet Perceptions of Nuclear Warfare," was fifty pages long.

Its insistent conclusion was that the Soviet leadership was all too inclined to believe its own propaganda about "aggressive imperialist circles" and that the West should be very wary of increasing such a dangerous paranoia in case it drove the Kremlin over the brink. The White House had, until then, fondly believed that, through the reports to Moscow of men like Anatoly Dobrynin, Soviet ambassador to Washington over more than two decades, the true picture of an essentially peace-loving and peace-seeking America would have been presented. It now transpired that for much of the time, even this respected veteran had been telling his Kremlin masters more or less what they wanted to hear.

President Reagan is said to have read these Gordievski reports from beginning to end, which was far from being his standard practice. The cautionary tale they contained sank in. Soon afterward, Reagan's famous "evil empire" onslaught against the Soviet Union began to be wound down, and eventually died almost completely.

But the impact of Gordievski's reporting was not confined to the political sphere. He had much of enormous value to tell the intelligence professionals in Britain and other Western countries. He could provide chapter and verse on how the strict policy followed by the British government in keeping down the numbers of Soviet intelligence officers in London since 1971 had damaged KGB operations. The tough British policy over expulsions had hurt on at least three fronts. First, by demoralizing and damaging the careers of those affected (three officers expelled from the UK in 1983 and 1984 became completely deskbound and, of three expelled from Denmark in the early 1970s, one took to drink and another suffered the equivalent of a breakdown). Second, by reducing the KGB's staffing levels, so that there were not enough people available for the jobs. Third, by limiting the officers who obtained British visas to those who had kept their noses clean rather than bolder souls who had built up some experience operating in foreign countries. Moreover, because he had worked on the British desk in the KGB department responsible for Britain, he was in a unique position to say authoritatively who was on the KGB's books or in its sights—and, sometimes equally important, who was not.

He was able to reassure MI6 that the KGB's London residency had been largely ineffective between 1982 and 1985. Most of its contacts were low-level with limited access to sensitive information; there was no high-level penetration of the British establishment. There was, moreover, a stark contrast between the persistence, dedication and occasional brilliance with which the KGB was capable of running its top-grade agents elsewhere and the routine level of the London residency's reporting, which often involved outright deception of Moscow. The residency would deceive the Center about the number and quality of agents on its books. The Center would deceive the Politburo by feeding it the information it thought it would want to hear. It was not unknown for reports to be complete fabrications by the residency, though more often they would be culled from the local press. On one occasion the London residency received a request from the Center to submit a report on Western views on Gorbachev's meetings with a delegation of the Socialist International in Moscow. As there was no information available, the residency simply invented a report and ascribed it to plausible-sounding sources.

Who was this Russian who, when still in his thirties, had started, out of sheer ideological conviction, to work secretly against the Soviet Union and who, before he was fifty, had succeeded in transforming Western perceptions of that regime? What can be told about Oleg Gordievski's life and work goes a long way toward explaining the outcome of his career.

He was born in Moscow in October 1938 and, as with certain KGB colleagues who trod the path to the West before him, the moral tug-of-war seems to have started almost at birth. His father was an officer in the NKVD (as the KGB was then styled) and had been a Communist party official since the early 1920s. He was an educated man, steeped in Russian culture, but he believed almost totally in the dictates of the Party press, even the justifications, which were to appear so incredible to the young Oleg, for the great purges.

His mother, on the other hand, came of more skeptical stock. She was from Turkestan in Central Asia and inherited from her own mother, an almost illiterate peasant woman, a simple unquestioning religious conviction. There is some evidence that both mother and grandmother conspired in a narrowly frustrated attempt to have the infant Oleg baptized. A two-way pull had started which was to last throughout Oleg's childhood and adolescence.

The family lived in a Moscow block of flats inhabited almost entirely by KGB officers. During the repeated purges of the intelligence services in the late 1930s, they often heard early morning hammerings on the doors of their neighbors as one or another of their KGB colleagues was carted away, never to reappear.

Even before the death of Stalin, the boy could listen to his parents arguing about the state of affairs in Russia, his mother always questioning Communist authority, his father, for the most part, defending it. But it was not until 1956 that the father was finally obliged to discuss Party affairs with the whole family. He could not very well avoid it. Khrushchev's famous speech to the Twentieth Party Congress denouncing the Stalinist terror was circulating around Moscow in pamphlet form. The Gordievski family was lent a copy, and the taboo was broken. Oleg's natural questioning of authority as a teenager was certainly deepened by the shock he received.

Nineteen fifty-six was also a crucial year for his own career. Whatever his stifled misgivings, he was ineluctably enrolled into the Party mainstream. That October, he entered the six-year course at the Moscow Institute of International Relations, which traditionally led to a posting in Soviet intelligence or regular diplomacy. Gordievski was already certain that his destiny lay abroad, though the form that destiny would finally take had not entered his wildest dreams.

For the moment, there was excitement enough within the Soviet orbit. This was, of course, the month of the Hungarian

revolution. Gordievski declared later that he had genuinely believed this to mark the beginning of a new era, but that he had
quickly suppressed these feelings when he observed the reaction of his fellow students to them. This was just as well, for,
a few days later, there came the news of the Soviet invasion to
crush the uprising.

In August 1961, during his last year at the institute, Gordievski was sent to the Soviet embassy in East Berlin for a spell of
apprentice training. He stayed there until January 1962. During
these six months his eyes were opened to a good deal more than
diplomatic practice. As the date indicates, he had arrived at a
momentous juncture. The Berlin Wall went up on the day after
his arrival. The unceasing campaign of lies which was promptly
produced to justify the monstrosity, the so-called need to keep
Western agent provocateurs at bay, may have impressed the
young Gordievski professionally, but it cannot have made him
feel any more comfortable about the superiority of the "workers' paradise" or the morals of those who ran it.

Another aspect of Gordievski's months in East Berlin must
have caused him to reflect. Though from his privileged position
at the Moscow Institute he had been able to get a glimpse of the
capitalist world through studying West German newspapers, it
was only now that the image became strong and clear. Every
day, he was able to watch Western television programs and read
the Western press as a whole. To an intelligent young man with
a questioning mind, the defects and, above all, the appalling
inefficiency of the system he served leaped out in contrast.

It was, therefore, a young man full of suppressed reflections
who returned to Moscow in 1962 to follow his father into the
KGB. After a twelve months' training course, he spent the first
three years of his career in Moscow Center, working in Department S of the First Chief Directorate on organizing Soviet
"illegals" (i.e., agents operating without official cover) in the
West. Then, in January of 1966, he received his first foreign
posting. It was a plum, Copenhagen, where he was able to
continue with the same work in the field, namely running and
expanding the KGB's undercover network in Denmark.

He stayed in the Danish capital until January 1970, and it was during these four years that his moral revulsion against the Communist regime became complete. This was no East Berlin, giving only tantalizing glimpses of the West, caught through the bars of a cage. In Copenhagen he was in the middle of the free world. All he had absorbed about the Stalin horror stories and the other excesses of recent Soviet history were put in a new perspective, and he recognized his true feelings toward the system he was supposed to believe in and defend.

In the summer of 1968 came the invasion of Czechoslovakia. It had the same indelible impact on Gordievski, the rising young KGB man watching the drama from Scandinavia, as it was having on Rezun, the rising young Red Army officer actually marching on Prague from the Carpathians.

For Gordievski, "The Czech crisis was the final decisive proof that, even under someone like Khrushchev, the system was simply incapable of change." He realized he would have to fight that system. "Just as Shostakovich, the composer, fought back with music and Solzhenitsyn, the writer, fought back with words, so I, the KGB man, could operate through my own intelligence world." But he was not yet ready psychologically to act on that decision.

He spent rather less than two years—from January 1970 to October 1972—working again at Moscow Center, and it was during this period that he managed to get his crucial transfer from administrative to political duties. Managing illegals from Department S was a humdrum desk job made even less attractive after four years on the same task in the field. The Third Department, which he now joined, demanded more brain-power, put to use at a much higher level. It had direct control over KGB operations in Britain, Ireland, Australasia and Malta, as well as Scandinavia and Finland.

The prime task faced by the Third Department during Gordievski's first assignment with it was to rebuild the London residency from the humiliating rubble it had been reduced to by the mass expulsion of 105 Soviet agents in September 1971, in the wake of the Lyalin disclosures.* This was not, Gordievski

*See pp. 257–61.

was later able to inform the British, the clean sweep of the entire Soviet espionage network that had been hoped for. About eight KGB officers and five GRU military intelligence men survived, because even Lyalin had not known of their existence. Nevertheless, the purge, the most drastic in the annals of the East-West espionage conflict, had truly horrified Moscow Center. Nor was horror the only reaction to what had happened. The Center also found itself numbed into a certain respect for a government which had the nerve and self-confidence to throw down such a challenge to Moscow.

The episode certainly helped to raise further, in Gordievski's eyes, the professional image of the British. He was already mulling over the problem of making some move toward the West on his next foreign assignment. In principle, he would have been prepared to talk either to the CIA or to MI6. By now, he had ample evidence, including the verdict of one of the rezidents during his Copenhagen years, who had also been in charge of the British desk in Moscow Center, that there was no risk to his own security in collaborating with the British. "I was confident that British intelligence was long since 'clean' of any Soviet agents and I was therefore safe in working for it. The time of the Philbys and Blakes was over."

When, therefore, Oleg Gordievski arrived back in Copenhagen in the autumn of 1972 for his second KGB spell of duty there, he was prepared to consider any Western contact on its merits. It was, in fact, the British who made the first move in what was to prove a long and cautious opening round. "I was very happy it should have been with the British—who have been allies of my country in two world wars—that contact was first established." Gordievski was well known on the diplomatic cocktail scene as an affable extrovert, and this was, therefore, the natural circuit on which to make the first attempts to cultivate him. It is likely that at this stage Gordievski was still wary, not of what he was doing, but of how and when to go about it. By 1975, however, he had begun cooperating with the British on a regular basis.

As Third Department officer in Copenhagen, Gordievski would have had detailed knowledge of the "legal" KGB network operating from the Soviet embassy, the "illegal" network (which he himself had once run) and the Danish citizens who were either actively working for Moscow or were dangerously susceptible, for one reason or another, to Soviet influence. He was also in a position to disclose much about KGB activities on the broader Scandinavian plane. It is virtually certain that the arrests of Colonel Bergling of Swedish Military Intelligence in 1978 and of the Norwegian Foreign Ministry spy, Miss Haavik, in the previous year stemmed from information provided by Gordievski.

Another clear debt that the Western alliance owes to Gordievski is for his role in netting the KGB's much bigger Norwegian fish, Arne Treholt. Treholt was finally arrested in 1984, caught in flagrante taking money from a KGB general in exchange for documents. On June 20, 1985, he was sentenced in Oslo to twenty years' imprisonment on charges of espionage dating back to 1975. The court heard that he, like his Norwegian Foreign Ministry colleague Miss Haavik, had been caught in the "honey trap": the KGB had secretly photographed him taking part in a sexual orgy and threatened to expose him unless he cooperated. Treholt, then in his midthirties and with a seemingly brilliant career ahead of him, did cooperate. One result was a steady stream of classified NATO documents not only dealing with the alliance's plans to defend its vulnerable northern flank against Soviet attack, but also giving details of secret discussions held between Norwegian ministers and other Western leaders, including Dr. Henry Kissinger, the West German Chancellor Helmut Schmidt and the British Foreign Secretary Lord Carrington. Another, and almost equally important, result of Treholt's recruitment was that the Soviet Union had gained a very important agent of influence in Oslo, for the young Foreign Ministry press officer was on excellent terms with nearly all the members of Norway's Labor government. Indeed, he was credited with being partly responsible for that government's decision to reject the deployment of any NATO nuclear missiles on Norwegian soil until an East-West war had actually broken out.

For Britain, however, Gordievski's greatest service was to

come after his return to Moscow Center in June 1978. It stemmed from a coup of internal office intrigue. Though a Scandinavian expert for all of his operational life (and he spoke some Swedish in addition to his fluent Danish), Gordievski managed to get himself transferred in 1981 to the British desk in the Third Department of the First Chief Directorate. He obviously engineered this with his own loyalties in mind, and with the ambition of a posting to London. Posted he was. In January 1982, a request for a visa for one Oleg Gordievski to be assigned to the Soviet mission in London was received at the British embassy in Moscow. It was a delightful New Year's surprise. The visa was not long in coming.

Gordievski arrived in London in June 1982, accompanied by his second wife* Leila and their two young children. He had the military rank of colonel in the KGB and was given the cover of an embassy counselor, the highest diplomatic slot normally reserved for an intelligence official. Contact with his MI6 controllers was simplified by the fact that one of his primary duties was to cultivate all manner of local information sources, always keeping on the lookout for potential KGB recruits.

In London, Gordievski quickly moved up the ladder to the top post of rezident. It is safe to assume that the British gave him a helping hand by providing him, as the officer responsible for political intelligence, with the best inside information to feed to his chiefs. Not surprisingly, Gordievski soon acquired the reputation of a particularly receptive and well-informed observer of the British scene. He had, after all, predicted Mrs. Thatcher's resounding victory in the 1983 elections, and assured Moscow that Arthur Scargill's miners' strike would eventually collapse. His contacts appeared to be paying handsome dividends for the Kremlin.

In 1983 Igor Titov, the deputy rezident and a potential rival

*His first marriage, which dated from 1963, was an unhappy one, and there were no children. He divorced, and married his second wife in 1978. She bore him two girls, Maria and Anna.

of Gordievski's for the top job, was expelled on the grounds that he had abused his "diplomatic position" by attempting to suborn an American student in Britain. The following year, the rezident himself, General Arkady Gouk, was sent packing in the wake of the Bettaney affair. (Michael Bettaney, a middle-ranking Security Service officer with access to the heart of the British intelligence establishment, had attempted to offer his services to the general. Gordievski was in a position to reveal these overtures and Bettaney was duly arrested and sentenced to twenty-three years' imprisonment. In stopping what could have developed into a major espionage case at the outset, Gordievski had performed another great service to the West.)

The great event of 1984 was the visit to Britain by Mikhail Gorbachev, which began on December 15. Gorbachev was then only a Politburo member but, as one of the Central Committee secretaries for ideology, already held a key position in the regime, and was widely touted as the coming man. (He duly succeeded the frail stopgap figure of Konstantin Chernenko as Party leader three months later.) Gordievski and his British helpers now came into their own. As deputy head of station responsible for the political line, Gordievski had to prepare the exhaustive personal briefs needed on the prime minister, the defense secretary, the speaker of the House of Commons and all the other leading figures whom Gorbachev would be seeing, as well as general background material. During the visit, he was also responsible for drawing up reports of the day's events, including British reactions, to be sent to Moscow. He was not always present when these reports were examined by the visitor late at night, but he soon learned that they were regarded as first-rate and were almost always transmitted without a word being altered.

As to the impression the visitor made on his colleague, one incident, more than anything else, revealed to Gordievski the caliber of the future general secretary. On the day Gorbachev was due to leave for Scotland, an urgent message arrived for him from Moscow announcing the death of Marshal Ustinov, minister of defense and full Politburo member. Should the visit be called off at once? His advisers, including Zamyatin, the future Soviet ambassador to London, urged an immediate return. Gorbachev stayed up until three in the morning discussing and pondering the problem. Then he announced his decision. He would go to Scotland as arranged but would cut the trip to one day instead of two. It was the act of a man who knew his mind and was, moreover, confident in his own judgment.

The success of the Gorbachev visit set the highest seal of approval on Gordievski's career. The next month, January 1985, he was summoned to Moscow and given plainly to understand that he would be promoted to head of station when Colonel Nikitenko was recalled. To this end he was initiated into the personal ciphers of the rezident, a sign of complete trust. Yet the blow which almost destroyed him fell only four months later.

On the morning of May 17, 1985, a personal telegram from Moscow Center arrived for him at the mission. It sounded normal enough. The message simply instructed him to return for final consultations before his formal appointment as rezident. There was no reason at the time to suspect a trap. His recent visit to Moscow, like all the previous ones, had gone swimmingly and there was no evidence known to him which might place him under suspicion. He decided therefore to comply with the summons and it is clear that his contacts would have dissuaded him from going back had they surmised that anything was wrong.

However, from the moment he landed in Moscow, it became obvious to Gordievski that he was indeed under suspicion. The high-level consultations for which he had been summoned back did not materialize; he was being watched; and, finally, he was interrogated about his loyalties. His inquisitors evidently failed to find the evidence they were looking for, since he remained at liberty, though, by this stage, his wife and children had been bundled back from London to Moscow and his moves were closely shadowed by the KGB.

Gordievski resolved to escape and seek safety in the West. He had to make the agonizing decision to leave his family behind, as he knew that, with the net closing behind him, it would have been an impossible operation to extricate a family of four, including two children. He therefore packed them off on holiday, his wife still ignorant of the true reason. Left behind in Moscow, Gordievski, despite the close surveillance maintained over him, showed the most extraordinary determination and professional skill in implementing the escape plan to the West, over which a veil still had to be drawn. His bid for freedom was successful. On September 12, the Foreign Office announced that Oleg Gordievski had sought, and been granted, political asylum in Britain.

Why had Gordievski suddenly fallen from grace to come under suspicion? The answer is not immediately clear and may have to await the arrival in the West of future defectors who were serving in the Moscow Center at the time. But it seems that there was no single authoritative tip-off which alerted the KGB. It is thought highly unlikely, for example, that Hans Tiedge, the senior West German counterintelligence official who defected to East Germany in August 1985, could, before that date, have been the source of any definite leak, because he would not have been informed of Gordievski's identity as a British agent. The explanation which is probably nearer the truth is a more general one, namely, that while making a final check on the track record of the rezident-designate in London, some analyst, putting together all the Soviet losses and information leakages which had taken place over the previous ten years in various Western countries, had pointed the finger at Oleg Gordievski as number 1 on a shortlist of suspects. That the evidence against him in Moscow was cumulative but circumstantial seems clear. The only surprise, perhaps, was that, in view of the risks he was always prepared to take, the KGB had been so late in questioning his loyalty. However, as other intelligence services, including the British, have learned to their cost, favored sons seem to lead a charmed life when they stray.

As an immediate operational result of Gordievski's formal defection, about thirty-seven Soviet KGB and GRU officers working in Britain under legal cover were expelled. They were given a civilized three weeks in which to leave. Those affected included six diplomats, seven officials of the Soviet Trade Mission and five journalists. It was the largest such operation carried out in Britain since the mass expulsion or exclusion of the 105 agents in 1971, though it had, of course, been exceeded across the Channel by the ejection of forty-seven Soviet spies from France in the wake of the Farewell affair.

So much for the short-term professional impact of Gordievski's defection to Britain, a move which he made because, in the words of Prime Minister Thatcher's statement, "he wished to become a citizen of a democratic country and live in a free society." His long-term impact has much to do with these words. Gordievski did not turn to the West out of pique, frustrated ambition or domestic strife, nor because of bribes or blackmail or the lure of a better existence.

The decision he made to collaborate with the British, as he emphasized to them shortly after taking that momentous step, had not been an easy one; nor should it be regarded as the result of irresponsibility or instability on his part. He had embarked on it, he said, only after prolonged spiritual and emotional struggle, and had come to realize that the only hope of progress for his country lay in democracy, and the tolerance and humanity which democracy would bring. If a man really believed that, Gordievski argued, he must show the courage of his convictions and act. In doing that, and in helping where he could to safeguard the safety and prosperity of the West, he saw a pledge that one day freedom might be restored to the peoples of the Soviet Union too.

Like Farewell, Gordievski rejected the system in which he had been reared and had prospered because he felt it had betrayed the Russian and East European peoples. One day, he hoped to see a root-and-branch reform of that system, which he felt was concerned only with self-preservation and which maintained its appallingly wasteful and inefficient rule through terror and lies. But, until that reform came about, he saw the Soviet regime not only as delinquent toward its own citizens but as a threat, because of its paranoia and its inherent expansionism, to the security of the world. Until such time as the Communist juggernaut rebuilt itself, his task was to explain the machine and its workings more closely to the West so that unnecessary collisions might be avoided. By explaining not just

Soviet ambitions and strengths, but also Soviet fears and weaknesses, he has tried to help the West "manage" relations with the Eastern bloc so as to create more stable conditions.

Gordievski believes that without such stability in East-West relations there is little prospect of the Soviet Union changing into a more open and agreeable society—one which will be less threatening to the West.

"For these reasons," he told me, "I argue that if the Soviet Union makes significant concessions on arms control, or introduces serious political reforms at home, the West should respond by showing itself willing to help the Soviet Union through increased trade and economic cooperation."

Gordievski is adamant, however, that Moscow has to make the first move. "This is not because Gorbachev is the *demandeur* on the international front, but because of his struggle at home. How can he persuade his key colleagues—let alone his opponents—that the Soviet Union must change its ways if the West is willing to give them what they want in any case?"

In view of all this, his advice to Western leaders has been unequivocal. "Meet Gorbachev head-on with straight talk," he tells them, "and never fudge the basic differences between East and West. Above all, in the meantime, remain strong on the military and nuclear fronts." Like any defector before him whose motive was largely ideological, Gordievski seeks not to demolish bridges between East and West, but to build them.

Notes

Chapter 1: Appointment at Chequers

1. *The Times* (London), October 8, 1945.
2. Stimson diary for June 6, 1945, quoted in Hugh Thomas, *Armed Truce 1945–46* (London, 1986), p. 442.
3. Svetlana Alliluyeva, *Twenty Letters to a Friend* (London, 1967), p. 199.

Chapter 2: The Cipher Clerk

1. Details of Gouzenko's early life and training as described by himself to the Royal Canadian Commission, who published their official report on June 27, 1946. An expanded version, *The Gouzenko Transcripts*, came out, also in Ottawa, in 1985.
2. Gouzenko, speaking on a Canadian radio phone-in, April 1968.
3. Igor Gouzenko, *This Was My Choice* (London, 1948), p. 248.
4. For the events which follow, see Royal Canadian Commission Report, especially pp. 641–46.
5. Boris Bajanov, one of Stalin's secretaries, who managed to flee to British India in 1928. See Gordon Brook-Shepherd, *The Storm Petrels* (London, 1977), pp. 10–71.
6. Apart from the details given in the 1946 and 1985 official Canadian reports, there are good descriptions in H. Montgomery Hyde, *The Atom Bomb Spies* (London, 1980), pp. 7–14; Malcolm MacDonald, *People and Places* (London, 1969), pp. 184–87; and Richard Hirsch, *The Soviet Spies* (London, 1947), pp. 3–18, who provided the first full account.
7. *The Mackenzie King Record*, ed. J. W. Pickersgill and D. F. Forster (Toronto, 1970), vol. 3, p. 9.
8. Mackenzie King, addressing the Canadian Parliament, March 18, 1946.
9. Mackenzie King, diary entry for September 24, 1945, quoted in Hyde, *Atom Bomb Spies*, p. 30.
10. MacDonald, *People and Places*, p. 192.
11. RCC Report, p. 231.
12. MacDonald, *People and Places*, p. 183.

Chapter 3: The Professor

1. RCC Report, pp. 31–32.
2. For example, Nigel West, *A Matter of Trust* (London, 1982), pp. 26–27.
3. Brook-Shepherd, *Storm Petrels*, pp. 168–70.
4. RCC Report, p. 450.
5. Ibid., p. 454.
6. Mackenzie King diary, quoted in Hyde, *Atom Bomb Spies*, p. 34.
7. For the most recent account of the Bentley case, see Robert T. Lamphere and Tom Schachtman, *The FBI-KGB War: A Special Agent's Story* (New York, 1986), pp. 36–41.
8. Hyde, *Atom Bomb Spies*, p. 55.
9. Text in Hirsch, *Soviet Spies*, pp. 133–34.
10. Quoted in *The Times* (London), March 18, 1947.

Chapter 4: The Wrecker

1. Harold A. R. Philby, *My Silent War* (New York, 1968), pp. 89–96.
2. For the first full account of the Agabekov affair, see Brook-Shepherd, *Storm Petrels*, pp. 95–138.
3. Philby, *My Silent War*, p. 91.
4. Ibid.
5. Ibid., p. 96.
6. Ismail Akhmedov, *In and Out of Stalin's GRU* (Frederick, Md., 1984), pp. 158–59.
7. Ibid.
8. In his memoirs (ibid., p. 188) Akhmedov strangely places this long session in the summer of 1948, and makes no mention of any meeting during the previous year.
9. Ibid., pp. 195–96.
10. Ibid., p. 197. In his own book, Philby does not even mention Akhmedov, let alone Philby's devious role in delay and obfuscation; a curious omission, in view of his readiness to boast of other achievements in the Communist cause.

Chapter 5: Tokyo

1. *The Times* (London), January 29, 1954.
2. *New York Times*, February 1, 1954.
3. *New York Herald Tribune*, February 2, 1954.
4. *New York Times*, February 5, 1954.
5. The account of Rastvorov's early life and career which follows is based on parts 2 and 3 of his three-part series of articles in *Life*, November–

December 1954. They are his only published writings, composed under professional guidance which he found very irksome. They contain many omissions and inaccuracies and he as good as disowned them in a conversation with the author on March 27, 1987. He confirmed these biographical details, however, with some additions.

6. Rastvorov to the author, March 27, 1987.
7. Ibid.
8. *Life* articles, December 6 and 13, 1954.
9. Rastvorov to the author, March 27, 1987.
10. *Life* article, December 13, 1954.
11. Ibid.
12. Rastvorov to the author, March 27, 1987.
13. *Life* article, December 6, 1954.
14. *Life* article, November 29, 1954.
15. *Scope of Soviet Activity in the United States,* hearings before Senate Judiciary subcommittee, February 8, 1956.
16. Ibid., pp. 18–19.

Chapter 6: Vienna

1. United Press, Vienna dispatch of February 20, 1954.
2. Peter Deriabin with Frank Gibney, *The Secret World* (New York, 1959; paperback, New York, 1982).
3. Deriabin in conversation with the author, April 4, 1987.
4. For the Orlov case, see Brook-Shepherd, *Storm Petrels,* pp. 183 et seq.
5. The details of Deriabin's childhood and youth which follow are based on his own account in *Secret World,* pp. 17 et seq. (paperback edition).
6. Ibid., p. 35.
7. Ibid., p. 114.
8. Ibid., p. 127.
9. Peter Deriabin, *Watchdogs of Terror* (New York, 1972), p. 355.
10. When asked by the author in 1987 why, if he had harbored any growing doubts about the system, he had enrolled voluntarily for this part-time course, Deriabin explained that he was obliged, as a Party member, to spend a fixed number of hours per week studying Party literature, so he had chosen to formalize the process by attending the institute. This would at least get him away from the stifling atmosphere of the Guard Directorate on three evenings a week. Also, he added frankly, he felt that the diploma might be useful for his career.
11. Deriabin, *Secret World,* p. 227.
12. The denunciation episode was described by Deriabin to the author on April 4, 1987.
13. Deriabin, *Secret World,* p. 282.

14. Deriabin to the author, April 4, 1987.
15. Ibid.
16. Ibid.
17. Ibid.

Chapter 7: Frankfurt

1. A flowery and somewhat different version of the encounter is given in Nikolai Khokhlov's own book, *In the Name of Conscience* (London, 1960). The book, which has scores of pages of re-created direct conversation, bears the heavy hallmarks of a ghostwritten work. It leaves big gaps, probably intentionally, on the planning details of Operation Rhein and is a total blank on the Western follow-up. A fuller account, though still with many omissions, was given in four articles published earlier under Khokhlov's name in the *Saturday Evening Post* in November and December of 1954.
2. Khokhlov, *Name of Conscience,* pp. 14–15.
3. Ibid., pp. 20–28, though details like this are omitted in the published version.
4. Ibid., pp. 36–48, gives a full account of his specialist training for the mission.
5. Khokhlov, in his book (ibid., pp. 71–73) and in the first of his *Saturday Evening Post* articles, claimed that it was he who handed the bomb over. This would seem to be inaccurate.
6. Khokhlov, *Name of Conscience,* pp. 82–85.
7. See ibid., pp. 98–99, for an account which omits all mention of the 1946 breach of security and its consequences and of the treatment of his Romanian wife.
8. Ibid., p. 139. The book omits his 1951 mission abroad.
9. Ibid., pp. 190–91.
10. Ibid., pp. 197–98.
11. Illustrations of the murder weapon and other special equipment were reproduced in the *Saturday Evening Post* articles.
12. Khokhlov himself published no details of the journeying before Frankfurt, nor, of course, of what happened after his defection.
13. Khokhlov, *Name of Conscience,* pp. 341–52.

Chapter 8: Canberra

1. Vladimir and Evdokia Petrov, *Empire of Fear* (New York and London, 1956), p. 22.
2. Ibid., p. 131.

3. *Report of the Australian Royal Commission on Espionage* (Sydney, 1955), p. 20 (henceforth cited as *Report*).
4. Petrov, *Empire of Fear*, p. 54.
5. Ibid., p. 124.
6. *Report*, p. 22.
7. Petrov, *Empire of Fear*, pp. 139–49.
8. *Report*, p. 20.
9. Petrov, *Empire of Fear*, p. 156.
10. Ibid., p. 160.
11. Ibid., p. 170.
12. Ibid., p. 207.
13. *Report*, p. 21.
14. Ibid., p. 335.
15. Petrov, *Empire of Fear*, p. 244.
16. Ibid., p. 258.
17. *Report*, p. 27.
18. He gave his own account of the affair in *The Petrov Story* (London, 1955).
19. Ibid., p. 117.
20. Ibid., p. 183.
21. Petrov, *Empire of Fear*, p. 310.
22. Ibid., p. 318.
23. Ibid., p. 329.
24. See on this not only *Report*, pp. 117–66, but Robert Manne, drawing on recently released ASIO archives and writing in *Quadrant*, April 1987.

Chapter 9: Penkovsky—Contact

1. Arkady Shevchenko to the author, June 16, 1987.
2. *The Penkovsky Papers* (New York and London, 1965) gave on pp. 233–45 a different batch of information. This dealt mainly with Soviet nuclear testing and space programs but included some technical details on missiles—especially on the development of the cruise weapon.
3. At Penkovsky's public trial in Moscow, staged in May 1963, the Soviet prosecutor admitted that "some five thousand separate photographed items" had been passed to the West by the accused.
4. See *Penkovsky Papers*, pp. 165–66.
5. Ibid., pp. 54–55.
6. Greville Wynne, *The Man from Moscow* (London, 1967), p. 20.
7. Phillip Knightley, *The Second Oldest Profession* (London, 1986), pp. 313–25, which deal with the Wynne/Penkovsky affair, average two factual errors per page.
8. Ibid., p. 319.
9. All these statements, ibid., p. 320.

10. Wynne, *Man from Moscow*, p. 43, and *Penkovsky Papers*, p. 99.
11. *Penkovsky Papers*, p. 100, but only quoting the wording at Penkovsky's trial.
12. Wynne, *Man from Moscow*, pp. 78–79, repeated in, among other works, Knightley, *Second Oldest Profession*, pp. 314–15.

Chapter 10: Penkovsky—Downfall

1. Wynne, *Man from Moscow*, pp. 197–98.
2. This reconstruction includes information supplied to the author by Yuri Nosenko, whose case is dealt with in chap. 12. Nosenko was serving at the time in the KGB's Second Chief Directorate, which, as the department responsible for internal counterintelligence, was at the heart of the investigation. He defected to the West less than eighteen months afterward, when the affair was fresh in his mind.
3. See *Penkovsky Papers*, pp. 267–84, for a summary of the trial proceedings.
4. Knightley, *Second Oldest Profession*, p. 327. His thesis largely reflects the grossly inaccurate portrait painted by Chapman Pincher in *Their Trade Is Treachery* (London, 1981). According to Pincher (quoting MI5 sources but *not* the experts in the matter, MI6, and, above all, Western military intelligence), almost all of Penkovsky's 5,500 documents were "chickenfeed" while his technical information was "several years old." Much of it, in fact, was from 1960 and 1961, that is, the very latest in the Soviet secret archives.

Chapter 11: The Dark Messenger

1. Anatoly Golitsyn, *New Lies for Old* (New York and London, 1984).
2. Deriabin to the author, April 3, 1987.
3. Ibid.
4. Shortly before Golitsyn arrived in Finland, the author himself had the benefit of a two-hour talk with President Kekkonnen, who left the impression of being nobody's fool and nobody's stooge. It is extremely unlikely that Golitsyn, for his part, ever met the president, beyond, perhaps, a formal embassy presentation.
5. See Chapman Pincher, *The Secret Offensive* (London, 1985), pp. 127–28, for a summary of the Pâques case.
6. See John Barron, *The KGB Today: The Hidden Hand* (New York, 1985), pp. 315–54, for a dramatized but useful account.
7. Pincher, *Their Trade Is Treachery*, p. 25.
8. Ibid., pp. 9–10.
9. See David C. Martin, *Wilderness of Mirrors* (New York, 1980), pp. 108–12, for an account of these events.
10. Golitsyn, *New Lies for Old*, p. 38.
11. Ibid., pp. 46–51.

12. Including the author, who paid some thirty visits to Hungary, Czechoslovakia and Yugoslavia between 1948 and 1970.

Chapter 12: The "Bone in the Throat"

1. Nosenko to the author, June 17, 1987.
2. Ibid.
3. All the biographical and family details which follow are from Nosenko to the author, June 17, 1987.
4. Hearings before the Select Committee on Assassinations of the U.S. House of Representatives, vol. 12, March 1979 (hereafter cited as Hearings, vol. 12), Nosenko's testimony, p. 479.
5. Ibid., p. 478.
6. Nosenko's revelations about his visit to England were made to the author, June 17, 1987.
7. Hearings, vol. 12, p. 594.
8. This account of what happened in Geneva in January 1962 was given by Nosenko to the author, June 17, 1987, and is not covered by anything published.
9. Ibid.
10. Ibid.
11. Hearings before the Select Committee on Assassinations, September 22, 25 and 26, 1978, vol. 4 (henceforth cited as Hearings, vol. 4), p. 187.
12. Ibid., pp. 302–13, the text of Oswald's Soviet Union entries.
13. Ibid., p. 304.
14. Ibid., p. 21.
15. Hearings, vol. 12, p. 601.
16. Hearings, vol. 4, p. 37.
17. Nosenko to the author, June 17, 1987.
18. Hearings, vol. 4, p. 238.
19. Nosenko to the author, June 17, 1987.
20. Hearings, vol. 12, p. 511.
21. Nosenko to the author, June 17, 1987.
22. Arkady Shevchenko to the author, June 16, 1987.
23. Hearings, vol. 12, p. 591.
24. Hearings, vol. 4, p. 96.
25. Nosenko to the author, June 17, 1987.
26. Hearings, vol. 4, p. 21.
27. Ibid., p. 37.

Chapter 14: The Under Secretary-General

1. The childhood details which follow are taken from Arkady N. Shevchenko, *Breaking with Moscow* (New York, 1985). (The page references are those in the Ballantine Books paperback edition of the same year.)

2. Ibid., p. 75.
3. Ibid., p. 76.
4. Shevchenko to the author, June 16, 1987.
5. Shevchenko, *Breaking with Moscow*, p. 205; Shevchenko, p. 24, extended this to forty years.
6. Ibid., p. 112.
7. Ibid., p. 115.
8. Ibid., p. 133.
9. Shevchenko to the author, June 16, 1987.
10. Ibid.
11. Shevchenko, *Breaking with Moscow*, pp. 117–18.
12. Ibid., p. 192.
13. Shevchenko to the author, June 16, 1987.
14. Ibid.
15. Ibid.
16. Ibid.
17. The sequence which follows is based on Shevchenko's own account—necessarily vague on some details—in *Breaking with Moscow*, pp. 1–64 and 357–486.
18. Ibid., p. 424.
19. Ibid., p. 435.
20. Ibid., p. 445.
21. Ibid., p. 455.
22. Waldheim's stiff resistance to Soviet pressure does not sit well with the persistent rumor that the secretary-general was beholden to the Russians, who had him in their power by threatening to disclose him, from documents on his army record in their possession, as a "war criminal."

Shevchenko, discussing this with the author on June 16, 1987, was dismissive of any such "blackmail hostage" theory. He commented: "When Waldheim was first proposed as UN secretary-general, we in Moscow, so far from supporting him, were negative. The Foreign Affairs Ministry had other candidates in mind, and the preference was for a friendly nonaligned nominee. But when it was clear he would emerge as the winner, we didn't object.

"As for the business of his record as a German army officer, I actually saw our Curriculum Vitae on Waldheim at the time. It mentioned that he had been wounded on the Russian front but there was no mention of war crimes.

"There was no question of him kowtowing to us while he was in office. In fact the KGB in New York was constantly complaining to me that Waldheim always froze the Soviet mission out of his inner circle of advisers and they would appeal to me for help."

23. Shevchenko, *Breaking with Moscow,* p. 469.
24. Shevchenko to the author, June 16, 1987.

Chapter 15: The Ideal Soldier

1. For these anecdotes the author is indebted to a senior officer who took a prominent part in Brave Defender.
2. This is the real identity of "Viktor Suvorov," as the defector has called himself when writing several recent books on the Soviet military and intelligence systems. Rezun authorized the author to disclose his proper name for the purposes of this present work.
3. See Viktor Suvorov, *Speznaz: The Story of the Soviet SAS* (London, 1987).
4. Ibid., Appendices A to D.
5. Ibid., pp. 49–50.
6. Ibid., p. 59.
7. Viktor Suvorov, *Aquarium* (London, 1985), pp. 23 et seq.
8. All the personal details which follow were given by Rezun to the author at a meeting stretching over several hours on December 16, 1987.
9. Ibid.
10. Viktor Suvorov, *The Liberators: My Life in the Soviet Army* (London, 1981), pp. 211–68 (page references are to the paperback edition of 1983).
11. Rezun to the author, December 16, 1987.
12. Suvorov, *Liberators,* pp. 266–67.
13. Ibid., pp. 227–28 and 237.
14. Rezun to the author, December 16, 1987.
15. *Aquarium,* pp. 6 et seq. Rezun has corrected several details in this book, which contained some errors deliberately made at the time.
16. Rezun to the author, December 16, 1987.
17. See, for example, Suvorov, *Aquarium,* pp. 237–45.
18. Rezun to the author, December 16, 1987.
19. Ibid.
20. Ibid.
21. Ibid.
22. Viktor Suvorov, *Inside Soviet Military Intelligence* (New York, 1985, Berkley paperback edition), pp. 58–82.
23. Ibid., pp. 95–121.
24. Suvorov, *Liberators,* pp. 9–10.

Chapter 16: "Active Measures"

1. Bittman's evidence was not made public until it was presented to the U.S. House of Representatives' Select Committee on Intelligence (Sub com-

mittee on Oversight) on February 6 and 19, 1980 (hereafter cited as Hearings).

2. Ibid., pp. 53–54.
3. Ibid., pp. 59–243.
4. Levchenko to the author, March 2, 1987.
5. Barron, *KGB Today*, pp. 44–45. Chapters 2, 3 and 4 of this strange intelligence pastiche deal with Levchenko's life and testimony and are solidly based on extensive talks with the defector. Levchenko himself has confirmed to the present author that the Barron version is factually accurate.
6. Hearings, p. 152.
7. Ibid., p. 140.
8. Barron, *KGB Today*, p. 57.
9. Hearings, p. 139.
10. Barron, *KGB Today*, p. 60.
11. Hearings, p. 157.
12. Barron, *KGB Today*, pp. 76–80, describes how King was trapped.
13. Levchenko to the author, March 2, 1987.
14. For the Soviet Union's strategic aims in Japan, see Hearings, p. 142.
15. Hearings, p. 143.
16. Barron, *KGB Today*, p. 82.
17. Levchenko to the author, March 2, 1987.
18. Barron, *KGB Today*, pp. 141–42, gives a full list.
19. Ibid., p. 153.

Chapter 17: "Farewell"—A French Connection

1. The most authoritative account of this network, based on Farewell's disclosures, was given in the French journal *Défense Nationale* for December 1983, by a "senior official." Its author, writing under the name of Henri Regnard, is generally believed to have been Raymond Nart himself. His article, "L'URSS et le Renseignement Scientifique, Technique, et Technologique," was reproduced in translation in the April 1984 volume of the American *Journal of Defense and Diplomacy.*
2. Quoted in the *Financial Times* (London), May 17, 1986.
3. Suvorov, *Inside Soviet Military Intelligence.*
4. Figures quoted in *Le Monde,* April 2, 1985.
5. Notably in Thomas Wolton, *Le KGB en France* (Paris, 1986), pp. 241–42, and repeated in the Western press.
6. Yurchenko defected back to the Soviet Union in November of 1985. There appears to have been a variety of reasons, all of them personal. A romance which he had hoped to cement with a Russian woman working at the Soviet embassy in Ottawa collapsed when she refused to claim asylum with him. Furthermore—a rare case among defectors—life in the United States appeared to him, on closer inspection, to be less attractive than it

had seemed. He was also irritated by the CIA's premature disclosure to the media of some of the information he had given them. In general his poor handling contributed largely to his redefection, simplified at the end by the fact that he was actually taken by his "minders" to eat in a Washington restaurant close to the Soviet embassy itself. He was thus able simply to excuse himself for a few minutes, and bolt. It is, however, generally accepted that this was also an "impulse decision." No adequate logical or professional grounds can be argued for the theory that he was, from the start, some sort of propaganda plant.

Selected Bibliography

(N.B. The comments offered below are the author's purely subjective opinions and relate to the value the author was able to find in connection with the present work.)

Akhmedov, Ismail. *In and Out of Stalin's GRU*. Frederick, Md., 1984. This wartime defector also testified before a Senate Judiciary subcommittee; see *Scope of Soviet Activity in the United States*, 84th Cong., 2d sess., 1956, especially pp. 57–75 and 4395–4398. (See chap. 4 of present work.)

Barron, John. *The Secret Work of Soviet Secret Agents*. New York, 1973. A good comprehensive survey of global KGB activity.

————. *The KGB Today: The Hidden Hand*. New York, 1983; paperback, 1985. Particularly useful on KGB "active measures," with much material provided by one of its former exponents, the defector Stanislav Levchenko. The section on Soviet scientific and industrial espionage has been overtaken by the revelations made shortly afterward by France's major KGB "agent in place," code-named "Farewell." (See chaps. 16 and 17 of present work.)

Bialoguski, Michael. *The Petrov Story*. London, 1955. Useful if self-important account by Petrov's chief link with Australian intelligence.

Boyle, Andrew. *The Climate of Treason*. London, 1979. Not, as claimed, the "definitive account" of the Philby-Burgess-Maclean saga but significant enough to have led to the public exposure of Anthony Blunt as a fourth major Soviet agent inside British intelligence.

Brook-Shepherd, Gordon. *The Storm Petrels*. London, 1977; New York, 1978. First study of the early Soviet defectors from 1928 to the outbreak of the Second World War.

Corson, W. R., and Crowley, R. T. *The New KGB: Engine of Soviet Power*. New York, 1985. A solid history of the KGB from the Lenin to the Andropov eras.

Dallin, David J. *Soviet Espionage*. New Haven, 1955. An excellent survey which covers the prewar period down to the early 1950s.

DERIABIN, Peter. *Watchdogs of Terror.* New York, 1972. A history of the Kremlin's internal security system from tsarist times to the Brezhnev era, based partly on the author's own service in the system. (See chap. 6 of present work.)

————, with Gibney, Frank. *The Secret World.* New York, 1959. A seminal work on the KGB in the early postwar period, told by a former KGB major.

DZHIRKVELOV, Ilya. *Secret Servant: My Life with the KGB and the Soviet Elite.* London, 1987. Interesting account of a KGB man's career, which ended with disinformation and espionage work under the cover of a Tass correspondent.

EPSTEIN, Edward Jay. *Legend: The Secret World of Lee Harvey Oswald.* New York, 1978. An unconvincing attempt to portray Oswald as a KGB agent in the assassination of President Kennedy. (See chap. 12 of present work.)

GOLDSCHMIDT, Bertrand. *Les Rivalités atomiques.* Paris, 1967. Interesting survey, from the French standpoint, of the technical background to the East-West nuclear espionage scene.

GOLITSYN, Anatoly. *New Lies for Old.* New York and London, 1984. Important in that it was the first exposure by a KGB agent of the thrust and global scope of Soviet disinformation; account does not tally when the author exaggerates his case to extravagant lengths. (See chap. 11 of present work.)

GOUZENKO, Igor. *This Was My Choice.* London, 1948. The GRU cipher clerk's account of his defection in Ottawa in September 1945 and his revelations about wartime Soviet penetration of Canadian and American targets, especially in the nuclear research field. See also Report of the Royal Canadian Commission, Ottawa, June 27, 1946, for the officially released details on the case. (See chaps. 2 and 3 of the present work.)

HINCHLEY, Vernon. *The Defectors.* London, 1967. A potpourri of intelligence cases from Gouzenko to the mid-1960s. The sequence is jumbled and contains little new material.

HIRSCH, Richard. *The Soviet Spies.* London, 1947. The first reconstruction of the Gouzenko affair, based on the Royal Canadian Commission's Report.

HYDE, H. Montgomery. *The Atom Bomb Spies.* London, 1980. An excellent survey with new material, notably the private diary of Mackenzie King, Canadian prime minister at the time of the Gouzenko affair. (See chaps. 1–3 of the present work.)

KAZNACHEEV, Alexsandr. *Inside a Soviet Embassy.* New York, 1962.

Memories of an unusual defector, trained as a regular diplomat and then "co-opted" for KGB disinformation activities in Burma in 1957. (See chap. 13 of present work.)

KHOKHLOV, Nikolai. *In the Name of Conscience.* New York, 1959; London, 1960. Autobiography of the first KGB-trained assassin to defect to the West. For operational and other reasons, the author suppressed or altered many details at the time and was himself unaware of the follow-up to his defection. Khokhlov later testified to the U.S. Senate Internal Security Subcommittee on May 21, 1954, and again on October 16, 1957. (See chap. 7 of present work.)

KNIGHTLEY, Phillip. *The Second Oldest Profession.* London, 1986. A sprightly study dedicated to the proposition that intelligence work is nowhere near as significant as its operators, and the general public, suppose. Marred by a tendency to make his thesis match the evidence available to the author. (See, especially, chaps. 4, 10 and 11 of present book.)

KRASNOV, Victor. *Soviet Defectors.* Stanford, Calif., 1985. A painstaking study of trends and motivation in postwar Soviet defection, notable mainly for its detailed statistical breakdown of the cases.

KRAVCHENKO, Victor. *I Chose Freedom.* New York, 1946; London, 1951. Moving autobiography of a defector so ideologically motivated that he risked seeking asylum at a time when America and the Soviet Union were firmly allied in war. (See chap. 2 of present work.)

MARTIN, David C. *Wilderness of Mirrors.* New York, 1980. A stimulating "journalist's" account of the postwar struggle between the CIA and the KGB, notable for some new material on the Golitsyn-Nosenko controversy. (See chaps. 2–3 of present work.)

NOEL-BAKER, Francis. *The Spy Web.* London, 1954. Lively essays on some wartime and early postwar espionage cases.

PENKOVSKY, Oleg. *The Penkovsky Papers.* New York and London, 1965. This is a flawed Cold War curiosity which has earned the unwarranted reputation of a complete and authoritative survey. It consists of disguised extracts from Penkovsky's debriefings while in Western hands with an officially supplied linking narrative. The record given is, in fact, full of gaps and the picture presented of Penkovsky is a very distorted one. (See chap. 9 of the present work.)

PETROV, Vladimir and Evdokia. *Empire of Fear.* New York and London, 1956. The rather entangled joint story of the husband and wife KGB team who defected within days of each other in Australia in 1954. Their personal tale is dramatic; however, their revelations are almost entirely of local interest, though these did lead to a thorough overhaul of Australian intelligence. Their book must be read in conjunction with the *Report of the Australian Royal Commission on Espionage* of August 22, 1985. (See chap. 8 of the present work.)

PHILBY, Harold A. R. ("Kim"). *My Silent War.* New York, 1968. These "memoirs" are an ingenious extension of the master spy's ideological crusade from his Moscow asylum. Every word has patently been cleared with his KGB masters. The book is written with verve and wit but is of historical value only where the stream of disinformation can be measured against such truth as is known. (See chap. 4 of present work.)

PINCHER, Chapman. *Their Trade Is Treachery.* London, 1981. *Too Secret Too Long.* London, 1984. Both books set out to buttress and develop, as regards the British services, the Golitsyn theory of massive high-level Soviet penetration of Western intelligence in the wartime and postwar period. The centerpiece is the attempt to prove, by circumstantial evidence, that Sir Roger Hollis, the onetime head of MI5, was a Soviet mole. Pincher produces much new detail on this and other cases but his central case suffers by relying much too heavily on the reminiscences of one long-retired former MI5 officer, Peter Wright of *Spy Catcher* fame. (See relevant material in chaps. 4, 9, 10, 11, 12, 13 and 18 of present work.)

ROMANOV, A. I. (pen name). *The Nights Are Longest There.* London, 1972. A former officer of the then NKVD describes his wartime and early postwar experiences in Soviet counterintelligence. Some revealing glimpses of the organization at work in the Soviet-occupied zone of Austria from 1945 to 1947.

SETH, Ronald. *Forty Years of Soviet Spying.* London, 1965. Workmanlike survey, all from published material, of KGB successes from tsarist days to the Vassall case of 1961.

SHEVCHENKO, Arkady N. *Breaking with Moscow.* New York, 1985. One of the most illuminating of all books by postwar defectors. The author, as under secretary-general of the United Nations, was the most senior Soviet political officer ever to work as an "agent in place" for the West until his final defection in 1978. He gives a withering exposure of the Kremlin's exploitation of the world body as a KGB bastion. Almost equally revealing are his reminiscences of serving as private secretary to the veteran Soviet foreign minister, Andrei Gromyko, in the early 1970s. (See chap. 14 of present work.)

SUVOROV, Viktor (pen name). *The Liberators: My Life in the Soviet Army.* London, 1981; New York, 1983. *Inside the Soviet Army.* London, 1982.

Inside Soviet Military Intelligence. London, 1984; New York, 1985. A trio of works, in different veins, by the former Red Army captain and GRU officer Vladimir Bogdanovich Rezun. The first is an anecdotal treatment, especially valuable for the 1968 invasion of Czechoslovakia, in which the author took part; the second is a handbook on the Soviet armed forces, with particular reference to the Speznaz troops; and the third, which overlaps at points with the second, examines the GRU. Each provides new material based on firsthand experience. *Aquarium.* London, 1985. *Speznaz: The Story of the Soviet SAS.* London, 1987. (See chap. 15 of present work.)

WINKS, Robin W. *Cloak and Gown.* New York, 1987. Stimulating study by an academic of other academics' involvement in intelligence from 1939 to 1961.

WOLTON, Thomas. *Le KGB en France.* Paris, 1986. A useful survey of postwar Soviet intelligence activity in France, though very inadequate on the one major French triumph in this field, the "Farewell" case. (See chap. 17 of present work.)

WYNNE, Greville. *The Man from Moscow.* London, 1967. A highly subjective account of the Penkovsky saga as recounted by the courageous and ill-fated British businessman who helped MI6 to establish and maintain contact with the Soviet colonel and who eventually stood trial in Moscow with him. (See chaps. 10 and 11 of present work.)

Appendix: *Plus ça change*

The Soviet secret police, while never changing its role, has frequently changed its name since the Bolshevik revolution of 1917–18.

It was first known by the initials VCHK or CHK (popularly called "Cheka"), which stood for Extraordinary Commission for the Struggle Against Counterrevolution, Speculation and Sabotage, a body set up on November 2, 1918.

This was replaced, on February 6, 1922, by the State Political Directorate, or GPU, to which an *O* was prefixed in 1923, to stand for United and mark the creation of the Union of Soviet Socialist Republics. The new label was intended to mask the Cheka's reign of terror, which, however, continued unchecked.

In July 1934, another cosmetic exercise was launched (this time to prepare for Russia's entry into the League of Nations) and the OGPU was transformed into the Directorate of the Commissariat of Internal Affairs, whose initials in Russian were NKVD.

In 1943, after a major wartime reorganization, the NKVD became the People's Commissariat of State Security or NKGB. This designation lasted only three years for, in 1946, the commissariat became a ministry under the title of MGB. So things remained until after Stalin's death in 1953 when, for twelve months, the Security Ministry was absorbed into the Interior Ministry (under Beria) and the initials changed accordingly to MVD.

Finally, after Beria's fall, all secret-police powers were transferred to a nonministerial body known as the Committee of State Security attached to the Council of Ministers, whose initials in Russian were the now familiar KGB.

By comparison, the military intelligence organization has followed a tranquil path. It started in 1920 as the Intelligence Directorate, or RU, of the Red Army and became GRU in 1943, when it was upgraded to a chief directorate.

Index

About the Author

After serving as a lieutenant colonel in the Allied Commission (Vienna) after the war, Gordon Brook-Shepherd became a much-traveled foreign correspondent and later deputy editor of the London *Sunday Telegraph*. A distinguished writer and authority on international affairs and nineteenth- and twentieth-century European history, he is the author of fourteen titles including *Uncle of Europe* (1975) and, most recently, *Royal Sunset* (1987). His book on the prewar Soviet defectors, *The Storm Petrels* (1977), is a direct forerunner to *The Storm Birds*. He was awarded the CBE in 1986.